# a colorful recipe sampler

**roasted pepper, pepperoncini, parmesan, and mozzarella pizza**

*See page 50*

# peach melba smoothie
## with raspberry coulis  *See page 5*

# cherry-cheese blintzes
## wrapped in freshly made crêpes *See page 25*

# lobster bisque
## with fresh tarragon ribbons

*See page 121*

lightly steamed
# shrimp shumai *See page 45*

# seafood stew
### with clams, mussels, shrimp, and fish fillet *See page 119*

grilled portobello
mushroom quesadillas
with mozzarella and roasted red peppers *See page 136*

# salmon
## with leeks and caviar
*See page 195*

eggs in hell

*See page 20*

# mushroom and goat cheese turnovers
## with an arugula and beet salad *See page 77*

# braised duck legs
## with egg noodles *See page 169*

# roasted leg of lamb
## with roasted garlic and rosemary
## and roasted cippolini onions

*See pages 270 and 281*

# chicken chaat
## on an iceberg bed *See page 92*

# fresh strawberry cobbler
### served warm and bubbling *See page 306*

**watermelon granita**
*See page 295*

**mint chocolate pot de crème**
*See page 298*

**orange pot de crème**
*See page 297*

# TOM VALENTI

# You Don't Have to Be Diabetic to Love This Cookbook

BY TOM VALENTI AND ANDREW FRIEDMAN

FOREWORDS BY
ROBIN GOLAND, M.D. AND ROBERT E. MICHLER, M.D.

NUTRITIONAL CONSULTANT: JOY PAPE

WORKMAN PUBLISHING • NEW YORK

*I dedicate this first to my family, who waved a red flag and
told me to watch my sugar (not that I always listened);
to my staff at Ouest, for their input and participation;
and, as always, to my wife, Abigail, whose patience, support,
and wisdom mean the world to me.*
—T.V.

---

*As always, to Caitlin, Declan, and Taylor,
and to the memory of my grandfather, Lew Serbin,
whose diabetes never, for a second, got him down.*
—A.F.

Copyright © 2009 by Tom Valenti and Andrew Friedman
Photography copyright © 2009 by Ben Fink

Library of Congress Cataloging-in-Publication Data is available.

ISBN 978-0-7611-5550-8 (pb)
ISBN 978-0-7611-5411-2 (hc)

Cover and book design: Lisa Hollander
Cover and interior photographs: Ben Fink
Illustrations: Steven Guarnaccia

Workman books are available at special discounts when purchased in bulk for premiums and sales promotions
as well as for fund-raising or educational use. Special editions or book excerpts can be created to specification.
For details, contact the Special Sales Director at the address below.

Workman Publishing Company, Inc.
225 Varick Street
New York, NY 10014-4381
www.workman.com

Manufactured in the United States of America
First printing May 2009
10 9 8 7 6 5 4 3 2 1

# acknowledgments

nobody writes a book on his or her own, and we'd like to give a public shout-out to our own "Diabetes Team." In order of appearance:

First and foremost, our editor, Suzanne Rafer had the fine idea to do this book, brought it to our door, then shepherded it from commencement to completion with great patience and care;

Suzanne and Tom never would have met without the intervention of Sheila Lukins, who recommended him as the right author for this book;

Peter Workman has given very special support to this project from its very first stages, and it's been appreciated at every turn;

David Black was very helpful in getting the deals done;

Joy Pape guided us down the path of modern diabetes thinking, and analyzed the nutritional content of the recipes;

Tom's former assistant, Scott Varricchio, ordered and organized the ingredients for most of our recipe-testing sessions—thanks for making life easy and damn you for moving to Florida;

Amy Tucker turned testing notes into recipes with style and grace;

Erin Klabunde, Suzanne's assistant, happily shuttled a seemingly endless procession of pages back and forth between writers and editor, and was always there in a pinch;

Copy editor Barbara Mateer and production editor Carol White did a great job of sanding and polishing the text to its final state;

Lisa Hollander, Workman's designer/art director, conceived the high-energy look of the book, Ben Fink took the photos that make the food look so irresistible, and was aided in his efforts by food stylist Jamie Kimm and prop stylist Sarah Abalan; Workman's photo department director Anne Kerman was also instrumental in guiding Ben and his team in everything from dish selection to the vision for the photos;

Steven Guarnaccia, your illustrations make me chuckle;

Thanks in advance to the marketing and publicity team—Kristin Matthews, Selina Meere, Melissa Possick, Melissa Broder, and David Schiller—for getting the word out, and to a fabulous sales team for getting the book on store shelves, both physical and virtual;

And, to all the loyal clients who have supported our restaurants; without them, we wouldn't have been able to pull this off.

# contents

## breakfast and brunch ................. 3

Smoothies, frittatas, Cherry-Cheese Blintzes, and Turkey Hash. Delicious and inviting ways to start the day.

## hors d'oeuvres, snacks, and finger foods ............................. 33

mushroom Bruschetta, Caramelized Onion Dip, Shrimp Shumai—even crispy crust pizzas. Contemporary nibbles that sound indulgent but are diabetes friendly.

## salads and starters .................. 57

here are classic salads—so fresh, so flavorful—plus a delightful array of first courses. Lemony Fennel Salad, Warm Artichokes with Artichoke Dressing and Parmesan, Beef Carpaccio with Arugula and Truffle Oil, Chicken Chaat—it's hard to choose.

## soups and stews ....................... 101

ladle out bowlsful of Creamless Creamy Mushroom Soup, Spicy Coconut Turkey Soup, hearty Seafood Stew, Jorge's Family Lunch Chicken Soup. Easy, filling, and oh so good.

## sandwiches, wraps, and quesadillas ................................. 135

a selection of sandwiches that will make you happy to the core—Southwestern Chicken and Avocado Wraps, Grilled Beef and Goat Cheese Quesadillas, Lobster Rolls, and Mushroom Burgers. They'll also make your life just a tad easier.

## pasta and risotto

the chapter you might not have expected in this cookbook. But pasta and risotto pose no problems in these dishes: Vegetable Lasagna, Linguine with Clams, Braised Duck Legs with Egg Noodles, Creamy Spinach Risotto, and Roasted Tomato, Black Olive, and Thyme Risotto.

## fish and shellfish

lean, light, nutritious, and—best of all—great tasting, fresh seafood can't be beat at dinnertime. Try Almond-Crusted Mahimahi, Snapper Piccata, Salmon with Leeks and Caviar, Bay Scallops Provençal, and Soft-Shell Crabs with Scallion Couscous and Curry Vinaigrette.

## poultry and meat

the special occasion dishes: Grilled Beef Tenderloin, Grilled Lamb Chops with Cauliflower Stew, Garlic-Roasted Pork Loin with Salsa Verde, Sauteed Chicken with Tangy Mushroom Sauce. Perfect for dinner parties.

## side dishes and accompaniments

dress up simple main dishes with just the right side: Creamed Spinach with Parmesan Cheese, Baked Spicy Sweet Potato Fries, Bacony Brussels Sprouts, and Garlicky Wilted Kale. Irresistible.

## desserts

the tasty and satisfying way to end the meal. Watermelon Granita. Mint Chocolate Pots de Crème. Blueberry Buckle and Strawberry Cobbler. Even Apple Turnovers with Walnuts and Cinnamon. There's no forgoing dessert.

## condiments and basics

better-than-store-bought chicken and beef stocks. Tomato Salsa and Onion Relish. Homemade Pesto and Herb Coulis. Packed with flavor, they will add punch to any main dish, sandwich, or side.

# foreword

### Robin Goland, M.D.

CODIRECTOR, NAOMI BERRIE DIABETES CENTER
PROFESSOR OF CLINICAL MEDICINE
COLUMBIA UNIVERSITY COLLEGE OF PHYSICIANS AND SURGEONS, NEW YORK

here is a scenario that is familiar to me: A doctor walks into the restaurant where a new patient and his or her family are eating dinner, and the new patient dives under the table. As the co-director of the Naomi Berrie Diabetes Center at the Columbia University Medical Center, the largest diabetes center in the New York metropolitan area, I've often had this experience. One of the biggest misconceptions about diabetes is that once someone has received this diagnosis, he or she is relegated to prisoner's rations and can never eat in a restaurant and enjoy "real" food again. How sad and how untrue! The patients who are hiding under the table are *new* patients at the Berrie Center; once they've received comprehensive diabetes and nutritional education, they know that there is no such thing as a "diabetic diet" and that any food can fit into their new healthier meal plan.

It's never easy to receive a diagnosis of a major chronic disease and diabetes can be particularly difficult. Many people with diabetes and their families believe that the treatment will likely be worse than the disease, and this mistaken idea is one of the major barriers to people receiving the care they need. It is far from the truth. If you've been told that your blood sugar is too high and you've been avoiding taking the next step and getting the needed treatment because you fear the dietary restrictions that will be coming your way, you should be reassured by this wonderful cookbook.

So many of my patients with diabetes are initially very apprehensive about making dietary changes. But Tom Valenti writes that as he adapted his eating to type 2 diabetes, rather than feeling sad and deprived, he actually began to feel better and to have more energy. Many people have this experience. They're also relieved that they're no longer ignoring their health and they and their loved ones can worry less about long-term complications.

Dealing with diabetes is a marathon, not a sprint. Dietary management of diabetes is not difficult. Moderation is key. A dietician and diabetes educator can help demystify diabetes and greatly assist in individualizing a meal plan. It's important to make small changes that can be sustained over a lifetime rather than a dramatic dietary overhaul that can at best be sustained for a few weeks or months. Importantly, as Tom Valenti stresses, people with diabetes continue to eat varied and delicious food, the same food enjoyed by their family and friends.

Tom Valenti offers delicious recipes coupled with helpful advice based on his own experience of living well and staying healthy with type 2 diabetes. As you'll learn, dietary management of type 2 diabetes often includes watching the carbohydrates as well as the fats and salt in the diet. People with type 1 diabetes, a form of diabetes that must be managed with insulin injections, will also find very helpful tips in the book, particularly in the detailed nutritional analyses of the recipes that can help guide their "carbohydrate counting"—matching the insulin dose to the carbohydrates they consume.

Having a chronic condition like diabetes can be isolating and lonely, and taking care of it is challenging. But there is much reason for hope: Doctors and scientists at the Berrie Center and elsewhere are working hard on finding a cure for diabetes.

Meanwhile, this important book will help people with diabetes and their families with its day-to-day management and will allow them to rediscover the joy of eating delicious food while still remaining in good health. And next time you're in a wonderful restaurant and your doctor walks by, you can happily recommend one of the great dishes you've selected!

# foreword

### Robert E. Michler, M.D.
SURGEON-IN-CHIEF
PROFESSOR AND CHAIRMAN, DEPARTMENTS OF SURGERY AND CARDIOTHORACIC SURGERY
CODIRECTOR, MONTEFIORE-EINSTEIN HEART CENTER, NEW YORK

bravo! At long last a cookbook designed around extraordinary flavor and delicious taste, yet precise in its attention to a diabetic person's needs. Renowned for his culinary skills and fabulous restaurants, Tom Valenti has created an artful selection of wonderful meals for every palate—to be equally enjoyed by the discriminating food connoisseur as well as the health-conscious individual. This is a cookbook for everyone in the family.

Many people experience the same shock and disappointment as Tom did upon learning of his diagnosis, but there is hope, and Tom himself is here to help you in a very personal way. Yes, you can live and enjoy life with diabetes. You are the one in control provided you make sensible choices and learn about taking care of this illness. As Tom says, "Get a grip. Making wise food choices are part of the solution and the solution can be fun!" And, remember, you are not alone. Nearly 8 percent of the United States population has diabetes— roughly 24 million people.

Diabetes is the result of a defect in insulin production or insulin activity, and produces abnormally high levels of blood sugar. There are two basic types of diabetes, type 1 or juvenile-onset diabetes and type 2 or adult-onset diabetes. Type 2 diabetes is much more common and accounts for 90 to 95 percent of all cases. As a heart surgeon, I have witnessed firsthand the effects of diabetes on heart disease. Managing the disease can significantly reduce these risks.

The steps to good health and treatment begin with you! Your physician is your guide and your coach, and it is likely that he or she will include a recommendation for exercise. Exercise must be part of your life's routine and I do not mean vigorous running or exhausting activity. Begin with walking, outside, in the shopping mall or wherever you can go for a good 10 to 15 minutes. While walking, you can spend time thinking about your lifestyle and what you should be adding or eliminating. You certainly need to add good eating habits and here in this wonderful cookbook you will find straightforward and easy ways to improve your health with delicious meals fit for all. With over 250 recipes, you will not yearn for options. In fact, the range of meals is quite extraordinary, from appetizers and snacks to poultry, fish, meat, and side dishes.

This book is an absolute must for young families. We face an epidemic of childhood obesity and we need to teach good eating habits to our children. Between 1980 and 2006, the prevalence of obesity in children ages 6 to 11 doubled, and the prevalence in children ages 12 to 19 more than tripled. There is a direct correlation between childhood obesity and obesity as an adult. The health risks associated with obesity include diabetes, heart disease, high blood pressure, bone and joint disease, to name just a few. These are frightening statistics and signal a significant change in the way families focus on diet and exercise. Tom Valenti's book will help families learn about good eating habits, the importance of calorie reduction, and how to prepare savory low-fat and reduced-sodium meals. Importantly, you need not dine alone; family and friends can now enjoy the same delicious meals and all can share the goal of a healthier lifestyle.

# "you mean I can't eat pasta anymore?"

believe it or not, that was the first thought that ran through my mind about fourteen years ago, when my doctor looked up from the results of some lab work, and confirmed what he and I both suspected: I had developed type 2 diabetes.

Nobody wants to hear that they have diabetes. It's one of those diseases that keeps on giving, putting you at risk for heart disease, circulatory complications, and diminished eyesight, to name just a few of its most regular partners in crime. But as my doctor began to run down the dos and don'ts that would define the rest of my days, my thoughts began to wander. You might say that I saw my life flash before my eyes—my *culinary* life. There were snippets from my childhood, like coming inside after predawn hockey practice in the brutal cold of upstate New York and tucking into a steaming hot bowl of oatmeal drizzled with maple syrup. Or enjoying one of the great pleasures of my family's home: pasta, which we consumed several times a week and which I continued to enjoy in such quantities and with such regularity as an adult that you could have made the case that it was one of the loves of my life.

I also thought about being a chef, my time spent mostly in the kitchen with anything my appetite might desire just a grab away—the end I'd tear off a loaf of bread when the daily delivery was made, or the bacon I'd nibble after I'd crisped a sheet pan's worth in the oven, or my thoughtless second helping of the nightly staff meal, or the second dinner I'd sit down to, hours later, in some late-night hangout with my culinary brothers and sisters.

Sitting in that doctor's office, the fluorescent lighting beaming down on me as I soaked up the news, I felt that stream of memories come to a screeching halt. I also felt a powerful sense of regret for all of the too-big meals and junk food I'd stuffed into my body; how much of my new predicament was determined by genetics and how much was due to poor decision making? I'd never know.

I left in a mild state of shock, and over the next few weeks it was a long, slow transition. I'd find myself casually helping myself to something, then remembering after one bite that I shouldn't be eating it. Or I'd go out to dinner and be so down about what I *couldn't* order that I hardly ordered anything at all. In time, I got over it, but not before I went through Dr. Kübler-Ross's five stages of grief: denial, anger, bargaining, depression, and finally, acceptance. The last stage was the most important. I regained my bearings and the problem-solving part of my brain kicked into gear.

## getting down to business

I'm a bit of an anomaly among chefs of my generation in that I never went to cooking school, so I've always had a tendency to wing things in the kitchen, questioning the conventional wisdom and going my own way. I decided to embrace this aspect of my nature and to try to have some fun with my lot in life, to make diabetes into a creative challenge rather than a test of my morale. The biggest concern was, of course, cutting back on carbohydrates, but I also did my best to up my intake of green veggies and to minimize salt and fat. Things went better than I could have hoped, in part because a few of my culinary predilections were so well suited to the task. For example, I've long had a fondness for using a lot of acidity in my cooking, mostly lemon juice and vinegar in all its forms, because they brighten almost anything, even long-simmered braises and creamy, emulsified dressings. I hadn't thought of it this way before, but they also happened to be a

fat-free, and virtually carb-free and calorie-free, way of upping the flavor ante in a limitless variety of recipes, which for a cook with diabetes is literally just what the doctor ordered. Similarly, my gravitation toward juxtaposing textures and temperatures on a single plate made for inherently interesting combinations that did not need to rely on an abundance of salt or sugar for their success.

I also often turn to bacon as a flavoring agent (although I have taken to replacing pork with the turkey variety), browning some in the pan or pot as the first step in many dishes. The smoky quality bacon imparts survives any cooking process, without exacting too much of a nutritional toll, and is perfectly in synch with the unique demands of diabetic dining.

Beyond discovering how useful my standard operating procedures were for my new scenario, I found that very often honoring the limits of diabetes simply meant rejiggering the proportions in a dish, emphasizing proteins and vegetables over pastas, grains, legumes, and so on. And, after eating like this for a while, something funny happened: I came not to mind it so much. One day I was making myself dinner and it occurred to me that accommodating the restrictions had become second nature, just like looking both ways before crossing the street; I had become conditioned to living with diabetes.

And after some more time, something even funnier happened. Even though I was technically infirm, I started to feel better than I ever had before. Sure, once in a while, my taste buds missed a few of the things I had given up, or minimized my intake of, but my body didn't miss them at all. Waking up with that heavy sensation in my gut from overindulging the night before was a thing of the past. My energy level was more constant. My weight went down. My skin even looked better.

## DIABETES DEFINED

Usually, we think of diabetes in terms of what we can and cannot eat. But in thinking about how to cook and eat with diabetes, it's useful to take a step back and understand exactly what diabetes is. My explanation will be somewhat general because (a) I'm not a doctor, and (b) I expect that *your* doctor has already explained much of this to you.

Basically, diabetes is a disease associated with insulin, the hormone that allows glucose (better known as sugar)—our primary source of energy—to leave our bloodstream and enter the cells to feed our body. Diabetes is caused when the body has a lack of insulin or inability to properly utilize it. The most common form of diabetes, affecting about 90 percent of people with diabetes, is type 2, caused by what's known as insulin resistance, which sounds like a political movement but really just means that our body's cells resist the effect of insulin so they fail to take in the glucose they need for energy.

Over time, our pancreas's insulin-producing cells begin to become exhausted and fail to produce enough insulin to keep our blood glucose levels in the normal range. Traditionally, type 2 diabetes was usually diagnosed in people over forty, but an increasing (and alarming) number of younger people have begun developing it year after year, which is really not surprising when you consider the diets of today's kids—especially the prevalence of junk food, sweets, huge high-calorie drinks, saturated fat, and trans fat—and how inactive many of them are.

The other main types of diabetes are type 1 (these people do not produce insulin, or produce very little insulin, and are usually but not always diagnosed at a young age) and gestational diabetes, which develops in women during pregnancy and can increase the risk of developing type 2 diabetes later in life.

All types of diabetes lead to the same danger zone: They cause too much glucose to remain in the bloodstream and, in time, the rising blood glucose levels can lead to complications such as blindness, heart disease, kidney failure, nerve damage, stroke, and, potentially, the amputation of limbs. For this reason, people with diabetes must monitor their intake of glucose and regularly monitor their blood glucose levels, keeping them as close to normal as possible. At the time of this writing, the American Diabetes Association (ADA) recommends that blood glucose levels be 70 to 130mg/dl (milligrams per deciliter) when fasting and before meals and less than 180mg/dl one to two hours after eating. The ADA also recommends that your A1C (a blood test that determines your average blood glucose level over the past two to three months) be less than 7.0 percent and your blood pressure be maintained below 130/80mm/Hg (commonly expressed as 130 over 80).

As dire as all of this sounds, the good news is that with careful diet and nutrition, sufficient physical activity, and most likely some medications, diabetes can be managed. The medical field has also created a new category to help people at risk ward off diabetes: pre-diabetes. Pre-diabetes means that your glucose levels are rising to above normal levels but are not quite high enough for you to be diagnosed with diabetes. This is generally determined by a simple blood-glucose test administered by your doctor. If you ever needed another reason to submit to an annual physical, or encourage those you love to do so, this is it, especially because it has been shown that type 2 diabetes can be prevented or delayed.

## EATING WITH DIABETES

As I've mentioned, there's no such thing as a set "one size fits all" diabetes diet, and that's even more true today than it was in the past. What most approaches to nutrition for people with diabetes have in common is the idea of "meal planning," which simply means planning what you are going to eat.

The one consideration that all people with diabetes *must* respect is regulating their intake of carbohydrates. The amount of carbohydrates one should consume varies according to that person's plan. Again, there's no set number; some diabetes educators and doctors recommend 45 to 65 grams of carbohydrates per meal and even suggest the slightly higher range of 60 to 75 grams per meal for men. But others find this too high or too low. Like all decisions about diabetes, figuring out the number of grams of carbohydrates that is right for you is a decision that should be made in consultation with your own health care team.

### CARBOHYDRATE CHOICES

One of the most popular plans at the moment is carb counting, which many people follow by reading nutrition labels to determine the carbohydrate content of the main ingredients in the food they plan to eat. This works especially well for people who take insulin and must adjust their insulin dosage to the total of carbohydrates they eat. Some people simplify the process by using a type of carb counting called carbohydrate choices, particularly as a tool for evaluating recipes from books and other sources. I like this method quite a bit. Simply put, one carbohydrate choice is approximately 15 grams of carbohydrates, roughly the amount found in one small apple or potato or a third of a cup of cooked rice.

Fiber is a mitigating factor in computing carbohydrate choices. Since fiber isn't digested by the body, if a dish contains more than 5 grams, that amount can be subtracted from the total number of carbohydrates before calculating carbohydrate choices.

Some people with diabetes don't count carbohydrates at all, choosing instead simply to cut back on portions from their pre-diabetes days. This is an imprecise method but can work if they're eating a sensible, well-balanced, and relatively low-carbohydrate diet to begin with.

### FOOD EXCHANGES

Even people who don't have diabetes have probably heard of the exchange system, the shorthand name for Exchange Lists for Meal Planning, which used to be the most popular approach and is still relied upon by many people with diabetes. The exchange system is a customized plan usually designed by the person who has diabetes in collaboration with a registered dietitian. The exchange system categorizes food into three main groups based on the three major nutrients: carbohydrates, protein, and fat. Those groups are subdivided into more precise categories, and within those categories are choices of similar foods that you can exchange for one another. (Personally, I find it easier to think of exchanges as allotments, as in "I'm allotted this many servings of vegetables per day, this many servings of meat per day, this many servings of starch per day, and so on.")

### THE FOOD PYRAMID

There are other approaches, such as the food pyramid. The most recent Department of Agriculture food pyramid divides food into six primary groups, suggesting a number of servings for each group per day. The pyramid system also emphasizes the importance of physical activity, reinforcing the message that a healthy lifestyle isn't only about monitoring food intake.

### WHAT'S ON THE PLATE?

Many diabetes educators will tell you that the most dependable road to success is the simplest one. Because most people don't tend to eat with a calculator and a nutritional analysis of each ingredient on hand, a clever soul created the so-called plate method, in which you imagine your plate divided into four quadrants: One fourth should be taken up with grains or starchy foods, such as rice, pasta, or starchy vegetables, such as corn, peas, or potatoes; one fourth should be filled with protein such as fish, poultry, meat, or tofu; the last two quadrants (that is, half of the plate) should be taken up by nonstarchy vegetables—broccoli, cauliflower, salad greens, and so on. Of course, it's a good idea to calculate the number of carbohydrates for all meals, but the plate method is a good starting point.

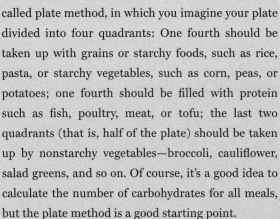

Whatever system you use, there are still no hard and fast limits because each person's plan is devised by his or her "team," comprising the person with diabetes, a doctor, a diabetes educator, and other advisors. The ultimate decision is made by you, the captain of the team, because you're the one who has to live with the eating plan.

This book shares some of my favorite recipes that I've developed since those formative days—about 250 of them—a surprisingly satisfying repertoire for gratifying cooking and eating within the bounds set, for you and me, by our shared situation. It is my fervent hope that in addition to pleasing you, the dishes here will be just as appealing to people who don't have diabetes, the ones you share a table with, either on a daily basis or for special occasions and holidays. As the title of this book promises, this is food that anybody can love.

## a secret about the diabetes diet

There's a common misconception out there that while diabetes is a disease that can be managed, it's a virtual death sentence for your dining pleasure. I'd like for this book to obliterate that way of thinking. When I signed on to write the book, the good people at Workman hired me my very own Certified Diabetes Educator, the endlessly energetic, helpfully opinionated Joy Pape. One of Joy's oft repeated mantras at our weekly recipe testing session was "There's no such thing as a diabetes diet."

There are a number of reasons why this is true: First of all, everyone's diabetes plan is different, arrived at through his or her own discipline, and advice of consulting health care professionals. There are also mitigating factors, such as age, amount of exercise, food preferences, whether or not medicine is being taken to manage the diabetes, and so on. Other factors that inform the eating habits of a person with diabetes might include budget, culture, religious guidelines, and so on.

What Joy meant was that, strictly speaking, there's nothing completely verboten for people with diabetes. Yes, putting a ceiling on your intake of carbohydrates is a must and, of course, fat and sodium should be minimized. But you can eat *a little* of almost anything, and if you're clever in the kitchen, a little can go an awfully long way. To me, this is one of the great revelations about eating that any person with diabetes can have because it directly refutes what I believe is the biggest concern most newly diagnosed people have about food: Will I be able to satisfy my cravings?

The range of recipes in this book has been designed to satisfy multiple cravings, from hot and spicy to sweet and sour; from cool and creamy to crunchy. About the only craving not indulged in these pages is the one for salt, but there's a very good reason for that (see A Note on Salt on page xvii).

By the same token my collaborator, Andrew Friedman, and I made it our mission to try to use only real foods in these recipes. One of the first things we did when we began thinking about the book was to consider whether or not to employ the ever-growing selection of imitation products on the market: fake mayonnaise, sugar-free preserves, tofu *everything*. We went to the supermarket and bought up a sampling of these products, then came back to one of my restaurants, Ouest, arranged them on a kitchen counter, and broke out a bucket of spoons. After about a half hour of taste testing these predominantly nasty specimens, we decided that we'd avoid most of them and cook with the actual ingredients we loved rather than use pale imitations. The few exceptions we made were using turkey bacon and sausage in place of their porky cousins and low or nonfat dairy products.

## how to use this book

I'm bringing the same attitude toward diabetes to this book that I've adopted in my own life:

I chose not to dwell on it. Oh, sure, from time to time I'll explain why I take a particular approach to a dish or point out things you can do to make it even healthier, but for the most part, I just want to focus on the food and the pleasure of eating, because that's what I try to do personally. I truly believe that the food tastes better if you don't constantly remind yourself why you've chosen it.

Put another way, I'd like this to be a cookbook that you turn to the way you would any other collection of recipes: as a source of dishes to serve yourself, your friends, and family. If you use it to serve people *without* diabetes as well as yourself, and if they don't perceive the food as "diabetes minded," the book will have achieved its ultimate mission. Also, while I don't have children of my own, I'd humbly suggest that the recipes in these pages might be used to show young eaters a healthful way of eating that won't leave them feeling diminished or deprived—a gift for life if ever there was such a thing.

## decisions, decisions

Scan through the lists of dishes at the beginning of each chapter and you'll notice that there are many more recipes offered in some categories than others: a plentitude of recipes for salads, soups, fish and shellfish main courses, and high-utility sides and accompaniments, for instance, versus a relatively small number of sandwich, poultry, and meat recipes. The reason for this is simple: The first categories listed are inherently more healthful than the second. There are more than thirty salads because they are low in fat (and most of the fat is "good fat," as explained in Fat Facts on page xvi), most of them feature loads of healthful greens, and many can be turned to as both a first course or a small meal, especially at lunch. By the same token, most fish and shellfish are better for you than most poultry or meat, so there are more of the former than the latter.

My presumption is that you've chosen this diabetes cookbook over others, or to complement your collection, because you want to be able to enjoy the recipes of a restaurant chef while staying true to your eating plan. Because everybody's plan is different, my overriding concern in developing all of the recipes was keeping the carbohydrate count down to a level that's safe for most people with diabetes. My second concern was keeping the sodium and fat content as low as possible, while still making the

dishes taste great, which means that some dishes have higher levels of fat and sodium than others. In other words, with more than two hundred recipes to choose from, there's plenty here to suit any plan, from the most conservative to the most inclusive. Another concern was to keep the recipes as accessible as possible, so although they draw on the knowledge and palate of a professional chef, they can be prepared by any home cook.

## UNDERSTANDING THE ANALYSIS

Each recipe in the book is accompanied by a nutritional analysis that offers counts of the following categories.

### CALORIES

Calories measure the energy provided by food. Though not necessarily from carbohydrates, consuming too many calories causes weight gain, so the calorie total should be considered when planning meals. For your reference, carbohydrates and proteins have 4 calories per gram; fat has 9 calories per gram; and alcohol has 7 calories per gram.

### FAT IN GRAMS (see Fat Facts, page xvi)

### TOTAL CARBOHYDRATES IN GRAMS

Along with fats and protein, carbohydrates are one of the three main nutrients in food and the most important category for people with diabetes to monitor while eating. Analyses of dietary fiber and total sugars in grams are included in the total carbohydrate count.

### PROTEIN IN GRAMS

The body uses proteins for cell structure, the production of hormones, and other important functions. Foods that provide protein include dairy products (cheese, milk, yogurt, and the like), dried beans, eggs, fish, poultry, meat, and soy.

### CHOLESTEROL IN MILLIGRAMS

Cholesterol is a fat-like substance that is used by the body to make hormones and build cell walls. Once thought to have the biggest influence on blood cholesterol levels, it's now thought that saturated fat is far more influential. For more, see Fat Facts on page xvi.

### SODIUM IN MILLIGRAMS

The sodium content of food is an important consideration for people with diabetes because many of the same diseases to which we are susceptible—heart disease, for example—can be aggravated by too much sodium in our diets. For more, see A Note on Salt on page xvii.

# breaking it down

because different people with diabetes follow different guidelines, there are three types of nutritional analyses offered for each recipe in these pages. There is a list of values for carbohydrates, fat, sodium, fiber, and so on. There is also a list of exchanges for people who still use that system.

The part of the breakdown that is the most prominent one is the number of carbohydrate choices in each dish. Because all people with diabetes, regardless of their personal eating plan, must regulate their intake of carbohydrates, think of carbohydrate choices as the executive summary, expressing the carbohydrate content of a serving in a succinct, single digit and/or fraction. This allows you to scan the book quickly, seeking recipes that meet your desired, or allowed, carbohydrate intake for any one meal or course, and then to examine the rest of the nutritional picture and make a decision.

# fat facts

there are recipes in this book that feature an amount of grams of fat and number of exchanges that might seem high, and relative to the conventional diabetes guidelines, they are. But the thinking on this has been evolving recently for the simple reason that fat does not affect blood glucose directly. It can of course contribute to weight gain, which isn't a good thing. But in the past several years, we've come to understand that there are "good fats" and "bad fats" as well as "good cholesterol" and "bad cholesterol."

It's not as confusing as it might sound. Here's how it all works.

There are three main types of fat in food. Each affects cholesterol (that is, blood lipid) levels in its own way:

First of all, many of the fats in the recipes in this book are monounsaturated fats, also known these days as "good fats," which raise the HDL (good cholesterol) and lower the LDL (bad cholesterol). These fats are found in canola, olive, and peanut oils; olives; avocados; and peanuts.

Somewhere on the middle of the good–bad fat scale are polyunsaturated fats. There are some that are considered not so good and others that are considered very good. The ones that are considered not so good are vegetable oils, such as corn oil, which may lower the LDL level but may also lower the HDL level. On the other hand, there are healthy polyunsaturated fats, specifically omega-3 fatty acids, which have been found to be very good for several reasons: They are heart healthy and they lower triglycerides—one of the bad cholesterols linked to heart disease (which tend to be high in many people with diabetes). Omega-3 fatty acids are found in fatty fish (most famously in salmon, but also in mackerel, sardines, and others) and in grass-fed beef. You can also find them in flax seeds and flaxseed oil, walnuts and walnut oil.

The bad fat—the one that raises blood cholesterol (both the good HDL and the bad LDL)—is saturated fat, which is mostly found in fatty meats and full-fat dairy products such as butter and full-fat cheeses. (It also turns up in coconut oil, palm oil, and palm-kernel oil, but none of those are used in this book.) In addition to the total fat content listed in the nutritional analysis for each recipe, you will also find a listing of how many of those grams are saturated fat.

It's also worth taking a moment to explain another fat, which we might call "the really bad fat," and that's trans fat. Trans fats exist in very small amounts in some dairy products and meats but otherwise are not a naturally occurring fat—in other words, they are for the most part

## A NOTE ON SALT

Whether you're dealing in the old-school world of exchanges or in the new-school counting carbs or carbohydrate choices, sodium doesn't figure into the equation. There's no "salt exchange" and the amount of sodium in a dish doesn't influence the number of carbohydrate choices in a given dish. But salt is an important consideration for anybody with diabetes because diabetes and heart disease go hand in hand, and some people with heart and blood pressure problems need to watch their sodium intake.

Even though I've had type 2 diabetes since 1997, it was a revelation to me when our Certified Diabetes Educator, Joy Pape, strolled into the test kitchen on Day One and informed me that the recommended intake of sodium for people *without* diabetes is no more than 2,300 milligrams per day, which translates to roughly one teaspoon of salt. (The amount for people with diabetes is roughly the same unless you have been advised a different amount by one or more members of your healthcare team.) This amount was, to put it mildly, shocking to me, more or less akin to learning the world was round instead of flat. (I was also stunned to learn that many ingredients, such as canned tomatoes, have a high amount of naturally occurring sodium.)

Now, I'm a chef and there are two things chefs use more of in their cooking than almost anybody in a home kitchen—butter and salt. The reason is simple: They make things taste better. I expected that we'd have to keep our use of butter in this book to a minimum, but salt? Salt is one of the most essential ingredients in cooking because it brings out the natural flavor of almost everything.

I'll be honest: I didn't know how we'd fare when it got down to testing recipes with minimal salt, but I resolved to give it a try. For the most part, I was surprised at how much you can accomplish with little or no salt.

There are, however, times when salt is essential to preparing a dish that's worth the trouble of cooking and eating. It's tough to imagine a piece of grilled meat without *any* salt or fresh, uncooked tomatoes that haven't been seasoned.

So, when you see salt in these recipes, it's there because I think it needs to be there. Most of the recipes in this book have a universally acceptable amount of sodium, but some have more. If the amounts provided don't fit your plan, you can by all means use less salt. If, on the other hand, you don't see any salt in a recipe, or notice that the amount is rather slight, it's not a mistake. That is all that's needed for that dish. However, if you are accustomed to salting food more liberally, I'll leave that decision for you, your doctor, and your culinary god to consider.

P.S. If you want to lower the amount of sodium in many of the recipes in this book, you can make your own stock using the recipes in the Basics chapter rather than the store-bought broths called for.

"changed fats." They are created when you process (hydrogenate) fats in order to cause them to remain solid at room temperature for use in such products as crackers, cookies, fried foods, snack foods, and some margarine. They have been associated with heart disease. You should avoid trans fats, even if you don't have diabetes.

Note: Some of the examples of fats above have been simplified. Because certain foods contain more than one type of fat, I have listed them based on which type they contain more of. For example, canola oil is composed of roughly two thirds monounsaturated fat and one third polyunsaturated fat, so it is listed under monounsaturated fat.

## the sidebars

Where appropriate, or necessary, I've provided the recipes in this book with one or more of the following features to share advice, information, and points of interest.

### A TIP FROM TOM

This is where I'll offer my professional advice on storing, preparing, or cooking specific ingredients or on kitchen techniques.

### VARIATIONS AND SUGGESTIONS

When possible, I'll maximize the value of recipes with ways to vary them from season to season or to accommodate your own personal taste. I'll also suggest ways to utilize the central idea or combination of a dish in other ways.

### SHOP RIGHT

If I think some notes about how or where to shop for an ingredient are in order, this is where you'll find them.

### DID YOU KNOW?

I'm endlessly fascinated by food science, culture, and history. This is where I'll share notes on ingredients and dishes.

### HOW LOW CAN YOU GO?

This is where I'll offer suggestions on how to lower the fat, carbohydrates, or other elements in a dish even further.

## READING THE NUMBERS

**IMPORTANT:** The nutritional values offered for each recipe are dependable but approximate. The reason for this is simple: If a recipe calls for, say, a medium-size tomato, there will always be a small variance in size between medium-size tomatoes. By the same token, no two brands of mayonnaise are identical, nor are the low-carb wraps made by different companies, or even different brands of turkey bacon. So, please know that while every effort has been made to give an accurate accounting of what goes into each and every dish, it's simply impossible to guarantee an exact amount in what you will produce at home.

**IMPORTANT, PART 2:** Throughout this book, I offer a number of options and variations for many of the recipes. The nutritional analyses provided refer only to the original recipes and do not include optional ingredients or variations, which will alter the nutritional analysis somewhat—in some cases they might raise the sodium count; in others the fat count; and so on—but not beyond what people with diabetes would normally allow themselves from time to time. Also, if an alternative for a particular ingredient is offered in the ingredient list, the analysis refers to the first ingredient listed; using an alternative might slightly change the nutritional makeup of the dish, but not substantially.

## notes on ingredients

Unless otherwise noted in the recipes, here's what I mean when I call for the following ingredients.

❖ Black pepper is freshly ground from a mill.

❖ Bread crumbs are dry, unseasoned bread crumbs.

❖ Butter is unsalted butter.

❖ Canola oil can be replaced by other neutral-flavored oils such as vegetable oil or grapeseed oil.

❖ Flour is all-purpose flour.

❖ Herbs are fresh.

❖ Lemon and lime juice are freshly squeezed and strained. Orange juice doesn't have to be freshly squeezed, but please don't use any made from concentrate.

❖ Parmesan cheese is Parmigiano-Reggiano cheese, which is generally considered the finest variation, with a pleasing salinity and crystalline quality. Similar, less expensive cheeses such as Grana Padano may be substituted, but do not use pregrated cheeses, especially the shelf-stabilized varieties sold in canisters.

❖ Milk is whole milk; low-fat milk is 1 percent milk.

❖ Salt is coarse, kosher salt.

❖ Sugar is granulated sugar.

❖ Wine should be dry for white and medium-bodied, not too tannic for red. Do *not* buy so-called cooking wine from the supermarket.

# You Don't
# Have to Be Diabetic
# to Love
# This Cookbook

# in this chapter

*"By eating breakfast,
I eliminated that mid- to late-morning
blood-sugar nosedive."*

# breakfast and brunch

When I became a professional chef, I pretty much gave up breakfast altogether. I just couldn't wrap my brain around the idea of keeping food in the house when I was bound for a workplace filled with hundreds of pounds of everything my taste buds might desire for the taking.

But when I was diagnosed with diabetes, I began eating breakfast more regularly. It wasn't until then that I truly came to understand that old saw about it being the "main meal." By eating breakfast, I eliminated that mid- to late-morning blood-sugar nosedive that used to possess me almost daily, sending me off in a near rabid search for the most convenient way to quell my appetite.

In hopes of making breakfast as appealing as possible, we developed the recipes in this chapter to be diverse and also pretty quick: Our assumption is that you don't have the luxury of time to whip up something in the morning. For most people, breakfast is the grab-and-go meal, so we conceived these offerings to aid in that frantic first dash of the day.

**A TIP FROM TOM**

**MAKING SMOOTHIES:**
If you find yourself drawn to smoothies for breakfast, or at other times of day, you might want to think about purchasing a blender with an ice-crushing feature—a stronger, more durable motor, with its own button on the control panel. Models with this option are often promoted on the box as being ideal for making frozen cocktails. The same attribute—the ability to produce a thick, slushy drink rather than simply liquefying the ice—makes them perfect for mixing up great smoothies.

Regardless of whether or not your blender has this ice-crushing option, if you find that the blender blade gets stuck when making smoothies try pulsing it rather than letting it run continuously. The start-stop pattern will often help keep solids from collecting around or under the blade.

Finally, if you add powdered supplements to your smoothies, do it while the blender motor is running, slowly adding them to the center vortex of the beverage; the powdered supplements will become better incorporated that way.

# smoothies

Over the past few years, smoothies have become an increasingly popular breakfast, for the same reason most things rise to the level of a trend: They fit the times in which we live. Smoothies are easy to make, quick to drink, relatively healthful, and can be carried out the door, if you make a minor investment in plastic cups and straws. (In other words, they're as good for your wallet as they are for your waistline.) They also have the very charming characteristic of welcoming customization. Just as people crave a tall, skinny, no-whip, decaf latte at Starbucks, they seek out an original Berry Lime Sublime with fiber boost and a little immunity dust at Jamba Juice.

Oh, and there's one other thing that makes smoothies appealing: Prepared correctly, with the right ratio of fruit to juice to milk to ice, they are delicious, refreshing, and appetite filling.

Here are some of my favorite smoothies. Feel free to add a scoop or two of your favorite (natural flavored) protein powder, some fiber, or another nutritional supplement to any of these.

**CARBOHYDRATE CHOICE: 1**

# kiwi mint smoothie

I still think of kiwis as those fuzzy fruits that first appeared on the scene here in the United States in the 1970s. They're not as fashionable as they once were, but I still find them bright and refreshing, especially when paired with mint as they are here. They're also very economical, as larger ones (perfect for smoothie making) are often available at a discounted rate.

The easiest way to peel a kiwi is to cut off the top and bottom, slip a tablespoon between the skin and the flesh, and run the spoon around to scoop out the flesh. **SERVES 4**

## INGREDIENTS

*1 medium-size kiwi, peeled*

*1 cup diced, fresh pineapple*

*1 medium-size banana*

*1½ cups large ice cubes*

*14 fresh mint leaves*

Put the kiwi, pineapple, banana, and ice in a blender and blend on low speed until smooth and you no longer hear the ice pieces shattering. Stop the motor and add 1 mint leaf at a time, pulsing just to chop and incorporate each leaf. Once all of the mint leaves have been added, divide the smoothie among 4 glasses and serve.

## nutritional information
(PER SERVING)

| | |
|---|---|
| Calories | 58 |
| Fat | 0 g |
| Saturated Fat | 0 g |
| Trans Fat | 0 g |
| Total Carbohydrates | 14 g |
| Dietary Fiber | 2 g |
| Total Sugars | 9 g |
| Protein | 1 g |
| Cholesterol | 0 mg |
| Sodium | 2 mg |

## exchanges

| | |
|---|---|
| Fruit | 1 |

CARBOHYDRATE CHOICE: 1

# peach melba smoothie

## WITH RASPBERRY COULIS

Like the famous sundae on which it is based, this smoothie has a topping of raspberry coulis.

**SERVES 4**

## INGREDIENTS

*½ cup fresh or frozen raspberries*

*1 tablespoon freshly squeezed lemon juice*

*1 tablespoon plus 1 teaspoon sugar*

*1 cup peeled, fresh peach slices (about 1 large peach)*

*½ cup nonfat, sugar-free vanilla yogurt*

*½ cup large ice cubes*

**1.** Make the coulis by putting the raspberries, lemon juice, sugar, and 1 tablespoon of cold water in a blender and pulsing to a thick, pourable consistency. Transfer the coulis to a bowl, using a rubber spatula to get as much as possible out of the blender, and clean out the blender.

**2.** Put the peach slices, yogurt, and ice in the blender and blend until thick and creamy and you no longer hear the ice pieces shattering. Divide the smoothies among 4 glasses and swirl some raspberry coulis over each serving.

## nutritional information
(PER SERVING)

| | |
|---|---|
| Calories | 55 |
| Fat | 0 g |
| Saturated Fat | 0 g |
| Trans Fat | 0 g |
| Total Carbohydrates | 13 g |
| Dietary Fiber | 2 g |
| Total Sugars | 10 g |
| Protein | 1 g |
| Cholesterol | 1 mg |
| Sodium | 16 mg |

## exchanges

| | |
|---|---|
| Fruit | 0.5 |
| Other Carbohydrates | 0.5 |

## nutritional information
(PER SERVING)

Calories.............................79
Fat........................................0 g
   Saturated Fat............0 g
   Trans Fat.....................0 g
Total Carbohydrates....18 g
   Dietary Fiber...............1 g
   Total Sugars...............13 g
Protein...................................1 g
Cholesterol......................0 mg
Sodium..............................1 mg

## exchanges

Fruit.........................................1
Other Carbohydrates....0.5

# pineapple and orange smoothie

Pineapple and orange have a great affinity for each other and are also available virtually year-round, making this a recipe for all seasons. Don't be daunted by the volume of pineapple; cube and freeze any remaining portions in a resealable plastic bag for future use. **SERVES 4**

### INGREDIENTS

*1 cup diced fresh pineapple*
*1 cup freshly squeezed orange juice*
*1 cup nonfat, sugar-free vanilla yogurt*
*1 cup large ice cubes*

Put the pineapple, orange juice, yogurt, and ice in a blender and blend on low speed until smooth and you no longer hear the ice pieces shattering. Divide the smoothie among 4 glasses and serve.

## nutritional information
(PER SERVING)

Calories.............................74
Fat........................................0 g
   Saturated Fat............0 g
   Trans Fat.....................0 g
Total Carbohydrates....17 g
   Dietary Fiber...............1 g
   Total Sugars...............13 g
Protein...................................2 g
Cholesterol........................1 mg
Sodium............................34 mg

## exchanges

Fruit.....................................0.5

# pineapple and banana smoothie

Here's a tropical treat that may have you reaching for little paper umbrellas. Be sure to purchase ripe bananas (recognizable by their brown spots) or let them ripen at home a day or two after buying them; bananas blend more easily when slightly softened. **SERVES 4**

### INGREDIENTS

*1½ cups diced fresh pineapple*
*1 cup freshly squeezed orange juice*
*½ large banana*
*1 cup large ice cubes*

Put the pineapple, orange juice, banana, and ice in a blender and blend on low speed until smooth and you no longer hear the ice pieces shattering. Divide the smoothie among 4 glasses and serve.

# apple and banana smoothie

many juice bars and smoothies joints use apple juice the way the rest of us use water: it's an ingredient in many concoctions, there to add volume and a touch of sweetness. This smoothie puts the apple flavor front and center. Be sure to make it with juice rather than cider. They're not as interchangeable as they sound. Cider hasn't been filtered, so it may contain pulp or sediment, not ideal for a smoothie. **SERVES 4**

## INGREDIENTS

*1⅓ cups unsweetened apple juice*
*1 large banana*
*⅔ cup plain nonfat yogurt*
*3 cups small ice cubes*

Put the apple juice, banana, yogurt, and ice in a blender and blend on low speed until smooth and you no longer hear the ice pieces shattering. Divide the smoothie among 4 glasses and serve.

## nutritional information
### (PER SERVING)

| | |
|---|---|
| Calories | 86 |
| Fat | 0 g |
| Saturated Fat | 0 g |
| Trans Fat | 0 g |
| Total Carbohydrates | 21 g |
| Dietary Fiber | 1 g |
| Total Sugars | 15 g |
| Protein | 2 g |
| Cholesterol | 1 mg |
| Sodium | 25 mg |

## exchanges

| | |
|---|---|
| Fruit | 1 |

# melon smoothie

Whichever kind of melon you choose to make this with, honeydew or cantaloupe, be sure to measure carefully; the high water content can result in a thin smoothie. The lime juice provides subtle but essential acidity to offset the sweet fruit. **SERVES 4**

## INGREDIENTS

*6 cups diced honeydew or cantaloupe*
*1 cup plain nonfat yogurt*
*2 teaspoons freshly squeezed lime juice*
*3 cups small ice cubes*

Put the honeydew, yogurt, lime juice, and ice in a blender and blend on low speed until smooth and you no longer hear the ice pieces shattering. Divide the smoothie among 4 glasses and serve.

## nutritional information
### (PER SERVING)

| | |
|---|---|
| Calories | 117 |
| Fat | 0 g |
| Saturated Fat | 0 g |
| Trans Fat | 0 g |
| Total Carbohydrates | 28 g |
| Dietary Fiber | 2 g |
| Total Sugars | 24 g |
| Protein | 4 g |
| Cholesterol | 1 mg |
| Sodium | 80 mg |

## exchanges

| | |
|---|---|
| Fruit | 1.5 |
| Nonfat Milk | 0.5 |

## nutritional information

(PER SERVING)

| | |
|---|---|
| Calories | 129 |
| Fat | 1 g |
| Saturated Fat | 0 g |
| Trans Fat | 0 g |
| Total Carbohydrates | 30 g |
| Dietary Fiber | 3 g |
| Total Sugars | 17 g |
| Protein | 3 g |
| Cholesterol | 3 mg |
| Sodium | 28 mg |

## exchanges

| | |
|---|---|
| Fruit | 2 |

---

**CARBOHYDRATE CHOICES: 2**

# coffee and banana smoothie

this one has it all: fruit, protein (in the form of milk), and coffee, with a subtle undercurrent of cocoa. It's a full breakfast in a glass; about the only thing it doesn't do is read the paper to you.   **SERVES 4**

### INGREDIENTS

*4 medium-size bananas*
*1½ cups brewed coffee*
*¾ cup low-fat (1 percent) milk*
*2 teaspoons unsweetened*
   *cocoa powder*
*1 cup small ice cubes*

---

Put the bananas, coffee, milk, cocoa powder, and ice in a blender and blend on low speed until smooth and you no longer hear the ice pieces shattering. Divide the smoothie among 4 glasses and serve.

## nutritional information

(PER SERVING)

| | |
|---|---|
| Calories | 129 |
| Fat | 2 g |
| Saturated Fat | 1 g |
| Trans Fat | 0 g |
| Total Carbohydrates | 22 g |
| Dietary Fiber | 2 g |
| Total Sugars | 18 g |
| Protein | 8 g |
| Cholesterol | 10 mg |
| Sodium | 95 mg |

## exchanges

| | |
|---|---|
| Fruit | 0.5 |
| Nonfat Milk | 1 |

---

**CARBOHYDRATE CHOICES: 1½**

# blueberry-ginger smoothie

blueberries and ginger are a surprising and decadent breakfast pairing, the kind of duo you expect to find in a cobbler or sorbet rather than a morning drink. This smoothie has extra healthful benefits as blueberries are rich in antioxidants such as vitamins C and E.   **SERVES 4**

### INGREDIENTS

*3 cups low-fat (1 percent) milk*
*2 cups fresh or frozen blueberries*
*¼ cup plus 2 tablespoons plain*
   *nonfat yogurt*
*A few drops of freshly squeezed*
   *lemon juice*
*A few drops of ginger "juice"*
   *(see facing page)*
*6 large ice cubes*

---

Put the milk, blueberries, yogurt, lemon juice, and ginger juice in a blender and blend on low speed until smooth and incorporated. With the motor running, add the ice cubes, one at a time, and blend until you no longer hear the ice pieces shattering. Divide the smoothie among 4 glasses and serve.

CARBOHYDRATE CHOICE: 1

# orange and yogurt parfait

When I was a kid I loved Creamsicles. I gave them up, with other childhood favorites, long before I learned I had diabetes. But my fond memory of them led me to develop this parfait, in which orange juice and orange liqueur are reduced together to make a potent syrup that's used to decorate a dish of yogurt and orange sections. A scattering of almonds adds visual interest and crunch.

The parfaits would also make a fine, light dessert, after a brunch or other meal. **SERVES 4**

## INGREDIENTS

2 cups plain low-fat yogurt

1 teaspoon almond extract

¼ cup slivered almonds

1 medium-size navel orange

3 tablespoons Grand Marnier

1. Put the yogurt and almond extract in a bowl and stir them together gently.

2. Put the almonds in a small pan and toast over medium heat, stirring to prevent scorching, until lightly browned and fragrant, about 2 minutes. Transfer the almonds to a cutting board, let cool, then coarsely chop them.

**A TIP FROM TOM**

**GINGER JUICE:** Uncooked fresh ginger can have a slightly bitter flavor, so in a recipe like this, it's best to extract the juice and discard the fibrous remains. Simply peel and mince some ginger and press it through a garlic press; the juice will be extracted. (Before using the garlic press, wash it in the dishwasher or in boiling water to eliminate any lingering garlic essence and keep the ginger flavor pure.)

To produce larger quantities of ginger juice for other recipes, gather peeled, minced ginger in the center of a piece of cheesecloth. Wrap the cheesecloth around the ginger and, working over a bowl, twist the ends over and over, as though wringing a towel, until juice begins to dip through the cheesecloth. You can use ginger juice to add a peppery flavor to vinaigrettes and marinades.

## nutritional information
### (PER SERVING)

| | |
|---|---|
| Calories | 158 |
| Fat | 5 g |
| Saturated Fat | 1 g |
| Trans Fat | 0 g |
| Total Carbohydrates | 16 g |
| Dietary Fiber | 2 g |
| Total Sugars | 12 g |
| Protein | 8 g |
| Cholesterol | 7 mg |
| Sodium | 86 mg |

## exchanges

| | |
|---|---|
| Fat | 0.5 |
| Fruit | 0.5 |
| Nonfat Milk | 1 |

3. Peel the orange and divide it into sections. Remove the orange sections from the membranes that connect them and set those "scraps" aside. Cut each orange section into small pieces. Squeeze the juice from the orange "scraps" into a saucepan. You should have about ¼ cup of juice. Add the Grand Marnier. Bring to a simmer over medium-high heat and cook until you have about 2 tablespoons of liquid left, 2 to 3 minutes.

4. To serve, divide the orange pieces among 4 attractive glasses or small bowls. Add the yogurt mixture and top with a drizzle of the orange syrup. Then, scatter the chopped almonds over each serving.

**variations and suggestions:** When they're in season (roughly December to July), you can make this with a scarlet-tinted blood orange for a more refined, bittersweet version. Pomelo, a relatively sweet variety of grapefruit that's available in the winter months, also works well.

CARBOHYDRATE CHOICES: 2; 1½ ADJUSTED FOR FIBER

# oatmeal

## WITH BROWN BUTTER AND STONE FRUITS

a s a boy, I craved oatmeal. I remember coming home from hockey practice, which began at what now seems the ungodly hour of 5:30 A.M., ravenously hungry from my predawn adventure on the ice, my muscles still aching from the exertion. My mom often had a pot of oatmeal on the stove, and the smell of those toasty oats wafting through the house drew me to the kitchen like a tractor beam. The craving still visits me every now and then, and when it does, I make this fruit-filled oatmeal. It hits all the right buttons with creamy grains and a range of sweetness from the cherries, peaches, and browned butter.

**SERVES 4**

## INGREDIENTS

2 tablespoons unsalted butter

1 cup rolled oats

Pinch of coarse salt

32 fresh sweet cherries,
    halved and pitted

2 medium-size fresh peaches, pitted
    and diced but not peeled

¼ cup slivered almonds

1. Melt the butter in a small, heavy-bottomed saucepan over low heat and cook, swirling occasionally, until it turns brown, about 8 minutes.

2. Meanwhile, bring 2 cups of water to a boil in a medium-size, heavy-bottomed saucepan over high heat. Stir in the oats and salt, lower the heat so the liquid is simmering, and continue to simmer, stirring occa-sionally, until the oatmeal is creamy but still slightly toothsome, about 5 minutes.

3. Remove the saucepan from the heat. Stir in the brown butter, then gently fold in the cherries, peaches, and almonds.

4. Divide the oatmeal and fruit among 4 bowls and serve.

### nutritional information
(PER SERVING)

| | |
|---|---|
| Calories | 235 |
| Fat | 10 g |
| Saturated Fat | 4 g |
| Trans Fat | 0 g |
| Total Carbohydrates | 31 g |
| Dietary Fiber | 5 g |
| Total Sugars | 14 g |
| Protein | 6 g |
| Cholesterol | 15 mg |
| Sodium | 31 mg |

### exchanges

| | |
|---|---|
| Fat | 1.5 |
| Fruit | 1 |
| Starch | 1 |

CARBOHYDRATE CHOICES: 1½

# asian shrimp toast

deep-fried shrimp toasts are a popular dim sum offering that I've adapted here in a less decadent form, using egg white instead of the entire egg, and lightly panfrying the toast rather than immersing it in a vat of sizzling oil. I actually prefer the result because you taste each ingredient cleanly and distinctly. The toasts are also very pretty thanks to their triangle shape and the way the flecks of color show through the cooked egg white. These are perfect for brunch, served from either a buffet or a basket in the center of the table. They're also a viable weekday treat, requiring only slightly more time to make than, say, French toast. **SERVES 4**

## nutritional information

**(PER SERVING— 6 TRIANGLES)**

| | |
|---|---|
| Calories | 244 |
| Fat | 11 g |
| Saturated Fat | 1 g |
| Trans Fat | 0 g |
| Total Carbohydrates | 21 g |
| Dietary Fiber | 0 g |
| Total Sugars | 4 g |
| Protein | 16 g |
| Cholesterol | 87 mg |
| Sodium | 360 mg |

## exchanges

| | |
|---|---|
| Fat | 1.5 |
| Starch | 1.5 |
| Lean Meat | 1.5 |

### INGREDIENTS

8 ounces shrimp (about 8 large shrimp), peeled, deveined, and coarsely chopped

¼ cup chopped napa cabbage

¼ cup coarsely chopped scallion greens

½ teaspoon minced garlic

½ teaspoon soy sauce

½ teaspoon Asian (dark) sesame oil

1 large egg white

2 tablespoons whole milk

6 thin slices white bread

2 tablespoons canola oil

1. Make sure all of the ingredients are cold. For the best results, also chill the food processor bowl and steel blade in the refrigerator or freezer briefly before using.

2. Put the shrimp, cabbage, scallion, garlic, soy sauce, sesame oil, and egg white in the food processor fitted with the steel blade. Pulse until everything is incorporated. Drizzle in the milk and pulse until just combined. Spread the shrimp mixture over 1 side of each slice of bread, pressing down gently to ensure the shrimp adheres to the bread.

3. Heat 1 teaspoon of canola oil in a heavy-bottomed, non-stick pan over medium-high heat. Arrange 1 slice of bread, with the shrimp mixture side down, in the pan and fry until the egg white is cooked and the shrimp mixture is firmly melded to the bread, about 3 minutes. Use a rubber spatula to turn the bread over and cook on the other side until toasted, about 2 minutes longer. Transfer the toast to a plate and loosely cover with aluminum foil to keep warm. Repeat with the remaining slices of bread and shrimp mixture, adding 1 teaspoon of oil to the pan before each toast.

4. Slice the toasts diagonally into 4 pieces each. Arrange on a plate or platter and serve.

# breakfast burritos

## WITH EGG WHITES AND SAUSAGE

**b**reakfast burritos are a modest form of early-morning rebellion. First of all, they are meant to be picked up, which wins them my love right off the bat because I've always enjoyed food that doesn't require silverware. Secondly, the idea of a burrito for breakfast is only about a half step removed from eating ice cream and cake at the crack of dawn. Burritos weren't invented with breakfast in mind. They're usually spicy, meat-filled things that are meant to be washed down with soda or beer. Make them with eggs and sausage, however, and they fit right in at the morning table.     **SERVES 4**

## nutritional information
### (PER SERVING)

Calories.................294
Fat............................16 g
   Saturated Fat............1 g
   Trans Fat..................0 g
Total Carbohydrates...20 g
   Dietary Fiber............11 g
   Total Sugars............3 g
Protein.....................19 g
Cholesterol..............28 mg
Sodium..................464 mg

## exchanges

Fat...............................2
Starch..........................1
Medium Fat Meat..........1
Lean Meat..................0.5

### INGREDIENTS

*1 tablespoon canola oil*

*2 spicy turkey sausage links*
   *(about 3 ounces each), diced*

*4 large egg whites, lightly beaten*

*4 low-carb tortillas*
   *(10 inches in diameter)*

*2 scallions, both white and green parts,*
   *thinly sliced*

*1 large ripe Hass avocado, pitted,*
   *peeled, and sliced*

*1 medium-size plum tomato, diced*

*¼ cup nonfat sour cream*

1. Heat the oil in a large, heavy-bottomed, nonstick pan over medium heat. Add the sausage and cook, stirring, until browned all over, about 6 minutes. Remove the sausage from the pan with a slotted spoon and drain on paper towels.

2. Add the egg whites to the same pan and cook, stirring occasionally, until they set up nicely to your taste, 3 to 4 minutes.

3. Place 1 tortilla on each of 4 plates. Use a rubber spatula to divide the egg whites among the centers of the tortillas. Top with some sausage, scallion, avocado, tomato, and sour cream. Roll the tortilla around the filling and tuck one end in to enclose it, leaving the other end open, like a cone. Repeat with the remaining tortillas. Serve the burritos with the seam side down.

### A TIP FROM TOM

**WORKING WITH AVOCADOS:** I'd dare say that there's no avocado recipe that doesn't require you to cut it in half and remove the pit before doing anything else. To accomplish this small feat, run a large, heavy knife around the avocado lengthwise, cutting all the way down to the pit, then twist and separate the halves. To remove the pit, hack the heel of your knife into the pit (take care when doing this; it's best to steady the avocado on the counter) and it should come right out with a tug. To remove the flesh from the skin, run a tablespoon between the two and dislodge the flesh.

**variations and suggestions:** Add some diced jalapeño pepper or grated pepper Jack cheese to bring a little spice to this burrito.

If you have company for brunch, you can simply set out all the filling ingredients and a stack of tortillas and invite your guests to make their own.

CARBOHYDRATE CHOICE: 1

# baked eggs

## WITH SPINACH

eggs Florentine is one of those superindulgent breakfast creations that really hits the spot. It's been freely adapted over the years but usually involves eggs, spinach, cheese, bread (an English muffin provides the base in many American kitchens), and a cream sauce. Of course, you and I can't shoot the works and eat the full on version, but this stripped down alternative takes the essence of the dish—the marriage of eggs and spinach—and makes it special in its own right with dolled up sautéed spinach and a scattering of Parmesan and bread crumbs that offer just enough representation of the original to satisfy the palate's expectation. **SERVES 4**

### nutritional information
(PER SERVING)

Calories.......................186
Fat..................................11 g
   Saturated Fat............3 g
   Trans Fat...................0 g
Total Carbohydrates.....11 g
   Dietary Fiber............3 g
   Total Sugars.............1 g
Protein...........................13 g
Cholesterol............220 mg
Sodium...................320 mg

### exchanges

Fat...................................1
Starch............................0.5
Medium Fat Meat.............1
Lean Meat.....................0.5
Vegetables......................1

### INGREDIENTS

1 recipe Ouest Spinach (page 283)
4 large eggs

¼ cup finely grated Parmesan
¼ cup dry bread crumbs

1. Preheat the oven to 350°F.

2. Put the spinach in a 12-inch, ovenproof, nonstick pan and heat over medium heat, stirring, for 2 minutes. Use a wooden spoon to spread the spinach evenly over the bottom of the pan.

3. Put the eggs in a bowl. Add ¼ cup of water and whisk together. Pour the eggs over the spinach and cook just

until the eggs begin to set, 2 to 3 minutes. Scatter the Parmesan and bread crumbs over the top and transfer the pan to the oven. Bake until the eggs are done, the cheese is melted, and the bread crumbs are golden, about 5 minutes.

4. Remove the pan from the oven. Use a rubber spatula to cut the eggs into 4 wedges, transfer 1 wedge to each of 4 plates, and serve.

CARBOHYDRATE CHOICE: 1

# open-faced spanish omelet

an omelet to me isn't so much about the vehicle (the egg), as the passengers (the filling), a predilection that became even more true when I began factoring diabetes into my menu planning: In the case of a vegetable omelet, eating more vegetable and less omelet was a very desirable objective. For that reason, I started making an omelet based on the Basque dish *piperade*, a stew of tomatoes, onions, and peppers. Rather than fill a rolled omelet with a mixture of those ingredients, I serve the "omelet" flat on the plate, and mound a stew of large-cut vegetables in the center. It's a very pretty composition, so it's suitable for entertaining, but it's also easy enough to make that you could call on it any day of the week.     **SERVES 4**

## INGREDIENTS

*2 tablespoons olive oil*

*2 large Spanish onions, cut into thick slices*

*1 green bell pepper, stemmed, seeded, and cut lengthwise into thick slices*

*2 large cloves garlic, minced*

*¼ cup tomato paste*

*1 medium-size plum tomato, diced, with its liquid*

*8 black olives, pitted and thinly sliced*

*Nonstick cooking spray*

*4 large eggs, beaten separately*

*2 tablespoons minced fresh flat-leaf parsley leaves*

## did you know?

Every time I look at the ingredients on a can of tomato paste I do a bit of a double take because the only thing this versatile product contains is tomatoes that have been cooked down and strained to remove the skin and seeds. Though it has an appearance, and name, that connote artificiality, it's actually very pure. Everything you see in its nutritional analysis is naturally occurring, including the sodium. Incidentally, along with beets and spinach, tomatoes contain a greater amount of sodium relative to other fruits and vegetables, so, when cooking with any of them go easy on the salt.

## nutritional information
(PER SERVING)

| | |
|---|---|
| Calories | 195 |
| Fat | 12 g |
| Saturated Fat | 3 g |
| Trans Fat | 0 g |
| Total Carbohydrates | 14 g |
| Dietary Fiber | 3 g |
| Total Sugars | 6 g |
| Protein | 8 g |
| Cholesterol | 215 mg |
| Sodium | 277 mg |

## exchanges

| | |
|---|---|
| Fat | 1.5 |
| Medium Fat Meat | 1 |
| Vegetables | 2 |

1. Heat the olive oil in a large, deep, heavy-bottomed pan over medium heat. Add the onions, bell pepper, and garlic to the pan and cook slowly, stirring, until they are very soft but not browned, about 15 minutes. Add the tomato paste and stir to coat the other ingredients. Stir in the tomato and olives and continue to cook, stirring occasionally, for 5 minutes longer.

2. Spray a heavy-bottomed nonstick pan with nonstick cooking spray. Add 1 egg and cook without stirring, so it more or less holds the shape of a circle, until it sets up nicely, 1 to 2 minutes. Use a spatula to slide the egg out of the pan and onto a plate and top it with a quarter of the onion and pepper stew. Repeat with the remaining eggs and pepper stew.

3. Scatter parsley over each omelet and serve.

# frittatas

a frittata is commonly referred to as an Italian omelet, but I usually just think of it as an open-faced one. If you've never made a frittata, it's a very cook-friendly way of making an omelet because it takes the dexterity out of the equation: There's no rolling or folding. You just beat the eggs, pour them into a pan, cook them partially on the stove top, add the desired filling(s), then finish the frittata in the oven. My approach to making frittatas is to minimize the amount of egg, specifically the yolks, so these are built on a foundation of whole eggs, egg whites, and water.

There are just three frittatas here, but once you master the formula, the sky is truly the limit. Experiment with this format and you'll soon find that you've created your own house favorites.

CARBOHYDRATE CHOICE: 0

# roasted tomato, goat cheese, and thyme frittata

adapt this frittata freely, using different cheeses and herbs. If you eliminate the tomato, replace the goat cheese with grated Gruyère, and add some diced, browned turkey bacon, you'll have an appealing approximation of a quiche lorraine.   **SERVES 8**

## INGREDIENTS

*1 teaspoon olive oil*
*3 large eggs plus 3 large egg whites*
*2 teaspoons fresh thyme leaves*
*Pinch of coarse salt*
*Pinch of freshly ground black*
   *pepper*
*1 recipe Roasted Plum Tomatoes*
   *(page 323), at room temperature*
*2 ounces crumbled goat cheese*
   *(about ½ cup), at room*
   *temperature*

1. Preheat the oven to 325°F.

2. Heat the olive oil in a 12-inch, ovenproof, heavy-bottomed, nonstick pan over medium heat.

3. Meanwhile, put the eggs, egg whites, and 3 tablespoons of water in a large bowl, add the thyme, salt, and pepper, and whisk together. Pour the egg mixture into the pan and cook until the eggs begin to set up, about 3 minutes. Scatter the tomatoes evenly on top of the eggs; they should sink about halfway into them, resting on the cooked bottom of the frittata.

4. Scatter the goat cheese over the frittata, transfer the pan to the oven, and bake the frittata until the eggs are completely set and the goat cheese is softened and slightly melted, about 4 minutes.

5. Remove the pan from the oven. Use a rubber spatula to cut the frittata into 8 wedges, transfer 1 wedge to each of 8 plates and serve. You can also serve the frittata family style by using the spatula to carefully slide it out onto a large plate or platter.

## nutritional information
**(PER SERVING)**

| | |
|---|---|
| Calories | 81 |
| Fat | 5 g |
| Saturated Fat | 2 g |
| Trans Fat | 0 g |
| Total Carbohydrates | 3 g |
| Dietary Fiber | 1 g |
| Total Sugars | 2 g |
| Protein | 6 g |
| Cholesterol | 88 mg |
| Sodium | 88 mg |

## exchanges

| | |
|---|---|
| Medium Fat Meat | 0.5 |
| High Fat Meat | 0.5 |
| Vegetables | 0.5 |

## nutritional information
(PER SERVING)

| | |
|---|---|
| Calories | 51 |
| Fat | 3 g |
| Saturated Fat | 1 g |
| Trans Fat | 0 g |
| Total Carbohydrates | 2 g |
| Dietary Fiber | 1 g |
| Total Sugars | 1 g |
| Protein | 6 g |
| Cholesterol | 82 mg |
| Sodium | 116 mg |

## exchanges

| | |
|---|---|
| Medium Fat Meat | 0.5 |
| Lean Meat | 0.5 |

CARBOHYDRATE CHOICE: 0

# asparagus and smoked salmon frittata

Smoked salmon and eggs is one of those simple, perfect breakfast combinations that's been around, and presumably will continue to be around, forever. This frittata adds asparagus to the time-tested mix, baking it into the eggs, with thin slices of salmon resting on top that all but melt into the frittata.

Timing is essential here: Be sure to drape the salmon over the frittata as soon as the pan comes out of the oven.

By the way, if you've ever wondered why smoked salmon looks raw, it's because the salmon is first cured, which "cooks" it. The smoke is applied by an indirect source, just to flavor the fish, so it never cooks in the traditional sense. **SERVES 8**

### INGREDIENTS

*8 spears pencil-thin asparagus*
*(about ½ pound), ends trimmed*
*1 teaspoon olive oil*
*3 large eggs plus 3 large egg whites*
*Pinch of coarse salt*
*Pinch of freshly ground black pepper*
*2 ounces very thinly sliced smoked*
*salmon*

1. Preheat the oven to 325°F.

2. Bring a large pot of water to a boil. Fill a large bowl halfway with ice water.

3. Cook the asparagus in the boiling water until tender, about 1 minute. Use tongs to remove the asparagus from the pot and transfer it to the ice water to stop the cooking and preserve the color. Once the asparagus has cooled, drain it and pat dry with paper towels.

4. Heat the olive oil in a 12-inch, ovenproof, heavy-bottomed, nonstick pan over medium heat.

5. Meanwhile, put the eggs, egg whites, and 3 tablespoons of water in a large bowl, add the salt and pepper, and whisk together. Pour the egg mixture into the pan and cook until the eggs begin to set up, about 3 minutes. Arrange the asparagus spears in the pan like the spokes of a wheel; they should sink about halfway into the eggs, resting on the cooked bottom of the frittata. Transfer the pan to the oven and bake the frittata until the eggs are completely set, about 4 minutes.

6. Remove the pan from the oven and drape the slices of salmon over the frittata in a single layer; this will warm the salmon just enough to meld the

flavors of the fish and the frittata. Use a rubber spatula to carefully slide the frittata out onto a large plate or platter. Using a serrated knife, cut the frittata into 8 wedges, making sure to include an asparagus spear in each wedge, and serve.

**variations and suggestions:** You can make a similar frittata by replacing the smoked salmon with very thin slices of Prosciutto di Parma. For a clever presentation, wrap the asparagus with the prosciutto just before adding it to the frittata.

**CARBOHYDRATE CHOICE: 0**

# broccoli rabe and turkey sausage frittata

broccoli rabe and sausage is the basis of a popular pasta dish from the Puglia region of Italy that's made with orecchiette, or ear-shaped pasta. The bitter *rappini* (as broccoli rabe is called back in Italy) and the fatty, slightly spicy sausage are perfect foils for each other. This frittata borrows that combination, relocating it to breakfast and substituting turkey sausage for the original's pork sausage. **SERVES 8**

## INGREDIENTS

*1 link (about 3 ounces) spicy turkey sausage*
*1 teaspoon olive oil*
*3 large eggs plus 3 large egg whites*
*Pinch of coarse salt*
*Pinch of freshly ground black pepper*
*½ recipe Broccoli Rabe with Olive Oil and Red Pepper (page 274), at room temperature*
*1½ teaspoons freshly grated Parmesan cheese*

1. Preheat the oven to 325°F.

2. Remove the sausage from the casing and crumble it into a small bowl or cut it into small dice.

3. Heat the olive oil in a 12-inch, ovenproof, heavy-bottomed, nonstick pan over medium heat. Add the sausage and cook until the fat is rendered and the sausage is nicely browned all over, about 6 minutes. Using a slotted spoon, transfer the sausage to a plate, leaving as much fat as possible behind in the pan.

## nutritional information
**(PER SERVING)**

| | |
|---|---|
| Calories | 85 |
| Fat | 5 g |
| Saturated Fat | 1 g |
| Trans Fat | 0 g |
| Total Carbohydrates | 3 g |
| Dietary Fiber | 0 g |
| Total Sugars | 1 g |
| Protein | 7 g |
| Cholesterol | 87 mg |
| Sodium | 148 mg |

## exchanges

| | |
|---|---|
| Fat | 0.5 |
| Medium Fat Meat | 0.5 |
| Vegetables | 0.5 |

4. Put the eggs, egg whites, and 3 tablespoons of water in a large bowl, add the salt and pepper, and whisk together. Pour the egg mixture into the pan and cook until the eggs begin to set up, about 3 minutes. Scatter the cooked sausage and broccoli rabe mixture evenly on top of the eggs; they should sink about halfway into them, resting on the cooked bottom of the frittata.

5. Scatter the Parmesan cheese over the frittata, transfer the pan to the oven, and bake the frittata until the eggs are completely set and the cheese is melted and lightly browned, about 4 minutes.

6. Remove the pan from the oven. Use a rubber spatula to cut the frittata into 8 wedges, transfer 1 wedge to each of 8 plates and serve. You can also serve the frittata family style by using the spatula to carefully slide it out onto a large plate or platter.

## nutritional information
(PER SERVING)

| | |
|---|---|
| Calories | 151 |
| Fat | 11 g |
|    Saturated Fat | 4 g |
|    Trans Fat | 0 g |
| Total Carbohydrates | 4 g |
|    Dietary Fiber | 1 g |
|    Total Sugars | 1 g |
| Protein | 9 g |
| Cholesterol | 222 mg |
| Sodium | 236 mg |

## exchanges

| | |
|---|---|
| Fat | 1 |
| Medium Fat Meat | 1 |
| High Fat Meat | 0.5 |
| Vegetables | 0.5 |

CARBOHYDRATE CHOICE: 0

# eggs in hell

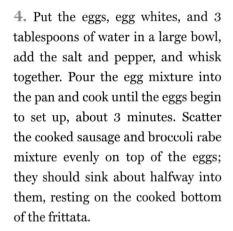

In his first cookbook, the great California chef Jeremiah Tower featured a dish called Eggs in Hell, Spanish-Style. I've long since forgotten exactly what it contained, or how it was made, but the name has stayed with me for years, an amusing moniker for a breakfast that sounds more like a Quentin Tarantino movie than something to eat. Eventually, I couldn't resist any longer: I devised my own interpretation of Eggs in Hell. It's devilishly red and appropriately spicy, with runny yolks that make it sinfully (get it?) fun to eat.

Note that you will need four attractive small baking dishes or ramekins in which to cook and serve this.

SERVES 4

## INGREDIENTS

1 tablespoon olive oil

½ small Spanish onion, finely diced

3 large cloves garlic, very thinly sliced

1 small plum tomato, cut into
    small dice with its seeds

¼ teaspoon coarse salt

2½ tablespoons cider vinegar

½ teaspoon crushed red pepper flakes

1½ tablespoons reduced-sugar
    tomato ketchup

¼ teaspoon freshly ground black
    pepper

1 tablespoon minced fresh cilantro
    leaves

4 large eggs

1 tablespoon minced fresh chives

1 ounce crumbled goat cheese,
    Jack, or queso blanco
    (about ¼ cup crumbled)

**1.** Preheat the oven to 350°F.

**2.** Heat the olive oil in a small heavy-bottomed, nonstick pan over medium heat. Add the onion and garlic and cook until softened but not browned, about 4 minutes. Stir in the tomato and salt and cook, stirring, for 2 minutes.

**3.** Stir in the cider vinegar, red pepper flakes, ketchup, black pepper, cilantro, and ½ cup plus 2 tablespoons of water and cook until warmed through, about 2 minutes.

**4.** Divide the mixture among 4 small baking dishes or ramekins and crack an egg over each serving. Set the ramekins on a baking sheet and bake until the egg whites are set but the yolks are still runny, 12 to 15 minutes.

**5.** Remove the baking sheet from the oven and use tongs or oven mitts to carefully transfer 1 ramekin to each of 4 plates. Scatter some chives and cheese over each dish and serve hot.

Eggs in

Hell

# flourless (egg) crêpes

I n 1977, in my first restaurant kitchen job, at L'Auberge du Cochon Rouge (the Inn of the Red Pig) in Ithaca, New York, I learned to hate crêpes. (Stay with me here; this story has a happy ending.) The restaurant did a brisk brunch business, and part of the good-natured punishment of my role as apprentice to the chef, Etienne Merle, was coming in at the crack of dawn on Saturday and Sunday to precook scores of crêpes, then working no fewer than eight pans during service in order to cook and fill the paper-thin pancakes to order. I felt like that performer on *The Ed Sullivan Show*, no doubt distantly related to an octopus, who spun plates at the end of all those long sticks.

It would have been nice if my chef, an otherwise fine man, had told me that you could make crêpes a day ahead, at a more civilized hour. I subsequently learned that lesson, which prompted me to rethink crêpes, and in time I devised a more user-friendly, and more healthful, way to make them, with nothing but eggs. That's right: A beaten egg thinned slightly with water will, when cooked in a pan over high heat, behave very much like a crêpe. It will hold its shape, support and contain a filling, and fold like a crêpe as well. So, here you have a selection of flourless, virtually carb-free crêpes.

## nutritional information
### (PER SERVING)

| | |
|---|---|
| Calories | 113 |
| Fat | 7 g |
| Saturated Fat | 3 g |
| Trans Fat | 0 g |
| Total Carbohydrates | 2 g |
| Dietary Fiber | 0 g |
| Total Sugars | 0 g |
| Protein | 10 g |
| Cholesterol | 223 mg |
| Sodium | 98 mg |

## exchanges

| | |
|---|---|
| Fat | 0.5 |
| Medium Fat Meat | 1.5 |

CARBOHYDRATE CHOICE: 0

## mozzarella, basil, and oregano crêpes

I f you like, expand on the Italian theme of these crêpes by adding some minced Prosciutto di Parma or chopped, sundried tomatoes along with the cheese. **SERVES 4**

### INGREDIENTS

*4 large eggs*

*1 teaspoon dried oregano*

*Pinch of coarse salt*

*Pinch of freshly ground black pepper*

*Nonstick cooking spray*

*2 ounces salt-free mozzarella cheese, cut into small cubes*

*20 fresh basil leaves, cut into chiffonade (see this page)*

1. Preheat the oven to 350°F.

2. Put the eggs and ¼ cup of cold water in a bowl and whisk them together. Whisk in the oregano and season with the salt and pepper.

3. Spray a nonstick, 12-inch pan with nonstick cooking spray and heat it over medium heat. Ladle about one quarter of the eggs into the pan and swirl to cover the bottom. Cook the egg until it begins to set up, 30 to 40 seconds. It's okay if the crêpe is still a little wet (undercooked) on top. Loosen the side of the crêpe with a rubber spatula and slide it off onto a plate. Repeat with the remaining eggs to make a total of 4 crêpes, spraying the pan with more nonstick cooking spray as necessary and stacking the crêpes.

4. Scatter a quarter of the mozzarella and basil over half of a crêpe. Fold the bare half of the crêpe over the filling and press down on it to flatten. Fold the crêpe in half again to form a triangle. Repeat with the remaining crêpes, mozzarella, and basil. Place the folded crêpes on a nonstick baking sheet and bake until the filling is warmed through, 5 to 6 minutes.

5. Put 1 crêpe on each of 4 plates and serve.

**CARBOHYDRATE CHOICE: 0**

# goat cheese and spinach crêpes

These very traditional crêpes can be augmented by adding sautéed button mushrooms or by seasoning the goat cheese with minced fresh garlic and herbs an hour or two before cooking the crêpes.      **SERVES 4**

## INGREDIENTS

*4 large eggs*

*Pinch of coarse salt*

*Pinch of freshly ground black pepper*

*Nonstick cooking spray*

*2 ounces crumbled goat cheese (about ½ cup), at room temperature*

*¾ cup drained steamed spinach (from about ¾ pound fresh spinach)*

1. Preheat the oven to 350°F.

## shop right

**MOZZARELLA:** No doubt because so many of us grew up seeing mozzarella breaded and fried in little batons, or grated and melted over pizza, it's still viewed as something of an industrial product in the United States, an impression furthered by the fact that until recently the only mozzarella available in supermarkets was the very firm, shrink-wrapped variety. But it's now much easier to find supermarket mozzarellas that lean toward the artisanal, which is good because mozzarella is meant to be eaten not long after it's produced. For a real treat, try to put your hands on some *burrata,* a cheese with a mozzarella exterior that gives way to a liquid center of mozzarella and cream.

## nutritional information
(PER SERVING)

| | |
|---|---|
| Calories | 118 |
| Fat | 8 g |
| Saturated Fat | 4 g |
| Trans Fat | 0 g |
| Total Carbohydrates | 2 g |
| Dietary Fiber | 1 g |
| Total Sugars | 0 g |
| Protein | 10 g |
| Cholesterol | 222 mg |
| Sodium | 171 mg |

## exchanges

| | |
|---|---|
| Fat | 0.5 |
| Medium Fat Meat | 1 |
| Vegetables | 0.5 |

## shop right

**OREGANO:** While I almost always use fresh herbs, I sometimes use dried oregano instead of fresh because it has a less intense flavor. In dishes such as this one, where the herb is stirred into a wet mixture, it also survives the cooking process better.

**2.** Put the eggs and ¼ cup of cold water in a bowl and whisk them together. Season the eggs with the salt and pepper.

**3.** Spray a nonstick, 12-inch pan with nonstick cooking spray and heat it over medium heat. Ladle about one quarter of the eggs into the pan and swirl to cover the bottom. Cook the egg until it begins to set up, 30 to 40 seconds. It's okay if the crêpe is still a little wet (undercooked) on top. Loosen the side of the crêpe with a rubber spatula and slide it off onto a plate. Repeat with the remaining eggs to make a total of 4 crêpes, spraying

the pan with more nonstick cooking spray as necessary and stacking the crêpes.

**4.** Scatter a quarter of the goat cheese and spinach over half of a crêpe. Fold the bare half of the crêpe over the filling and press down on it to flatten. Fold the crêpe in half again to form a triangle. Repeat with the remaining crêpes, goat cheese, and spinach. Place the folded crêpes on a nonstick baking sheet and bake until the filling is warmed through, 5 to 6 minutes.

**5.** Put 1 crêpe on each of 4 plates and serve.

## nutritional information
(PER SERVING)

| | |
|---|---|
| Calories | 127 |
| Fat | 9 g |
| Saturated Fat | 4 g |
| Trans Fat | 0 g |
| Total Carbohydrates | 2 g |
| Dietary Fiber | 0 g |
| Total Sugars | 0 g |
| Protein | 10 g |
| Cholesterol | 230 mg |
| Sodium | 181 mg |

## exchanges

| | |
|---|---|
| Fat | 0.5 |
| Medium Fat Meat | 1 |
| High Fat Meat | 0.5 |

CARBOHYDRATE CHOICE: 0

# pepper jack, cilantro, and chive crêpes

for a fun, communal experience, serve these crêpes open-faced, with such garnishes as nonfat sour cream, Asparagus Guacamole (page 35), and Salsa (page 318) alongside, and let people add the filling to the crêpes, then fold them up themselves. If you have an open kitchen, and some confidence at the stove, you can also make these to order, taking requests from each guest. **SERVES 4**

## INGREDIENTS

*4 large eggs*
*1 teaspoon minced fresh chives*
*Pinch of coarse salt*
*Pinch of freshly ground black pepper*
*Nonstick cooking spray*
*2 ounces pepper Jack cheese, cut into
    small cubes (about ½ cup)*
*¼ cup minced fresh cilantro leaves*

**1.** Preheat the oven to 350°F.

2. Put the eggs and ¼ cup of cold water in a bowl and whisk them together. Whisk in the chives and season with the salt and pepper.

3. Spray a nonstick, 12-inch pan with nonstick cooking spray and heat it over medium heat. Ladle about one quarter of the eggs into the pan and swirl to cover the bottom. Cook the egg until it begins to set up, 30 to 40 seconds. It's okay if the crêpe is still a little wet (undercooked) on top. Loosen the side of the crêpe with a rubber spatula and slide it off onto a plate. Repeat with the remaining eggs to make a total of 4 crêpes, spraying the pan with more nonstick cooking spray as necessary and stacking the crêpes.

4. Scatter a quarter of the pepper Jack and cilantro over half of a crêpe. Fold the bare half of the crêpe over the filling and press down on it to flatten. Fold the crêpe in half again to form a triangle. Repeat with the remaining crêpes, pepper Jack and cilantro. Place the folded crêpes on a nonstick baking sheet and bake until the filling is warmed through, 5 to 6 minutes.

5. Put 1 crêpe on each of 4 plates and serve.

CARBOHYDRATE CHOICES: 2

# cherry-cheese blintzes

i didn't even know what a blintz was until I moved to one of the brunch capitals of the world, the Upper West Side of Manhattan, where New Yorkers line up outside any number of eateries, even in the brutal dead of winter, to wait for a place to read their Sunday *Times* in the company of their fellow bed-headed, groggy-eyed city dwellers.

Cheese blintzes are well worth rediscovering, or trying for the first time, because they are fun. In fact, if they weren't warm, or the filling wasn't tucked into a pancakelike wrapper, their dessertlike qualities—a predominance of cream, often topped with fruit, not unlike a sundae—might be more apparent.

## plan ahead

The unfilled blintzes may be made up to 2 hours ahead of time and kept between sheets of wax paper at room temperature.

## nutritional information

| | |
|---|---|
| Calories | 305 |
| Fat | 16 g |
| Saturated Fat | 9 g |
| Trans Fat | 0 g |
| Total Carbohydrates | 29 g |
| Dietary Fiber | 2 g |
| Total Sugars | 14 g |
| Protein | 11 g |
| Cholesterol | 154 mg |
| Sodium | 286 mg |

## exchanges

| | |
|---|---|
| Fat | 3 |
| Fruit | 1 |
| Starch | 0.5 |
| Medium Fat Meat | 0.5 |

The trick to the blintzes here is that they use nonfat and low-fat dairy options for the filling, then minimize the fat even further by putting the fruit, in this case cherries, inside, rather than spooning it over the top. This means you need less of the cheese and sour cream mixture to fill the blintz.

These are perfect for a weekend or holiday brunch or buffet. **SERVES 4**

### INGREDIENTS

2 large eggs

3 tablespoons low-fat (1 percent) milk

½ teaspoon baking powder

¼ cup plus 2 tablespoons all-purpose flour

¾ cup whipped full-fat cream cheese

½ cup nonfat sour cream

¼ cup low-fat cottage cheese

40 fresh sweet cherries, halved and pitted

1 tablespoon unsalted butter

1. Put the eggs, milk, baking powder, flour and 3 tablespoons of water in a bowl and whisk well. (You can also do this in a blender.) Let stand for 30 minutes at room temperature.

2. Meanwhile, put the cream cheese, sour cream, and cottage cheese in a bowl and stir together with a rubber spatula until well incorporated. Gently fold in the cherries, taking care not to crush them.

3. Preheat the oven to 350°F.

4. Melt 1 teaspoon of butter in an 8-inch, heavy-bottomed, nonstick pan over medium-high heat, swirling it to cover the surface of the pan. Ladle in about 2 tablespoons of batter and swirl to coat the bottom of the pan.

Cook the blintz until the top begins to set and the bottom is golden, about 5 minutes. Use a spatula to help slide the blintz out of the pan and onto a large plate. Repeat to make 7 more blintzes, adding more butter as necessary and stacking the blintzes between layers of paper towels or wax paper.

5. To assemble the blintzes, spoon approximately ¼ cup of filling onto each. Roll the blintzes tautly around the filling and arrange them in a baking dish, seam side down, without crowding. Bake the blintzes until warmed through and lightly golden, 7 to 8 minutes.

6. To serve, use a rubber spatula to divide the blintzes evenly among 4 plates.

variations and suggestions: When it comes to fruit and cream combinations, berries get all the attention. Most people's minds go to strawberries, blueberries, and raspberries when looking for something to top with fresh or whipped heavy cream. But I've always felt that cherries have an even greater affinity for cream. For a healthful alternative, skip the blintzes and enjoy a cup of low-fat vanilla yogurt with fresh, sweet cherries; for a less healthful version, cherries and full-fat, Greek-style yogurt are a match made in heaven. You can't eat too much, but a little goes a very long way.

CARBOHYDRATE CHOICES: 2

# whole wheat banana pancakes

**m**y coauthor, Andrew Friedman, makes his twin children whole-grain pancakes on weekends, using a recipe from the pages of the *Gourmet* cookbook. The combination of whole wheat flour and cornmeal makes for an unusually textured, and relatively light, pancake. This recipe is based on that one, although it goes easy on the sugar and adds a mashed banana for creaminess and, of course, the flavor of the fruit itself.

**SERVES 6**

## nutritional information
(PER SERVING—ABOUT 3 SMALL PANCAKES)

| | |
|---|---|
| Calories | 297 |
| Fat | 16 g |
| Saturated Fat | 4 g |
| Trans Fat | 0 g |
| Total Carbohydrates | 33 g |
| Dietary Fiber | 4 g |
| Total Sugars | 7 g |
| Protein | 8 g |
| Cholesterol | 85 mg |
| Sodium | 328 mg |

## exchanges

| | |
|---|---|
| Fat | 2.5 |
| Nonfat Milk | 0.5 |
| Starch | 1.5 |
| Fruit | 0.5 |
| Medium Fat Meat | 0.5 |

## INGREDIENTS

2 large eggs, separated

1½ cups low-fat (1 percent) milk

¼ cup canola oil

1¼ cups whole wheat flour

⅓ cup yellow cornmeal

2 teaspoons baking powder

1½ teaspoons sugar

Pinch of coarse salt

1 medium-size ripe banana
    (see next page), mashed with a fork

2 tablespoons (¼ stick) unsalted
    butter

shop right

**BANANAS: Just** as very ripe, or even overripe, bananas are crucial to the success of banana bread, using soft, superripe bananas is the way to go here. The banana's texture makes it easy to mix in with the other ingredients, and its pronounced sweetness helps make up for the relatively small amount of granulated sugar in the recipe.

1. Put the egg yolks, milk, and oil in a large bowl and whisk them together.

2. Put the whole wheat flour, cornmeal, baking powder, sugar, and salt in another bowl and stir them together, then stir them into the wet ingredients. Let the batter stand for 5 minutes.

3. Put the egg whites in a blender and whip until stiff peaks form. With the motor running, blend in the batter, then quickly blend in the banana.

4. Melt 1 tablespoon of the butter in a 12-inch nonstick pan over medium heat. Add small ladlefuls of batter to the pan. When the pancakes begin to bubble and the bottoms are golden brown, about 3 minutes, carefully turn them over with a spatula. Cook each pancake until it is set, about 2 minutes longer. Transfer the pancakes to a plate and cover them loosely with aluminum foil to keep warm while you make the rest of the pancakes, adding more butter to the pan when it gets dry.

5. Divide the pancakes among 4 plates and serve.

CARBOHYDRATE CHOICE: ½

# grilled asparagus
## WITH MUSHROOM-TRUFFLE VINAIGRETTE AND A POACHED EGG

Unless you treat yourself *way* better than I do, this is a special-occasion breakfast or brunch dish, rather than the kind of thing you throw together on a typical weekday to hold you over until lunchtime rolls around. You can serve this as a salad with lunch or dinner, with or without the eggs. You can also scatter pine nuts over each serving.

This is best enjoyed in the springtime, especially if you have access to farm-fresh asparagus and eggs and an outdoor grill. If you want to cash in some carbs, smear a thin slice of country bread with olive oil, grill it until nicely marked, and spread some high-quality ricotta cheese on top. Eat this outside, and you'll feel like you're on vacation.                                    **SERVES 4**

## INGREDIENTS

12 spears jumbo asparagus (about 1 pound), peeled with ends trimmed

3 tablespoons extra-virgin olive oil

1½ tablespoons freshly squeezed lime juice

1½ teaspoons finely grated lime zest

¼ teaspoon coarse salt

¼ teaspoon freshly ground black pepper

1 small clove garlic, thinly sliced

4 large white button mushrooms, stems trimmed, thinly sliced

1 tablespoon minced shallot or white onion

2 teaspoons chopped fresh flat-leaf parsley leaves

1 teaspoon white truffle oil

4 large eggs, poached (see this page)

1. Bring a large pot of water to a boil. Fill a large bowl halfway with ice water.

2. Cook the asparagus in the boiling water until just tender to a knife tip, about 1 minute. Use tongs to remove the asparagus from the pot and transfer it to the ice water to stop the cooking and preserve the color. Once the asparagus has cooled, drain it and pat dry with paper towels.

3. Preheat a gas grill to medium or build a fire in a charcoal grill, letting the coals burn down until covered with white ash. If using a grill pan, preheat the pan over medium-high heat.

4. Meanwhile, put 1 tablespoon of the olive oil, the lime juice, lime zest, ⅛ teaspoon of the salt, and ⅛ teaspoon of the pepper in a baking dish and whisk together. Add the asparagus spears and roll them in the vinaigrette to coat, then set aside.

5. Heat the remaining 2 tablespoons of olive oil in a large, heavy-bottomed pan over low heat. Add the garlic to the pan and cook until lightly browned, about 1 minute. Add the mushrooms, season with the remaining ⅛ teaspoon salt and ⅛ teaspoon pepper, and stir for 1 minute. Add the shallot and parsley and cook, stirring, for 2 minutes longer. Remove the pan from the heat and stir in the white truffle oil. Set aside, covered, to keep the mushrooms warm.

6. Grill the asparagus, turning them as they lightly blacken, until lightly charred all over, about 5 minutes.

7. Divide the asparagus among 4 plates. Spoon the mushrooms over the asparagus, top with a poached egg, and serve.

## nutritional information
(PER SERVING)

| | |
|---|---|
| Calories | 197 |
| Fat | 16 g |
| Saturated Fat | 3 g |
| Trans Fat | 0 g |
| Total Carbohydrates | 6 g |
| Dietary Fiber | 2 g |
| Total Sugars | 2 g |
| Protein | 8 g |
| Cholesterol | 215 mg |
| Sodium | 188 mg |

## exchanges

| | |
|---|---|
| Fat | 2.5 |
| Medium Fat Meat | 1 |
| Vegetables | 1 |

## poaching eggs

To poach eggs, pour 2 quarts of water into a pot large enough to hold the eggs. Add ½ cup distilled white vinegar and bring to a simmer over medium-high heat. Crack an egg into a small bowl and then carefully let it slide into the water so that it maintains its shape. Continue with the eggs, first cracking each into the bowl before adding it to the water. Let the eggs poach (do not let the whites touch) until the whites are firm and the yolk is warmed, 2 to 3 minutes. Remove the eggs one at a time with a slotted spoon, letting any excess water run off.

## nutritional information
**(PER SERVING WITH AN EGG )**

| | |
|---|---|
| Calories | 218 |
| Fat | 9 g |
| Saturated Fat | 2 g |
| Trans Fat | 0 g |
| Total Carbohydrates | 12 g |
| Dietary Fiber | 2 g |
| Total Sugars | 3 g |
| Protein | 24 g |
| Cholesterol | 247 mg |
| Sodium | 404 mg |

## exchanges

| | |
|---|---|
| Starch | 0.5 |
| Lean Meat | 1.5 |
| Medium Fat Meat | 1 |
| High Fat Meat | 0.5 |
| Vegetables | 0.5 |

**CARBOHYDRATE CHOICE: 1 (WITH OR WITHOUT THE EGG)**

# turkey hash

Plenty of bistros and brasseries serve gourmet versions of corned beef hash these days; in fact, some historical tomes suggest that the dish has its origins as a means of using leftovers in French kitchens. But to me, it's the stuff of American diners, meant to be cooked on a flattop griddle, with the egg sizzling right alongside. If you long ago kissed this breakfast indulgence good-bye, then try this more healthful recipe made with turkey instead of beef, a minimum of potato, and turkey bacon to add just enough smoky goodness.

The key to success here is that I don't even try to replicate the guilty pleasure of the original. This hash is cleaner and leaner than the traditional version; the (optional) egg is poached rather than fried. The lighter treatment suits the hash very well, as does the last-second scattering of sliced scallions to add an extra note of freshness, as well as some oniony crunch.

**SERVES 4**

## INGREDIENTS

½ cup minced turkey bacon
   (from about 4 slices)
⅔ cup diced Spanish onion
   (from 1 medium-size onion)
½ cup diced cooked Idaho potato
1 clove garlic, minced
⅔ cup low-sodium, store-bought
   chicken broth

1 cup hand-shredded turkey
   (from about 2 ounces roasted
   turkey breast)
Pinch of coarse salt
Pinch of freshly ground black pepper
4 scallions, both white and green parts,
   thinly sliced
4 poached eggs (optional; see previous
   page for poaching instructions)

**1.** Heat a nonstick pan over low heat. Add the turkey bacon and cook until browned and the fat is rendered, about 8 minutes. Add the onion, potato, and garlic and cook until softened but not browned, 3 to 4 minutes. Add the broth and cook, stirring, until reduced and thickened, 3 to 4 minutes.

2. Remove the pan from the heat. Add the turkey and stir just to warm it through. Season the hash with the salt and pepper.

3. To serve, divide the hash among 4 large plates. Top with a scattering of scallions and a poached egg, if desired.

**variations and suggestions:** You can also bake this hash. Preheat the oven to 350°F. Then, prepare the hash through Step 2 and divide it among 4 small baking dishes or ramekins and crack an egg over each serving. Set the ramekins on a baking sheet and bake until the egg whites are set but the yolks are still runny, 12 to 15 minutes.

## nutritional information
(PER SERVING WITHOUT AN EGG)

| | |
|---|---|
| Calories | 47 |
| Fat | 4 g |
| Saturated Fat | 1 g |
| Trans Fat | 0 g |
| Total Carbohydrates | 11 g |
| Dietary Fiber | 2 g |
| Total Sugars | 2 g |
| Protein | 18 g |
| Cholesterol | 36 mg |
| Sodium | 257 mg |

## exchanges

| | |
|---|---|
| Fat | 0.5 |
| Starch | 0.5 |
| Lean Meat | 1.5 |
| High Fat Meat | 0.5 |
| Vegetables | 0.5 |

# in this chapter

*"The good news is that
all of these recipes pack a lot of flavor
into relatively small bites. "*

# hors d'oeuvres, snacks, and finger foods

● thought about slapping a skull and cross-bones on the first page of this chapter, or perhaps a sign warning you to "Enter at Your Own Risk." Not because the recipes that follow are especially heavy on carbohydrates but because they represent a different kind of risk: By their very nature, these dishes are meant to be consumed without thought, munched on while socializing at a cocktail party, or while watching the ball game, the Oscars, or some other communal event.

That informal indulgence runs counter to the rigidly defined lives that most people with diabetes lead when it comes to food and eating. I mean, what good is it to know how many carbs each portion of an hors d'oeuvre contains if you're going to lose track of how much you've eaten? By the same token, do you really want to be standing around the snack bar silently tracking how many nibbles of pizza you've consumed, like a card counter at a Vegas blackjack table?

I suggest that you devise a special dining plan for parties, especially the ones you throw yourself. One strategy might be to know how much of each hors d'oeuvre you can have and put your full allotment on a small plate that you snack from gradually. Another is to select only the lowest carb items to cook and serve, so the downside of overindulging isn't too steep. Another good trick is to augment the hors d'oeuvres you cook with raw vegetables such as halved cherry tomatoes and sliced, chilled fennel.

Or you can do like that Vegas card counter and just keep a mental tally of what you've eaten, but do yourself a favor—if you lose track, round up, not down, before digging in again.

The good news is that all of these recipes pack a lot of flavor into relatively small bites, so whatever approach you adapt, I dare say that even if you sample only a few nibbles, you'll be more than satisfied.

## CARBOHYDRATE CHOICE: ½

# caramelized onion dip

i don't know about you, but I have fond memories of those insanely creamy onion dips made by mixing an envelope of soup mix with sour cream, or sour cream and mayonnaise. (Does anybody else out there recall eating it out of a scooped-out loaf of bread at a party sometime around 1978?) The only problem with the originals is that they're mostly prohibitively fatty and based on a high-sodium concoction featuring MSG, chemicals, and artificial colors. Seeking a more healthful alternative, I thought to caramelize fresh onions to coax out a flavor that would be different, but comparably powerful, to those dips. Caramelizing extracts a natural sweetness that, when blended with very small amounts of olive oil, cream cheese, sour cream, and mayonnaise, requires little else for a rich result.

Use this as a dip for raw vegetables, such as celery, endive, zucchini, or yellow squash. It can also be spread on flatbread. (None of the serving suggestions are included in the nutritional information.)

**MAKES ABOUT 1 CUP; SERVES 4 (¼ CUP EACH)**

## nutritional information
(PER SERVING)

| | |
|---|---|
| Calories | 86 |
| Fat | 6 g |
| Saturated Fat | 1 g |
| Trans Fat | 0 g |
| Total Carbohydrates | 7 g |
| Dietary Fiber | 1 g |
| Total Sugars | 3 g |
| Protein | 1 g |
| Cholesterol | 5 mg |
| Sodium | 80 mg |

## exchanges

| | |
|---|---|
| Fat | 1 |
| Vegetables | 1 |

**INGREDIENTS**

1 teaspoon canola oil

2 medium-size Spanish onions,
    thinly sliced

1 tablespoon plus 1 teaspoon full-fat
    whipped cream cheese

1 tablespoon olive oil

1 tablespoon nonfat sour cream

1 tablespoon reduced-fat
    mayonnaise

1 teaspoon Dijon mustard

½ teaspoon balsamic vinegar

Pinch of cayenne pepper

Vegetable crudités or flatbread,
    for serving

**1.** Heat the canola oil in a deep, wide, heavy-bottomed pan over low heat. Add the onions and cook slowly and patiently, letting them caramelize to a deep, golden brown, 40 to 45 minutes, stirring occasionally. Add a few drops of water when necessary to keep the onions from scorching or sticking. Remove the pan from the heat and let the onions cool.

**2.** Transfer the cooled onions to a food processor fitted with a steel blade and add the cream cheese, olive oil, sour cream, mayonnaise, mustard, balsamic vinegar, and cayenne pepper. Pulse until just thoroughly combined, smooth, and creamy. Transfer the dip to a serving dish, scraping down the side of the processor bowl with a rubber spatula to get out as much as possible. Serve the dip with vegetable crudités or spread on flatbread.

plan ahead

The dip can be made up to 1 day before you plan to serve it and kept refrigerated in an airtight container. Let it come to room temperature before serving.

CARBOHYDRATE CHOICE: 0

# asparagus guacamole

Years ago, a friend of mine who was shedding pounds on the Weight Watchers plan told me that he'd made a guacamole using asparagus in place of avocado. I scoffed, opining that maybe he'd never had real guacamole, because I couldn't imagine asparagus standing in for that full, fatty, palate-coating avocado. So, you can imagine my surprise when I gave it a whirl and discovered that you can indeed make a fairly delicious guacamole

### A TIP FROM TOM

**CHILE AND PEPPER SEEDS:** Most of the heat in chiles and peppers such as jalapeños or Serranos comes from the seeds, so leave some or all of them in when a spicier dish is desired, and remove them all for a minimum of heat.

using asparagus. It's not as rich and creamy as the original—nor is it by any means authentic—but the flavor and color come very close, largely because the acid in the lime and heat of the jalapeño go quite a ways toward making up the difference.

Serve this as a dip, or use it in tacos, burritos, and other Mexican dishes. **MAKES ABOUT 1 CUP; SERVES 4 (¼ CUP EACH)**

### INGREDIENTS

*30 spears pencil-thin asparagus (about 2 pounds), ends trimmed*

*½ cup loosely packed fresh cilantro leaves*

*¼ cup plus 2 tablespoons olive oil*

*1 tablespoon plus 1 teaspoon freshly squeezed lime juice*

*¾ teaspoon ground cumin*

*¼ teaspoon minced seeded jalapeño pepper*

*¼ cup diced seeded plum tomato*

**1.** Bring a large skillet of water to a boil. Fill a large bowl halfway with ice water.

**2.** Cook the asparagus in the boiling water until tender, about 1 minute. Use tongs to remove the asparagus from the skillet and transfer it to the ice water to stop the cooking and preserve the color. Once the asparagus has cooled, drain it and pat dry with paper towels.

**3.** Cut the asparagus into 1-inch pieces. Transfer the asparagus to a blender and add the cilantro, olive oil, lime juice, cumin, and jalapeño. Blend until just thick and creamy but do not overprocess or the Asparagus Guacamole will turn watery.

**4.** Transfer the Asparagus Guacamole to a serving bowl. Carefully fold in the tomato. Serve immediately.

## nutritional information
**(PER SERVING)**

| | |
|---|---|
| Calories | 170 |
| Fat | 15 g |
| Saturated Fat | 2 g |
| Trans Fat | 0 g |
| Total Carbohydrates | 11 g |
| Dietary Fiber | 7 g |
| Total Sugars | 2 g |
| Protein | 2 g |
| Cholesterol | 0 mg |
| Sodium | 129 mg |

## exchanges

| | |
|---|---|
| Fat | 3 |
| Vegetables | 0.5 |

**CARBOHYDRATE CHOICE: 1; 0 ADJUSTED FOR FIBER**

# "real" guacamole

here is a more traditional guacamole made with actual avocados and lots of cilantro, lime juice, and red onion. It has the wonderful, palate-coating quality of the real thing, and a little of it can make a big impact in sandwiches, on burgers, and of course as a dip.

**MAKES ABOUT 2 CUPS; SERVES 4 (½ CUP EACH)**

## INGREDIENTS

2 medium-size ripe Hass avocados, pitted and peeled

¼ cup chopped seeded plum tomato

¼ cup finely diced red onion

¼ cup minced fresh cilantro leaves

2 tablespoons freshly squeezed lime juice

2 teaspoons minced seeded jalapeño pepper

¼ teaspoon coarse salt

Pinch of ground cumin

Using a fork, mash the avocado in a medium-size bowl. Use a rubber spatula to gently fold in the tomato, onion, cilantro, lime juice, jalapeño, salt, and cumin. Serve immediately.

**CARBOHYDRATE CHOICE: 1; ½ ADJUSTED FOR FIBER**

# mediterranean pinwheels

garlic-and-herb goat cheese and assorted roasted vegetables come together seamlessly when rolled together into a multigrain wrap that's sliced and served in pinwheels. The secret to the pinwheels' success is the garlic and thyme infused oil that's drizzled over the vegetables just before they go into the oven.

Note that you will need toothpicks.

**MAKES 24 PINWHEELS; SERVES 12**

## INGREDIENTS

5 medium-size cloves garlic

½ pound goat cheese,
    at room temperature

8 large fresh basil leaves, coarsely
    chopped, plus 12 large fresh basil
    leaves

½ cup extra-virgin olive oil
    (divided use)

Freshly ground black pepper

1 medium-size green zucchini, cut
    lengthwise into ¼-inch-thick slices

1 medium-size yellow zucchini, cut
    lengthwise into ¼-inch-thick slices

1 medium-size eggplant,
    cut lengthwise into ¼-inch-thick
    slices

2 large portobello mushrooms,
    stems trimmed

2 small plum tomatoes, seeded and
    cut into ¼-inch-thick slices

Leaves from ½ bunch fresh thyme

½ teaspoon coarse salt

4 multigrain wraps
    (10 inches in diameter)

2 ounces salt-free mozzarella,
    thinly sliced

1. Preheat the oven to 350°F.

2. Mince 2 of the garlic cloves and put them in a bowl. Add the goat cheese, chopped basil, 2 teaspoons of the olive oil, and a pinch of pepper and mix together with a rubber spatula or knead with immaculately clean (or latex-gloved) hands. Cover and keep refrigerated while you prepare the vegetables, or for up to 4 hours.

3. Arrange the zucchini, yellow squash, eggplant, mushrooms, and tomatoes in a single layer on a non-stick baking sheet; use 2 baking sheets if necessary to keep from crowding or overlapping.

4. Mince the remaining 3 garlic cloves. Pour the remaining olive oil in a bowl and add the garlic, thyme, salt and a pinch of pepper. Drizzle the seasoned oil over the vegetables. Bake the vegetables until softened and just barely browned, 30 to 45 minutes.

5. To make the wraps, spread one quarter of the goat cheese mixture in the center of each wrap. Slice the

mushrooms diagonally and divide them and the rest of the vegetables among the wraps, placing each grouping neatly across the center third of the wrap. Top with the mozzarella and basil leaves. Roll the wraps over once, tuck in the top and bottom to enclose the filling, then continue to roll until sealed.

**6.** Secure each wrap at 1-inch intervals with toothpicks. Cut off and discard the very ends of each wrap, then cut each wrap crosswise into 6 pieces. Arrange the pinwheels on a serving platter or plate and serve.

---

CARBOHYDRATE CHOICE: 1

# mushroom bruschetta

## WITH ARUGULA

a bruschetta is an Italian hors d'oeuvre featuring a slice of toasted bread topped with just about anything but usually diced tomatoes or sautéed chicken livers. This bruschetta is made with a savory mushroom sauté and topped with arugula. Instead of the usual thick piece of bread, it uses very thinly sliced baguette for a melba toast–like effect. The bread is toasted to make it crisp enough to hold the topping without becoming soggy. (If you prefer, you can use actual melba toast in place of the fresh bread.)

To lower the amount of carbs and fat per serving, use this recipe to serve six people rather than four.     **MAKES 12 BRUSCHETTE; SERVES 4**

---

### nutritional information

(PER SERVING— 3 BRUSCHETTE)

| | |
|---|---|
| Calories | 134 |
| Fat | 8 g |
| Saturated Fat | 1 g |
| Trans Fat | 0 g |
| Total Carbohydrates | 12 g |
| Dietary Fiber | 1 g |
| Total Sugars | 2 g |
| Protein | 4 g |
| Cholesterol | 0 mg |
| Sodium | 328 mg |

### exchanges

| | |
|---|---|
| Fat | 1.5 |
| Starch | 0.5 |
| Vegetables | 1 |

---

### INGREDIENTS

*12 very thin slices French bread, toasted*
*1 recipe Mushroom Duxelles (page 326)*

*2 tablespoons thinly sliced arugula*

---

Top each slice of toast with some of the Mushroom Duxelles followed by a scattering of arugula. Arrange the bruschette on a serving platter or plate and serve.

## nutritional information

**(PER SERVING— 3 MUSHROOMS)**

| | |
|---|---|
| Calories | 109 |
| Fat | 2 g |
| Saturated Fat | 0 g |
| Trans Fat | 0 g |
| Total Carbohydrates | 11 g |
| Dietary Fiber | 0 g |
| Total Sugars | 4 g |
| Protein | 13 g |
| Cholesterol | 32 mg |
| Sodium | 355 mg |

## exchanges

| | |
|---|---|
| Lean Meat | 1 |
| Vegetables | 1 |

## shop right

**CRABMEAT:** Not all crabmeat is created equal. For dishes where the crab is front and center and largely unadorned, the gold standard is large-lump Maine or Chesapeake Bay crabmeat. But for a recipe like this, where the crab is cooked in a mixture of milk, cheese, and bread crumbs, more generic lump crabmeat will do just fine. (The one crabmeat variety you should avoid is "mock," those pink and white striped batons usually made from Alaskan pollock, a white fish, with the flavor and color doctored to resemble crab.) Regardless of the caliber of the crab, be sure to pick through the meat for shell and cartilage fragments.

**CARBOHYDRATE CHOICE: 1**

# crabmeat-stuffed mushroom caps

Like the Caramelized Onion Dip on page 34, these are a bit of a throwback to the cocktail parties of the 1960s and 1970s. We tend to make fun of the food trends of that era, but there was a reason they once ruled: They are mostly easy to make and delicious. These stuffed caps use the whole mushroom—the stems get chopped up and mixed with the crab filling—and have true retro charm. **MAKES 12 STUFFED MUSHROOMS; SERVES 4**

## INGREDIENTS

12 large white button mushroom caps (about 1 pound), stems removed and set aside

½ cup whole milk

2 teaspoons cornstarch

¼ teaspoon coarse salt

¼ teaspoon freshly ground black pepper

6 ounces fresh crabmeat (see this page)

3 tablespoons dry, unseasoned bread crumbs or panko (see facing page)

1 tablespoon chopped fresh flat-leaf parsley leaves

2 teaspoons freshly grated Parmesan cheese

1 teaspoon finely grated lemon zest

1 small clove garlic, minced

1. Preheat the oven to 400°F.

2. Put the mushroom stems in a food processor and pulse to a fine dice but not so much that they turn to paste. Transfer the diced stems to a nonstick pan and cook, stirring, over medium heat until dry but not scorched, 3 to 4 minutes. Transfer the cooked stems to a mixing bowl and set aside.

3. Bring the milk to a boil in a small, heavy-bottomed pot. Stir in the cornstarch, salt, pepper, and 1 tablespoon of water. Reduce the heat and let simmer until slightly thickened, about 2 minutes, then pour the mixture over the mushrooms. Add the crabmeat, bread crumbs, parsley, Parmesan cheese, lemon zest, and garlic. Using immaculately clean (or latex-gloved)

hands or a wooden spoon, mix the filling together.

**4.** Arrange the mushroom caps, stem side up, on a baking sheet. Spoon the crab filling into the mushrooms. Cover the mushrooms loosely with aluminum foil and bake for 10 minutes. Remove the foil and continue to bake until nicely browned on top, 4 to 5 minutes longer. Arrange the mushrooms on a serving platter or plate and serve.

CARBOHYDRATE CHOICES: 1½

# spanakopita

these spinach and feta pies have always struck me as a perfect food: loaded with spinach and just enough feta to add creaminess and a touch of saltiness to each and every bite. Making spanakopita is also a good way to become proficient with store-bought phyllo dough, one of the most amazing conveniences you'll find in any supermarket, and endlessly useful for wrapping up sautéed vegetables, seasoned ground meats, and melted cheese. Some of my favorite fillings include Broccoli Rabe with Olive Oil and Red Pepper (page 274; chop the broccoli rabe after draining it in Step 2) and duxelles (page 326) with crumbled goat cheese.

**MAKES 8 SPANAKOPITA; SERVES 4**

## INGREDIENTS

*1 tablespoon canola oil*

*1 large clove garlic, minced*

*1 pound spinach, well rinsed in several changes of cold water, tough stems discarded*

*Pinch of coarse salt*

*Pinch of freshly ground black pepper*

*Pinch of ground nutmeg*

*6 sheets phyllo dough (see page 78), thawed if frozen*

*2 tablespoons unsalted butter, melted*

*2 ounces crumbled feta cheese (about ½ cup)*

## nutritional information
(PER SERVING—
2 SPANAKOPITA)

| | |
|---|---|
| Calories | 260 |
| Fat | 15 g |
| Saturated Fat | 7 g |
| Trans Fat | 0 g |
| Total Carbohydrates | 25 g |
| Dietary Fiber | 3 g |
| Total Sugars | 1 g |
| Protein | 8 g |
| Cholesterol | 28 mg |
| Sodium | 462 mg |

## exchanges

| | |
|---|---|
| Fat | 2.5 |
| Other Carbohydrates | 1.5 |
| Medium Fat Meat | 0.5 |
| Vegetables | 1 |

A TIP FROM TOM

**DRAINING COOKED GREENS:** If you choose to refrigerate the prepared spinach for a period of time, you can take advantage of the opportunity to extract as much liquid as possible, which will help focus the flavor in the finished dish and keep the phyllo from becoming soggy. Put the spinach in a colander and top it with a few saucers or other small plates to weight it down. Set the colander in a bowl and put the entire setup in the fridge. The longer the plates sit on top of the spinach, the more water they'll force out.

You can use this technique whenever refrigerating cooked greens that will be used in a similar fashion.

1. Heat the oil in a heavy-bottomed pan over medium heat. Add the garlic and cook for 1 minute. Add the spinach, season with the salt, pepper, and nutmeg and cook until the spinach wilts and turns dark green, 2 to 3 minutes.

2. Spread the spinach out on a plate or platter and let it cool completely. Drain any liquid that accumulates. The spinach can be covered and refrigerated for up to 24 hours. Drain any additional liquid that gathers during that time.

3. Preheat the oven to 375°F.

4. To assemble the spanakopita, place a sheet of phyllo on a work surface. Using a pastry brush and working along one of the long edges, brush some of the melted butter over half of the sheet of phyllo, then fold it in half lengthwise over the buttered side, pressing down to make one thick sheet. Mound about an eighth of the spinach and feta about an inch from the short edge closest to you. Starting from the lower left corner, fold the phyllo diagonally up over the filling so that the corner touches the right edge of the phyllo; it will form a triangle. Keep folding the triangle upward, as though folding a flag, until you have about an inch of dough remaining at the top. Brush the exposed phyllo with butter and fold it over to make a triangle-shaped packet. Repeat with the remaining phyllo, spinach, and feta.

5. Arrange the spanakopita in a single layer on a nonstick or aluminum foil–lined baking sheet and bake until lightly browned and cooked through, 12 to 15 minutes.

6. Arrange the spanakopita on a serving platter or plate and serve hot.

Spanakopita

# lobster vol-au-vents

french for windblown, *vol-au-vent* is a catch-all name for a small, round, hollowed-out piece of baked puff pastry into which any number of fillings can be spooned or piped. This elegant canapé is the perfect thing to serve at a dinner party, and goes down great with some chilled Champagne.

**MAKES 3 DOZEN VOL-AU-VENTS; SERVES 12**

### INGREDIENTS

*1 cup chopped, cooked, and chilled lobster meat (from about 4 ounces shelled meat; (see this page)*
*3 tablespoons reduced-fat mayonnaise*
*1 tablespoon Dijon mustard*
*1 tablespoon chopped shallot*
*2 tablespoons minced celery*

*2 teaspoons freshly squeezed lemon juice*
*½ teaspoon minced fresh tarragon leaves*
*1 piece (9½ by 9 inches) store-bought puff pastry, thawed if frozen*
*1 large egg yolk, beaten with 1 tablespoon water*

1. To make the filling, put the lobster, mayonnaise, mustard, shallot, celery, lemon juice, and tarragon in a bowl and stir together. The filling can be covered and refrigerated for up to 8 hours. Let come to room temperature before proceeding.

2. To prepare the pastry, preheat the oven to 350°F.

3. Use a 1½-inch cutter to punch 3 dozen circles out of the puff pastry. Score a small circle in the center of each puff pastry circle, using a ½-inch cutter, only marking the dough, not cutting all the way through. Arrange the circles, a few inches apart, on a nonstick baking sheet and brush them with the egg yolk mixture.

4. Bake the pastry circles until they are puffy and golden-brown, about 15 minutes. Let the pastries cool on the baking sheet. They can be baked up to 2 hours ahead of time and held at room temperature.

5. When ready to fill, press down on the "perforated" small circle in

## nutritional information
(PER SERVING— 3 VOL-AU-VENTS)

| | |
|---|---|
| Calories | 78 |
| Fat | 5 g |
| Saturated Fat | 1 g |
| Trans Fat | 0 g |
| Total Carbohydrates | 6 g |
| Dietary Fiber | 0 g |
| Total Sugars | 1 g |
| Protein | 3 g |
| Cholesterol | 26 mg |
| Sodium | 159 mg |

## exchanges
| | |
|---|---|
| Fat | 1 |
| Other Carbohydrates | 0.5 |

## shop right
**LOBSTER MEAT:** If you purchase fish and shellfish from a reputable fishmonger that sells foods prepared on the premises, you might find cooked, shelled, chopped lobster meat in the refrigerator case. If so, there's absolutely nothing wrong with buying the prepared meat for a recipe like this one that calls for only a small quantity that is served cold.

To cook and shell your own lobster, follow the instructions in the recipe on page 86.

the center of each larger pastry circle to form an indentation. Use a small spoon to generously fill the indentation with lobster mixture. Arrange the vol-au-vents on a serving platter or large plate and serve.

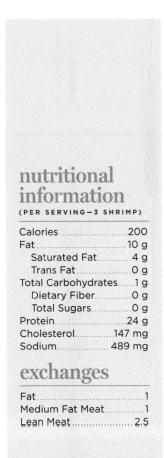

## nutritional information

(PER SERVING—3 SHRIMP)

| | |
|---|---|
| Calories | 200 |
| Fat | 10 g |
|   Saturated Fat | 4 g |
|   Trans Fat | 0 g |
| Total Carbohydrates | 1 g |
|   Dietary Fiber | 0 g |
|   Total Sugars | 0 g |
| Protein | 24 g |
| Cholesterol | 147 mg |
| Sodium | 489 mg |

## exchanges

| | |
|---|---|
| Fat | 1 |
| Medium Fat Meat | 1 |
| Lean Meat | 2.5 |

CARBOHYDRATE CHOICE: 0

# shrimp

## WITH GOAT CHEESE, BASIL, AND PROSCIUTTO

the first time I made these I got nostalgic for the food writing of the 1980s, when one of the most-oft-repeated phrases in restaurant criticism was "explosions in the mouth." I never much cared for the expression, but I have to say, these shrimp, which are curled around basil and goat cheese, then wrapped with prosciutto, do just that: When you bite into them, wave after wave of flavor and texture is unleashed. Salty ham gives way to crunchy shrimp and then herbaceous basil and creamy cheese—a guaranteed crowd-pleaser if there ever was one. **MAKES 12 SHRIMP; SERVES 4**

### INGREDIENTS

*3 ounces goat cheese, at room temperature*

*12 large shrimp (about 12 ounces), peeled and deveined*

*12 large fresh basil leaves*

*6 large slices Prosciutto di Parma (about 1½ ounces), cut crosswise in half*

*1 tablespoon olive oil*

**1.** Stuff some goat cheese into the cavity in the back of each shrimp (where it was deveined). Wrap a basil leaf lengthwise around each shrimp to hold the goat cheese in place, making sure that the leaf slightly overlaps the end of the shrimp. Wrap the entire shrimp with a piece of prosciutto.

**2.** Heat 1 teaspoon of the olive oil in a heavy-bottomed nonstick pan over medium-high heat. Add some of the shrimp with the seam of the prosciutto facing down and cook, turning, until the prosciutto is fused around the shrimp and crisp all over, 3 to 4 minutes. (The shrimp will be cooked through, too.) Transfer the shrimp to paper towels to drain. Repeat with the remaining shrimp, adding more olive oil to the pan as necessary.

3. Arrange the shrimp on a serving platter or plate and serve.

**variations and suggestions:** Make these shrimp the centerpiece of a salad by serving them over a bed of arugula and dressing them with a drizzle of balsamic vinegar.

CARBOHYDRATE CHOICES: 2

# shrimp shumai

Shrimp *shumai* are small dumplings that are a mainstay of any dim sum menu. I've always loved ordering them in Chinatown, and I also appreciate their ease of preparation at home because the filling does not need to be cooked before the dumplings are assembled.

**MAKES 16 DUMPLINGS; SERVES 4**

## INGREDIENTS

8 ounces shrimp (about 8 large shrimp), peeled and deveined, coarsely chopped
¼ cup chopped napa cabbage
¼ cup coarsely chopped scallion greens
½ teaspoon minced garlic
½ teaspoon Asian (dark) sesame oil
¼ teaspoon low-sodium soy sauce
16 wonton wrappers

1. To make the filling, put the shrimp, cabbage, scallion, garlic, sesame oil, and soy sauce in a bowl and stir together gently.

2. Divide the filling evenly among the wrappers. Dampen your finger with a little water and run it around the edge of the wrapper. Pull the wrapper up over the filling, gathering the edges together, and crimp around the top to seal the edges together neatly and firmly. Repeat with the remaining wrappers.

3. Bring a large pot of water to a boil

### nutritional information
(PER SERVING— 4 DUMPLINGS)

| | |
|---|---|
| Calories | 230 |
| Fat | 2 g |
| Saturated Fat | 0 g |
| Trans Fat | 0 g |
| Total Carbohydrates | 35 g |
| Dietary Fiber | 1 g |
| Total Sugars | 0 g |
| Protein | 16 g |
| Cholesterol | 86 mg |
| Sodium | 262 mg |

### exchanges

| | |
|---|---|
| Starch | 2 |
| Lean Meat | 1.5 |

and cook the *shumai* in the boiling water until they float, 5 to 6 minutes, or steam them, without crowding, in a bamboo steaming basket set over boiling water, 6 to 8 minutes. Arrange the *shumai* on a serving platter or plate and serve.

### variations and suggestions:

❖ You can vary the *shumai* by adding minced cilantro or replacing the shrimp with crumbled turkey sausage.

❖ You can also make summer rolls based on this recipe. To do this you will need four 9-inch round rice paper wrappers. Cut the shrimp into larger pieces and cook them in a tablespoon of olive oil in a large, nonstick pan over medium heat, along with a thinly sliced clove of garlic, just until the shrimp turns firm and pink, 2 to 3 minutes. Transfer the shrimp mixture to a bowl and toss them with the cabbage, scallion, sesame oil, and soy sauce. Stir in ½ teaspoon of distilled white vinegar. Let the filling rest while you prepare the rice wrappers: Fill a large, wide-mouthed bowl with warm water. Working with one wrapper at a time, soak it until soft and pliable. Fill the wrappers and roll them up, tucking in the ends to encase the filling as you roll, and then serve the summer rolls.

CARBOHYDRATE CHOICE: 0

# deviled eggs

When I was a kid, deviled eggs were one of my favorite things to eat at picnics and barbecues, something to grab and devour on the run between possessions on the touch football field. I (meaning we) might not be able to eat that many deviled eggs now, but they're so easy and quick to produce, that I find the reward well worth the meager effort.

MAKES 8 DEVILED EGGS; SERVES 4

## nutritional information

(PER SERVING—
2 EGG HALVES)

| | |
|---|---|
| Calories | 112 |
| Fat | 8 g |
| Saturated Fat | 2 g |
| Trans Fat | 0 g |
| Total Carbohydrates | 4 g |
| Dietary Fiber | 0 g |
| Total Sugars | 1 g |
| Protein | 7 g |
| Cholesterol | 217 mg |
| Sodium | 237 mg |

## exchanges

| | |
|---|---|
| Fat | 1 |
| Medium Fat Meat | 1 |

### INGREDIENTS

*4 large eggs, hard-cooked (see next page)*
*2½ tablespoons Dijon mustard*
*2½ tablespoons full-fat mayonnaise*

*1 teaspoon minced fresh dill*
*Pinch of freshly ground black pepper*
*Pinch of paprika*

1. Peel the eggs and cut them in half lengthwise. Carefully remove the yolks and transfer them to a bowl. Set the whites on a plate or small serving platter.

2. Mash the yolks with a fork. Add the mustard, mayonnaise, dill, pepper, and paprika to the yolks. Stir together.

3. Fill the cavity in each egg white half with the yolk mixture, using a small spoon or a pastry bag fitted with a small, plain tip. Set on a platter to serve.

# pizzas

**p**izza is pretty much off-limits to you and me, but if you make your own—rolling the dough out as thinly as possible—it can be visited from time to time in the form of an hors d'oeuvre. You can also buy ready-made dough at many supermarkets, and most pizzerias will be happy to sell you some, but I can't vouch for its nutritional makeup.

Here are a few pizzas that I love.

**CARBOHYDRATE CHOICES: 1½**

## goat cheese and mushroom pizza

**MAKES ONE 12-INCH PIZZA; SERVES 6 AS AN HORS D'OEUVRE**

**i**t sounds pretty specific, but a goat cheese and mushroom pizza is actually a very adaptable affair. The recipe here calls for the most accessible, generic ingredients—white button mushrooms and vacuum-packed goat cheese, both readily available in any supermarket in the land—and will for sure produce a mouth-watering, people-pleasing pizza. But you can also take the theme and run with it, calling on any number of wild mushrooms, or an assortment, and selecting an artisanal goat's milk cheese or an aged variety, as well. If you really want to pull out the jams, perhaps for a New Year's Eve celebration, shave some fresh white truffle over the pizza just before serving. Truffles are famously expensive, so if you opt to do this, I have one final suggestion: Call me.

**plan ahead**

The deviled eggs can be covered loosely with plastic wrap and refrigerated for up to 12 hours.

**hard-cooked eggs**

To hard-cook eggs, put them in a small, heavy-bottomed pot and cover them with cold water. Set the pot over high heat and bring to a boil. Turn off the heat and cover the pot for 15 minutes. Drain the hot water and run cold water over the eggs until cooled.

**nutritional information**
(PER 2 SLICE SERVING)

Calories....................268
Fat...............................17 g
  Saturated Fat..........6 g
  Trans Fat......0 g
Total Carbohydrates....21 g
  Dietary Fiber.............1 g
  Total Sugars.............2 g
Protein........................9 g
Cholesterol................18 mg
Sodium....................219 mg

**exchanges**

Fat..............................2
Starch.........................1
High Fat Meat............0.5
Vegetables.................0.5

### INGREDIENTS

*3 tablespoons olive oil*

*1 large clove garlic, minced*

*8 ounces white button mushrooms, stems trimmed, very thinly sliced*

*1 tablespoon fresh thyme leaves*

*1 recipe Basic Pizza Dough (page 52)*

*Flour, for dusting*

*About ¼ cup cornmeal, for dusting*

*¾ cup crumbled goat cheese (about 3 ounces)*

*¼ cup coarsely grated Parmesan cheese (about 1 ounce)*

**1.** Heat 1 tablespoon of the olive oil in a heavy-bottomed pan over medium heat. Add the garlic and cook until softened but not browned, about 2 minutes. Add the mushrooms and cook, stirring, until softened and beginning to give off their liquid, about 5 minutes. Stir in the thyme and remove the pan from the heat. Let the mushrooms cool, then carefully drain the liquid from the pan.

**2.** Preheat the oven to 450°F, or 500°F if it goes that high. Set a pizza stone or inverted baking sheet on the center rack.

**3.** Roll the Pizza Dough out on a lightly floured work surface as thinly as possible to a diameter of about 12 inches.

**4.** Carefully remove the stone to a heatproof surface and dust with cornmeal. Transfer the dough to the stone and rub the remaining 2 tablespoons of olive oil over the surface of the dough. Scatter the cooked mushrooms and the goat cheese on top, then scatter the Parmesan cheese over them.

**5.** Bake the pizza until the cheese is bubbly and the crust underneath turns a nice golden brown, 12 to 15 minutes. Remove the stone from the oven and very carefully transfer the pizza to a cutting board. Use a pizza slicer or a sharp knife to cut the pizza into 12 very thin, long triangles. Arrange the pieces on a serving platter or plate and serve.

**CARBOHYDRATE CHOICES: 1½**

# red onion and soppressata pizza

**MAKES ONE 12-INCH PIZZA; SERVES 6 AS AN HORS D'OEUVRE**

You can make this pizza with spicy or sweet *soppressata*—I prefer the hot because it provides contrast to the sweet red onion.

## INGREDIENTS

*1 tablespoon olive oil*

*½ small red onion, very thinly sliced*

*2 large cloves garlic, very thinly sliced*

*1 tablespoon tomato paste*

*¾ cup your favorite store-bought tomato sauce*

*¼ teaspoon dried oregano*

*Pinch of crushed red pepper flakes*

*1 recipe Basic Pizza Dough (page 52)*

*Flour, for dusting*

*About ¼ cup cornmeal, for dusting*

*½ ounce hot or sweet soppressata (see this page), very thinly sliced*

*¼ cup coarsely grated Parmesan cheese (about 1 ounce)*

1. Heat the olive oil in a wide, deep, heavy-bottomed pan over medium heat. Add the onion and garlic and cook very gently, stirring often, until very soft but not browned, about 4 minutes. Add the tomato paste and stir to coat. Stir in the tomato sauce, oregano, and red pepper flakes, increase the heat to medium-high, and let come to a simmer. Reduce the heat to medium and let simmer until the sauce is infused with flavor, about 10 minutes. (The sauce can be cooled and refrigerated in an airtight container for up to 2 days. Let come to room temperature before proceeding.)

2. Preheat the oven to 450°F, or 500°F if it goes that high. Set a pizza stone or inverted baking sheet on the center rack.

3. Roll the Pizza Dough out on a lightly floured work surface as thinly as possible to a diameter of about 12 inches.

4. Carefully remove the stone to a heatproof surface and dust with cornmeal. Transfer the dough to the stone and ladle the sauce over it, spreading the onions and garlic out evenly. Top with the *soppressata*, then scatter the Parmesan cheese over the top.

5. Bake the pizza until the cheese is bubbly and the crust underneath turns a nice golden brown, 12 to 15 minutes. Remove the stone from the oven and very carefully transfer the pizza to a cutting board. Use a pizza slicer or a sharp knife to cut it into 12 very thin, long triangles. Arrange the pieces on a serving platter or plate and serve.

## nutritional information
### (PER 2 SLICE SERVING)

| | |
|---|---|
| Calories | 178 |
| Fat | 8 g |
| Saturated Fat | 2 g |
| Trans Fat | 0 g |
| Total Carbohydrates | 22 g |
| Dietary Fiber | 1 g |
| Total Sugars | 3 g |
| Protein | 6 g |
| Cholesterol | 6 mg |
| Sodium | 397 mg |

## exchanges

| | |
|---|---|
| Fat | 1.5 |
| Starch | 1 |
| Vegetables | 0.5 |

## shop right

**SOPPRESSATA:** *Soppressata* is a beloved pork salami made of a variety of parts of the pig (I'll spare you the litany; you know what they say about sausage making) and seasoned with an enticing blend of spices and aromatics that varies from brand to brand. It comes in sweet and hot varieties. If possible, buy it from the deli counter and have it sliced to order, although a few companies like Citterio now sell prepackaged, presliced versions that aren't bad at all. If you can't find *soppressata* in your local supermarket, you can replace it in this and many other recipes with other hard salamis.

## nutritional information
**(PER 2 SLICE SERVING)**

Calories......................215
Fat..............................12 g
  Saturated Fat...........4 g
  Trans Fat...................0 g
Total Carbohydrates...19 g
  Dietary Fiber.............2 g
  Total Sugars.............3 g
Protein.........................9 g
Cholesterol.................12 mg
Sodium....................451 mg

## exchanges

Fat................................2
Starch...........................1
Lean Meat..................0.5
Vegetables..................0.5

CARBOHYDRATE CHOICE: 1

# roasted pepper, pepperoncini, parmesan, and mozzarella pizza

**MAKES ONE 12-INCH PIZZA;
SERVES 6 AS AN HORS D'OEUVRE**

if you love the variety of peppers, then do try this colorful pizza, which attains an impressive spectrum of flavor with very few ingredients. I recommend grilling rather than baking the pizza: The charred flavor really complements the heat of the peppers.

### INGREDIENTS

*1 recipe Basic Pizza Dough (page 52)*
*Flour, for dusting*
*About ¼ cup cornmeal, for dusting
  (optional)*
*1½ tablespoons olive oil*
*Pinch of coarse salt*
*2 roasted red peppers, homemade
  (page 324) or store-bought,
  thinly sliced*
*10 pepperoncini peppers, thinly
  sliced, rinsed and drained to
  remove seeds and brine*
*½ cup coarsely grated Parmesan
  cheese (about 2 ounces)*
*2 ounces salt-free mozzarella,
  coarsely grated (½ cup)*

1. If baking the pizza, preheat the oven to 450°F, or 500°F if it goes that high. Set a pizza stone or inverted baking sheet on the center rack. If grilling the pizza, preheat a gas grill to medium or build a fire in a charcoal grill, letting the coals burn down until covered with white ash.

2. Roll the Pizza Dough out on a lightly floured work surface as thinly as possible to a diameter of about 12 inches. Rub the olive oil over the surface of the pizza and season it with the salt.

3. If baking the pizza, carefully remove the stone to a heatproof surface and dust with cornmeal. Transfer the dough to the stone. If grilling the pizza, transfer the dough to the grill.

4. Bake or grill the pizza crust until it is just firm enough to hold its shape, about 6 minutes.

5. Return the stone and crust to the work surface, scatter the roasted peppers and pepperoncini over the crust, and top with the Parmesan and mozzarella cheeses.

6. Return the pizza to the oven or grill, cover the grill, if using, and cook the pizza until the dough is nicely charred on the bottom and the

cheese is melted and bubbly, about 7 minutes. Remove the stone from the oven and very carefully transfer the pizza to a cutting board. Use a pizza slicer or a sharp knife to cut it into 12 very thin triangles. Arrange the pieces on a serving platter or plate and serve.

CARBOHYDRATE CHOICE: 1

# broccoli rabe and sausage calzone

like the frittata on page 19, this empanada-like variation on a pizza adapts the combination of broccoli rabe and sausage, here rounding out the flavors and textures with creamy ricotta cheese, fragrant basil, and hot pepper flakes. It is especially satisfying during the colder months of the year.

**MAKES 2 CALZONES; SERVES 6 AS AN HORS D'OEUVRE**

## INGREDIENTS

*1 teaspoon olive oil*

*1 link (about 4 ounces) Italian-style turkey sausage, casing removed, crumbled*

*1 recipe Basic Pizza Dough (page 52)*

*Flour, for dusting*

*¼ cup low-fat ricotta cheese*

*½ recipe Broccoli Rabe with Olive Oil and Red Pepper (page 274), coarsely chopped*

*¼ cup freshly grated Parmesan cheese (about 1 ounce)*

*2 tablespoons coarsely chopped fresh basil leaves*

*Pinch of crushed red pepper flakes*

*About ¼ cup cornmeal, for dusting*

**1.** Heat the olive oil in a heavy-bottomed pan over medium-high heat. Add the sausage and cook, breaking it up with a fork or wooden

## nutritional information
(PER SERVING—1 PIECE)

| | |
|---|---|
| Calories | 221 |
| Fat | 11 g |
| Saturated Fat | 3 g |
| Trans Fat | 0 g |
| Total Carbohydrates | 19 g |
| Dietary Fiber | 0 g |
| Total Sugars | 2 g |
| Protein | 12 g |
| Cholesterol | 20 mg |
| Sodium | 320 mg |

## exchanges

| | |
|---|---|
| Fat | 2 |
| Starch | 1 |
| Medium Fat Meat | 0.5 |
| Lean Meat | 0.5 |
| Vegetables | 0.5 |

spoon, until browned and the fat has rendered, about 7 minutes. Remove the sausage from the pan with a slotted spoon and drain on paper towels.

**2.** Preheat the oven to 450°F, or 500°F if it goes that high. Set a pizza stone or inverted baking sheet on the center rack.

**3.** Divide the Pizza Dough into 2 pieces and roll out one of them on a lightly floured work surface as thinly as possible to a diameter of about 6 inches. Put half of the sausage, ricotta, broccoli rabe, Parmesan cheese, basil, and red pepper flakes on half of the rolled out dough and fold the other half over to encase it.

Crimp the dough together at the seam to seal it. Repeat with the remaining dough and other ingredients.

**4.** Very carefully use a sharp knife to score the top of the calzones in thirds. Sprinkle the cornmeal on the pizza stone, then set the calzones on it. Bake the calzones until they are golden brown and you can see the juices of the sausage and broccoli rabe bubbling within, about 10 minutes.

**5.** Transfer the calzones to a cutting board and let rest for 5 minutes. Cut them along the score marks into 3 pieces each. Arrange the pieces on a serving platter or plate and serve.

CARBOHYDRATE CHOICES (ENTIRE RECIPE): 6

# basic pizza dough

this is a very basic recipe for pizza dough. If ever there was a time to judiciously add more salt to a recipe, this is it: The dough will taste much better with just a half teaspoon added.

MAKES ENOUGH DOUGH FOR ONE 12-INCH PIZZA CRUST

## INGREDIENTS

1 cup unbleached flour, plus more
  for dusting
Pinch of coarse salt

¾ teaspoon active dry yeast
5 tablespoons plus 1 teaspoon warm water
1½ tablespoons olive oil

---

1. Put the yeast in a bowl. Whisk in 2 tablespoons of warm water, then 1 tablespoon of the olive oil. Let stand until the liquid begins to foam, about 10 minutes.

2. Meanwhile put the flour and salt in the bowl of a stand mixer fitted with a dough hook and mix until thoroughly incorporated.

3. When ready, pour the yeast mixture into the center of the flour and mix until incorporated. Add 3 tablespoons plus 1 teaspoon more warm water to the flour and mix again until the dough pulls together into a single, unified mass.

4. Turn the dough out onto a lightly floured work surface and knead until you have a smooth ball that's elastic but not sticky, about 7 minutes.

5. Rub the surface of a clean stainless-steel or plastic mixing bowl with the remaining ½ tablespoon (1½ teaspoons) of olive oil and transfer the ball of dough to the bowl. Cover with a clean kitchen towel and let rise at room temperature until it has doubled in size, about 90 minutes, then punch the dough down. The dough can be refrigerated, covered, for 24 hours or frozen for up to 1 month. Let it thaw to room temperature before using.

# beef and vegetable kebabs

i'm not exaggerating when I say that the humble bamboo skewer might be one of the most diabetes friendly of all cooking implements, because it allows you to pick up your food—in this case grilled beef and vegetables—

## nutritional information
(FOR ENTIRE RECIPE)

Calories....................588
Fat................................20 g
  Saturated Fat............3 g
  Trans Fat....................0 g
Total Carbohydrates...89 g
  Dietary Fiber............3 g
  Total Sugars.............4 g
Protein.........................13 g
Cholesterol..................0 mg
Sodium........................124 mg

## exchanges

Fat....................................4
Starch..............................5

## nutritional information
(PER SERVING—1 KEBAB)
(SEE NOTE)

Calories....................166
Fat..................................9 g
  Saturated Fat............2 g
  Trans Fat....................0 g
Total Carbohydrates.....5 g
  Dietary Fiber............1 g
  Total Sugars.............2 g
Protein.........................13 g
Cholesterol..................38 mg
Sodium........................155 mg

## exchanges

Fat....................................1
Lean Meat.......................2
Vegetables...................0.5

without the need for bread or a breadlike wrapper. Skewers also, of course, let you grill bite-size pieces, reducing the cooking time for a perfect party food that can, essentially, be made to order. To that end, this recipe can be multiplied as much as you'd like.

Note that you will need four 8-inch bamboo skewers. **SERVES 4**

## INGREDIENTS

2 tablespoons freshly squeezed
   lemon juice
1½ tablespoons extra-virgin olive
   oil
1 tablespoon minced garlic
1 tablespoon Dijon mustard
Pinch of coarse salt
Pinch of freshly ground black pepper

8 ounces filet mignon, in 1-inch chunks
¼ pound small cremini mushrooms,
   stems trimmed
½ small Spanish onion,
   cut into 1½-inch dice
½ red or green bell pepper, stemmed,
   seeded, and cut into 1½-inch dice

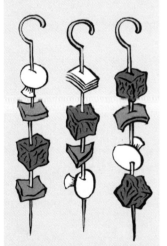

**1.** Put the lemon juice, olive oil, garlic, mustard, salt, and pepper in a bowl and stir them together. Add the beef and let marinate for at least 1 hour or up to 4 hours.

**2.** Soak the bamboo skewers in cold water for about an hour; this will prevent them from scorching or catching fire when grilled.

**3.** Preheat a gas grill to medium or build a fire in a charcoal grill, letting the coals burn down until covered with white ash. If using a grill pan, preheat the pan over medium-high heat.

**4.** Skewer alternating pieces of beef, mushroom, onion, and bell pepper on each skewer, pressing them together firmly to get as much as possible on each skewer. Grill until the beef is nicely charred and cooked through, turning the kebabs as each side is done, about 8 minutes total cooking time.

**5.** Arrange the kebabs on a serving platter or plate and serve hot.

**note:** If you'd like to serve these kebabs as a main course, two kebabs will make one serving.

CARBOHYDRATE CHOICE: 0

# chile and cumin lamb skewers

1amb is such an elegant meat, often a go-to selection for holidays and special events, that we can sometimes forget how well it takes to less refined, big-flavored treatments. Here, lamb is marinated in lime with jalapeño, then charred on a grill. The result is basically a glorified bar snack: spicy, fragrant, and addictive. You can multiply the recipe to serve as many people as you want (also see Note, facing page).

Note that you will need four 8-inch bamboo skewers.          **SERVES 4**

## INGREDIENTS

*Juice of 3 limes*
*¼ cup extra-virgin olive oil*
*1 tablespoon ground cumin*

*½ jalapeño pepper, seeded and minced*
*8 ounces lamb shoulder or leg,*
  *in 1-inch chunks*

1. Put the lime juice, olive oil, cumin, and jalapeño in a bowl and stir them together. Add the lamb and let marinate for at least 1 hour or up to 4 hours.

2. Soak the bamboo skewers in cold water for about an hour; this will prevent them from scorching or catching fire when grilled.

3. Preheat a gas grill to medium or build a fire in a charcoal grill, letting the coals burn down until covered with white ash. If using a grill pan, preheat the pan over medium-high heat.

4. Skewer the lamb pieces and grill until nicely charred and cooked through, turning the kebabs as each side is done, about 8 minutes total cooking time.

5. Arrange the kebabs on a serving platter or plate and serve hot.

## nutritional information
(PER SERVING—1 SKEWER)
(SEE NOTE)

Calories........................212
Fat...............................17 g
    Saturated Fat...........3 g
    Trans Fat..................0 g
Total Carbohydrates.....3 g
    Dietary Fiber.............1 g
    Total Sugars.............1 g
Protein.........................12 g
Cholesterol..............36 mg
Sodium.....................38 mg

## exchanges
Fat...............................3
Lean Meat...................1.5

# in this chapter

*"Everything from
a bowl of simply dressed mixed greens to
sashimi-style fish . . ."*

# salads and starters

i don't know of a category of dishes that better fits our needs than the extended family of salads and starters. I refer to them that way because that's the way we've taken to thinking of them, at restaurants *and* in homes, where a first course can be everything from a bowl of simply dressed mixed greens to sashimi-style fish to tea-smoked duck garnished with ingredients you'd be hard-pressed to pronounce properly or to identify in a culinary lineup.

This chapter includes mostly classic salads—you know, a bunch of leafy goodness with a vinaigrette of some kind—because they are such a bull's-eye for dining with diabetes: loaded with tasty fresh green vegetables; often featuring just enough protein; and voluminous enough to satisfy, even as a light meal.

I've also included some dishes that would be better characterized as starters, such as an assortment of raw-fish preparations (lots of protein without the fat required for cooking) and a few composed and warm salads. You might want to save these for entertaining, although the more conventional ones would also make me plenty happy if I found myself a guest at your table.

**CARBOHYDRATE CHOICES: 1½; 1 ADJUSTED FOR FIBER**

# raw vegetable salad

One of the more endearing food traditions for Tuscans is their love of raw spring and summer vegetables. Baby artichoke salads and uncooked fava beans tossed with Pecorino Romano cheese are two of the quintessential dishes of the region. Thinking about this one day, I decided to bring those vegetables together, along with some others that can be enjoyed without being blanched or sautéed, and before I knew it I had concocted this salad of shaved asparagus and artichokes, and freshly shucked peas and favas, with frisée lettuce providing the perfect, slightly bitter backdrop.

Not only should you make this in the late spring and early summer, but you can *only* make it then, when these ingredients are in season. The peas are especially important; try to purchase them from a farm or farmers' market and eat them as soon as possible. If you can't get the peas, add more favas or leave them out.

By the way, I didn't forget pepper in the ingredients list; its heat would only distract from the clean, springlike flavor here. SERVES 4

## INGREDIENTS

*4 baby artichokes, stems trimmed, top ½ inch cut off, toughest outer leaves removed*

*¼ cup plus 3 tablespoons freshly squeezed lemon juice*

*4 jumbo asparagus spears, ends trimmed, tips cut off and reserved for another use*

*¼ cup plus 2 tablespoons extra-virgin olive oil*

*Finely grated zest of 1 lemon*

*4 cups loosely packed frisée lettuce*

*½ cup shucked and skinned fava beans, from about 1 pound favas in the pod*

*½ cup fresh peas, from about ½ pound peas in the pod*

*¼ cup freshly grated Pecorino Romano cheese (about 1 ounce)*

1. Shave the artichokes very thinly horizontally, preferably using a man- doline. Put the artichokes in a bowl and add cold water to cover. Add 1

tablespoon of the lemon juice to the water to prevent the artichokes from browning.

2. Use a vegetable peeler to thinly slice the asparagus lengthwise.

3. Make the vinaigrette by putting the olive oil, the remaining ¼ cup and 2 tablespoons of lemon juice, and the lemon zest in a large bowl and whisking until well blended. Drain the artichokes, pat them dry with paper towels, and add them to the bowl with the vinaigrette along with the asparagus, frisée, fava beans, and peas. Toss together well but gently; you want the frisée to remain nicely fluffy and the vegetables to retain their shape and crunch.

4. Mound a pile of salad on each of 4 plates. Sprinkle the cheese on top and serve.

CARBOHYDRATE CHOICE: 1

# lemony fennel salad

t he faint anise flavor of raw fennel is so delicious and refreshing that the addition of garlic, herbs, and a simple lemon dressing is all that's required to turn it into the basis of a salad. SERVES 4

## INGREDIENTS

1½ fennel bulbs (about 18 ounces total), very thinly sliced, ideally using a mandoline

5 large cloves garlic, very thinly sliced

¼ cup extra-virgin olive oil

Juice of ½ large lemon

Pinch of coarse salt

Pinch of freshly ground black pepper

1 teaspoon minced fresh chives

1 teaspoon minced fresh flat-leaf parsley leaves

1. Put the fennel and garlic in a stainless steel bowl and let chill in the refrigerator for 1 hour.

2. Put the olive oil and lemon juice in another stainless steel bowl, add the salt and pepper, and whisk together.

## did you know?

Fava beans aren't actually beans; they're a vetch, a twining (climbing) plant. They are, like beans, legumes but thrive in cooler climates, which is why they're considered a spring, rather than summer, delicacy.

Working with favas is a two-step process. First you must remove the outer pod. You can run a paring knife along the seam before pulling the pod apart, but be careful not to cut into the favas themselves. Each fava bean is encased in a thick, light green skin that you can remove by pressing the bean between your thumb and forefinger until the green treasure that looks like a lima bean pops out. Some people like to split each fava, which you can do by gently separating the bean with your fingers.

## nutritional information
(PER SERVING)

| | |
|---|---|
| Calories | 173 |
| Fat | 14 g |
| Saturated Fat | 2 g |
| Trans Fat | 0 g |
| Total Carbohydrates | 11 g |
| Dietary Fiber | 4 g |
| Total Sugars | 0 g |
| Protein | 2 g |
| Cholesterol | 0 mg |
| Sodium | 97 mg |

## exchanges

| | |
|---|---|
| Fat | 3 |
| Vegetables | 2 |

Pour the dressing over the fennel and garlic, and toss well. Add the chives and parsley and toss again.

3. Divide the salad among 4 small plates and serve.

**variations and suggestions:** In addition to serving this on its own, you can use it as an accompaniment to grilled shrimp or skin-on striped bass.

# asparagus
## WITH LEMON VINAIGRETTE AND A WARM PROSCIUTTO CHIP

I'm always on the lookout for perfect pairings, and one definition to me is two ingredients that complement each other in as many ways as possible. Case in point: plump, green, clean-tasting asparagus and thinly sliced, pink, crisped Prosciutto di Parma. Add some lettuce and lemon vinaigrette to complete the salad and we're in business. The impress-your-friends (but easy-to-make) prosciutto chip makes this a natural for entertaining, but you can, of course, enjoy it any time you like.

For a clever lunch or dinner take on ham and eggs, top the asparagus with a fried or poached egg; I prefer poached because the runny yolk alongside both the asparagus and the prosciutto is sublime, adding two more perfect pairings to the same plate.

**SERVES 4**

## nutritional information
(PER SERVING)

| | |
|---|---|
| Calories | 117 |
| Fat | 8 g |
| Saturated Fat | 1 g |
| Trans Fat | 0 g |
| Total Carbohydrates | 7 g |
| Dietary Fiber | 4 g |
| Total Sugars | 2 g |
| Protein | 5 g |
| Cholesterol | 7 mg |
| Sodium | 238 mg |

## exchanges

| | |
|---|---|
| Fat | 1.5 |
| Lean Meat | 0.5 |
| Vegetables | 1 |

### INGREDIENTS

*6 spears jumbo asparagus (about 1⅓ pounds), peeled with ends trimmed*

*2 tablespoons chopped fresh flat-leaf parsley leaves*

*1 tablespoon plus 1 teaspoon freshly squeezed lemon juice*

*1 tablespoon extra-virgin olive oil*

*1 tablespoon finely grated Parmesan cheese*

*1 tablespoon canola oil*

*4 thin slices Prosciutto di Parma (about 1 ounce total)*

*2 tablespoons minced fresh shallot*

*4 cups loosely packed frisée lettuce*

1. Bring a medium-size pot of water to a boil over high heat. Fill a large bowl halfway with ice water.

2. Cook the asparagus in the boiling water until al dente, about 8 minutes. Use tongs to remove the asparagus from the pot and transfer it to the ice water to stop the cooking and preserve the color. Once the asparagus has cooled, drain it and pat dry with paper towels.

3. Place 1 tablespoon of parsley, 2 teaspoons of the lemon juice, the olive oil, and Parmesan cheese in a bowl and whisk together (you can use the same bowl that held the ice water if you wipe it out). Add the asparagus and gently turn to coat with the dressing.

4. Heat the canola oil in a wide, nonstick pan over medium heat. Add 2 slices of the prosciutto and cook until crisp on both sides, 30 to 40 seconds per side, turning with tongs or a rubber spatula. Transfer the prosciutto to paper towels to drain. Repeat with the remaining 2 slices of prosciutto.

5. When all of the prosciutto has been cooked, add the shallot, the remaining 1 tablespoon of the parsley, and the remaining 2 teaspoons of the lemon juice to the hot pan and swirl to combine with any fat remaining from the prosciutto, about 20 seconds.

6. Put the frisée in a bowl, pour the warm shallot vinaigrette over it, and toss to coat.

7. Place 4 stalks of asparagus on each of 4 salad plates. Divide the frisée among the plates, arranging it next to the asparagus. Lean a prosciutto crisp against each salad and serve immediately.

CARBOHYDRATE CHOICE: ½

# asparagus salad

## WITH AN EGG WHITE DRESSING

i f you ever find yourself in the mood for something unabashedly old-fashioned, keep this simple asparagus starter in mind. Whisking hard-cooked egg whites into the dressing doesn't just add texture; it's also a subtle way of bringing some protein to the plate. **SERVES 4**

## nutritional information
(PER SERVING)

Calories......................105
Fat...............................5 g
   Saturated Fat............1 g
   Trans Fat...................0 g
Total Carbohydrates....8 g
   Dietary Fiber.............2 g
   Total Sugars.............3 g
Protein.........................8 g
Cholesterol...........107 mg
Sodium..................199 mg

## exchanges

Fat.................................1
Vegetables......................1
Lean Meat...................0.5

## did you know?

Mimosa isn't just a drink made from orange juice and Champagne. It's also the classic French culinary term for a garnish of minced, hard-cooked egg yolks, a nod to the small yellow flower of the same name.

## INGREDIENTS

20 large asparagus spears (about 1 pound), peeled with ends trimmed

5 large hard-cooked eggs (see page 47)

¼ cup minced red onion

2 tablespoons full-fat mayonnaise

1 rib celery, finely diced

1 tablespoon freshly squeezed lemon juice

1 tablespoon chopped fresh flat-leaf parsley leaves

2 teaspoons Dijon mustard

1. Bring a medium-size pot of water to a boil over high heat. Fill a large bowl halfway with ice water.

2. Cook the asparagus in the boiling water until al dente, about 8 minutes. Use tongs to remove the asparagus from the pot and transfer it to the ice water to stop the cooking and preserve the color. Once the asparagus has cooled, drain it and pat dry with paper towels.

3. Peel the eggs, cut them in half, and separate the whites from the yolks. Mince all of the whites and 2 of the yolks and set them aside separately. (Discard the remaining 3 yolks or save them for another use.)

4. Put the onion, mayonnaise, celery, lemon juice, parsley, mustard, and 1 tablespoon of water in a bowl and whisk together until blended. Gently stir the egg whites into the dressing.

5. To serve, put 5 asparagus stalks on each of 4 plates. Spoon the dressing over the asparagus and garnish with the minced egg yolks.

**CARBOHYDRATE CHOICE: 1; ½ ADJUSTED FOR FIBER**

# puntarelle

## WITH ANCHOVY SAUCE

a n Italian chicory that's in season during the late fall and winter, puntarelle has a very compelling flavor, like a cross between celery and Belgian endive. It's not something you'll find at every supermarket; look for it instead at farmers' markets and Italian grocers. If you can't find puntarelle, replace it with peeled, shaved celery stalks, Belgian endive, and/or fennel; you can even use a combination of all three because the dressing will pull the flavors together.

**SERVES 4**

### INGREDIENTS

*2 pounds puntarelle (1 large head),*
  *outer green leaves discarded,*
  *separated into stalks, and thinly*
  *sliced lengthwise*
*¼ cup olive oil*

*1 large clove garlic, minced*
*2 anchovy fillets from a can or*
  *jar, rinsed and drained*
*½ teaspoon red wine vinegar*

1. Arrange the puntarelle slices on a large serving plate in a single layer.

2. Heat the olive oil in a small, heavy-bottomed pan over medium heat. Add the garlic and anchovies and cook, mashing the anchovies with a spoon until they dissolve into the oil, about 3 minutes. Stir in the vinegar.

3. Drizzle the anchovy sauce over the puntarelle and serve family-style from the center of the table.

## nutritional information
(PER SERVING)

Calories......................195
Fat................................14 g
  Saturated Fat...........2 g
  Trans Fat..................0 g
Total Carbohydrates...17 g
  Dietary Fiber...........7 g
  Total Sugars.............0 g
Protein..........................3 g
Cholesterol..................2 mg
Sodium....................192 mg

## exchanges

Fat.................................2.5
Vegetables.....................3

## nutritional information
### (PER SERVING)

| | |
|---|---|
| Calories | 22 |
| Fat | 2 g |
|   Saturated Fat | 0 g |
|   Trans Fat | 0 g |
| Total Carbohydrates | 2 g |
|   Dietary Fiber | 0 g |
|   Total Sugars | 0 g |
| Protein | 1 g |
| Cholesterol | 0 mg |
| Sodium | 9 mg |

## exchanges

| | |
|---|---|
| Fat | 0.5 |
| Vegetables | 0.5 |

**A TIP FROM TOM**

**MICROPLANE ZESTER:** For grating cheese and zest, there's nothing like a Microplane zester. Originally a woodworking tool, this narrow, blade-lined "file" is easy to manipulate (you run it over what you want to grate, rather than vice versa) and produces delicate, consistent flakes.

**CARBOHYDRATE CHOICE: 0**

# kale salad

## WITH PINE NUTS AND RICOTTA SALATA

i was looking for a prominent way to include kale, a high-fiber, nutrient-rich leafy green, in this book when I remembered this classic Italian salad. It's one of those simple, perfect concoctions in which every ingredient makes an important contribution: the slightly bitter kale is offset by sweet currants, toasted pine nuts, and salty ricotta salata cheese. By using white rather than red wine vinegar, the vinaigrette perks up these qualities without distracting from them. **SERVES 4**

### INGREDIENTS

3 tablespoons pine nuts

8 cups loosely packed kale (from about 1 small bunch), stems discarded, cut into chiffonade (see page 22)

2 tablespoons dried currants

3 tablespoons extra-virgin olive oil

1 tablespoon white wine vinegar

2 tablespoons coarsely grated ricotta salata

1. Put the pine nuts in a small pan and toast over medium heat, shaking the pan frequently to prevent scorching, until lightly browned and fragrant, about 3 minutes. Transfer the pine nuts to a salad bowl and let cool.

2. Once the pine nuts are cool, add the kale and currants to the bowl. Add the olive oil and vinegar and toss well.

3. Mound some salad in the center of each of 4 salad plates. Dust with the cheese and serve.

CARBOHYDRATE CHOICE: ½

# brussels sprouts salad

most of us think of brussels sprouts as a vegetable to be cooked and eaten hot, as in the side dish on page 275. But brussels sprouts are also wonderful cold, shaved paper-thin and dressed with lemon juice and olive oil. I've never much cared for raw artichoke salad prepared this way but I happen to *love* raw brussels sprouts salad made with these ingredients, and the fact that the thin shavings naturally curl makes for an effortlessly attractive presentation, especially when showered with a snowy blanket of finely grated cheese.

**SERVES 4**

## nutritional information
**(PER SERVING)**

| | |
|---|---|
| Calories | 184 |
| Fat | 16 g |
| Saturated Fat | 4 g |
| Trans Fat | 0 g |
| Total Carbohydrates | 7 g |
| Dietary Fiber | 2 g |
| Total Sugars | 2 g |
| Protein | 4 g |
| Cholesterol | 8 mg |
| Sodium | 184 mg |

## exchanges

| | |
|---|---|
| Fat | 3 |
| Vegetables | 1 |

## INGREDIENTS

12 large brussels sprouts
(about ½ pound), ugly outer
leaves removed
Pinch of coarse salt
3 cloves garlic, smashed and
peeled

¼ cup extra-virgin olive oil
2 tablespoons freshly squeezed
lemon juice
Pinch of freshly ground black pepper
1 ounce Pecorino Romano cheese,
finely grated (about ¼ cup)

1. Thinly slice the brussels sprouts, ideally with a mandoline. Put the slices in a large bowl.

2. Put the garlic in a small bowl, add the salt, and mash to a paste, using the back of a spoon. Add the olive oil and lemon juice and whisk. Drizzle the dressing over the sprouts and toss to coat. Season the sprouts with pepper and toss again.

3. Divide the brussels sprouts among 4 salad plates. Shower the cheese on top and serve.

# antipasto salad

## WITH A CHERRY PEPPER VINAIGRETTE

i love snacking on the elements of an Italian antipasti spread: cold cuts, mozzarella and Parmesan cheese, olives, and peppers. This dish collects all of those addictive treats together in a salad with (what else?) a red wine vinaigrette. But not just any red wine vinaigrette: This one's spiced up with chopped hot cherry peppers that also paint the entire salad a beautiful, streaky red.

**SERVES 4**

## nutritional information
### (PER SERVING)

| | |
|---|---|
| Calories | 339 |
| Fat | 26 g |
| Saturated Fat | 7 g |
| Trans Fat | 0 g |
| Total Carbohydrates | 13 g |
| Dietary Fiber | 5 g |
| Total Sugars | 7 g |
| Protein | 14 g |
| Cholesterol | 31 mg |
| Sodium | 391 mg |

## exchanges

| | |
|---|---|
| Fat | 4.5 |
| High Fat Meat | 1.5 |
| Vegetables | 2 |

### INGREDIENTS

¼ cup extra-virgin olive oil

2 tablespoons seeded, chopped hot cherry pepper from a jar (about 1 large pepper)

2 tablespoons plus 2 teaspoons red wine vinegar

1 tablespoon plus 1 teaspoon chopped fresh flat-leaf parsley leaves

1 tablespoon grated Parmesan cheese

Pinch of freshly ground black pepper

8 cups crisp salad greens, such as escarole hearts, romaine lettuce, or frisée lettuce

¼ pound salt-free mozzarella, cut into ½-inch cubes

2 ounces sweet or hot soppressata, or combination of the two (see page 49), cut into long, thin strips

4 black olives, pitted and coarsely chopped

2 Roasted Bell Peppers (page 324), thinly sliced

¼ cup chopped red onion

1. To make the vinaigrette, put the olive oil, cherry pepper and its liquid, vinegar, parsley, Parmesan cheese, and black pepper in a bowl and whisk together.

2. Put the greens, mozzarella, *soppressata*, olives, red bell pepper, and onion in a salad bowl. Drizzle the vinaigrette on top and toss to coat well.

3. Divide the salad among 4 plates, making sure to get a good mix of ingredients on each plate, and serve.

CARBOHYDRATE CHOICE: 1; ½ ADJUSTED FOR FIBER

# warm artichokes

## WITH ARTICHOKE DRESSING AND PARMESAN

**1** et's not kid ourselves: the *warm,* in the name of this dish is a healthier sounding euphemism for *fried.* But never fear because there's just a modicum of oil used for frying, as the artichokes are cooked and quartered, then crisped on the cut sides only. A few artichokes are blended right into the dressing, acting as a surprising emulsifying agent. Add some Parmesan shards and some greens and you have the makings of a memorable salad that features hot and cold, creamy and crunchy, and often all of this in every bite. **SERVES 4**

### INGREDIENTS

8 small artichokes, trimmed

½ lemon plus 2 tablespoons freshly
   squeezed lemon juice

½ teaspoon coarse salt

¼ teaspoon coriander seeds

2 tablespoons Dijon mustard

1 medium-size clove garlic, peeled

¼ cup low-sodium, store-bought
   chicken broth

1 cup olive oil

½ teaspoon freshly ground black pepper

1 teaspoon canola oil

1 large bunch arugula

1 head escarole, trimmed

2 ounces Parmesan cheese,
   cut into shards or coarsely
   grated

1 teaspoon white truffle oil

**1.** Put the artichokes in a pot. Add enough cold water to just cover them. Squeeze the juice from the half lemon into the water, catching the seeds in your hand, then add the lemon rind to the pot. Add ¼ teaspoon of salt, bring to a boil, lower the heat, and let the artichokes simmer until they are tender when pierced with a knife tip, 10 to 12 minutes.

**2.** Place the artichokes in a colander and let drain and cool in the sink.

**3.** Meanwhile, put the coriander seeds in a small pan and toast over medium heat, shaking the pan to prevent scorching, until the coriander is fragrant, about 2 minutes. Transfer the coriander to a small bowl and set aside to cool.

## shop right

**TRUFFLE OIL:** Truffle oil is one of the most maligned condiments on the market today, largely because we all fell in love with it about ten years ago, overused it, and got sick of it. But the truth is that used in small doses, while no substitute for the real thing, truffle oil does have a haunting quality it can add to dishes. Just a few drops of truffle oil over artichokes can perfume them with an intense, alluring aroma.

**4.** To make the dressing, coarsely chop 3 of the artichokes and put them in a standing blender. Add the toasted coriander seeds, mustard, garlic, and broth and blend. With the motor running, slowly add the olive oil in a thin stream until a thick, creamy emulsion forms. Add the remaining 2 tablespoons of lemon juice and a pinch of the black pepper.

**5.** Line a large plate with paper towels. Quarter the remaining artichokes. Heat the canola oil in a wide, deep, heavy-bottomed pan over medium-high heat. Add the arti-chokes, cut side down, and cook until just golden brown, 30 to 45 seconds. Transfer the artichokes to the paper towel–lined plate and season the cut sides with the remaining ¼ teaspoon of salt.

**6.** To assemble the salads, put the arugula and escarole in a bowl and toss with the artichoke dressing. Divide them among 4 salad plates. Top with the fried artichoke quarters. Garnish with Parmesan shards, a few drops of truffle oil, and a scattering of the remaining black pepper.

## nutritional information
(PER SERVING)

| | |
|---|---|
| Calories | 134 |
| Fat | 11 g |
| Saturated Fat | 2 g |
| Trans Fat | 0 g |
| Total Carbohydrates | 8 g |
| Dietary Fiber | 2 g |
| Total Sugars | 4 g |
| Protein | 2 g |
| Cholesterol | 0 mg |
| Sodium | 215 mg |

## exchanges

| | |
|---|---|
| Fat | 2 |
| Vegetables | 1 |

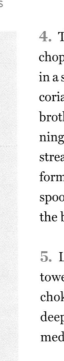

CARBOHYDRATE CHOICE: ½

# tomatoes and cucumbers

**WITH SHERRY VINAIGRETTE**

the best time to make this salad is at the height of summer, preferably as soon as you've returned from the farm stand, farmers' market, or your own backyard garden with an armful of fresh, fragrant tomatoes in tow. (Okay, tomatoes are really a fruit, but I think of them as a vegetable, and I'll bet you do, too.) It doesn't take much to coax the most out of these ingredients: A quick sherry vinaigrette with lemon juice and garlic does the trick.

**SERVES 4**

## INGREDIENTS

*3 tablespoons extra-virgin olive oil*

*2 tablespoons sherry vinegar*

*¼ teaspoon freshly squeezed lemon
juice*

*¼ teaspoon minced garlic*

*¼ teaspoon coarse salt*

*Pinch of freshly ground black pepper*

*6 medium-size plum tomatoes,
cut into large dice*

*1 small red onion, cut into large
dice*

*½ English (seedless) cucumber,
peeled and cut into large dice
(about 1½ cups dice)*

Put the olive oil, sherry vinegar, lemon juice, and garlic in a large bowl and whisk them together. Season with the salt and pepper. Add the tomatoes, onion, and cucumber and toss gently but thoroughly. Divide the salad among 4 plates and serve or serve family style from the bowl.

### variations and suggestions:

This salad is a perfect vehicle for crumbled feta, goat cheese, or blue cheese.

Because this salad has many of the same ingredients as gazpacho—tomatoes, cucumbers, olive oil, sherry vinegar, garlic, and red onion—it occurred to me to blend it up and see if I ended up with something like gazpacho, which after all is referred to as a "liquid salad" in Spain. With a little doctoring, like the addition of more olive oil to advance the emulsification and some jalapeño pepper for heat, it comes pretty close. There's no bread in this gazpacho, which makes it a bit unorthodox, but it's perfectly appropriate to our mission here.

For four servings, add the following to the salad while it's still in the bowl: 2 tablespoons extra-virgin olive oil; 1 tablespoon red wine vinegar; and 1½ teaspoons chopped seeded jalapeño pepper. Toss the salad and transfer it to a food processor. Pulse until it has the consistency of a wet salsa, then divide it among 4 bowls and serve. You can also blend the gazpacho in a standing blender but the result will be a more watery, less chunky gazpacho.

### did you know?

In Spain, many tapas bars ladle gazpacho into glasses and invite you to drink it like a beverage, a cooling, refreshing Andalusian alternative to iced tea or lemonade. If you'd like to do the same, blend your gazpacho first in a food processor and then a blender for the finest, most drinkable result.

CARBOHYDRATE CHOICE: 1

# winter salad

## WITH HINTS OF SUMMER

One of my favorite summer salads features tomatoes, red onions, blue cheese, and a simple red wine vinaigrette. I got to wondering if I could take the same summery ingredients and make them the basis of a winter salad, and this is the result. The off-season tomatoes are roasted to draw out their flavor, and the red onion slices are lightly charred (a grill pan is fine for this, especially if your actual grill is surrounded by snow drifts). The dressing is made with balsamic vinegar and mustard so it stands up to the other ingredients. **SERVES 4**

### INGREDIENTS

2 teaspoons Dijon mustard

2 teaspoons balsamic vinegar

¼ cup olive oil

½ teaspoon freshly squeezed lemon
   juice

Pinch of freshly ground black pepper

5 cups loosely packed arugula

8 Roasted Plum Tomato halves
   (page 323)

4 Grilled Red Onion slices
   (page 321), cut in half and
   separated

4 slices (¼ inch thick) French
   bread, toasted and cut into
   small cubes

¼ cup crumbled Roquefort or
   other blue cheese (about
   1 ounce)

1. Whisk the mustard and balsamic vinegar together in a large bowl. Slowly whisk in the olive oil, adding it in a thin stream, to make an emulsified dressing, then whisk in the lemon juice. Season with the pepper.

2. Add the arugula, tomatoes, onion slices, and bread cubes to the bowl and toss well. Divide the salad among 4 plates, scatter some blue cheese over each salad, and serve.

CARBOHYDRATE CHOICE: 1; ½ ADJUSTED FOR FIBER

# salad of chicories, roquefort, and roasted garlic

One of the challenges in putting together a classic salad, by which I mean one based on greens, is avoiding monotony, so the more textures and temperatures the better. This salad has a little of everything: two members of the chicory family to keep the palate engaged; soft, warm garlic confit; crunchy croutons; and creamy, potent blue cheese. With all of that action, a straightforward Red Wine Vinaigrette is all that's required to dress it, adding a little oil and acid to the mix. **SERVES 4**

## INGREDIENTS

*1 cup Roasted Garlic cloves (page 321)*

*About ½ cup country bread cubes (1-inch cubes; you can leave the crust on)*

*1 medium-size head chicory, outer leaves removed, separated into leaves*

*1 medium-size head escarole, outer leaves removed, separated into leaves*

*1 tablespoon grated Parmesan cheese*

*½ cup crumbled Roquefort, or other blue cheese (about 2 ounces)*

*¼ cup plus 2 tablespoons Red Wine Vinaigrette (page 315)*

*Pinch of freshly ground black pepper*

*1 tablespoon minced fresh flat-leaf parsley leaves*

1. Preheat the oven to 250°F.

2. Put the garlic and bread cubes in a nonstick baking pan and warm in the oven for 2 to 3 minutes.

3. Put the chicory, escarole, Parmesan and Roquefort cheeses in a bowl. Drizzle the vinaigrette on top and toss well. Add the warmed garlic and bread cubes, season with the pepper, and toss again. Divide among 4 salad plates and scatter some parsley over each serving.

## nutritional information
### (PER SERVING)

| | |
|---|---|
| Calories | 250 |
| Fat | 20 g |
| Saturated Fat | 5 g |
| Trans Fat | 0 g |
| Total Carbohydrates | 13 g |
| Dietary Fiber | 5 g |
| Total Sugars | 1 g |
| Protein | 7 g |
| Cholesterol | 14 mg |
| Sodium | 414 mg |

## exchanges

| | |
|---|---|
| Fat | 3 |
| High Fat Meat | 0.5 |
| Vegetables | 1.5 |

## shop right

**BLUE CHEESE:** Thanks to the snowballing interest in cheese in the United States, there are countless varieties of blue cheese available today, ranging from the mild American Point Reyes to the club-you-over-the-head richness of British Stilton. In the kitchen, my personal "top 3" blues are the classics: French Roquefort, Italian Gorgonzola, and American Maytag blue. They're all easy to find, even in many supermarkets these days, and are middle-of-the-road in flavor and texture. Experiment with other cheeses on your cheese boards, or in restaurants, but stick to these three in cooking and you won't go wrong.

**CARBOHYDRATE CHOICE: ½**

# warm spinach salad

## WITH BACON VINAIGRETTE

If there were a recipe Hall of Fame, I'd nominate the classic warm spinach and bacon salad for enshrinement. The simple perfection of sautéed diced bacon and fresh spinach leaves, tossed with a vinaigrette made from the bacon drippings themselves, with nothing but red onion and hard-cooked egg to complete the composition is something I never get tired of. This less fatty version uses turkey bacon in place of the porky stuff and turns the cooking liquid into a dressing of mustard and sherry vinegar, making up for the missing fat with extra flavor and creaminess. **SERVES 4**

## INGREDIENTS

¼ cup extra-virgin olive oil

6 slices turkey bacon, finely diced
  (about ¾ cup)

2 tablespoons plus 2 teaspoons
  sherry vinegar

1 tablespoon plus 1 teaspoon
  Dijon mustard

1 tablespoon minced fresh flat-leaf
  parsley leaves

Pinch of freshly ground black pepper

8 cups loosely packed spinach,
  tough stems discarded

1 small red onion, thinly sliced

¼ teaspoon coarse salt

2 large hard-cooked eggs (see page 47),
  thinly sliced crosswise

1. Heat 1 tablespoon of the olive oil in a nonstick pan over medium heat. Add the turkey bacon and cook until browned and the fat is rendered, about 8 minutes. Using a slotted spoon, transfer the bacon to paper towels to drain.

2. Pour the hot oil from the pan into a large heatproof mixing bowl. Add the remaining 3 tablespoons of olive oil and the sherry vinegar and mustard and whisk together. Whisk in the parsley and the pepper.

3. Add the spinach, onion, and bacon to the bowl. Season with the salt and toss well.

**4.** Divide the salad among 4 salad plates. Garnish each plate with some of the egg slices. Serve while the dressing is still warm.

**variations and suggestions:** This salad is also delicious made with curly endive or frisée lettuce in place of spinach. A few ounces of crumbled goat cheese, tossed in just before serving, is also a welcome addition.

CARBOHYDRATE CHOICE: 0

# raw mushroom salad

With all the varieties of wild mushrooms on the market today, I sometimes feel like the plain, old button mushroom has become the Rodney Dangerfield of 'shrooms: It don't get no respect. Well, here's one chef who's not afraid to say that he still loves the button mushroom, which is delicious in soups and pastas—to name just two places I still like to use it. For further proof of its value, here's a salad that uses the mushrooms uncooked, dressing them with a lemony vinaigrette and topping them with some arugula and Parmesan. **SERVES 4**

## nutritional information
(PER SERVING)

| | |
|---|---|
| Calories | 103 |
| Fat | 9 g |
| Saturated Fat | 2 g |
| Trans Fat | 0 g |
| Total Carbohydrates | 3 g |
| Dietary Fiber | 0 g |
| Total Sugars | 1 g |
| Protein | 3 g |
| Cholesterol | 5 mg |
| Sodium | 360 mg |

## exchanges

| | |
|---|---|
| Fat | 1.5 |
| Lean Meat | 0.5 |
| Vegetables | 0.5 |

### INGREDIENTS

1 small clove garlic, minced

2½ tablespoons freshly squeezed lemon juice

2 tablespoons extra-virgin olive oil

½ teaspoon coarse salt

¼ teaspoon freshly ground black pepper

4 large white button mushrooms, stems trimmed, thinly sliced

4 cups loosely packed arugula

1 ounce Parmesan cheese, cut into shards with a vegetable peeler

**1.** Put the garlic, lemon juice, olive oil, salt, and pepper in a large bowl and whisk together.

**2.** Fan out the slices of 1 mushroom on each of 4 salad plates. Drizzle about 2 teaspoons of vinaigrette over the mushroom on each plate.

**3.** Put the arugula in the bowl with the remaining vinaigrette and toss. Arrange the arugula over the mushrooms. Garnish with Parmesan shards and serve.

# mushroom and farro salad

farro is a firm, nutty grain—and a close relative to spelt—that has been popular in Italy for thousands of years but only became popular in the United States in the past decade or so. This year-round, room-temperature salad offsets farro's earthiness, and that of the mushrooms, with balsamic vinegar, feta cheese, and fresh parsley; a perfect dish for potluck dinners and picnics (in the summer). It also makes wonderful leftovers that can be served alongside everything from chicken to sliced cold roast beef.   SERVES 4

## shop right

**BALSAMIC VINEGAR:** The very best balsamic vinegars are aged for years, if not decades, in wood barrels and, not unlike fine wines or sherries, take on complex flavors and nuances. Those vinegars are also famously expensive and are used almost comically sparingly. For most cooking, including all of the recipes in this book, I do *not* recommend such an investment. But I also urge you not to use the least expensive brands of balsamic vinegar, many of which are pale imitations of the real thing. A good rule of thumb is to select balsamic vinegars that bear the phrase Aceto Balsamico Tradizionale di Modena or Aceto Balsamico Tradizionale di Reggio Emilia on the label. Both are protected designations of origin— the surest sign of quality.

## INGREDIENTS

¼ pound uncooked farro

1 medium-size carrot, cut crosswise
  into 2 or 3 large pieces

1 medium-size Spanish onion,
  cut into 4 large pieces

1 large rib celery, cut crosswise into
  2 or 3 large pieces

3 cloves garlic, crushed and peeled

1½ teaspoons Porcini Powder
  (page 325)

¼ cup olive oil

2 fresh thyme sprigs

6 ounces shiitake and/or oyster
  mushrooms, stems trimmed

3 tablespoons crumbled feta cheese

3 tablespoons chopped fresh flat-leaf
  parsley leaves

2 tablespoons plus 2 teaspoons
  balsamic vinegar

1 tablespoon plus 1 teaspoon extra-
  virgin olive oil

½ teaspoon coarse salt

Pinch of freshly ground black pepper

12 Belgian endive spears
  (from about 2 endives)

1. Preheat the oven to 350°F.

2. Put the farro in a pan and toast over low heat, shaking the pan to prevent scorching, until the farro is lightly toasted and fragrant, 10 to 15 minutes.

3. Transfer the farro to a heavy-bottomed pot. Add the carrot, onion, celery, 2 of the garlic cloves, the Porcini Powder, and 3½ cups of water. Bring to a simmer over medium-high heat, and let simmer until the farro is al dente, about 45 minutes.

4. Meanwhile, roast the mushrooms: Put the regular olive oil, remaining garlic clove, and the thyme in a wide, shallow bowl. Dip the mushrooms in the olive oil mixture, then remove them, letting any excess oil run back into the bowl. Arrange the mushrooms on a baking sheet without crowding and bake until golden brown and starting to crisp around the edges, about 15 minutes. (Discard the olive oil mixture.) Let the mushrooms cool, then cut them into ¼-inch dice.

5. When the farro is done, use tongs to remove the vegetables and discard them. If there is any water left in the farro drain it. You should have about 2 cups of cooked farro.

6. To serve, put the diced mushrooms in a large bowl. Add the farro, feta, parsley, balsamic vinegar, and extra-virgin olive oil. Season with the salt and pepper and toss. Divide the salad among 4 salad plates. Arrange 3 endive spears alongside the salad on each plate.

**variations and suggestions:** To incorporate some crunch, cut the carrot, onion, and celery into ¼-inch dice and add them to the farro raw at the end when you mix the salad rather than cooking them.

Mushroom & Farro Salad

## nutritional information
(PER SERVING)

| | |
|---|---|
| Calories | 358 |
| Fat | 21 g |
| Saturated Fat | 4 g |
| Trans Fat | 0 g |
| Total Carbohydrates | 38 g |
| Dietary Fiber | 6 g |
| Total Sugars | 5 g |
| Protein | 9 g |
| Cholesterol | 6 mg |
| Sodium | 421 mg |

## exchanges

| | |
|---|---|
| Fat | 4 |
| Starch | 1 |
| Vegetables | 3 |

## nutritional information
(PER SERVING)

Calories.........................181
Fat................................16 g
   Saturated Fat...........4 g
   Trans Fat..................0 g
Total Carbohydrates.....6 g
   Dietary Fiber..............1 g
   Total Sugars.............3 g
Protein............................5 g
Cholesterol................13 mg
Sodium....................297 mg

## exchanges

Fat....................................3
Medium Fat Meat..........0.5
Vegetables......................1

**CARBOHYDRATE CHOICE: ½**

# warm mushroom salad

## WITH SUNFLOWER SEEDS, SPINACH, AND ARUGULA

One of the most efficient techniques in the kitchen is making a pan sauce in the same skillet in which you seared a piece of meat or fish. This recipe calls on a similar method to make a warm vinaigrette, adding some olive oil and vinegar to a pan in which mushrooms have been quickly sautéed. The mushrooms and vinaigrette top a bed of spinach and arugula, and the salad is finished with a scattering of feta cheese and sunflower seeds.

I have to give credit where credit is due: this is based on a very similar salad served by my friend Tammy at the Riverside Cafe in upstate New York.

**SERVES 4**

### INGREDIENTS

2 cups loosely packed spinach leaves, well rinsed, tough stems discarded, patted dry

2 cups loosely packed arugula

3 tablespoons extra-virgin olive oil

1 medium-size shallot, minced

1 large clove garlic, minced

8 ounces white button mushrooms, stems trimmed, thinly sliced

¼ teaspoon coarse salt

Pinch of freshly ground black pepper

1 teaspoon balsamic vinegar

1 teaspoon red wine vinegar

2 ounces feta cheese, crumbled (about ½ cup)

2 tablespoons dry-roasted, unsalted sunflower seeds

1. Toss the spinach and arugula together and divide them among 4 salad plates. Set aside.

2. Heat 1½ teaspoons of the olive oil in a heavy-bottomed, nonstick pan over medium heat. Add the shallot and garlic and cook just until they begin to sizzle about 30 seconds. Add the mushrooms, season with the salt and pepper, stir, and cook for 30 seconds.

3. Remove the pan from the heat. Add the remaining 2½ tablespoons of the olive oil and the vinegars to the mushrooms. Swirl to make a quick, warm vinaigrette.

4. Spoon the mushrooms and vinaigrette over the greens on each plate. Scatter some feta cheese and sunflower seeds over each salad and serve.

**CARBOHYDRATE CHOICES: 1½**

# mushroom and goat cheese turnovers

## WITH AN ARUGULA AND BEET SALAD

mushrooms, goat cheese, and beets are a tried and true salad combination that I don't think will ever go out of style. I like incorporating the turnovers because salads are often the first thing served at a meal, and I still crave a piece of bread alongside. The phyllo more than satisfies that urge with a fraction of the carbohydrate cost. **SERVES 4**

### INGREDIENTS

1 medium-size red beet
  (about 12 ounces), well scrubbed,
  root end trimmed
¼ cup extra-virgin olive oil
1½ tablespoons unsalted butter,
  at room temperature,
  plus 1 tablespoon butter, melted
1 small clove garlic, minced
6 ounces white button mushrooms,
  stems trimmed, coarsely chopped
¼ teaspoon fresh thyme leaves
¼ teaspoon coarse salt

⅛ teaspoon freshly ground
  black pepper
⅛ teaspoon Porcini Powder
  (page 325; optional)
4 sheets phyllo dough (see next page),
  thawed if frozen
2 ounces crumbled goat cheese
  (about ½ cup)
2 tablespoons freshly squeezed
  lemon juice
⅛ teaspoon white truffle oil (optional)
2 cups loosely packed arugula

### nutritional information
(PER SERVING)

| | |
|---|---|
| Calories | 352 |
| Fat | 27 g |
| Saturated Fat | 10 g |
| Trans Fat | 0 g |
| Total Carbohydrates | 22 g |
| Dietary Fiber | 3 g |
| Total Sugars | 9 g |
| Protein | 7 g |
| Cholesterol | 30 mg |
| Sodium | 358 mg |

### exchanges

| | |
|---|---|
| Fat | 4.5 |
| Other Carbohydrates | 0.5 |
| High Fat Meat | 0.5 |
| Vegetables | 2 |

**WORKING WITH PHYLLO:** If you purchase frozen phyllo dough, be sure to move it from the freezer to the refrigerator the night before you plan to cook, or the morning of the day you will use it, because phyllo is one of the few kitchen items that can't be hurried along by the trusty "defrost" button on your microwave. (Leftover thawed phyllo can be kept for several weeks in an airtight bag in the fridge.)

When working with phyllo dough, be sure to set it on a clean, dry surface and cover it with a damp paper towel to keep it from drying out and cracking, which can happen in record time. But don't overdampen the towel; it doesn't take much moisture to turn the delicate sheets gummy. As you fill and fold up the turnovers or other items, periodically wipe down the work surface to be sure it's dry when you lay down the next sheet of phyllo.

1. Preheat the oven to 350°F.

2. Cut 1 piece (about 8 by 8 inches) of aluminum foil and place the beet in the center. Rub the beet with 1 tablespoon of the olive oil. Gather up the edges of the foil to encase the beet. Bake the beet until tender when pierced with a knife, but very much holding its shape, 35 to 40 minutes. Remove the beet from the oven and increase the oven temperature to 375°F.

3. Unwrap the beet, and let cool. When the beet is cool enough to handle, using a paring knife, remove the skin, cut the beet into ¼-inch dice, and set aside.

4. Heat 1 tablespoon of the olive oil and the 1½ tablespoons of butter in a heavy-bottomed pan over medium heat. Add the garlic and cook until softened but not browned, about 2 minutes. Add the mushrooms, thyme, salt, pepper, and Porcini Powder, if using, and cook until the mushrooms are just cooked through, 3 to 4 minutes. Transfer the mushroom mixture to a bowl and let cool, then drain off any liquid that accumulates.

5. To assemble the turnovers, place a sheet of phyllo on a work surface. Using a pastry brush and working along one of the long edges, brush some of the melted butter over half of the sheet of phyllo, then fold it in half lengthwise over the buttered side. Mound some of the mushroom mixture and one quarter of the goat cheese about an inch from the short edge closest to you. Starting from the lower left corner, fold the phyllo diagonally up over the filling so that the corner touches the right edge of the phyllo; it will form a triangle. Keep folding the triangle upward, as though folding a flag, until you have about an inch of dough remaining at the top. Brush the exposed phyllo with butter and fold it over to make a triangle-shaped packet. Repeat with the remaining phyllo, mushroom mixture, and cheese.

6. Place the turnovers in a single layer onto a nonstick or foil-lined baking sheet and bake until lightly browned, 12 to 15 minutes.

7. While the turnovers are baking, put the remaining 2 tablespoons of olive oil in a medium-size bowl. Whisk in the lemon juice and truffle oil, if using. Add the arugula and toss to coat. Gently toss in the diced beets.

8. When the turnovers are done, place 1 on each of 4 salad plates. Mound some arugula and beet salad alongside and serve.

MAKING THE (SUSHI) GRADE:

# seviches, carpaccios,

## AND OTHER RAW FISH PREPARATIONS

**a**ssuming you like them to begin with, raw fish dishes are a diabetic diner's dream come true. The combination of uncooked fish (requiring no fat for cooking) with the vibrant flavor of the marinades and some vegetables and herbs makes seviches and carpaccios easy prepping and ideal eating. Here are a handful of dishes that take advantage of this winning approach.

### did you know?

In a seviche, raw fish or shellfish is "cooked" by the chemical reaction that occurs when it comes into contact with an acidic marinade. The longer the fish marinates, the more "cooked" it becomes. Seviches turn up on the menus of French and American restaurants these days, but they originated in a country about whose food most of us know very little: Peru.

**CARBOHYDRATE CHOICES: 2**

## shrimp seviche

### WITH GRAPEFRUIT AND LETTUCE

**g**rapefruit sections and cilantro give this seviche a hard-to-place, vaguely South American quality. The bitter grapefruit proves the perfect counterpoint to the natural sweetness of the shellfish, and the lemon juice binds them together seamlessly.       **SERVES 4**

### INGREDIENTS

*1 tablespoon plus 2 teaspoons extra-virgin olive oil*

*8 large shrimp, peeled, deveined, cut in half crosswise, and thinly sliced lengthwise*

*Pinch of freshly ground black pepper*

*2 tablespoons plus 1 teaspoon freshly squeezed lemon juice*

*8 grapefruit sections, peeled and diced*

*1 tablespoon minced red onion*

*2 teaspoons chopped fresh chives*

*1 teaspoon coarsely chopped fresh cilantro leaves*

*1½ cups loosely packed Bibb or Boston lettuce*

---

**1.** Rub ½ teaspoon of the olive oil in the center section of each of 4 cold salad plates. Arrange the shrimp slices in a single layer in each center over the oil, dividing them evenly. Season the shrimp with some pepper and drizzle 1 teaspoon of the lemon juice over the shrimp slices on each plate. Scatter the grapefruit, onion, chives, and cilantro over the shrimp.

### nutritional information

(PER SERVING)

| | |
|---|---|
| Calories | 200 |
| Fat | 7 g |
| Saturated Fat | 1 g |
| Trans Fat | 0 g |
| Total Carbohydrates | 23 g |
| Dietary Fiber | 3 g |
| Total Sugars | 17 g |
| Protein | 13 g |
| Cholesterol | 0 mg |
| Sodium | 1 mg |

### exchanges

| | |
|---|---|
| Fat | 1.5 |
| Fruit | 1.5 |

## shop right

**HEAD-ON SHRIMP:** If you can, buy shrimp with the heads on; there's no surer sign of freshness. If you can't find pristine, fresh shrimp for this and other raw presentations, use thinly sliced sea scallops or fluke.

## nutritional information

(PER SERVING)

| | |
|---|---|
| Calories | 164 |
| Fat | 8 g |
| Saturated Fat | 1 g |
| Trans Fat | 0 g |
| Total Carbohydrates | 4 g |
| Dietary Fiber | 0 g |
| Total Sugars | 0 g |
| Protein | 19 g |
| Cholesterol | 37 mg |
| Sodium | 368 mg |

## exchanges

| | |
|---|---|
| Fat | 1.5 |
| Lean Meat | 2 |

**2.** Cover the plates tautly with plastic wrap, so that the herbs are pressed into the shrimp. Refrigerate for 30 minutes to 1 hour.

**3.** Just before removing the seviche from the refrigerator, put the remaining tablespoon of olive oil in a medium-size bowl. Add the remaining 1 tablespoon of lemon juice and whisk. Add the lettuce and toss to coat with the dressing.

**4.** To serve, remove the plastic wrap from the seviche plates. Mound some lettuce in the center, on top of each serving of shrimp, and serve.

CARBOHYDRATE CHOICE: 0

# bay scallop seviche

bay scallops are tiny as pencil erasers and nicely toothsome. In many ways, they're one of the ultimate candidates for the seviche treatment because their natural size ensures that each and every one will get full exposure to the marinade and because they readily take on other flavors. I like to go in a spicy direction with bay scallops, adding jalapeño pepper and crushed red pepper flakes. A perfect dish for entertaining, this is best served in martini glasses, which will show off the colors of the citrus juice, jalapeño, and red pepper flakes popping against the white scallops. **SERVES 4**

## INGREDIENTS

*1 pound bay scallops*
*¼ cup celery ribs (first halved lengthwise and sliced)*
*2 tablespoons olive oil*
*1 tablespoon plus 2 teaspoons freshly squeezed lime juice*
*1 tablespoon plus 1 teaspoon freshly squeezed lemon juice*
*1 tablespoon minced red onion*
*1 teaspoon seeded, diced jalapeño pepper (leave some or all of the seeds in for a spicier dish)*
*½ teaspoon chopped fresh cilantro leaves*
*½ teaspoon crushed red pepper flakes*
*⅜ teaspoon coarse salt*
*Pinch of freshly ground black pepper*

Put the scallops in a medium-size mixing bowl. Add the celery, olive oil, lime juice, lemon juice, onion, jalapeño, cilantro, red pepper flakes, salt, and black pepper and toss well. Cover and refrigerate for 10 minutes to 1 hour, then divide the scallops among 4 glasses or bowls and serve.

CARBOHYDRATE CHOICE: 0

# salmon seviche

though I use the name seviche for this dish, there's nothing even vaguely Peruvian about it; it's really a stylish way of presenting the popular flavors of a salmon tartare—extra-virgin olive oil, lemon juice, capers, and onion. You can, of course, dice the salmon instead of slicing it and mold this in small, chilled bowls tartare style instead.

**SERVES 4**

## INGREDIENTS

*4 teaspoons extra-virgin olive oil*

*12 ounces sushi-grade salmon fillet, thinly sliced*

*½ teaspoon coarse salt*

*2 teaspoons freshly squeezed lemon juice*

*2 teaspoons capers or osetra caviar (optional)*

*2 teaspoons minced Spanish onion*

*1 teaspoon finely diced celery*

*½ teaspoon chopped fresh chives*

*½ teaspoon mustard oil (optional; see this page)*

Rub ½ teaspoon of the olive oil in the center of each of 4 cold salad plates. Arrange the salmon slices in a single layer in each center over the oil, pressing them together to cover the surface of the plates. Season the salmon with the salt and drizzle the lemon juice and remaining 2 teaspoons of olive oil over the fish. Scatter the capers or caviar, if using, and the onion, celery, chives and mustard oil, if using, over the salmon slices. Serve the salmon immediately or cover the plates tautly with plastic wrap and refrigerate the salmon for up to 20 minutes. Remove the plastic wrap from the seviche plates and serve.

To facilitate thinly slicing the salmon, wrap it in plastic wrap and firm it in the freezer, 10 to 20 minutes.

**variations and suggestions:** If you opt for the capers (instead of the caviar), cut some Belgian endive diagonally into thin slices and scatter it over the seviche.

## nutritional information
(PER SERVING)

| | |
|---|---|
| Calories | 200 |
| Fat | 14 g |
| Saturated Fat | 3 g |
| Trans Fat | 0 g |
| Total Carbohydrates | 0 g |
| Dietary Fiber | 0 g |
| Total Sugars | 0 g |
| Protein | 17 g |
| Cholesterol | 50 mg |
| Sodium | 291 mg |

## exchanges

| | |
|---|---|
| Fat | 2 |
| Lean Meat | 2.5 |

## mustard oil

Mustard oil is not very common in American kitchens, but is readily available from Indian grocers and specialty food Web sites. It's made with pressed mustard seeds and has a potent, pleasingly hot flavor. Even just a few drops make an impact.

## nutritional information
### (PER SERVING)

| | |
|---|---|
| Calories | 177 |
| Fat | 13 g |
| Saturated Fat | 2 g |
| Trans Fat | 0 g |
| Total Carbohydrates | 3 g |
| Dietary Fiber | 1 g |
| Total Sugars | 1 g |
| Protein | 12 g |
| Cholesterol | 33 mg |
| Sodium | 395 mg |

## exchanges

| | |
|---|---|
| Fat | 2 |
| Lean Meat | 1.5 |

**CARBOHYDRATE CHOICE: 0**

# salmon carpaccio

the combination of lemon and lime juice brings out the best in the salmon here. It's an accessible way of imitating the flavor of the Asian fruit *yuzu*, which has become a popular restaurant ingredient but is inconvenient, or impossible, for most home cooks to find.

**SERVES 4**

### INGREDIENTS

*8 ounces sushi-grade salmon fillet*

*2 tablespoons minced shallot*

*2 tablespoons freshly squeezed lemon juice*

*1 tablespoon freshly squeezed lime juice*

*1 tablespoon chopped fresh chives*

*1 tablespoon extra-virgin olive oil*

*1 tablespoon mustard oil (see previous page), or an additional tablespoon extra-virgin olive oil*

*1 lemon, rind, membranes, and seeds removed and discarded, sections chopped*

*¾ teaspoon coarse salt*

*⅛ teaspoon freshly ground black pepper*

1. Wrap the salmon in plastic wrap and place it in the freezer until well chilled, 10 to 20 minutes, to firm up and make it easier to slice. Remove the plastic and cut the salmon into ¼-inch-thick slices.

2. Arrange the salmon slices in a single layer in the center of each of 4 cold salad plates, pressing them together to cover the surface of the plates.

3. Put the shallot, lemon juice, lime juice, chives, olive oil, mustard oil, and chopped lemon in a bowl and stir together to create a marinade.

4. Season the salmon with the salt and pepper. Drizzle the marinade over the salmon. Cover the plates loosely with plastic wrap and refrigerate the salmon for 30 minutes. Remove the plastic wrap from the plates and serve.

### variations and suggestions:

❖ You can refrigerate the salmon longer than indicated here, but the acid will begin to cook the fish, as in a seviche.

❖ You can also garnish each serving with minced hard-cooked egg whites after the salmon has marinated.

CARBOHYDRATE CHOICE: 0

# marinated salmon

## WITH WATERCRESS, CUCUMBER, AND CREME FRAICHE

You don't need to look any further than Scandinavian cuisine to know that certain fish have a great affinity with cream, and salmon is one of them. This starter offers a fresh take on salmon and cream, pairing raw fish with a salad of watercress, cucumber, and celery that's dressed with crème fraîche and lemon juice.     **SERVES 4**

### INGREDIENTS

*8 ounces sushi-grade salmon fillet*

*2 tablespoons extra-virgin olive oil*

*¼ teaspoon coarse salt*

*2 tablespoons plus 2 teaspoons
    freshly squeezed lemon juice*

*⅛ teaspoon freshly ground
    black pepper*

*2 large ribs celery*

*1 bunch watercress, stems discarded*

*1 small English (seedless) cucumber,
    peeled, cut in half lengthwise,
    and thinly sliced*

*3 tablespoons crème fraîche
    (see next page)*

*1 tablespoon American sturgeon roe
    (caviar)*

1. Wrap the salmon in plastic wrap and place it in the freezer until well chilled, 10 to 20 minutes, to firm it up and make it easier to slice. Remove the plastic and cut the salmon into ¼ inch–thick slices.

2. Rub ½ teaspoon of the olive oil in the center of each of 4 cold small plates, then sprinkle them with the salt. Arrange the salmon in a single layer on each plate over the oil. Sprinkle 1½ teaspoons of the lemon juice, 1 teaspoon of the olive oil, and some of the pepper over each plate of salmon. Cover the plates tautly with plastic wrap and refrigerate the salmon for 90 minutes.

3. Meanwhile, bring a medium-size pot of water to a boil. Fill a medium-size bowl halfway with ice water.

4. Cook the celery in the boiling water for 25 to 30 seconds. Drain it and transfer it to the ice water to stop the cooking and preserve the color. Drain the ice water and cut the celery diagonally into ¼-inch pieces.

5. Put the celery, watercress, and cucumber in a bowl.

## nutritional information
(PER SERVING)

| | |
|---|---|
| Calories | 232 |
| Fat | 18 g |
| Saturated Fat | 5 g |
| Trans Fat | 0 g |
| Total Carbohydrates | 3 g |
| Dietary Fiber | 1 g |
| Total Sugars | 2 g |
| Protein | 13 g |
| Cholesterol | 57 mg |
| Sodium | 253 mg |

## exchanges

| | |
|---|---|
| Fat | 3 |
| Lean Meat | 1.5 |
| Vegetables | 0.5 |

## nutritional information
(PER SERVING)

| | |
|---|---|
| Calories | 270 |
| Fat | 19 g |
| Saturated Fat | 2 g |
| Trans Fat | 0 g |
| Total Carbohydrates | 2 g |
| Dietary Fiber | 1 g |
| Total Sugars | 0 g |
| Protein | 21 g |
| Cholesterol | 32 mg |
| Sodium | 260 mg |

## exchanges

| | |
|---|---|
| Fat | 3.5 |
| Lean Meat | 2.5 |

**6.** In another bowl, stir together the crème fraîche, sturgeon caviar, the remaining 2 teaspoons of lemon juice, and 1 teaspoon of warm water. Pour the dressing over the vegetables and toss.

CARBOHYDRATE CHOICE: 0

# fresh tuna
### WITH SOY AND GINGER

i've never broken out the bamboo mats and sticky rice, but I do happen to love sushi, and this is my nod to some of its most popular flavors, painting sushi-grade slices of tuna with a soy-ginger dressing.

SERVES 4

### INGREDIENTS

*12 ounces sushi-grade tuna*

*¼ cup canola oil*

*2 tablespoons low-sodium soy sauce*

*2 large cloves garlic, minced*

*1 tablespoon minced peeled fresh ginger*

*1 tablespoon white sesame seeds*

*½ small English (seedless) cucumber, very thinly sliced*

*Pinch of coarse salt*

*2 tablespoons thinly sliced scallions, white and light green parts only*

**7.** To serve, remove the plastic wrap from the plates. Mound some of the watercress salad in the center, on top of each serving of salmon, and serve.

**1.** Wrap the tuna in plastic wrap and place it in the freezer until well chilled, 10 to 20 minutes, to firm up and make easier to slice. Remove the plastic and cut the salmon into ¼-inch-thick slices.

**2.** Put the oil, soy sauce, garlic, ginger, and sesame seeds in a bowl and stir together to make a dressing.

**3.** Arrange overlapping slices of the cucumber in the center of each of 4 salad plates. Arrange overlapping slices of the tuna over the cucumbers on each plate and spoon some dressing over the tuna and around the perimeters of the plates. Sprinkle some salt over the tuna, garnish with the scallions, and serve.

CARBOHYDRATE CHOICE: ½

# cold poached bluefish

## WITH CUCUMBER AND LIGHTLY PICKLED VEGETABLES

a study in efficiency, and a wonderful make-ahead starter for a brunch or dinner party, this recipe poaches bluefish off the stove by pouring a hot, vinegary liquid over it. Once cooled and refrigerated overnight, the fish is gently pickled as are the carrot, shallots, and fennel. The poaching solution also dresses the julienned cucumber over which the fish is draped, and the marinated vegetables are drained and garnish the dish.       **SERVES 4**

### INGREDIENTS

*4 very thin, sushi-grade bluefish fillets*
   *(about 4 ounces each), with the*
   *skin on*
*⅔ cup white wine vinegar*
*½ medium-size fennel bulb,*
   *thinly sliced*
*1 medium-size carrot, peeled and*
   *cut crosswise into ⅛-inch rounds*

*2 medium-size shallots, thinly sliced*
*¼ cup loosely packed fresh flat-leaf*
   *parsley leaves*
*1 tablespoon black peppercorns*
*1 tablespoon mustard seeds*
*¼ teaspoon coarse salt*
*1 large Kirby cucumber, peeled, seeded*
   *(see next page), and cut into julienne*

1. Use a paring knife to lightly score the skin side of the fillets at 1-inch intervals, taking care not to cut into the flesh (this will keep the fish from curling when poached). Put the fillets skin side up in a baking dish or other heatproof vessel just large enough to hold them in a single layer.

2. Put the vinegar, fennel, carrot, shallots, parsley, peppercorns, mustard seeds, and salt in a large pot.

Add 3 cups of cold water and bring to a boil over high heat. Remove the pot from the heat.

3. As soon as the boiling stops, gently pour the mixture over and around the fish. Cover the dish tautly with plastic wrap, let cool, and refrigerate for at least 4 hours, or overnight.

4. When ready to serve, put the cucumber in a small bowl. Spoon a

### nutritional information
(PER SERVING)

| | |
|---|---|
| Calories | 170 |
| Fat | 5 g |
|     Saturated Fat | 1 g |
|     Trans Fat | 0 g |
| Total Carbohydrates | 7 g |
|     Dietary Fiber | 2 g |
|     Total Sugars | 2 g |
| Protein | 24 g |
| Cholesterol | 67 mg |
| Sodium | 217 mg |

### exchanges

| | |
|---|---|
| Fat | 0.5 |
| Lean Meat | 3 |
| Vegetables | 1 |

**A TIP FROM TOM**

**SEEDING CUCUMBERS:** To seed a cucumber, cut it in half lengthwise, then use a tablespoon to scoop out the seeds from each half. If a recipe calls for peeling the cucumber, do yourself a favor and peel it before halving it; it's much easier to handle then.

tablespoon or 2 of the poaching liquid (taking care not to include any solids such as the peppercorns and mustard seeds) over the cucumbers and gently toss them. Divide the cucumbers evenly among 4 dinner plates, neatly arranging the slices in a stack in the center.

**5.** Use a slotted spoon to remove the fish from the baking dish, wiping off any solids, and drape 1 fillet over the cucumbers on each plate. Use the slotted spoon to remove the fennel, carrot, and shallots from the dish and scatter them decoratively over the fish or arrange them around the fish and cucumber for a more elegant presentation. Serve the bluefish cold.

**variations and suggestions:** You can also make this dish with bass or snapper.

CARBOHYDRATE CHOICE: 0

# warm lobster salad

## WITH ASPARAGUS AND A LEMON-BUTTER SAUCE

Pairing lobster and melted butter results in a simple perfection, and so does a coupling of asparagus and lemon juice. This salad combines the two duos and they add up to more than the sum of their parts because the asparagus and lobster make their own kind of magic. This is truly one of those dishes where the quality of the raw ingredients is paramount: Only make this with fresh, perfectly cooked lobster and plump, green, in-season asparagus.

**SERVES 4**

## INGREDIENTS

*1 live lobster (about 1½ pounds)*

*12 spears jumbo asparagus, peeled with ends trimmed*

*2 tablespoons (¼ stick) cold unsalted butter, cut into small cubes*

*3 tablespoons freshly squeezed lemon juice*

*Pinch of coriander seeds*

*Pinch of minced fresh tarragon leaves*

*2 tablespoons plus 1 teaspoon extra-virgin olive oil*

*Pinch of freshly ground black pepper*

1. Bring a large stockpot full of water to a boil over high heat. Add the lobster to the boiling water and cook until the shell turns bright red, 6 minutes. Remove the pot from the heat and let the lobster sit in the pot for about 90 seconds.

2. Fill a large bowl halfway with ice water. Using tongs, remove the lobster from the pot and immerse it in the ice water.

3. Once the lobster has cooled, drain the water. Take the head of the lobster in one hand and the tail in the other and twist them in opposite directions until the upper and lower halves come apart. Using a large, heavy knife, and working over a bowl or baking dish to collect the juice, split the lobster tail in half lengthwise. Remove the meat from the body of the lobster. Crack the claws and remove the meat from within. Cut the lobster meat into 1-inch dice and set it aside. Also set aside about ¼ cup of the juice from the lobster. Remove and discard the gray-green tomalley (liver) and red roe (if any), along with the shells. (This step can be performed up to 24 hours ahead of time. Store the lobster meat and juice in separate airtight containers in the refrigerator. Let come to room temperature before proceeding.)

4. Bring a large pot of water to a boil.

Cook the asparagus in the boiling water until al dente, about 8 minutes. Fill a large bowl halfway with ice water. Use tongs to remove the asparagus from the pot and transfer it to the ice water to stop the cooking and preserve the color. Once the asparagus has cooled, drain it and pat dry with paper towels.

5. Put the lobster juice in a pan and bring to a boil over high heat. Remove the pan from the heat, add the butter, and whisk until it melts and is incorporated into the lobster juice. Add 2 tablespoons of the lemon juice and stir. Swirl in the coriander seeds and tarragon. Add the lobster meat to the pan and let warm through.

6. Whisk together 1 tablespoon of the olive oil and the remaining 1 tablespoon of lemon juice in a large bowl, then add the asparagus and gently toss to coat. Put 3 asparagus spears in the center of each of 4 plates. Top the asparagus with the lobster meat. Spoon the sauce over the lobster. Drizzle 1 teaspoon of olive oil over each salad and around the plate, top with a scant sprinkling of black pepper, and serve.

variations and suggestions: If you like, top each salad with some black caviar and/or a small herb salad of chervil, chives (cut into 1-inch lengths), and fresh flat-leaf parsley.

## nutritional information
(PER SERVING)

| | |
|---|---|
| Calories | 179 |
| Fat | 14 g |
| Saturated Fat | 5 g |
| Trans Fat | 0 g |
| Total Carbohydrates | 4 g |
| Dietary Fiber | 2 g |
| Total Sugars | 2 g |
| Protein | 10 g |
| Cholesterol | 55 mg |
| Sodium | 127 mg |

## exchanges

| | |
|---|---|
| Fat | 2.5 |
| Vegetables | 0.5 |
| Lean Meat | 1 |

## nutritional information
### (PER SERVING)

Calories......................294
Fat..............................22 g
   Saturated Fat............3 g
   Trans Fat...................0 g
Total Carbohydrates.....6 g
   Dietary Fiber..............1 g
   Total Sugars..............1 g
Protein.........................17 g
Cholesterol..............81 mg
Sodium...................431 mg

## exchanges

Fat................................4
Lean Meat.......................2
Vegetables..................0.5

**CARBOHYDRATE CHOICE: ½**

# warm lobster

## WITH HARICOTS VERTS, RED AND GREEN LETTUCES, AND A MUSTARD VINAIGRETTE

I don't usually insist on "cheffy" or "restaurant" presentations in my cookbooks, but the elegance of this salad is so easy to duplicate at home that I strongly recommend you follow the instructions here, especially if you are serving this at a dinner party. That said, you could of course serve this as more of a composed salad, arranging the lobster and haricot verts over a bed of lettuces. To make this a main course, increase the portions to one lobster per person.

**SERVES 4**

### INGREDIENTS

*4 ounces haricots verts, ends trimmed*
*2 live lobsters (about 1¼ pounds each)*
*3 tablespoons freshly squeezed lemon juice*
*2 tablespoons Dijon mustard*
*½ clove garlic, minced*
*⅓ cup plus 2 teaspoons extra-virgin olive oil*

*1 tablespoon chopped chives*
*Pinch of freshly ground black pepper*
*Pinch of cayenne pepper*
*1 medium-size Hass avocado (optional)*
*1 cup loosely packed red and green leaf lettuces*
*2 tablespoons minced shallots*

1. Bring a large pot of water to a boil. Cook the haricots verts in the boiling water until al dente, about 3 minutes.

2. Fill a large bowl halfway with ice water. Drain the haricots verts and transfer them to the ice water to stop the cooking and preserve their color.

Drain the ice water and set the beans aside. (The beans can be patted dry with paper towels and refrigerated in an airtight container for up to 24 hours. Let come to room temperature before proceeding.)

3. Bring a large stockpot full of water to a boil over high heat. Add

the lobsters to the boiling water and cook until the shell turns bright red, 6 minutes. Remove the pot from the heat and let the lobsters sit in the pot for about 90 seconds.

4. Fill a large bowl halfway with ice water. Using tongs remove the lobsters from the pot and immerse them in the ice water.

5. Once the lobsters have cooled, drain the water. Take the head of one lobster in one hand and the tail in the other and twist them in opposite directions until the upper and lower halves come apart. Using a large, heavy knife, split the lobster tail in half lengthwise. Remove the meat from the body of the lobster. Crack the claws and remove the meat from within in single, unbroken pieces if possible. Remove and discard the gray-green tomalley (liver) and red roe (if any) along with the shells. Repeat with the remaining lobster. (This step can be performed up to 24 hours ahead of time. Store the lobster meat in an airtight container in the refrigerator. Let come to room temperature before proceeding.)

6. To make the dressing put the lemon juice, mustard, and garlic in a small bowl and whisk together. Still whisking, slowly pour in ⅓ cup of the olive oil in a thin stream to make an emulsion. Whisk in the chives, black pepper, and cayenne.

7. Cut the avocado in half and remove and discard the pit and the peel. Slice the avocado lengthwise ¼-inch thick. Put the slices from one quarter of the avocado in the center of each of 4 plates and gently press down on them to fan them out.

8. Brush the lobster tail and claw meat with some of the dressing. Cut each lobster tail in half and arrange one half tail and one lobster claw on top of each avocado fan. Toss the haricots verts with a few tablespoons of the dressing and tuck them in the curve of each lobster tail half.

9. Roll up the lettuce leaves and tuck them in with the haricots verts. Drizzle the remaining dressing over each salad and drizzle ½ teaspoon of olive oil on top of each. Sprinkle the shallot over each salad and serve.

**CARBOHYDRATE CHOICES: 1½**

# cold sesame noodles

I had never had cold sesame noodles until I moved to New York City, but it wasn't long before I loved the creamy tahini that hugs the pasta and the refreshing crunch of the cucumber that's usually included as a garnish. This is my version of cold sesame noodles, with the cucumbers and cabbage taking a more voluminous role to make up for the relatively small amount of noodles.

**SERVES 4**

## INGREDIENTS

¼ cup tahini

3 tablespoons rice wine vinegar

2 tablespoons low-sodium soy sauce

Few drops of hot sauce

4 cups hand-shredded chicken white meat (from leftover roasted or poached chicken)

4 cups shredded napa cabbage

2 cups cooked rice noodles

1 English (seedless) cucumber, cut in half and julienned

¼ cup chopped roasted unsalted peanuts

¼ cup chopped fresh cilantro leaves

1. Put the tahini, rice wine vinegar, soy sauce, hot sauce, and ¼ cup plus 2 tablespoons hot water in a small bowl and whisk together well.

2. Put the chicken, cabbage, and noodles, in a large bowl. Pour the tahini dressing over the noodles, chicken, and cabbage and toss well.

3. Divide the noodle mixture among 4 salad plates and garnish with the cucumber, peanuts, and cilantro, then serve.

CARBOHYDRATE CHOICE: ½

# asian chicken salad

my answer to the classic Chinese chicken salad features lots of crunchy vegetables and all the expected flavors—garlic, ginger, soy, and hoisin sauce—plus a few you might not expect, such as serrano pepper and American hot sauce. The amount of hoisin is relatively small here; while this condiment registers as sweet to the palate, it's actually rather high in sodium. If you are so able, another teaspoon or two of hoisin adds a nice touch. If you like, top each serving with crisp rice noodles and/or crushed peanuts.

**SERVES 4**

## nutritional information
(PER SERVING)

| | |
|---|---|
| Calories | 104 |
| Fat | 3 g |
| Saturated Fat | 0 g |
| Trans Fat | 0 g |
| Total Carbohydrates | 9 g |
| Dietary Fiber | 2 g |
| Total Sugars | 6 g |
| Protein | 10 g |
| Cholesterol | 24 mg |
| Sodium | 194 mg |

## exchanges

| | |
|---|---|
| Fat | 0.5 |
| Lean Meat | 1.5 |
| Vegetables | 1 |

## INGREDIENTS

*1 cup hand-shredded chicken white meat (from leftover roasted or poached chicken)*

*2 cups loosely packed shredded napa cabbage*

*2 Belgian endives, trimmed and cut lengthwise into thin strips*

*2 teaspoons minced serrano pepper*

*½ cup chopped scallions, both white and green parts*

*½ cup diced red bell pepper*

*2 teaspoons minced garlic*

*2 teaspoons minced peeled fresh ginger*

*2 teaspoons honey*

*2 teaspoons low-sodium soy sauce*

*1 teaspoon hoisin sauce*

*1 teaspoon hot sauce*

*2 teaspoons rice wine vinegar*

*1 teaspoon Asian (dark) sesame oil*

1. Put the chicken, cabbage, endive, and serrano pepper in large bowl.

2. Heat a large, heavy-bottomed pan over medium heat. Add the scallions, red bell pepper, garlic, and ginger and cook, stirring, until the vegetables are warmed through but still crunchy, about 2 minutes. Add the honey, soy sauce, hoisin sauce, and hot sauce. Cook, stirring, just to mix, about 1 minute. Add the rice wine vinegar and sesame oil.

3. Pour the warm vinaigrette over the chicken and vegetables and toss well. Divide the salad among 4 plates and serve.

CARBOHYDRATE CHOICE: 0

# chicken chaat

The Indian dish chicken *chaat* features the combination of heat and acidity that I love. It's spicy and fragrant, but—because the chicken is steamed—also very clean and fresh. Picking the chicken up with lettuce leaves makes it a fun social centerpiece to a meal for family or friends, keeping things casual.

SERVES 4

## INGREDIENTS

¾ cup coarsely chopped Spanish onion (from 1 medium-size onion)

2 tablespoons chopped fresh cilantro leaves

½ medium-size clove garlic, minced

1 tablespoon olive oil

1 teaspoon freshly squeezed lime juice, plus 4 lime halves for garnish

1 tablespoon freshly squeezed lemon juice

1 teaspoon garam masala, available at specialty food stores and Indian markets

1 teaspoon chopped hot green pepper, such as serrano

1 teaspoon red chile powder

¼ teaspoon coarse salt

1 pound skinless, boneless chicken breast, steamed (page 245), sliced lengthwise, and cut into ¼-inch pieces

8 iceberg lettuce leaves

Put the onion, cilantro, garlic, olive oil, lime juice, lemon juice, garam masala, green pepper, chile powder, and salt in a large bowl and mix to create a sauce. Add the chicken and toss well. Divide the chicken among 4 small plates and serve with iceberg lettuce leaves and lime halves. Use the lettuce to scoop up bites of the salad.

CARBOHYDRATE CHOICE: 1

# caesar-inspired chicken salad

Y ou can't eat a true Caesar salad on a diabetic diet: The raw egg and anchovies alone are cause to run for the hills, not to mention the generous piles of Parmesan. But you can sure hit all the flavor buttons associated with a Caesar by minimizing the cheese and maximizing the vinegar, lemon juice, and black pepper. My second inspiration here is the two decade old trend of restaurants offering to add grilled chicken to a Caesar. It's got nothing to do with the classic, but it tastes good and puts this salad into main course territory, if you want to serve or eat it that way. I make my Caesar salad with iceberg rather than romaine lettuce because I happen to love the crunch, but you could certainly use romaine instead.     SERVES 4

---

## INGREDIENTS

*2 tablespoons freshly squeezed lemon juice*

*1 teaspoon Dijon mustard*

*¼ teaspoon red wine vinegar*

*1 small clove garlic, minced*

*¼ cup plus 2 tablespoons extra-virgin olive oil*

*1 tablespoon chopped fresh flat-leaf parsley leaves*

*2 tablespoons grated Parmesan cheese, plus more if desired*

*1 tablespoon freshly ground black pepper, plus more if desired*

*1 head iceberg lettuce, cut into large wedges*

*8 ounces steamed chicken white meat (page 245), shredded by hand (about 2 cups)*

*1 slice whole wheat bread, toasted and cut into small croutons*

---

Put the lemon juice, mustard, red wine vinegar, and garlic in a bowl. Slowly whisk in the olive oil, adding it in a thin stream, to make an emulsion. Let sit for 10 to 15 minutes for the flavor to develop, then whisk in

## nutritional information
(PER SERVING)

| | |
|---|---|
| Calories | 321 |
| Fat | 23 g |
| Saturated Fat | 4 g |
| Trans Fat | 0 g |
| Total Carbohydrates | 11 g |
| Dietary Fiber | 3 g |
| Total Sugars | 4 g |
| Protein | 17 g |
| Cholesterol | 36 mg |
| Sodium | 146 mg |

## exchanges

| | |
|---|---|
| Fat | 4.5 |
| Lean Meat | 1.5 |
| Vegetables | 1 |

the parsley, Parmesan cheese, and pepper. Taste for seasoning, adding more Parmesan and/or pepper, if desired. To serve, divide the lettuce among 4 salad plates. Drizzle the vinaigrette over it and top with the chicken and croutons.

**variations and suggestions:** This can also be served as a salad with a grilled chicken breast over it, or alongside, in place of the shredded chicken.

## nutritional information
### (PER SERVING)

| | |
|---|---|
| Calories | 195 |
| Fat | 13 g |
| Saturated Fat | 5 g |
| Trans Fat | 0 g |
| Total Carbohydrates | 7 g |
| Dietary Fiber | 1 g |
| Total Sugars | 3 g |
| Protein | 14 g |
| Cholesterol | 34 mg |
| Sodium | 196 mg |

## exchanges

| | |
|---|---|
| Fat | 1.5 |
| Lean Meat | 1 |
| High Fat Meat | 0.5 |
| Vegetables | 0.5 |

# roasted turkey, spinach, grapes, and goat cheese

f you consider salads as a place to get creative with your leftovers, then you'll love this refrigerator raid of a salad that uses cold roasted turkey, spinach, green grapes, and goat cheese—all stuff you're likely to have around or that can be replaced with something you do: chicken for turkey, other greens for the spinach, red grapes or sliced green apple for the grapes, and blue cheese for the goat's milk variety. Whisking the cheese right into the dressing makes this quick and decadent, an irresistible combination.     **SERVES 4**

## INGREDIENTS

2 tablespoons olive oil

1 tablespoon Dijon mustard

2 ounces crumbled goat cheese (about ½ cup), at room temperature

4 ounces leftover turkey white meat, shredded by hand (about 1 cup)

½ cup halved seedless green grapes

4 cups loosely packed baby spinach leaves or finely sliced large spinach leaves with the heavy stems removed

1. Put the olive oil and mustard in a large bowl and whisk them together. Whisk in the goat cheese to make a thick, creamy dressing. If it seems too thick, whisk in 1 or 2 teaspoons of hot water.

2. Add the turkey and grapes to the bowl and toss to coat with the dressing. Finally, add the spinach and toss to coat it well. Divide the salad among 4 plates and serve.

CARBOHYDRATE CHOICE: 0

# beef carpaccio

## WITH ARUGULA AND TRUFFLE OIL

Sometimes, carpaccios are served with a small salad at their center, but I like to reverse expectations, making the carpaccio itself the finishing touch to a salad of arugula, dressed with a lemon vinaigrette, that has been perfumed with truffle (oil), and garnished with pine nuts. Draping a thin sheet of pounded-out uncooked filet mignon over the salad turns the dish into a little culinary gift.                    **SERVES 4**

### did you know?

According to legend, carpaccio was created at Harry's Bar in Venice, devised to accommodate a customer seeking a meal of raw meat. The bar's owner selected the name because he found the colors of the dish reminiscent of the palate of Venetian painter, Vittore Carpaccio. Since then, carpaccios have been freely adapted to include everything from seafood to other meats.

### INGREDIENTS

¼ cup pine nuts (optional)

4 slices (1 ounce each) top-quality
   filet mignon

1⅓ cups loosely packed arugula

2 teaspoons extra-virgin olive oil

½ teaspoon freshly squeezed lemon
   juice

½ teaspoon truffle oil

Pinch of coarse salt

Pinch of freshly ground black pepper

1 ounce Parmesan cheese, coarsely
   grated (about ¼ cup)

1. If using the pine nuts, toast them in a heavy-bottomed pan over medium heat, shaking the pan frequently to prevent scorching, until golden brown and fragrant, about

3 minutes. (Take extra care when toasting pine nuts; they burn very easily.) Transfer the pine nuts to a heatproof bowl to cool and set aside.

2. Place 1 piece of filet between 2 pieces of plastic wrap and pound it with a meat mallet or the bottom of a small, heavy-bottomed pot until paper-thin. Set aside and repeat with the remaining pieces of filet.

3. Put the arugula in a large bowl. Drizzle the olive oil, lemon juice, and truffle oil over it and toss well.

4. Divide the salad among 4 salad plates, mounding it in the center. Drape a piece of filet over each salad, covering it. Season with the salt and pepper. Scatter the Parmesan cheese and pine nuts, if using, over each dish, and serve.

**CARBOHYDRATE CHOICE: 1/2**

# thai beef salad

## WITH LIME JUICE, WATERCRESS, AND PLUMS

Charred, lime-marinated beef meets peppery watercress and an assortment of hot and sweet ingredients here. The sliced plums add a surprising tartness to the beef drippings in the dressing, which helps make it a uniquely hearty salad—a perfect light lunch, or even dinner. **SERVES 4**

**A TIP FROM TOM**

**HOT ENOUGH?:** To determine if a charcoal grill is ready for cooking, see page 151.

### INGREDIENTS

8 ounces beef strip steak or flank steak

¼ cup plus 2 tablespoons freshly squeezed lime juice

Pinch of freshly ground black pepper

1 tablespoon low-sodium soy sauce

2 teaspoons Asian fish sauce

2 teaspoons rice wine vinegar

1 teaspoon minced peeled fresh ginger

½ teaspoon crushed red pepper flakes

5 cups loosely packed watercress, tough stems discarded

1 cup shredded napa cabbage

1 cup loosely packed fresh cilantro leaves

2 medium-size firm, tart plums, very thinly sliced

½ medium-size red onion, thinly sliced

1 medium-size radish, very thinly sliced

1. Put the beef in a shallow baking dish. Pour the ¼ cup of lime juice over the meat and sprinkle with the pepper. Turn the meat over to coat on all sides. Let marinate for 15 minutes at room temperature.

2. Preheat a gas grill to high or build a fire in a charcoal grill, letting the coals burn until covered with white ash. If using a grill pan, preheat the pan over high heat.

3. Grill the beef until nicely charred on both sides, about 7 minutes per side. Transfer to a plate and let cool.

4. Meanwhile, put the remaining 2 tablespoons of lime juice and the soy sauce, fish sauce, rice wine vinegar, ginger, and red pepper flakes in a large bowl and whisk together.

5. Slice the meat crosswise into thin slices and add it to the bowl with the dressing, along with any juices that accumulated on the plate while the meat was cooling. Add the watercress, cabbage, cilantro, plums, onion, and radish to the bowl. Toss well, then divide the salad among 4 plates and serve.

## nutritional information
### (PER SERVING)

| | |
|---|---|
| Calories | 123 |
| Fat | 3 g |
| Saturated Fat | 1 g |
| Trans Fat | 0 g |
| Total Carbohydrates | 10 g |
| Dietary Fiber | 1 g |
| Total Sugars | 5 g |
| Protein | 14 g |
| Cholesterol | 19 mg |
| Sodium | 407 mg |

## exchanges

| | |
|---|---|
| Fruit | 0.5 |
| Lean Meat | 2 |
| Vegetables | 0.5 |

CARBOHYDRATE CHOICE: ½

# lamb salad

## WITH RED PEPPERS, OLIVES, AND FETA

grilled red bell peppers, kalamata olives, and feta cheese are one of those trios that you can use any number of ways with great success. One of my favorite backdrops is grilled thinly sliced lamb, because the lamb's delicate flavor and texture strike the perfect balance, complementing and completing the bell peppers, olives, and feta without competing the way, say, beef might. I'm not alone in my affection for this dish, which I've served in a number of guises over the past decade—it's a perennial favorite at Ouest.

SERVES 4

## shop right

**FETA CHEESE:**
Although feta cheese is most closely associated with Greek food, it is now produced in many countries including the U.S.A. My favorite fetas are the creamy varieties produced in France. Apparently, Greece doesn't appreciate people with my preference: In 2005, after a protracted battle, the European Union's highest court awarded Protected Designation of Origin status to Greek feta cheese, meaning that in Europe the French cannot market their cheese under the name of feta. Only fetas produced according to certain traditional methods in specific regions of Greece can be sold as feta in Europe.

## INGREDIENTS

12 ounces boneless lamb loin roast

¼ cup plus 1 tablespoon extra-virgin olive oil

3 large cloves garlic, mashed to a paste with ¼ teaspoon coarse salt, plus 1 small garlic clove, minced

¼ teaspoon freshly ground black pepper

Pinch of cayenne pepper

3 kalamata olives, pitted and minced

3 tablespoons freshly squeezed lemon juice

1 teaspoon chopped fresh flat-leaf parsley leaves

1 large red bell pepper

4 cups loosely packed salad greens, such as mesclun

¼ cup crumbled feta cheese (about 1 ounce)

1. Put the lamb in a shallow baking dish and set it aside.

2. Whisk together 2 tablespoons of the olive oil, the mashed garlic, ⅛ teaspoon of the black pepper, and the cayenne in a small bowl. Pour the mixture over the lamb. Cover the dish loosely with plastic wrap and let marinate in the refrigerator for at least 2 hours and up to 8 hours.

3. When ready to proceed, put the remaining 3 tablespoons of olive oil, the minced garlic, olives, lemon juice, and parsley in a bowl and whisk together to make a dressing. Set aside.

4. Preheat a gas grill to high or build a fire in a charcoal grill, letting the coals burn down until covered with white ash. If using a grill pan, place the pan over medium-high heat.

5. Remove the lamb from the marinade, brushing off the mashed garlic, and grill until nice marks form on both sides, 2 to 3 minutes per side for medium-rare. Set the lamb aside to rest.

6. Meanwhile, grill the red bell pepper, turning it as it blackens, until charred all over, about 8 minutes. Put the pepper in a heatproof bowl, cover it with plastic wrap, and let steam in its own heat for 5 minutes. Remove the plastic wrap and, when cool enough to handle, using a paring knife, remove the skin from the pepper. Slice the pepper open and remove and discard the seeds. Cut the pepper into thin strips and let cool to room temperature. (The lamb and pepper can be tightly wrapped in plastic separately and refrigerated overnight. Let them come to room temperature before serving.)

7. To serve, thinly slice the lamb. Toss the greens with all but 2 tablespoons of the dressing. Overlap slices of lamb on one side of each of 4 salad plates. Mound some greens on the other side of the plate. Drizzle the remaining dressing over the lamb. Scatter a tablespoon of feta over each plate, drape the pepper strips over the salad, and serve.

## nutritional information
(PER SERVING)

| | |
|---|---|
| Calories | 364 |
| Fat | 27 g |
| Saturated Fat | 7 g |
| Trans Fat | 0 g |
| Total Carbohydrates | 8 g |
| Dietary Fiber | 2 g |
| Total Sugars | 4 g |
| Protein | 22 g |
| Cholesterol | 73 mg |
| Sodium | 323 mg |

## exchanges

| | |
|---|---|
| Fat | 4 |
| Very Lean Meat | 2.5 |
| Medium Fat Meat | 0.5 |
| Vegetables | 1 |

# in this chapter

*"A beautiful bowlful of soup
brings together a perfect combination of
flavors and texture."*

# soups and stews

i loved the extended family of soups and stews long before I developed diabetes. But most soups and stews happen to be friendly to our way of life: For the most part, they're primarily made up of liquid, which means that a bowlful can really tamp down the appetite without the intake of huge amounts of, well, anything.

The flip side is that soups can become as monotonous as the act of eating them. That repetitive up and down of the spoon threatens to lull you right to sleep if what's in the bowl isn't worth the trouble. So, my goal with any soup or stew is to keep it interesting, both with compelling textures and the inclusion of some heat, or spice, or acid, or all of the above.

Soups and stews are also among the most leftover friendly categories of food. Many soups can be refrigerated for a few days, and often stews actually improve after a day or two in the fridge. This means that they can be prepared in advance for entertaining or everyday dinners—just one more reason to like them.

## nutritional information
### (PER SERVING)

Calories......................133
Fat................................9 g
   Saturated Fat...........1 g
   Trans Fat..................0 g
Total Carbohydrates... 10 g
   Dietary Fiber.............2 g
   Total Sugars..............5 g
Protein..........................3 g
Cholesterol..............4 mg
Sodium.................546 mg

## exchanges

Fat..................................1.5
Vegetables.....................1.5

**CARBOHYDRATE CHOICE: ½**

# chilled cucumber soup

## WITH AN HERB AND RED ONION SALAD

looking for pure, summer refreshment? Try a cold puree of cucumber, enlivened with lemon juice and sour cream. The cilantro and red onion salad, mounded like an island in the center of the bowls, takes the soup to another level, providing a freshness and crunch just waiting to be stirred in.

**SERVES 4**

### INGREDIENTS

8 cups plus 3 tablespoons diced, peeled English (seedless) cucumbers (from about 4 cucumbers)

1 teaspoon coarse salt

2 tablespoons plus 1 teaspoon extra-virgin olive oil

¾ cup minced Spanish onion (from 1 medium-size onion)

1 medium-size clove garlic, minced

1½ cups store-bought low-sodium chicken broth

2 tablespoons freshly squeezed lemon juice

¼ cup nonfat sour cream

¼ cup coarsely chopped fresh cilantro leaves

¼ cup coarsely chopped fresh dill

3 tablespoons diced red onion

1. Put the 8 cups of cucumber into a large, heatproof bowl, season with the salt, and stir. Set aside.

2. Heat 1 tablespoon of the olive oil in a wide, deep, heavy-bottomed pan over medium-high heat. Add the Spanish onion and garlic and cook until softened, but not browned, about 4 minutes. Add the chicken broth, bring it to a boil, then lower the heat and let simmer until almost dry, about 5 minutes. Pour the onion mixture over the cucumbers and let sit for 10 minutes.

3. Transfer the cucumber mixture to a food processor Add the lemon juice and sour cream, and process until uniformly blended and smooth. Work in batches if necessary. Cover and refrigerate until cold, at least 2 hours or up to 8 hours.

**4.** When ready to serve, put the remaining 3 tablespoons of cucumber in a small bowl. Add the cilantro, dill, red onion, and the remaining 1 tablespoon plus 1 teaspoon of olive oil. Stir together gently.

**5.** To serve, divide the soup among 4 bowls and put a small mound of cucumber and red onion salad in the center of each serving.

**variations and suggestions:** For a more substantial soup, arrange strips of smoked salmon over each serving or dice some cured salmon and toss it into the cilantro and dill salad.

CARBOHYDRATE CHOICE: 1

# tomato consommé

One of my favorite ways to capture the essence of a tomato is in tomato water, which I extract by chopping tomatoes, seasoning them liberally with salt and pepper, setting them in a cheesecloth-lined colander, then serving the juices released by the tomatoes. Tomato consommé is another way of getting to a similar place but without the high sodium. **SERVES 6**

## nutritional information
### (PER SERVING)

| | |
|---|---|
| Calories | 154 |
| Fat | 6 g |
| Saturated Fat | 1 g |
| Trans Fat | 0 g |
| Total Carbohydrates | 14 g |
| Dietary Fiber | 3 g |
| Total Sugars | 9 g |
| Protein | 8 g |
| Cholesterol | 13 mg |
| Sodium | 659 mg |

## exchanges

| | |
|---|---|
| Fat | 1 |
| Lean Meat | 0.5 |
| Vegetables | 2 |

### INGREDIENTS

2 tablespoons olive oil

3 large ribs celery, coarsely chopped

2 small carrots, coarsely chopped

½ medium-size Spanish onion, coarsely chopped

4 ounces (½ cup) tomato paste

⅔ cup dry white wine

¼ cup distilled white vinegar

10 medium-size ripe plum tomatoes, coarsely chopped

6 fresh tarragon sprigs

2 fresh thyme sprigs

1 tablespoon plus 1 teaspoon whole black peppercorns

1 teaspoon sugar

1 teaspoon coarse salt

1 bay leaf, preferably fresh

1 cup tomato juice

4 ounces skinless, boneless dark or white meat chicken, or 4 ounces ground chicken or turkey

4 large egg whites, with their shells

## plan ahead

The consommé can be refrigerated in an airtight container for up to 1 week or frozen for up to 3 months. Let come to room temperature before gently reheating.

## did you know?

The purpose of the raft that forms on top of the consommé and is held together by the proteins in the eggs is to draw out any impurities in the other ingredients. This is an essential technique shared by all classic consommé recipes. (The raft also intensifies the flavor of the soup.) The raft is not meant to be eaten—after all, it does contain eggshells— but it must be kept in place while ladling out the liquid to avoid returning any of the undesirable elements back to the broth.

1. Heat the olive oil in a large, heavy-bottomed soup pot over medium heat. Add half of the celery, half of the carrots, and the onion and cook, stirring, until softened but not browned, about 4 minutes. Lower the heat, add the tomato paste, and cook for 2 minutes, stirring to coat. Pour in the white wine and vinegar and cook, stirring to loosen any flavorful bits stuck to the bottom of the pot.

2. Add the tomatoes, 3 sprigs of the tarragon, the thyme, 1 tablespoon of the peppercorns, and the sugar, salt, and bay leaf. Cook, stirring, for 3 minutes. Pour in 2 cups of water and the tomato juice; if the tomatoes aren't very juicy, add another cup of water. Increase the heat to high, bring to a boil, then lower the heat, and let simmer gently, uncovered, for 1 hour.

3. Strain the contents of the pan through a fine-mesh strainer set over a bowl, pressing down with a ladle or the back of a wooden spoon to extract as much of the flavorful liquid as possible. Let cool. (To cool quickly, set the bowl in a larger bowl full of ice water and stir.)

4. Wipe out the soup pot, return the strained broth to the pot, and rewarm it over low heat.

5. Meanwhile, put the chicken, egg whites and shells, and the remaining carrots, celery, and the remaining 1 teaspoon of black peppercorns in a food processor and pulse for 30 to 40 seconds to puree.

6. Using a whisk, stir the pureed chicken, carrots, and celery into the tomato broth for a few seconds. Let cook over low heat for about 25 minutes. During this time, a white mass (the raft) will form on the surface of the consommé. Once it has, let it cook very gently until the center of the raft develops a crust, about 90 minutes. Using a slotted spoon, gently cut out and remove a circle from the top of the raft that is large enough to accommodate a small ladle, about 4 inches. Ladle the liquid out through this hole and into a cheesecloth-lined strainer or colander set over a bowl. You should have about 7 cups of consommé. To serve, divide the soup among 6 bowls.

variations and suggestions: You can serve the tomato consommé as a broth in its own right or add finely minced vegetables or even poached shellfish to the bowls.

# yellow tomato soup

**y**ellow tomatoes are readily available but remain a surprise at the table. They vary from the ubiquitous red tomatoes not just in color but also in flavor, with a lower acidity and a pronounced sweetness. This quick, bright soup takes full advantage of those qualities and lends itself to the addition of other ingredients (see Variations and Suggestions). **SERVES 4**

## INGREDIENTS

2 pounds yellow tomatoes, coarsely chopped (about 8 cups)

1 teaspoon coarse salt

1 tablespoon olive oil

2 cups coarsely chopped Spanish onion (from about 1½ large onions)

1 large clove garlic, minced

Pinch of freshly ground black pepper

2 cups store-bought low-sodium chicken broth, vegetable broth, or water (use water if lower sodium is desired)

1. Put the tomatoes in a bowl, season them with the salt, and set aside.

2. Heat the olive oil in a heavy-bottomed soup pot over medium-low heat. Add the onions and garlic and cook until softened but not browned, 6 to 8 minutes. Stir in the tomatoes and pepper. Cook the tomatoes, stirring occasionally, until they are tender, 10 to 12 minutes.

3. Add the chicken broth to the pot, bring it to a simmer, and let simmer for 5 minutes. Remove the pot from the heat.

4. Working in batches, puree the soup in a blender or food processor (see page 102 for a safety note on blending hot liquids). Serve the soup warm or chill it and serve cold, divided among 4 bowls.

**variations and suggestions:** You can also make this soup with red tomatoes. To add another visual element and complementary flavor to the bowl, drizzle a tablespoon of Homemade Pesto (page 317) decoratively over each serving.

## nutritional information
(PER SERVING)

| | |
|---|---|
| Calories | 97 |
| Fat | 4 g |
| Saturated Fat | 1 g |
| Trans Fat | 0 g |
| Total Carbohydrates | 13 g |
| Dietary Fiber | 3 g |
| Total Sugars | 3 g |
| Protein | 4 g |
| Cholesterol | 2 mg |
| Sodium | 588 mg |

## exchanges

| | |
|---|---|
| Fat | 0.5 |
| Vegetables | 2.5 |

## plan ahead

The soup can be refrigerated in an airtight container overnight; reblend it if necessary to reincorporate the solids and liquid. Let the soup come to room temperature before reheating, if desired.

## nutritional information
### (PER SERVING)

| | |
|---|---|
| Calories | 103 |
| Fat | 3 g |
| Saturated Fat | 0 g |
| Trans Fat | 0 g |
| Total Carbohydrates | 14 g |
| Dietary Fiber | 5 g |
| Total Sugars | 5 g |
| Protein | 6 g |
| Cholesterol | 2 mg |
| Sodium | 466 mg |

## exchanges

| | |
|---|---|
| Fat | 0.5 |
| Starch | 0.5 |
| Vegetables | 0.5 |

# green pea soup

you might do a bit of a double take when you scan the ingredients list for this recipe and see that I call for *frozen* peas. What kind of fancy-pants, big-city chef uses frozen peas? Well, you might be surprised at how many of us do just that because the truth about peas is that as soon as they're cut off from the vine their natural sugars begin turning to starch, sapping away the peas' essential sweetness. Unless you're harvesting them from your own backyard garden, by the time they reach your kitchen, they taste nowhere near as fresh as you'd expect. In contrast, frozen peas, especially the ones sold as petit pois, capture peas at their peak. In salads, such as the one on page 58, where the peas are served raw, I insist on fresh peas, but for making soups and sauces, frozen peas aren't just a viable alternative; they're often the best choice you can make. This soup illustrates this principle beautifully; it has just six ingredients, but the result tastes farm fresh. **SERVES 4**

## INGREDIENTS

*1 bag (16 ounces) frozen peas*

*2 teaspoons canola oil*

*1 large Spanish onion, diced*

*2 large cloves garlic, crushed and peeled*

*2 cups store-bought low-sodium chicken broth*

*¾ teaspoon coarse salt*

1. Bring a large pot of water to a boil. Fill a large bowl halfway with ice water.

2. Cook the peas in the boiling water for 1 minute. Drain the peas and transfer them to the ice water to stop the cooking and preserve their color. Drain the peas again and set them aside.

3. Heat the oil in a large, heavy-bottomed saucepan over low heat. Add the onion and garlic and cook gently, stirring occasionally, until very soft but not browned, about 15 minutes. Add the peas and cook for 2 minutes longer. Stir in the chicken broth and salt and let it come just to a simmer, then remove the pan from the heat.

4. Working in batches, puree the soup in a blender or food proces-

sor (see page 102 for a safety note on blending hot liquids). Serve the soup warm or chill it and serve cold, divided among 4 bowls.

### variations and suggestions:

❖ Mound some cooked, chilled lobster meat or shrimp, dressed with a few drops of lemon juice, in the center of wide, shallow soup bowls and ladle the chilled pea soup around it. You can also top this soup with a chiffonade of fresh mint.

❖ Serve the soup as an hors d'oeuvre, spooning it into shot glasses and garnishing it with a little crème fraîche.

**plan ahead**

**The soup can be refrigerated in an airtight container overnight. Let the soup come to room temperature before reheating, if desired.**

CARBOHYDRATE CHOICE: 1

# french onion soup

## WITH GRUYERE AND THYME

i never went to cooking school, but I'm told that much is made of the importance of veal stock in a classic French onion soup. I'd always believed that myself, until we tried making the soup with low-sodium, store-bought beef broth. The result was so potent, so deeply flavored, and so instantly recognizable as French onion soup, that I think we've had it wrong all along: Caramelizing the onions—cooking them slowly to release their natural sugar and turn them soft and amber colored—is the main thing you have to do to make a terrific French onion soup. Caramelize them long and slow and patiently, until you can't caramelize them any more. Do that, and you'll be amazed at how good this soup is. SERVES 4

### INGREDIENTS

¼ cup olive oil

4 large Spanish onions, thinly sliced

1 cup dry white wine

4 cups store-bought low-sodium beef broth

4 fresh thyme sprigs

1 bay leaf, preferably fresh

2 ounces grated Gruyère cheese (about ½ cup)

2 tablespoons grated Parmesan cheese

## nutritional information
(PER SERVING)

| | |
|---|---|
| Calories | 335 |
| Fat | 20 g |
| Saturated Fat | 5 g |
| Trans Fat | 0 g |
| Total Carbohydrates | 16 g |
| Dietary Fiber | 3 g |
| Total Sugars | 7 g |
| Protein | 12 g |
| Cholesterol | 17 mg |
| Sodium | 180 mg |

## exchanges

| | |
|---|---|
| Fat | 3.5 |
| High Fat Meat | 1.5 |
| Vegetables | 2.5 |

1. Heat the olive oil in a large, heavy-bottomed saucepan over low heat. Add the onions and cook, stirring periodically, until they are well caramelized, about 45 minutes. If they begin to scorch or stick to the pan, add a few drops of water occasionally, but only just enough to keep the onions from sticking.

2. Preheat the broiler.

3. Pour the white wine into the pan with the onions and stir with a wooden spoon to loosen any flavorful bits stuck to the bottom. Increase the heat to high and let boil until the wine has completely cooked out, about 8 minutes. Add the beef broth, thyme, and bay leaf. Bring to a boil, then lower the heat and let simmer for 15 minutes. (The soup can be made up to this point, cooled, and refrigerated in an airtight container for up to 2 days. Let come to room temperature before proceeding.)

4. Remove and discard the thyme sprigs and bay leaf. Spoon the soup into 4 ovenproof bowls or crocks and arrange the crocks on a baking sheet. Top each bowl with 2 tablespoons of the Gruyère cheese then 1½ teaspoons of Parmesan cheese. Place under the broiler and broil just until the cheeses are melted (the Parmesan should brown nicely), about 2 minutes. Use oven mitts to transfer each bowl to a small plate. Serve immediately.

CARBOHYDRATE CHOICES: 2½; 2 ADJUSTED FOR FIBER

# ribollita

a typically descriptive Italian name for this soup, *ribollita* means twice boiled. It's meant to be prepared one day and then cooked again the next. *Ribollita* is one of those charmingly adaptable dishes that every cook interprets as he or she sees fit; but there's always one thing in common and that's good news for people with diabetes: This is a vegetable-packed soup that really gets the most out of each vegetable. As they spend the night in the fridge, the flavors meld, and the vegetables, softened up from the "first boil," begin to fall apart. The result is a beautiful bowlful of soup that brings the word *rustic* to life—a coming together of flavors and textures perfect for cooking and eating in the wintertime. 

SERVES 4

## INGREDIENTS

2 tablespoons olive oil

1 large Spanish onion,
    cut into small dice

2 large ribs celery, cut crosswise
    into ¼-inch pieces

1 large leek, white and light green
    parts only, thinly sliced
    crosswise, rinsed and
    drained

2 large cloves garlic,
    crushed and peeled

Pinch of coarse salt

Pinch of freshly ground black pepper

1 small Yukon Gold potato,
    peeled and cut into medium-size
    dice

3 very ripe plum tomatoes, coarsely
    chopped, with their juice

½ medium-size savoy cabbage,
    core removed and discarded,
    coarsely chopped

½ bunch kale, stems and tough
    center stalks removed and
    discarded, coarsely chopped

½ cup canned cannellini beans,
    rinsed and drained

1 quart store-bought low-sodium
    vegetable broth

½ cup finely grated Parmesan
    cheese

¼ cup minced fresh flat-leaf
    parsley leaves

1. Heat the olive oil in a large, heavy-bottomed soup pot over medium-high heat. When the oil is hot but not yet smoking add the onion, celery, leek, and garlic and season with the salt and pepper. Cook, stirring, until the vegetables are softened but not browned, about 6 minutes.

2. Add the potato and cook for 2 to 3 minutes. Add the tomatoes, cabbage, kale, and beans and cook, stirring, for 2 to 3 minutes. Pour the broth into the pot, stir gently, and bring to a boil over high heat. Lower the heat and let simmer very gently, covered, for 2 hours.

3. Remove the pot from the heat and let the soup cool, then refrigerate it in an airtight container (or cover and refrigerate it right in the pot) for at least 12 hours or up to 2 days. The soup can also be frozen in an airtight container for up to 1 month; let thaw before proceeding.

4. When ready to serve, gently reheat the soup over medium heat. Ladle some soup into 4 wide, shallow bowls. Scatter 2 tablespoons of the Parmesan cheese and 1 tablespoon of the parsley over the top of each portion and serve.

## nutritional information
(PER SERVING)

| | |
|---|---|
| Calories | 259 |
| Fat | 9 g |
| Saturated Fat | 2 g |
| Trans Fat | 0 g |
| Total Carbohydrates | 36 g |
| Dietary Fiber | 7 g |
| Total Sugars | 9 g |
| Protein | 9 g |
| Cholesterol | 5 mg |
| Sodium | 432 mg |

## exchanges

| | |
|---|---|
| Fat | 1.5 |
| Starch | 0.5 |
| Lean Meat | 0.5 |
| Vegetables | 4 |

## nutritional information

(PER SERVING)

| | |
|---|---|
| Calories | 120 |
| Fat | 2 g |
| Saturated Fat | 0 g |
| Trans Fat | 0 g |
| Total Carbohydrates | 21 g |
| Dietary Fiber | 2 g |
| Total Sugars | 3 g |
| Protein | 5 g |
| Cholesterol | 3 mg |
| Sodium | 455 mg |

## exchanges

| | |
|---|---|
| Fat | 0.5 |
| Starch | 1 |
| Vegetables | 1 |

## plan ahead

The soup can be refrigerated in an airtight container overnight. Let come to room temperature and gently reheat before serving.

**CARBOHYDRATE CHOICES: 1½**

# potato leek soup

Years ago, I wrote a cookbook featuring a recipe for potato leek soup that was basically a bowl of mashed potatoes with some creamed leeks added to it, a delicious soup that my customers loved, but which I never ate myself for the simple reason that I couldn't. But I do eat a version of potato leek soup at home, one that has a greater ratio of leeks and broth to potato than you'll find in most. It's a different potato leek soup, but satisfying on its own terms. It's also a house favorite of mine: On my riverside property in upstate New York, I gather wild leeks (ramps) every spring. If you have access to these seasonal gems, packed with sweet, oniony flavor, this soup will take on a life of its own; you might even find yourself doing as I've done on more than one occasion and making it with no potatoes at all. **SERVES 4**

## INGREDIENTS

1½ teaspoons canola oil

6 ounces leeks, white and light green parts only, coarsely chopped (about 3 cups), well rinsed, and drained

¾ pound Idaho potatoes, peeled and cut into large dice

3 cups store-bought low-sodium chicken broth

¾ teaspoon coarse salt

Pinch of freshly ground black pepper

1. Heat the oil in a heavy-bottomed soup pot over medium heat. Add the leeks and cook, stirring occasionally, until softened but not browned, about 5 minutes.

2. Add the potatoes, chicken broth, salt, and pepper and bring to a boil over high heat. Lower the heat and let simmer until the potatoes are soft when pierced with a knife, 20 to 25 minutes. Working in batches, transfer the soup to a blender or food processor and puree until smooth and creamy (see page 102 for a safety note on blending hot liquids). If necessary, return the soup to the pot and reheat it briefly. Divide the soup among 4 wide, shallow bowls, and serve.

**nutritional information**
(PER SERVING)

| | |
|---|---|
| Calories | 244 |
| Fat | 17 g |
| Saturated Fat | 5 g |
| Trans Fat | 0 g |
| Total Carbohydrates | 14 g |
| Dietary Fiber | 5 g |
| Total Sugars | 2 g |
| Protein | 11 g |
| Cholesterol | 22 mg |
| Sodium | 235 mg |

**exchanges**

| | |
|---|---|
| Fat | 2.5 |
| Vegetables | 2 |

**CARBOHYDRATE CHOICE: 1; ½ ADJUSTED FOR FIBER**

# savoy cabbage soup
## WITH RYE CROUTONS AND BACON

like the *ribollita* on page 108, this is a soup that improves after a day or two in the refrigerator, as the vegetables begin to break down and the smokiness from the ham hock and bacon grows more and more potent. Because this is a soup that you can keep coming back to, I suggest doubling or tripling the recipe and having a stash of it on hand for a few days. **SERVES 4**

### INGREDIENTS

2 tablespoons unsalted butter

2 tablespoons canola oil

¼ teaspoon sugar

1 large savoy cabbage, core removed
    and discarded, shredded

¼ teaspoon freshly ground black pepper

Pinch of ground allspice

1½ quarts store-bought low-sodium
    beef broth diluted with 1 cup
    water

1 ham hock

2 slices turkey bacon, finely
    diced

1 slice rye bread, crust removed

1. Put the butter and oil in a heavy-bottomed soup pot and cook over low heat until the butter melts.

2. Add the sugar and cook, stirring, until it browns, about 5 minutes. Add the cabbage and cook very gently, stirring, over low heat, until it begins to wilt, 8 to 10 minutes. Add the pepper and allspice and stir to coat the cabbage with the spices.

3. Pour in the diluted stock, add the ham hock, and bring the liquid to a simmer over medium heat. Cover and continue to let simmer until the cabbage is softened and the flavors are well integrated, about 1 hour. (The soup can be cooled and refrigerated for up to 2 days. It does not freeze well. Let come to room temperature before reheating.)

4. Meanwhile, brown the turkey bacon in a nonstick pan over low heat until crisp, about 7 minutes. Using a slotted spoon, transfer the bacon to paper towels to drain.

**5.** Toast the bread and cut it into ¼-inch croutons.

**6.** To serve, remove and discard the ham hock or set it aside for another use. Ladle the soup into 4 wide, shallow bowls and garnish with the bacon and croutons.

**variations and suggestions:** If you like, omit the bacon, and shred and return the meat from the ham hock back to the soup instead.

CARBOHYDRATE CHOICE: 1

# mushroom barley soup
## WITH PARSLEY AND PINE NUTS

 don't know about you, but most of my experiences of mushroom barley soup involve either a can or a seat at a diner. You don't see this supposed classic in very many places anymore, but I think it's still as welcome as ever in a home setting—making it with fresh ingredients, and a barley that retains a little of its toothsome quality, elevates it, as do the wide variety of finishing touches you can add. Here, a drizzling of parsley puree and a scattering of toasted pine nuts do wonders for such an unassuming standard. You can also give it a quick, refreshing makeover with a more distinct mushroom, such as cremini or oyster, finishing it with other herbs or herb purees, or replacing the barley with a different grain: Mushroom couscous soup, anyone? **SERVES 4**

## INGREDIENTS

2 tablespoons olive oil

1 medium-size Spanish onion, cut into small dice

1 large rib celery, cut into small dice

8 ounces white button mushrooms, brushed clean, stems trimmed, thinly sliced

Pinch of coarse salt

Pinch of freshly ground black pepper

1 quart store-bought low-sodium beef broth

¼ cup pearl barley

¼ cup pine nuts

¼ cup Parsley Puree (page 316)

1. Heat the olive oil in a large, heavy-bottomed soup pot over medium-high heat. Add the onion and celery and cook, stirring, until the vegetables are lightly browned, about 7 minutes. Add the mushrooms and season with the salt and pepper. Cook until they begin to give off their liquid, about 6 minutes.

2. Add the beef broth and barley and bring to a boil over high heat. Lower the heat so the liquid is simmering, cover the pot, and continue to let simmer until the barley is softened but still a bit al dente, about 40 minutes.

3. Put the pine nuts in a heavy-bottomed pan and toast over medium heat, shaking the pan frequently to prevent scorching, until the pine nuts are golden brown and fragrant, about 3 minutes.

4. To serve, ladle the soup into 4 wide, shallow soup bowls. Scatter a tablespoon of toasted pine nuts and drizzle a tablespoon of the Parsley Puree decoratively over each portion and serve.

## plan ahead

The soup can be cooled and refrigerated in an airtight container for up to 3 days, or frozen for up to 1 month. Let the soup come to room temperature and gently reheat it. Toast the pine nuts right before serving.

CARBOHYDRATE CHOICE: 1

# creamless creamy mushroom soup

i've always been a bit suspicious of "less" foods: sugar*less* candy, meat-*less* meat loaf, and so on. My antennae for culinary chicanery begin to tilt and whirl whenever I hear such constructions. That said, I have found that, of the entire genre, it's most plausible to concoct a creamless version of a creamy food, and moreover that it turns out to be a very appealing thing to do. When something is creamy without the presence of dairy, it offers the best of both worlds—palate-coating texture without the residual heaviness and guilt that come with eating cream-laden foods.

All of which brings me to this cream-free but luscious puree of mushrooms, garlic, thyme, and olive oil. Not a drop of cream in sight, but in this case, "less" is definitely more. **SERVES 4**

## nutritional information
(PER SERVING)

| | |
|---|---|
| Calories | 181 |
| Fat | 14 g |
| Saturated Fat | 2 g |
| Trans Fat | 0 g |
| Total Carbohydrates | 11 g |
| Dietary Fiber | 1 g |
| Total Sugars | 5 g |
| Protein | 4 g |
| Cholesterol | 0 mg |
| Sodium | 377 mg |

## exchanges

| | |
|---|---|
| Fat | 2.5 |
| Vegetables | 2 |

## INGREDIENTS

¼ cup olive oil

¾ cup diced Spanish onion
 (from 1 medium-size onion)

2 large cloves garlic, minced

3 fresh thyme sprigs

7½ cups diced white button mushrooms
 (from about 1½ pounds)

Pinch of freshly ground black pepper

1 tablespoon Porcini Powder (page 325)

¾ teaspoon coarse salt

plan ahead

**The soup can be cooled and refrigerated in an airtight container overnight. Let come to room temperature before reheating.**

1. Heat 2 tablespoons of the olive oil in a heavy-bottomed soup pot over medium heat. Add the onion and garlic and cook until softened but not browned, about 4 minutes. Add the thyme, mushrooms, pepper, and 1½ cups of water. Bring to a boil and let boil until the flavors meld, about 5 minutes. Use tongs or a slotted spoon to fish out and discard the thyme sprigs.

2. Working in batches, transfer the mushroom mixture with its liquid to a blender or food processor. (See page 102 for a safety note on blending hot liquids.) Add the remaining 2 table-spoons of olive oil, the Porcini Powder, and salt divided among the batches until all is used up. Puree or process the soup until smooth and creamy.

3. Carefully wipe out the pot and return the soup to it to reheat it, if necessary. Ladle the soup into 4 bowls and serve.

**variations and suggestions:** You can make or garnish this soup with your favorite roasted mushrooms and/or a drizzle of white truffle oil.

**CARBOHYDRATE CHOICES: 2½; 2 ADJUSTED FOR FIBER**

# butternut squash soup

While I love a thick, porridgelike pureed butternut squash soup, I've also learned to appreciate the autumnal flavor of the squash in a thinner, more diabetes-appropriate version. I'm also a huge fan of the soup's fiery orange hue, diminished not at all by the consistency here, and the way the soup welcomes any number of herbs, from sage and thyme to a drizzle of Parsley Puree (page 316). **SERVES 4**

## INGREDIENTS

1 medium-size butternut squash
  (about 2½ pounds)

2 teaspoons unsalted butter

Pinch of freshly ground black pepper,
  or more to taste

2 slices turkey bacon (optional)

1 tablespoon olive oil

1 large Spanish onion, peeled and
  cut into small dice

3 fresh marjoram sprigs, plus leaves
  for serving

1 bay leaf, preferably fresh

3 cups store-bought low-sodium
  chicken broth

1 tablespoon heavy (whipping) cream

½ teaspoon coarse salt, or more to taste

½ teaspoon sugar, or more to taste

1. Preheat the oven to 400°F.

2. Cut the butternut squash in half lengthwise. Scoop out and discard the seeds. Place the squash halves cut-side up in a baking dish. Place 1 teaspoon of butter in each hollowed-out seed cavity and season the cut sides of the squash with the pepper. If using, arrange 1 slice of turkey bacon lengthwise down the center of each squash half. Bake the squash until a sharp, thin-bladed knife pierces it easily in the center, 35 to 40 minutes.

3. Remove the squash from the oven. Discard the bacon or chop it into bits (see Variations and Suggestions). Once the squash has cooled slightly, use a tablespoon to scoop out the flesh, including any melted butter in the seed cavity. Set the squash flesh aside and discard the skins.

4. Heat the olive oil in a medium-size, heavy-bottomed pot over medium heat. Add the onion and cook, stirring, until softened but not browned, about 4 minutes. Stir in the marjoram sprigs and bay leaf, then add the squash. Cook, stirring to integrate the flavors and keep the squash from scorching, for 1 to 2 minutes. Stir in the chicken broth, increase the heat to high, bring to a boil, then lower the heat and let simmer for 15 minutes.

5. Use tongs or a slotted spoon to fish out and discard the marjoram sprigs and bay leaf. Working in batches, transfer the soup to a food processor and process for several minutes until uniformly thick and creamy. (See page 102 for a safety note on blending hot liquids). Add the cream, salt, and sugar to the last batch.

6. Return the soup to the pot and gently reheat it. Taste for seasoning,

## nutritional information
(PER SERVING)

| | |
|---|---|
| Calories | 220 |
| Fat | 7 g |
| Saturated Fat | 3 g |
| Trans Fat | 0 g |
| Total Carbohydrates | 38 g |
| Dietary Fiber | 6 g |
| Total Sugars | 9 g |
| Protein | 6 g |
| Cholesterol | 13 mg |
| Sodium | 335 mg |

## exchanges

| | |
|---|---|
| Fat | 1.5 |
| Vegetables | 5.5 |

## plan ahead

The soup can be cooled and refrigerated in an airtight container for up to 3 days, or frozen for up to 1 month. Let come to room temperature before reheating.

adding more salt, pepper, and/or sugar if necessary. Divide the soup among 4 wide, shallow bowls. Garnish with marjoram leaves and serve.

**variations and suggestions:** If using the bacon, after the squash has baked, drain the bacon, chop it up, and scatter it over the soup.

CARBOHYDRATE CHOICE: 1

# manhattan clam chowder

long before there were the Yankees and the Red Sox, another rivalry existed between New York and New England: the intense and often nasty regard in which each region holds the other's version of clam chowder. In New England, the land of cream-based chowder, contempt for the tomato-based Manhattan version seems to run deeper than vice versa. Perhaps New Yorkers aren't nearly as invested in our local shellfish and, more to the point, there's no real certainty that Manhattan clam chowder even originated here. (Some people say it was first concocted in Connecticut.) Regardless of its birthplace, I do have a fondness for Manhattan clam chowder and am happy to share my version of it.

**SERVES 4**

## INGREDIENTS

3 medium-size plum tomatoes, diced

1 teaspoon distilled white vinegar

¼ teaspoon coarse salt

¼ teaspoon minced fresh marjoram leaves

⅛ teaspoon freshly ground black pepper

1 teaspoon olive oil

2 slices turkey bacon, finely diced

½ small Spanish onion, finely diced

3 medium-size cloves garlic, finely sliced, plus 1 clove, crushed and peeled

2 ribs celery, finely diced

1 small Idaho or russet potato, peeled and cut into ¼-inch dice (about ⅔ cup dice)

1 cup bottled clam juice

1 cup store-bought low-sodium chicken broth

⅛ teaspoon crushed red pepper flakes

3 tablespoons dry white wine

24 Manila clams (see page 162), scrubbed under cold running water

1. Put the plum tomatoes in a bowl with the vinegar, salt, marjoram, and pepper. Toss and set aside to marinate.

2. Heat the olive oil in a large, heavy-bottomed saucepan over medium heat. Add the turkey bacon and cook until browned and the fat has rendered, about 7 minutes. Add the onion, sliced garlic, and celery and cook until softened but not browned, about 4 minutes. Add the marinated tomatoes and the potato and cook, stirring, for 2 minutes. Add the clam juice, chicken broth, red pepper flakes, and ½ cup of water. Bring to a simmer and let simmer until the tomatoes have broken down completely, 20 to 25 minutes.

3. Meanwhile, in a separate, heavy-bottomed pot heat the white wine and crushed garlic clove over medium-high heat until the wine just begins to simmer. Add the clams, cover the pot, and cook until the clams open, about 5 minutes; discard any clams that do not open. Remove the pot from the heat and let the clams cool.

4. When cool enough to handle, remove the clams from the shells and add them to the soup. Discard the shells. Strain the clam cooking liquid and stir it into the soup. Divide the soup among 4 bowls and serve.

Manhattan Clam Chowder

CARBOHYDRATE CHOICE: 1

# new england clam chowder

m y take on New England clam chowder is made with fresh clams, milk in place of the traditional cream, and some chicken broth to balance the salty clam broth. Although less rich than the classic, the flavor is satisfying with the bacon and celery more pronounced than in traditional versions.           SERVES 4

## nutritional information
### (PER SERVING)

| | |
|---|---|
| Calories | 235 |
| Fat | 9 g |
| Saturated Fat | 3 g |
| Trans Fat | 0 g |
| Total Carbohydrates | 19 g |
| Dietary Fiber | 2 g |
| Total Sugars | 5 g |
| Protein | 17 g |
| Cholesterol | 49 mg |
| Sodium | 337 mg |

## exchanges

| | |
|---|---|
| Fat | 1.5 |
| Nonfat Milk | 0.5 |
| Starch | 0.5 |
| Lean Meat | 1.5 |
| Vegetables | 0.5 |

## INGREDIENTS

1 tablespoon olive oil

2 slices turkey bacon, cut into small dice

1 tablespoon butter

1 cup finely diced Spanish onion (from about 1 small onion)

1 cup finely diced celery (from about 2 ribs)

3 medium-size cloves garlic, finely sliced, plus 1 clove, crushed and peeled

1½ tablespoons all-purpose flour

1 cup bottled clam juice

1 cup whole milk

1 cup store-bought low-sodium chicken broth

1 small Idaho or russet potato, peeled and cut into ¼-inch dice (about ⅔ cup dice)

⅛ teaspoon celery seed

⅛ teaspoon fresh thyme leaves

Pinch of freshly ground black pepper

3 tablespoons dry white wine

24 Manila clams (see page 102), scrubbed under cold running water

1. Heat the olive oil in a large, heavy-bottomed saucepan over medium heat. Add the turkey bacon and cook until browned and the fat has rendered, about 7 minutes. Stir in the butter and cook until it melts, then add the onion, celery, and garlic. Cook until softened but not browned, about 4 minutes. Sprinkle the flour on top and cook, stirring, for 3 to 4 minutes without browning the flour.

2. Slowly stir in the clam juice, then add the milk, chicken broth, potato, celery seed, thyme, and pepper. Bring to a simmer and let simmer gently for 15 minutes.

3. Meanwhile, in a separate heavy-bottomed pot, heat the white wine and crushed garlic clove over medium-high heat, until the wine just begins to simmer. Add the clams, cover the pot, and cook until the clams open, about 5 minutes; discard any clams that do not open. Remove the pot from the heat and let the clams cool.

4. When cool enough to handle, remove the clams from the shells and add them to the soup. Discard the shells. Strain the clam cooking liquid and stir it into the soup. Divide the soup among 4 bowls and serve.

CARBOHYDRATE CHOICE: 1

# seafood stew

here's a seaside fisherman's stew with plenty of garlic, saffron, and heat. If you like, you can add half a cup of cooked rice, orzo, tubetti, or angel hair pasta before serving. To make it more of a meal, you can also split a lobster tail and poach it in the broth during the last few minutes of cooking.     **SERVES 6**

## INGREDIENTS

¼ cup olive oil

1 medium-size Spanish onion,
    cut into ½-inch dice

8 cloves garlic, thinly sliced

3 tablespoons tomato paste

1 teaspoon fresh thyme leaves

¼ teaspoon saffron threads

½ teaspoon crushed red pepper flakes

1¼ cups store-bought low-sodium
    vegetable broth diluted with
    1¼ cups water

1½ cups dry white wine

¼ cup distilled white vinegar

3 medium-size plum tomatoes,
    coarsely chopped, with their juice

1 cup organic tomato juice

½ teaspoon coarse salt

½ teaspoon freshly ground black pepper

18 small clams, or 9 regular clams
    (about 1 pound; see page 162),
    scrubbed under cold running water

12 mussels (about 12 ounces), scrubbed
    under cold running water and
    bearded

1½ pounds firm-fleshed fish fillet such as
    bass or snapper, cut in 1-inch cubes

6 medium-size to large shrimp
    (about 6 ounces), with tails, peeled,
    deveined, and cut in half lengthwise

1 tablespoon extra-virgin olive oil

2 tablespoons chopped fresh flat-leaf
    parsley leaves

1. Heat the olive oil in a heavy-bottomed soup pot over medium heat. Add the onion and garlic and cook until softened but not browned, about 4 minutes.

2. Add the tomato paste, thyme, saffron, and red pepper flakes and cook, stirring to coat the other ingredients with the tomato paste, about 3 minutes.

3. Add the vegetable broth, wine, vinegar, tomatoes, tomato juice, ¼ teaspoon of the salt, and the black pepper and bring to a simmer, then

## nutritional information
(PER SERVING)

| | |
|---|---|
| Calories | 361 |
| Fat | 14 g |
| Saturated Fat | 2 g |
| Trans Fat | 0 g |
| Total Carbohydrates | 11 g |
| Dietary Fiber | 1 g |
| Total Sugars | 4 g |
| Protein | 35 g |
| Cholesterol | 97 mg |
| Sodium | 541 mg |

## exchanges

| | |
|---|---|
| Fat | 2.5 |
| Lean Meat | 4 |
| Vegetables | 1.5 |
| Alcohol | 0.5 |

lower the heat and let simmer for 15 minutes. (The soup can be made up to this point, cooled, and refrigerated in an airtight container for up to 2 days, or frozen for up to 2 months. Let come to room temperature, then gently reheat before proceeding.)

**4.** Add the clams and mussels, submerging them with a spoon, and cook, uncovered, until they open, about 5 minutes; discard any that do not open. Season the soup with the remaining ¼ teaspoon of salt and add the fish and shrimp to the pot, gently poaching them until the fish is opaque and the shrimp are firm and pink, 3 to 4 minutes.

**5.** Divide the stew among 6 wide, shallow bowls. Drizzle some olive oil and scatter some parsley over each serving.

## nutritional information
**(PER SERVING)**

| | |
|---|---|
| Calories | 125 |
| Fat | 3 g |
| Saturated Fat | 1 g |
| Trans Fat | 0 g |
| Total Carbohydrates | 14 g |
| Dietary Fiber | 1 g |
| Total Sugars | 1 g |
| Protein | 10 g |
| Cholesterol | 131 mg |
| Sodium | 367 mg |

## exchanges

| | |
|---|---|
| Starch | 0.5 |
| Lean Meat | 0.5 |
| Medium Fat Meat | 0.5 |
| Vegetables | 0.5 |

**CARBOHYDRATE CHOICE: 1**

# lemony shrimp and asparagus soup

this soup takes the traditional Greek avgolemono, a broth into which lemon juice and eggs are stirred, and adds asparagus for fiber, shrimp for extra texture and protein, and a small amount of pasta, which is a classic touch. Personally, I love the way the eggs and lemon get along; you wouldn't think they would, but in this context it's like they were made for each other. **SERVES 4**

## INGREDIENTS

4 spears large asparagus, thick ends trimmed

2 cups store-bought low-sodium chicken broth

¼ cup dry pastina or other very small pasta

2 medium-size cloves garlic, thinly sliced

½ teaspoon coarse salt

8 ounces shrimp (about 8 large shrimp), peeled, tails removed, deveined, and quartered

2 large eggs, beaten

2 teaspoons freshly squeezed lemon juice

2 teaspoons grated Parmesan cheese

Pinch of freshly ground black pepper

1. Bring a medium-size pot of water to a boil over high heat. Cook the asparagus in the boiling water until al dente, about 8 minutes.

2. Fill a large bowl halfway with ice water. Use tongs to transfer the asparagus to the ice water. Once the asparagus has cooled, drain it and pat dry with paper towels. Cut the asparagus crosswise into 1-inch pieces and set aside.

3. Pour the chicken broth and 1 cup of water into a large, heavy-bottomed saucepan. Add the pastina, garlic, and salt. Bring to a simmer and continue to let simmer until the pasta is al dente, 10 to 12 minutes.

4. Add the shrimp and cook for 30 seconds. Stir in the eggs; they will form ribbons quickly. Stir in the lemon juice, Parmesan cheese, and pepper. Add the asparagus and cook until warmed through, about 1 minute. Divide the soup among 4 bowls and serve.

**CARBOHYDRATE CHOICE: 1**

# lobster bisque

i think that the potent, haunting essence of lobster that's released by cooking its shells is one of the most beguiling effects you can conjure in any cooking, and one of my favorite ways to harness it is in a bisque. A classic bisque has much more cream than this one, but I think you won't miss it because that lobster flavor carries the day.          **SERVES 6**

## INGREDIENTS

2 live lobsters (about 1½ pounds each)

3 tablespoons olive oil

¼ cup tomato paste

Pinch of sugar

2 plum tomatoes, coarsely chopped

2 sprigs fresh tarragon plus 2
   tablespoons tarragon leaves

2 sprigs fresh flat-leaf parsley

2 fresh thyme sprigs

2 large cloves garlic, very thinly sliced

⅓ cup dry white wine

2 teaspoons distilled white vinegar

3 tablespoons all-purpose flour

⅔ cup heavy (whipping) cream

1 tablespoon black peppercorns

½ teaspoon coarse salt

1½ cups cooked, long-grain rice
   (from ¾ cup uncooked rice)

## nutritional information
(PER SERVING)

| | |
|---|---|
| Calories | 300 |
| Fat | 17 g |
| Saturated Fat | 7 g |
| Trans Fat | 0 g |
| Total Carbohydrates | 20 g |
| Dietary Fiber | 1 g |
| Total Sugars | 2 g |
| Protein | 14 g |
| Cholesterol | 90 mg |
| Sodium | 427 mg |

## exchanges

| | |
|---|---|
| Fat | 3.5 |
| Starch | 1 |
| Lean Meat | 1 |
| Vegetables | 0.5 |

1. Bring a stockpot full of water to a boil over high heat. Add the lobsters to the boiling water and cook until the shells turn bright red, 6 minutes. Remove the pot from the heat and let the lobsters sit in the pot for about 90 seconds.

2. Fill a large bowl halfway with ice water. Using tongs, remove the lobsters from the pot and immerse them in the ice water.

3. Once the lobsters have cooled, drain the water. Take the head of one lobster in one hand and the tail in the other and twist them in opposite directions until the upper and lower halves come apart. Using a large, heavy knife, split the lobster tail in half lengthwise. Remove the meat from the body of the lobster. Crack the claws and remove the meat from within. Cut the lobster meat into 1-inch dice and set it aside. Remove the gray-green tomalley (liver) and red roe (if any) from the lobster shells and set them and the shells aside separately. Repeat with the remaining lobster. (This step can be performed up to 24 hours ahead of time. Reserve the lobster meat, shells, tomalley and roe in separate airtight containers in the refrigerator. Let come to room temperature before proceeding.)

4. Heat the olive oil in a medium-size, heavy-bottomed pot over high heat. Add the lobster shells to the pot and cook, stirring, for 2 to 3 minutes. Lower the heat and add the tomato paste and sugar. Stir to coat the lobster shells with the tomato paste and cook for 2 to 3 minutes longer.

5. Place the tomatoes, lobster roe (if any), tarragon sprigs, parsley, thyme, and garlic in a small bowl and stir to mix.

6. Add the white wine, vinegar, and tomato mixture to the pot with the lobster shells and stir. Sprinkle the flour on top and cook, stirring, for 2 minutes. Add 3 cups of water and the cream, peppercorns, and salt. Bring to a simmer over medium heat and simmer gently, without boiling, for 15 minutes, adding the tomalley for the last 5 minutes of cooking. Taste the bisque; if the lobster flavor isn't prominent, continue simmering until it is, about 5 minutes longer. As soon as you can taste the lobster, remove the pot from the heat; if overcooked the flavor can become murky.

7. Strain the bisque into a bowl, pressing down on the solids to extract as much flavorful liquid as possible. Discard the solids. You should have 2½ to 3 cups of liquid. (The bisque can be cooled and refrigerated in an airtight container for up to 2 days. It does not freeze well. Let come to room temperature before proceeding.)

8. Return the bisque to the pot. Stir in the rice and tarragon leaves. Warm the bisque over low heat for about 5 minutes. To serve, ladle some bisque into each of 6 bowls and garnish with the lobster meat.

CARBOHYDRATE CHOICE: ½

# jorge's family lunch chicken soup

t his recipe was introduced to me by Ouest's sous chef Jorge Carrera. This easy-to-make soup is truly a meal, with chicken breast and vegetables in a fragrant, spicy broth. The fun part is that each person gets to season the soup to his or her own taste with lime juice, cilantro, and hot sauce, turning this into a real conversation piece. I also recommend it to you as the ultimate chicken soup the next time you have a cold. **SERVES 4**

## nutritional information
(PER SERVING)

| | |
|---|---|
| Calories | 163 |
| Fat | 8 g |
| Saturated Fat | 2 g |
| Trans Fat | 0 g |
| Total Carbohydrates | 9 g |
| Dietary Fiber | 2 g |
| Total Sugars | 4 g |
| Protein | 14 g |
| Cholesterol | 28 mg |
| Sodium | 348 mg |

## exchanges

| | |
|---|---|
| Fat | 1.5 |
| Lean Meat | 1 |
| Vegetables | 1 |

## INGREDIENTS

2 tablespoons extra-virgin olive oil

1 medium-size Spanish onion, minced

3 medium-size cloves garlic, minced

4 cups store-bought low-sodium chicken broth

1 skinless, boneless half chicken breast (about 6 ounces)

2 ribs celery, finely diced

1 large carrot, peeled and finely diced

1 tablespoon tomato paste

¼ teaspoon coarse salt

⅛ teaspoon freshly ground black pepper

2 lime halves, plus lime halves, for serving

3 tablespoons chopped fresh cilantro leaves, plus more for serving

Hot sauce

1. Heat the olive oil in a heavy-bottomed soup pot over medium heat. Add half of the onion and the garlic and cook until softened but not browned, about 4 minutes.

2. Pour in the chicken broth and bring to a simmer. Add the chicken breast and poach gently for about 7 minutes. Add the celery and carrot and continue to simmer for 7 minutes.

**3.** Remove the pot from the heat. Using tongs or a slotted spoon, transfer the chicken breast to a cutting board. When the chicken is cool enough to handle, shred it by hand. You should have about 1¼ cups of chicken.

**4.** Return the pot to the stove top over medium-high heat. Stir in the tomato paste. Add the shredded chicken to the pot and let it warm for a minute or 2. Stir in the salt and pepper and squeeze the juice from the 2 lime halves into the soup. Add the cilantro and a few shakes of hot sauce.

**5.** Divide the soup among 4 bowls and serve it, with more lime halves, the remaining minced onion, some cilantro, and hot sauce alongside.

CARBOHYDRATE CHOICE: 1

# chicken "pot pie"

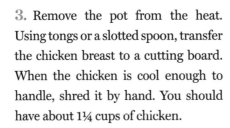

this variation on a chicken pot pie is a chicken stew made with all the familiar ingredients, but not served in a doughy dish. Instead, serve a small cheddar biscuit alongside for dunking, crumbling into the bowl, or mopping up any sauce left behind after the rest of the stew is gone.

SERVES 4

## nutritional information
(PER SERVING)

| | |
|---|---|
| Calories | 442 |
| Fat | 28 g |
| Saturated Fat | 10 g |
| Trans Fat | 0 g |
| Total Carbohydrates | 20 g |
| Dietary Fiber | 4 g |
| Total Sugars | 6 g |
| Protein | 28 g |
| Cholesterol | 86 mg |
| Sodium | 425 mg |

## exchanges

| | |
|---|---|
| Fat | 5 |
| Starch | 0.5 |
| Lean Meat | 2.5 |
| Vegetables | 2.5 |

## INGREDIENTS

*1 cup frozen peas*
*2 skinless, boneless half chicken breasts*
    *(about 6 ounces each)*
*¼ cup olive oil*
*6 ribs celery, thinly sliced crosswise*
*2 large carrots, peeled and thinly*
    *sliced crosswise*
*1 large Spanish onion, cut into small dice*
*2 cups sliced white button or cremini*
    *mushrooms (from about 12*
    *mushrooms)*

*¼ cup all-purpose flour*
*4 tablespoons (½ stick) unsalted butter*
*4 cups store-bought low sodium*
    *chicken broth*
*2 tablespoons grated Parmesan cheese*
*1 tablespoon fresh thyme leaves*
*½ teaspoon coarse salt*
*¼ teaspoon freshly ground black*
    *pepper*
*4 Cheddar Biscuits*
    *(recipe follows; optional)*

1. Bring a small pot of water to a boil. Fill a bowl halfway with ice water.

2. Cook the peas in the boiling water for 1 minute. Drain the peas and transfer them to the ice water to stop the cooking and preserve their color. Drain the ice water and set the peas aside.

3. Bring another small pot of water to a boil. Add the chicken breasts and let poach gently for about 15 minutes. Using tongs or a slotted spoon, transfer the chicken to a plate to cool. When the chicken is cool enough to handle, shred it by hand. You should have about 2½ cups of chicken.

4. Heat the olive oil in a large, heavy-bottomed saucepan over medium-high heat. Add the celery, carrots, and onion and cook, without browning, for 4 minutes. Add the mushrooms and cook for 2 minutes.

5. Sprinkle the flour over the vegetables and stir to cook the flour without letting it brown. Add the butter and cook, stirring gently, until the butter melts and blends into the flour.

6. Slowly add the chicken broth, one cup at a time, stirring until a thick sauce forms. Add the shredded chicken and the peas to the pot and cook for 1 minute. Stir in the Parmesan cheese, thyme, salt, and pepper.

7. Divide the stew among 4 wide, shallow bowls and top each serving with a biscuit, if desired.

**CARBOHYDRATE CHOICES: 2**

# cheddar biscuits

These biscuits are delicious just as they are, but you can give them even more flavor by adding a pinch of cayenne pepper or some minced chives—stir them in after the buttermilk in Step 2.

**MAKES 4 BISCUITS**

## INGREDIENTS

1 cup all-purpose flour

2 teaspoons baking powder

½ teaspoon baking soda

Pinch of coarse salt

2 tablespoons cold unsalted
    butter, cut into small cubes

3 ounces cheddar cheese,
    grated (about 2 cups)

1 tablespoon finely grated
    Parmesan cheese

¾ cup low-fat buttermilk

1. Position a rack in the center of the oven and preheat it to 450°F.

2. Put the flour, baking powder, baking soda, and salt in a bowl and stir or swirl them together. Add the

## nutritional information
(PER SERVING)

| | |
|---|---|
| Calories | 277 |
| Fat | 14 g |
| Saturated Fat | 9 g |
| Trans Fat | 0 g |
| Total Carbohydrates | 27 g |
| Dietary Fiber | 1 g |
| Total Sugars | 2 g |
| Protein | 11 g |
| Cholesterol | 41 mg |
| Sodium | 624 mg |

## exchanges

| | |
|---|---|
| Fat | 1.5 |
| Starch | 1.5 |
| High Fat Meat | 1 |

**A TIP FROM TOM**

You can leave out the biscuit or serve this with your favorite crackers or bread instead; for this reason the nutritional analyses for the biscuit and stew are presented separately.

butter, a few cubes at a time, and work it into the dry ingredients with your fingertips until the mixture resembles coarse cornmeal. Stir in the cheddar and Parmesan cheeses, then add the buttermilk slowly, stirring, until it is just incorporated and the mixture comes together into a uniform dough.

3. Shape the dough into 4 mounds, arranging them about 2 inches apart on a nonstick baking sheet. Bake the biscuits until nicely golden, 15 to 18 minutes.

4. Using a spatula, transfer the biscuits to a wire rack. Let cool and serve warm or at room temperature.

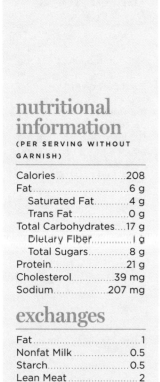

## nutritional information

(PER SERVING WITHOUT GARNISH)

| | |
|---|---|
| Calories | 208 |
| Fat | 6 g |
| Saturated Fat | 4 g |
| Trans Fat | 0 g |
| Total Carbohydrates | 17 g |
| Dietary Fiber | 1 g |
| Total Sugars | 8 g |
| Protein | 21 g |
| Cholesterol | 39 mg |
| Sodium | 207 mg |

## exchanges

| | |
|---|---|
| Fat | 1 |
| Nonfat Milk | 0.5 |
| Starch | 0.5 |
| Lean Meat | 2 |

**CARBOHYDRATE CHOICE: 1**

# spicy coconut turkey soup

i came up with this soup as an unusual way to use Thanksgiving turkey leftovers, which often find themselves in a slightly richer version of chicken noodle soup. We don't associate turkey with Asian flavors, but I decided to take that direction and ended up with this variation on a noodle soup. If you have houseguests for the holiday, they'll be pleasantly surprised.    **SERVES 4**

## INGREDIENTS

4 cups store-bought low-sodium chicken broth

2 large cloves garlic, crushed

2 bay leaves, preferably fresh

2 ounce piece of peeled fresh ginger, minced (about 2 tablespoons)

1 piece lemongrass, white part only, crushed

Zest of ½ lime

¼ teaspoon crushed red pepper flakes

⅛ teaspoon Asian fish sauce

2 cups skim milk

¼ cup unsweetened coconut milk

6 ounces diced leftover roast turkey (about 1½ cups)

4 ounces rice vermicelli, cooked

Optional garnishes: thinly sliced scallion, thinly sliced cucumber, sliced shiitake mushrooms, thinly sliced cilantro leaves, lime wedges

1. Put the chicken broth, garlic, bay leaves, ginger, lemongrass, lime zest, red pepper flakes, and fish sauce in a soup pot and bring to a boil over high heat. Lower the heat and add the skim milk and coconut milk. Let simmer gently for 15 to 20 minutes.

2. Strain the soup and return it to the pot over medium heat. Add the turkey and the vermicelli to the soup and let them warm through, 4 minutes.

3. Ladle the soup into 4 soup bowls and serve with the desired garnishes.

**CARBOHYDRATE CHOICE: 1**

# turkey chili

here's another dish designed for using turkey leftovers, this one a hot and spicy chili. It's the kind of thing you'd usually make with beef, which is why dark-meat turkey is recommended. If this sounds like something you might like to serve up on the day after Thanksgiving, then by all means pick up the necessary ingredients when you do your holiday shopping. You can also double or triple this recipe for a few days' worth of snacking. **SERVES 6**

## INGREDIENTS

6 ripe plum tomatoes, coarsely chopped, with their juice

1 teaspoon coarse salt

¼ cup canola oil

4 cloves garlic, thinly sliced

2 ribs celery, diced

1 medium-size Spanish onion, diced

1 jalapeño pepper, cut crosswise into large slices (seed the jalapeño or leave the seeds in for a hotter chili)

2 tablespoons tomato paste

2 tablespoons coarsely chopped chipotle pepper with its adobe sauce

1 tablespoon chili powder

½ teaspoon cayenne pepper

¼ teaspoon ground cumin

¼ teaspoon freshly ground black pepper

2 cups store-bought low-sodium chicken broth, or more to taste

12 ounces diced leftover roast turkey, preferably dark meat

¼ cup canned white beans, rinsed and drained

¼ cup minced fresh cilantro leaves

Optional garnishes: minced red onion, nonfat sour cream, grated Jack or cheddar cheese

## nutritional information
**(PER SERVING WITHOUT GARNISH)**

| | |
|---|---|
| Calories | 239 |
| Fat | 13 g |
| Saturated Fat | 2 g |
| Trans Fat | 0 g |
| Total Carbohydrates | 11 g |
| Dietary Fiber | 3 g |
| Total Sugars | 4 g |
| Protein | 20 g |
| Cholesterol | 44 mg |
| Sodium | 490 mg |

## exchanges

| | |
|---|---|
| Fat | 2 |
| Lean Meat | 2 |
| Vegetables | 1.5 |

1. Put the tomatoes in a bowl, add the salt, and toss to mix. Set the tomatoes aside while you begin making the chili.

2. Heat the oil in a large pot. Add the garlic, celery, onion, and jalapeño and cook, stirring, until the vegetables are softened but not browned, about 7 minutes. Add the salted tomatoes, tomato paste, and chipotle and stir to coat the vegetables with them. Cook for about 2 minutes. Stir in the chili powder, cayenne, cumin, and black pepper and cook for 1 minute.

3. Stir in the chicken broth, bring it to a gentle simmer, and let simmer until the chili is slightly thickened and flavorful, about 20 minutes. Stir in the turkey and beans and let warm through, 2 to 3 minutes. Stir in the cilantro.

4. Divide the chili among 4 bowls. Set out red onion, sour cream, and/ or cheddar cheese, if desired, for garnishing each serving to taste.

## nutritional information

**(PER SERVING)**

| | |
|---|---|
| Calories | 287 |
| Fat | 14 g |
| Saturated Fat | 4 g |
| Trans Fat | 0 g |
| Total Carbohydrates | 13 g |
| Dietary Fiber | 3 g |
| Total Sugars | 6 g |
| Protein | 27 g |
| Cholesterol | 37 mg |
| Sodium | 116 mg |

## exchanges

| | |
|---|---|
| Fat | 1.5 |
| Lean Meat | 3.5 |
| Vegetables | 2.5 |

CARBOHYDRATE CHOICE: 1

# ropa vieja

One of the all-time great names ever given to a dish is that of the Cuban beef and pepper stew known as *ropa vieja,* which means old clothes, a nod to the resemblance of the pulled beef to tattered, raglike garments. *Ropa vieja* is one of those dishes that vary from household to household in Cuba, but the essentials are flank steak, bell peppers, and onion. I add a little distilled white vinegar to perk up what can sometimes be a one-dimensional affair in unfamiliar hands, and while tomatoes are thought of as optional in this dish's homeland, I find them essential for the sweetness and acidity they add. Another revision I've made to the classic recipe is that after the beef is cooked, I discard the vegetables from the cooking liquid, and add sautéed fresh onions and peppers for more flavor, color, and snap in the finished dish. If you can, make this a day ahead and refrigerate it overnight; the meat will become more tender and the flavors will intensify considerably. **SERVES 4**

## INGREDIENTS

2 tablespoons plus 1 teaspoon olive oil

1 pound flank steak, cut crosswise into
2 pieces

Pinch of coarse salt, or more as needed

Pinch of freshly ground black pepper,
or more as needed

2 bell peppers, green, red, or 1 of each,
stemmed, seeded, 1 cut into large
dice, 1 sliced lengthwise

2 large Spanish onions, 1 cut into large
dice, 1 cut in half and thinly sliced

1 teaspoon distilled white vinegar

1 bay leaf, preferably fresh

Pinch of ground cumin

3 cloves garlic, thinly sliced

½ tablespoon tomato paste

2 plum tomatoes, peeled
(see this page) and coarsely chopped

1. Heat 1 tablespoon of the olive oil in a medium-size, heavy-bottomed pot set over high heat. Season the flank steak with the salt and pepper and add it to the pot. Brown the meat on all sides, about 5 minutes. Transfer the meat to a plate and set it aside.

2. Add 1 tablespoon of the olive oil to the pot and heat it over medium heat. Add the diced bell pepper and diced onion and cook, stirring, until they just begin to brown, about 4 minutes. Add the vinegar and stir, scraping up any flavorful bits stuck to the bottom of the pot. Pour in 2 cups of water, raise the heat to high, and bring the water to a boil. Add the bay leaf and cumin.

3. Return the flank steak to the pot. If the liquid does not come up to the top of the steak, add just enough water to cover it. When the liquid returns to a boil, cover the pot, lower the heat, and let simmer until the meat is almost falling apart, about 2½ hours. Remove the pot from the heat and let the meat cool in the liquid.

4. Transfer the meat to a plate. Strain the cooking liquid and discard the solids. Set the liquid aside. Shred the meat by hand, pulling off and discarding any remaining fat. The strands of meat should resemble pulled pork. (The meat and cooking liquid can be cooled, covered, and refrigerated separately overnight. Let come to room temperature before proceeding.)

5. Wipe out the pot, add the remaining teaspoon of olive oil, and heat over medium-low heat. Add the sliced onions, sliced bell pepper, and the garlic and cook, stirring occasionally, until the onion and pepper are very soft, but not browned, about 20

A TIP FROM TOM

**PEELING AND SEEDING TOMATOES:** To peel tomatoes, bring a large pot of water to a boil. Fill a large bowl halfway with ice water. Carefully remove the stem, if any, from each tomato and cut a shallow X on the bottom (opposite the stem end), just deep enough to penetrate the skin. When the water boils, add the tomatoes and cook for 1 minute. Using tongs or a slotted spoon, transfer the tomatoes to the ice water. As the tomatoes cool, the skins will begin to peel away. Remove the tomatoes from the water and remove the skins.

To seed a peeled or unpeeled tomato, simply cut off the top ¼ inch, invert the tomato over a bowl or the kitchen sink, and gently squeeze the tomato until the seeds run out.

minutes. Add the tomato paste and stir to coat. Add the tomatoes and 3 cups of the reserved cooking liquid. Raise the heat to high, bring to a boil, then lower the heat and let simmer until thickened and nicely flavored, about 15 minutes. Return the meat to the pot and stir it into the stew. Taste for seasoning, adding more salt and/or pepper as necessary. Divide the *ropa vieja* among 4 plates and serve.

## nutritional information
(PER SERVING)

| | |
|---|---|
| Calories | 395 |
| Fat | 16 g |
|   Saturated Fat | 3 g |
|   Trans Fat | 0 g |
| Total Carbohydrates | 25 g |
|   Dietary Fiber | 5 g |
|   Total Sugars | 11 g |
| Protein | 28 g |
| Cholesterol | 55 mg |
| Sodium | 322 mg |

## exchanges

| | |
|---|---|
| Fat | 1.5 |
| Lean Meat | 2.5 |
| Vegetables | 3.5 |
| Alcohol | 0.5 |

**CARBOHYDRATE CHOICES: 1½; 1 ADJUSTED FOR FIBER**

# hearty beef and vegetable stew

i bring two of my favorite tricks of the trade to this otherwise straightforward beef stew: the addition of turkey bacon for a bit of smoke and some distilled white vinegar to add an acidic tang. Let the stew simmer as gently as possible to keep the meat from toughening up. **SERVES 4**

## INGREDIENTS

2 tablespoons canola oil

¼ cup diced turkey bacon
  (from about 2 slices)

12 ounces beef stew meat

Pinch of coarse salt

Pinch of freshly ground black pepper

2 tablespoons plus 1½ teaspoons all-purpose flour

3 medium-size carrots, peeled and cut diagonally into 1-inch pieces

3 ribs celery, peeled and cut diagonally into 1-inch pieces

2 large Spanish onions, cut into large dice

3 tablespoons tomato paste

6 plum tomatoes, coarsely chopped, with their juice

2 tablespoons distilled white vinegar

1 cup robust red wine

1 quart store-bought low-sodium beef broth

3 fresh thyme sprigs

1 bay leaf, preferably fresh

1. Heat the oil in a large, heavy-bottomed pot over medium-high heat. Add the bacon and cook until browned and the fat is rendered, about 7 minutes.

2. Add the beef and season it with the salt and pepper. Sprinkle the flour over the meat and brown the meat on all sides, about 8 minutes. Transfer the meat to a plate or bowl.

3. Add the carrots, celery, and onions to the pan. Cook, stirring, until they begin to soften, about 8 minutes. Add the tomato paste, stir to coat the vegetables, and cook for 2 minutes. Add the tomatoes, vinegar, and red wine, bring to a simmer, and scrape up any flavorful browned bits stuck to the bottom of the pot. Let simmer until the liquids are reduced by half, about 5 minutes. Add the beef broth, thyme, bay leaf, and browned beef. Bring to a simmer and let simmer until the stew is nicely thickened and the flavors are incorporated, about 1 hour.

4. Remove and discard the thyme sprigs and bay leaf. Divide the stew among 4 bowls and serve.

## plan ahead

The stew can be refrigerated in an airtight container for up to 2 days or frozen for up to 1 month; reheat gently before serving.

CARBOHYDRATE CHOICE: ½

# veal meatballs en brodo

the kind of dish my grandmother used to make, this is straight-up Italian-American fare, meaning big flavors, arrived at in a straightforward fashion. It doesn't sound like much—the name just means veal meatballs in broth—but meatballs alone can be a treat, so this may surprise you with its charm, depth, and ability to satisfy. The meatballs are seasoned with Parmesan, parsley, mustard, and oregano, and the broth is a simple elevation of the store-bought stuff, infused with red pepper flakes, olive oil, and garlic. To me, this is what home tastes like, and I've found the same is true of most people, even if they don't share my ancestry.        SERVES 4

## nutritional information

| | |
|---|---|
| Calories | 335 |
| Fat | 24 g |
| Saturated Fat | 4 g |
| Trans Fat | 0 g |
| Total Carbohydrates | 7 g |
| Dietary Fiber | 1 g |
| Total Sugars | 1 g |
| Protein | 23 g |
| Cholesterol | 60 mg |
| Sodium | 281 mg |

## exchanges

| | |
|---|---|
| Fat | 4 |
| Lean Meat | 2 |
| Vegetables | 0.5 |

## INGREDIENTS

6 tablespoons olive oil

2 cloves garlic, minced, plus
  2 cloves, crushed and
  peeled

¼ cup diced Spanish onion

10 ounces ground veal

2 tablespoons dried bread
  crumbs

2 tablespoons grated Parmesan
  cheese, plus more for garnish
  (optional)

1½ tablespoons chopped fresh
  flat-leaf parsley leaves

1 large egg white

1 teaspoon Dijon mustard

¼ teaspoon chopped fresh oregano

Pinch of coarse salt

Pinch of freshly ground black
  pepper

2½ cups store-bought, low sodium
  chicken broth

¼ teaspoon crushed red pepper
  flakes

2 cups loosely packed escarole

1. Heat 1 tablespoon of the olive oil in a wide, deep, heavy-bottomed pan over medium-high heat. Add the minced garlic and the onion and cook until softened but not browned, about 4 minutes. Remove the pan from the heat and transfer the onion mixture to a large bowl. Let cool.

2. Add the veal, bread crumbs, Parmesan cheese, parsley, egg white, mustard, oregano, salt, and pepper to the bowl with the onion mixture. Using immaculately clean hands, knead everything together, then chill the meat mixture in the refrigerator for 20 to 30 minutes.

3. Put the chicken broth, 2 table- spoons of the olive oil, the crushed garlic, and red pepper flakes in a large pot and bring to a boil over high heat. Lower the heat until the liquid is simmering. Add the escarole to the pot and let simmer until wilted, about 1 minute, then remove the pot from the heat.

4. Shape the meat mixture into 16 small meatballs, each about 1 inch in diameter.

5. Heat 3 tablespoons of the remaining olive oil in a large, ovenproof, nonstick pan over medium-high heat until hot and shimmering. The pan should be large enough to hold all of the meatballs in a single layer.

Add the meatballs and cook just until nicely browned all over, only about 15 to 20 seconds per "side" (about 1½ minutes total); the meatballs will finish cooking in the broth.

**6.** Put 4 meatballs at the bottom of each of 4 soup bowls. Ladle the escarole soup over the meatballs and sprinkle with more Parmesan to taste, if desired. Serve immediately.

**variations and suggestions:** You can also form the meat mixture into 4 patties and grill them—do it quickly to avoid overcooking the lean meat. Serve the veal burgers with the following salad:

### INGREDIENTS

*1 English (seedless) cucumber, thinly sliced crosswise*

*½ medium-size red onion, thinly sliced*

*¼ cup extra-virgin olive oil*

*Juice of ½ lemon*

*¼ teaspoon coarse salt*

*¼ teaspoon freshly ground black pepper*

*1 tablespoon grated Parmesan*

*1 tablespoon chopped fresh flat-leaf parsley*

Put the cucumber, onion, olive oil, lemon juice, salt, pepper, Parmesan, and parsley in a bowl, toss, and serve.

**SERVES 4**

### A TIP FROM TOM

**WORKING WITH VEAL:** Be careful not to overcook the veal, which is naturally very lean. For a more traditional meatball, make them with one third ground veal, one third ground beef, and one third ground pork and brown them a bit longer.

# in this chapter

*"There's a lot here
that will do what any good sandwich does:
Put a smile on your face."*

# sandwiches, wraps, and quesadillas

**i**f you're wondering what a chapter on sandwiches, quesadillas, and wraps is doing in this book, the answer is that I did it for love. I've always loved sandwiches, for all the reasons most people do: They are, in many ways, the foods that inspire nostalgia, evoking fond memories of everything from brown-bag school lunches to outdoor picnics. They're also incredibly convenient: I've eaten sandwiches at restaurant staff meetings, in front of the television, behind the wheel of my car, and even walking down the street. If you're a busy person—and aren't we all?—sandwiches make life just a tad easier.

From a flavor and texture standpoint, sandwiches and their extended family of quesadillas, wraps, and burgers (all represented in the following pages) have one thing in common: They essentially force their respective, often disparate, ingredients together. One of their charms is that they put between two pieces of bread (on top of one slice in the case of an open-face) or within the confines of a tortilla or wrap, all the things that might normally be scattered over a plate—meat, vegetables, a sauce or condiment, and bread.

Of course, you won't find some of my all-time favorite sand-wiches here. There's no Italian combo or Ruben because they're way too fatty and salty for people like us. But there's a lot here that will do what any good sandwich does: Put a smile on your face, and make you happy to the core, even if you're eating them, literally, on the run.

**CARBOHYDRATE CHOICES: 1¹/₂; 1 ADJUSTED FOR FIBER**

# grilled portobello mushroom quesadillas

here's a vegetarian quesadilla that makes its mark with an enticing range of textures. You can riff on this theme by replacing the mozzarella with goat cheese and adding Roasted Garlic (page 321) and thyme—all classic mushroom accompaniments—to the filling. **SERVES 4**

## nutritional information
(PER SERVING)

| | |
|---|---|
| Calories | 253 |
| Fat | 10 g |
| Saturated Fat | 3 g |
| Trans Fat | 0 g |
| Total Carbohydrates | 23 g |
| Dietary Fiber | 11 g |
| Total Sugars | 6 g |
| Protein | 18 g |
| Cholesterol | 15 mg |
| Sodium | 158 mg |

## exchanges

| | |
|---|---|
| Fat | 1.5 |
| Starch | 1 |
| Vegetables | 2 |

## INGREDIENTS

*4 large portobello mushroom caps*

*1 teaspoon extra-virgin olive oil*

*Coarse salt*

*4 low-carb wraps*
  *(10 inches in diameter)*

*4 ounces fresh salt-free mozzarella,*
  *thinly sliced*

*8 fresh basil leaves, torn by hand*

*2 roasted red bell peppers, store-bought*
  *or homemade (page 324),*
  *thinly sliced*

1. Build a fire in a charcoal grill, letting the coals burn down until covered with white ash or preheat a gas grill to medium. If using a grill pan, preheat the pan briefly over medium-high heat.

2. Brush each mushroom cap with olive oil, season them with a pinch of salt, and grill until grill marks form and the mushrooms are tender, 4 to 5 minutes per side. Transfer the mushrooms to a plate and let cool. Leave the fire burning. When cool enough to handle, thinly slice the mushrooms.

3. Arrange the mushroom slices over the bottom half of each wrap. Top with the mozzarella, basil, and roasted pepper slices. Fold the top of the wraps over the filling.

4. Grill the wraps just long enough to warm the filling through and melt the cheese so it holds the quesadillas together, about 1 minute per side.

5. Put 1 quesadilla on each of 4 plates and serve.

variations and suggestions: You can smear Homemade Pesto (page 317) on the wraps instead of using fresh basil.

CARBOHYDRATE CHOICES: 3½ WITH BREAD (3 ADJUSTED FOR FIBER)

# mushroom burgers

there was a big "mushrooms-for-beef" restaurant trend a few years ago that found mushroom "burgers" and "steaks" on menus all over the land. It got a little out of hand, but now that it's died down we can appreciate the essential truth behind the fad: Mushrooms do, indeed, do a pretty good imitation of beef, especially if you amp up their flavor as we do here with onion, garlic, reduced wine and broth, and porcini mushroom powder. Try to include a mix of at least two different types of mushroom; this will add complexity to the patties.

I don't insist on bread here: You can serve the burgers on their own, wrapped in a lettuce leaf, or on a hamburger bun as I do with all the fixings. I like it open-face on 7-grain bread, for just enough of a "roll" effect. **SERVES 4**

## nutritional information

(PER SERVING WITH BREAD; WITHOUT GARNISHES)

| | |
|---|---|
| Calories | 380 |
| Fat | 11 g |
| Saturated Fat | 1 g |
| Trans Fat | 0 g |
| Total Carbohydrates | 53 g |
| Dietary Fiber | 5 g |
| Total Sugars | 7 g |
| Protein | 15 g |
| Cholesterol | 54 mg |
| Sodium | 983 mg |

## Exchanges

| | |
|---|---|
| Fat | 1.5 |
| Starch | 2.5 |
| Vegetables | 2 |

## INGREDIENTS

1½ large Spanish onions, minced (about 2 cups)

3 large cloves garlic, minced

2 tablespoons dry white wine

1 tablespoon distilled white vinegar

½ cup store-bought low-sodium chicken broth

1 pound assorted mushrooms, such as white button, oyster, and shiitake

1⅔ cups dry, unseasoned bread crumbs

1 large egg plus 1 large egg white, at room temperature

1 tablespoon fresh thyme leaves

2 teaspoons Porcini Powder (page 325)

1 teaspoon coarse salt

½ teaspoon freshly ground black pepper

2 tablespoons olive oil

4 slices 7-grain light bread, toasted

Optional garnishes: lettuce leaves, sliced tomato, sliced red onion

1. Heat a heavy-bottomed saucepan over medium heat and add the onions, garlic, white wine, and vinegar. Cook until the wine evaporates, then pour in the broth and bring to a simmer. Continue to simmer until the broth is reduced by about half, about 4 minutes. Remove the pan from the heat, set aside, and let cool.

2. Put the mushrooms in a food processor and pulse to a fine dice, but not so much that they turn to a paste.

3. Working in batches, put the diced mushrooms in a nonstick pan and cook, stirring with a rubber spatula, over medium heat until dry but not scorched, 3 to 4 minutes. Put the cooked, diced mushrooms in a large mixing bowl; add the onion and garlic mixture and the bread crumbs, egg and egg white, thyme, Porcini Powder, salt, and pepper. Stir until well incorporated. Divide the mushroom mixture into 4 equal portions and shape each one into a patty. Set aside on a plate for 10 to 12 minutes.

4. Heat 1 tablespoon of the olive oil in a wide, deep, heavy-bottomed nonstick pan over medium-high heat. Add 2 patties to the pan and cook until browned and beginning to crisp, 3 to 4 minutes per side. Repeat with the remaining 1 tablespoon of oil and patties. You can also cook all 4 patties in 2 pans simultaneously.

5. Serve the mushroom burgers on the bread slices and with lettuce, tomato, and red onion, if desired.

**CARBOHYDRATE CHOICES: 1½; 1 ADJUSTED FOR FIBER**

# swiss, avocado, and sprouts sandwiches

t he ingredients in this sandwich come together as they do in few sandwiches I know, largely thanks to the tahini dressing. If you like warm sandwiches, heat these in a low oven for a few minutes or one at a time in a toaster oven for about ten seconds at high heat: The Swiss cheese will melt slightly and all of the flavors will be even more fully integrated when you eat the sandwich.    **SERVES 4**

## nutritional information
### (PER SERVING)

Calories ...................... 266
Fat ............................. 17 g
   Saturated Fat ........... 4 g
   Trans Fat ................. 0 g
Total Carbohydrates ... 22 g
   Dietary Fiber ............ 7 g
   Total Sugars ............. 3 g
Protein ...................... 11 g
Cholesterol ............... 12 mg
Sodium .................. 467 mg

## Exchanges

Fat ............................. 2.5
Starch ......................... 1
Medium Fat Milk .......... 0.5
Vegetables ................. 0.5

---

### INGREDIENTS

8 slices multigrain bread, toasted

2 tablespoons plus 2 teaspoons
   Tahini Dressing (page 314)

4 thin slices Swiss cheese
   (about ½ ounce each)

1 medium-size Hass avocado, halved,
   pitted, and very thinly sliced

2 plum tomatoes, seeded and
   thinly sliced crosswise

4 thin slices Spanish onion

4 cups loosely packed alfalfa
   sprouts

Pinch of coarse salt

---

1. Arrange 4 slices of the toast on a work surface and spread half of the Tahini Dressing over them. Top each piece of toast with 1 slice of Swiss cheese, one quarter of the avocado, one quarter of the tomato, 1 slice of the onion, one quarter of the sprouts, and a pinch of salt.

2. Spread the remaining dressing on the remaining 4 slices of toast and invert them onto the sandwiches. Press down gently on each sandwich, cut it in half diagonally, and serve.

variations and suggestions: Sliced turkey gets along great with the ingredients in these sandwiches.

## nutritional information
### (PER SERVING)

Calories......................355
Fat.............................25 g
   Saturated Fat...........5 g
   Trans Fat.................0 g
Total Carbohydrates...25 g
   Dietary Fiber...........16 g
   Total Sugars.............3 g
Protein......................13 g
Cholesterol..............15 mg
Sodium..................329 mg

## exchanges

Fat.............................3.5
Starch...........................1
High Fat Meat..............0.5
Vegetables..................0.5

**CARBOHYDRATE CHOICES: 1½; 1 ADJUSTED FOR FIBER**

# avocado, jack cheese, tomato, and red onion quesadillas

i don't do a lot of vegetarian cooking, but I have dabbled in it enough to have developed a philosophy: Bringing a wide range of textures to the plate is essential when there's no meat to be found. In this case, the creamy avocado, molten cheese, crunchy onion, and crisp grilled tortilla keep the palate so occupied that it barely has time to notice the absence of poultry or beef. Of course, none of that would matter if the combination of flavors didn't deliver the goods in the first place and, fortunately, it does. **SERVES 4**

## INGREDIENTS

1 small red onion, cut into thick slices

1 tablespoon olive oil

2 ounces pepper Jack cheese, thinly sliced with an old-fashioned cheese slicer

4 low-carb wraps (10 inches in diameter)

2 Hass avocados, halved, pitted, and very thinly sliced

1 small plum tomato, seeded and very thinly sliced

¼ cup plus 2 tablespoons pickled jalapeño pepper, drained

1. Build a fire in a charcoal grill, letting the coals burn down until covered with white ash or preheat a gas grill to medium. If using a grill pan, preheat the pan briefly over medium-high heat.

2. Brush the onion slices with some of the olive oil. Set them on the grill and grill until lightly charred and slightly softened, about 3 minutes per side. Set the onion aside and let cool, then coarsely chop it. Leave the fire burning.

3. Arrange a slice of pepper Jack on the bottom half of 1 wrap. Top with overlapping slices of avocado, then

tomato, chopped onion, jalapeño, and more cheese. Fold the top half of the wrap over the filling. Brush the outside of the wrap lightly with some of the remaining olive oil. Repeat with the remaining wraps and fillings.

**4.** Grill the quesadillas until golden brown on both sides and the cheese is melted, gooey, and holds the quesadillas together, about 3 minutes per side.

**5.** Serve each quesadilla whole on its own plate or slice each crosswise into 3 pieces.

**variations and suggestions:** For a nonvegetarian option, use this recipe as a guideline to make a chicken, turkey bacon, and white cheddar quesadilla, adding an ounce of hand-shredded, leftover roasted or poached chicken and 1 slice of crisp, cooked turkey bacon to each sandwich and replacing the pepper Jack cheese with white cheddar.

CARBOHYDRATE CHOICES: 2

# clts

## (CRAB, LETTUCE, AND TOMATO SANDWICHES)

this was originally conceived as a soft-shell crab BLT, but when the crab came off the grill crunchy and slightly smoky, I realized that the bacon would be completely superfluous. The mayonnaise and mustard dressing does double duty here, first smeared on the bread, then diluted with hot water and drizzled over the open-face sandwich as a sauce.

**SERVES 4**

### INGREDIENTS

¼ cup canola oil

4 soft-shelled crabs (about 3 ounces each), cleaned (see this page)

4 slices country bread

3 tablespoons full-fat mayonnaise

3 tablespoons Dijon mustard

8 leaves Boston or Bibb lettuce

8 slices beefsteak tomato

A TIP FROM TOM

**CLEANING SOFT-SHELL CRABS:** This will sound like I'm kidding, but I'm not: The easiest way to clean soft-shell crabs is to have your fishmonger do it for you. However, it's not difficult to clean soft-shells yourself: Use a pair of kitchen shears to cut across the body, removing the eyes and mouth. Reach into the opening and pull out the small sack inside. Turn the crab over, belly-down on the work surface, lift the soft shell and remove the feathery gills underneath. Finally, pull away the armorlike "apron" and discard it.

## nutritional information

Calories......................368
Fat.............................20 g
   Saturated Fat...........2 g
   Trans Fat..................0 g
Total Carbohydrates...27 g
   Dietary Fiber.............2 g
   Total Sugars.............4 g
Protein.......................19 g
Cholesterol..............69 mg
Sodium...................842 mg

## exchanges

Fat................................3.5
Starch...........................1.5
Lean Meat.....................1.5
Vegetables....................0.5

## how low can you go?

To lower the carbohydrates, you can leave out the bun and serve this as a lobster salad, adding greens and serving some crackers alongside.

1. Heat the oil in a heavy-bottomed pan over medium-high heat. Add the crabs, top side down, and cook until nicely browned and crisp, about 1 minute. Turn the crabs over and cook on the other side for about 1 minute.

2. Toast or grill the bread with no butter or oil, until lightly browned on both sides.

3. Put the mayonnaise and mustard in a small bowl and whisk them together.

4. To serve, smear some mayonnaise and mustard dressing over each piece of bread. Top each slice with a crab, 2 leaves of lettuce, and 2 tomato slices. Place 1 sandwich on each of 4 plates. Whisk 1 tablespoon of hot water into the remaining dressing and drizzle it over and around the sandwich on each plate.

**CARBOHYDRATE CHOICES: 1½**

# lobster rolls

there are a number of ways of making a lobster roll: The two most popular are serving big pieces of the crustacean brushed with hot butter or cooling it, chopping it, and dressing it with lots of mayonnaise and celery. The cold version we offer here uses a minimum of mayonnaise, augmenting it with lots of lemon juice, and the celery flavor is deepened by the addition of celery salt and celery seed. The result is a sandwich more refreshing than the original, maybe even better suited to the hot summer days for which it was created in the first place.

**SERVES 4**

## INGREDIENTS

2 live lobsters (1½ pounds each)

3 tablespoons freshly squeezed
   lemon juice

1 tablespoon reduced fat
   mayonnaise

2 ribs celery, finely diced, plus
   pale yellow leaves from a
   bunch of celery, for garnish

⅛ teaspoon celery seed

⅛ teaspoon celery salt

4 hot dog buns

1. Bring a large stockpot full of water to a boil over high heat. Add the lobsters to the boiling water and cook until the shells turn bright red, 6 minutes. Remove the pot from the heat and let the lobsters sit in the pot for about 90 seconds.

2. Fill a large bowl halfway with ice water. Using tongs, remove the lobsters from the pot and immerse them in the ice water.

3. Once they have cooled, drain the water. Take the head of one lobster in one hand and the tail in the other and twist them in opposite directions until the upper and lower halves come apart. Using a large, heavy knife, split the lobster tail in half lengthwise. Remove the meat from the body of the lobster. Crack the claws and remove the meat from within. Cut the lobster meat into 1-inch dice and set it aside. Remove and discard the gray-green tomalley (liver) and red roe (if any) along with the shells. Repeat with the remaining lobster. (The lobster meat can be refrigerated in an airtight container for up to 24 hours before making the rolls. Let come to room temperature before proceeding.)

4. Put the lemon juice and mayonnaise in a bowl and whisk them together. Add the diced lobster, celery, celery seed, and celery salt. Stir together gently, cover with plastic wrap, and refrigerate to chill for at least 1 hour and up to 4 hours.

5. To serve, open the hot dog buns and toast or grill the insides. Put 1 bun on each of 4 plates and press the rolls open. Pile the lobster mixture on top, scatter the celery leaves over the sandwiches, and serve.

**variations and suggestions:** If you are pressed for time, or if lobster is a bit of an indulgence for you, this can also be made with crab or shrimp.

## nutritional information
(PER SERVING)

| | |
|---|---|
| Calories | 200 |
| Fat | 3 g |
| Saturated Fat | 1 g |
| Trans Fat | 0 g |
| Total Carbohydrates | 24 g |
| Dietary Fiber | 1 g |
| Total Sugars | 4 g |
| Protein | 18 g |
| Cholesterol | 71 mg |
| Sodium | 508 mg |

## exchanges

| | |
|---|---|
| Starch | 1.5 |
| Lean Meat | 1.5 |

## how low can you go?

For lower fat and calories, omit the pesto and coarsely chop and scatter the basil over the sandwich.

## nutritional information
(PER SERVING)

| | |
|---|---|
| Calories | 279 |
| Fat | 17 g |
| Saturated Fat | 5 g |
| Trans Fat | 0 g |
| Total Carbohydrates | 16 g |
| Dietary Fiber | 3 g |
| Total Sugars | 5 g |
| Protein | 14 g |
| Cholesterol | 23 mg |
| Sodium | 431 mg |

## exchanges

| | |
|---|---|
| Fat | 3 |
| Starch | 0.5 |
| Very Lean Meat | 1 |
| Medium Fat Meat | 0.5 |
| Vegetables | 1 |

CARBOHYDRATE CHOICE: 1

# open-face smoked salmon and basil sandwiches

In this sandwich, the thin slices of smoked salmon function more like a cold cut than a piece of fish, the pesto stands in for a condiment like mustard or mayonnaise, and the fresh basil replaces the greens—the textures and format are very familiar, but the flavors are fresh and unexpected.

SERVES 4

## INGREDIENTS

¼ cup Homemade Pesto (page 317)

4 thin slices pumpernickel bread, toasted

2 roasted red bell peppers, store-bought or homemade (page 324), cut into 4 slices each

3 ounces fresh mozzarella, thinly sliced

4 ounces thinly sliced smoked salmon

12 fresh basil leaves

Spread the Pesto on each of the bread slices. Place 1 slice of bread on each of 4 plates. Top each with slices of pepper, then the mozzarella. Drape some salmon over the cheese on each plate. Garnish each sandwich with 3 basil leaves and serve.

CARBOHYDRATE CHOICE: 1; ½ ADJUSTED FOR FIBER

# fresh tuna salad wraps

this is another popular staff meal served at Ouest. If you're used to tuna salad made with canned fish, the fresh flavor of this one will be a revelation. For a more healthful option, omit the wraps and spoon some of the salad in each lettuce leaf, roll it up, and eat. **SERVES 4**

## INGREDIENTS

8 ounces fresh tuna

2 teaspoons freshly squeezed lemon juice

Pinch of coarse salt

Pinch of freshly ground black pepper

2 tablespoons olive oil

½ medium-size red bell pepper, stemmed, seeded, and finely diced

½ medium-size green bell pepper, stemmed, seeded, and finely diced

½ medium-size yellow bell pepper, stemmed, seeded, and finely diced

½ small red onion, finely diced

4 low-carb wraps (10 inches in diameter)

Lettuce leaves (optional), for serving

1. Preheat the oven to 350°F.

2. Put the tuna in a small baking dish and sprinkle the lemon juice over it. Season the tuna with the salt and pepper. Bake the tuna until cooked through, about 15 minutes.

3. While the tuna is baking, heat the olive oil in a medium-size, heavy-bottomed pan over medium-high heat. Add the red, green, and yellow bell peppers and the onion to the pan and cook until softened but not browned, about 5 minutes. Transfer the peppers and onions to a bowl and let cool.

4. Remove the tuna from the oven, let it cool, then flake it into the bowl with the vegetables and toss. Divide the tuna salad evenly among the 4 wraps. Roll up the wraps, tucking in the ends to seal the filling, and serve.

**variations and suggestions:** You can also add chopped cherry peppers for heat or add a drizzle of Parsley Puree (page 316).

## nutritional information
(PER SERVING OF SALAD)

| | |
|---|---|
| Calories | 257 |
| Fat | 12 g |
| Saturated Fat | 2 g |
| Trans Fat | 0 g |
| Total Carbohydrates | 17 g |
| Dietary Fiber | 9 g |
| Total Sugars | 2 g |
| Protein | 21 g |
| Cholesterol | 22 mg |
| Sodium | 169 mg |

## exchanges

| | |
|---|---|
| Fat | 1.5 |
| Starch | 1 |
| Lean Meat | 2 |
| Vegetables | 0.5 |

## plan ahead

The tuna salad can be refrigerated in an airtight container for up to 24 hours.

**CARBOHYDRATE CHOICES: 2; 1 ADJUSTED FOR FIBER**

# southwestern chicken and avocado wraps

This wrap achieves a Southwestern effect by tossing cubed, breaded chicken with many of the signature ingredients of that region such as avocado, tomato, and cumin. Feel free to add anything you might roll into a burrito—hot chiles, sour cream, or shredded cheese. **SERVES 4**

## nutritional information
**(PER SERVING)**

Calories................................379
Fat..........................................17 g
   Saturated Fat.................2 g
   Trans Fat.......................0 g
Total Carbohydrates....27 g
   Dietary Fiber...............11 g
   Total Sugars..................2 g
Protein...................................30 g
Cholesterol........................49 mg
Sodium..............................323 mg

## exchanges

Fat..........................................2.5
Starch....................................1.5
Lean Meat................................2

### INGREDIENTS

½ cup dry, unseasoned bread
   crumbs

1 large egg white beaten with
   1 tablespoon cold water

2 skinless, boneless chicken breast
   halves (about 6 ounces each)

1 tablespoon canola oil

½ large Hass avocado

1 tablespoon extra-virgin olive oil

1 tablespoon freshly squeezed
   lemon juice

½ plum tomato, seeded and diced

½ teaspoon ground cumin

Coarse salt and freshly ground
   black pepper

4 low-carb wraps
   (10 inches in diameter)

**1.** Put the bread crumbs on a plate. Pour the egg white-water mixture into a wide, shallow bowl. One at a time, dip the chicken in the egg mixture, letting any excess drip off, then dredge in the bread crumbs pressing down just firmly enough for the crumbs to adhere.

**2.** Heat the oil in a large, nonstick pan over medium-high heat. Add the chicken and cook until golden on both sides and cooked through, about 5 minutes per side. Transfer the chicken to a cutting board and let it cool.

**3.** Meanwhile, cut the avocado in half and remove the pit and peel. Dice the avocado.

**4.** When cool enough to handle, cut the chicken into ½-inch dice. Put the diced chicken in a bowl. Add the avocado, olive oil, lemon juice, tomato, and cumin. Stir to mix well, then season with a pinch of salt and pepper.

**5.** Divide the chicken mixture evenly among the 4 wraps. Roll up the wraps, tucking in the ends to seal in the filling, and serve.

CARBOHYDRATE CHOICES: 1 ½

# turkey burgers

lower in fat than their beef counterparts, turkey burgers are a popular alternative that might be even more popular if they didn't have such a tendency to dry out when cooked. (Part of the challenge is that, unlike beef, turkey cannot be served rare or even medium-rare due to salmonella concerns.) The burgers here are less apt to dry out thanks to the oil and soy sauce. Serve these with such traditional burger garnishes as lettuce (or arugula), grilled red onion, and sliced cheese. **SERVES 4**

## INGREDIENTS

1 pound lean ground turkey

¼ cup dry, unseasoned bread crumbs

3 tablespoons minced Spanish onion

2 tablespoons canola oil

1 tablespoon chopped fresh flat-leaf parsley leaves

2 teaspoons minced garlic

1 teaspoon low-sodium soy sauce

½ teaspoon coarse salt

¼ teaspoon freshly ground black pepper

8 slices 7-grain light bread, toasted

Optional garnishes: lettuce leaves or arugula, grilled red onion, sliced cheese

## nutritional information

(PER SERVING WITH 2 SLICES BREAD; WITHOUT GARNISH)

| | |
|---|---|
| Calories | 363 |
| Fat | 18 g |
| Saturated Fat | 3 g |
| Trans Fat | 0 g |
| Total Carbohydrates | 24 g |
| Dietary Fiber | 2 g |
| Total Sugars | 3 g |
| Protein | 25 g |
| Cholesterol | 90 mg |
| Sodium | 623 mg |

## exchanges

| | |
|---|---|
| Fat | 2.5 |
| Starch | 1.5 |
| Lean Meat | 3 |

## shop right

**PURCHASING GROUND TURKEY:** Pay attention to the packaging of ground turkey to make sure you're getting the same quality of meat you usually insist on, be it organic, antibiotic free, or whatever other modifier is important to you. At home, I purchase boneless poultry, grind it myself in a food processor, and freeze it in resealable plastic bags. (If you wish to do the same, pulse the processor just until the turkey is ground but do not overprocess it.)

1. Put the turkey, bread crumbs, onion, oil, parsley, garlic, soy sauce, salt, and pepper in a large bowl and knead them together. Form into 4 patties. Wrap the patties with plastic wrap and refrigerate for 1 to 2 hours to develop the flavor and give them a chance to set.

2. Build a fire in a charcoal grill, letting the coals burn down until covered with white ash or preheat a gas grill to medium. If using a grill pan, preheat the pan briefly over medium-high heat.

3. Grill the patties until cooked through, 4 to 5 minutes per side. Let the burgers rest for 2 to 3 minutes before serving on the bread with your choice of garnishes.

**CARBOHYDRATE CHOICE: 1; ½ ADJUSTED FOR FIBER**

# grilled beef and goat cheese quesadillas

there's no particular cut of beef specified in the ingredient list for this recipe, and that's by design. This is meant to be as casual or upscale as you'd like. Grilled on their own and then again inside the quesadillas, flank or hangar steak will come through just fine here, but a New York strip or rib eye would elevate this to another level. It's a great way to use leftover meat from that steak house dinner you had the night before. And, it's also a very flexible recipe; for instance, you can use the same quantities of meat and cheese to make, say, a sausage and mozzarella quesadilla.      **SERVES 4**

## INGREDIENTS

*6 ounces beefsteak of your choice for grilling*

*2 tablespoons olive oil*

*Coarse salt and freshly ground black pepper*

*1 medium-size red onion, cut crosswise into 1-inch slices*

*4 low-carb tortillas (8 inches in diameter)*

*4 ounces goat cheese*

*1 roasted red bell pepper, store-bought or homemade (page 324), sliced*

1. Build a fire in a charcoal grill, letting the coals burn down until covered with white ash or preheat a gas grill to medium. If using a grill pan, preheat the pan briefly over medium-high heat.

2. Brush the beef with some of the olive oil and season it with a pinch of salt and pepper. Grill the meat until nicely charred and cooked to medium-rare, about 5 minutes on each side. Transfer to a cutting board and let rest for 5 minutes. Leave the fire burning.

3. While the beef is cooking brush the onion slices with some of the olive oil. Once the beef is off the grill and resting, place the onion slices on the grill and grill until lightly charred and slightly softened, about 3 minutes per side. Transfer the grilled onion to the cutting board.

4. Thinly slice the beef across the grain. Coarsely chop the onion. Arrange some beef slices in an overlapping pattern on the bottom half of a tortilla. Layer one quarter of the goat cheese on top, then one quarter of the red pepper and the chopped onion. Fold the top half of the tortilla over the filling and brush it lightly with some of the remaining olive oil. Repeat with the remaining tortillas and fillings.

5. Grill the quesadillas until golden brown on both sides and the cheese is melted, gooey, and holds the quesadillas together, about 3 minutes per side.

6. Serve each quesadilla whole on its own plate or slice each crosswise into 3 pieces.

## nutritional information
(PER SERVING)

| | |
|---|---|
| Calories | 377 |
| Fat | 22 g |
| Saturated Fat | 9 g |
| Trans Fat | 0 g |
| Total Carbohydrates | 19 g |
| Dietary Fiber | 9 g |
| Total Sugars | 4 g |
| Protein | 26 g |
| Cholesterol | 44 mg |
| Sodium | 269 mg |

## exchanges

| | |
|---|---|
| Fat | 1.5 |
| Starch | 1 |
| Lean Meat | 1.5 |
| High Fat Meat | 1 |
| Vegetables | 1 |

# steak house sandwich wraps

a steak house experience in the confines of a wrap; here's grilled filet mignon and a tomato and onion salad all rolled into one. While we're making a steak sandwich, why not borrow from Philadelphia and add a little cheese, in this case smoked mozzarella?   SERVES 4

## nutritional information
### (PER SERVING)

| | |
|---|---|
| Calories | 358 |
| Fat | 15 g |
| Saturated Fat | 3 g |
| Trans Fat | 0 g |
| Total Carbohydrates | 20 g |
| Dietary Fiber | 9 g |
| Total Sugars | 4 g |
| Protein | 35 g |
| Cholesterol | 60 mg |
| Sodium | 621 mg |

## exchanges

| | |
|---|---|
| Fat | 1.5 |
| Starch | 1 |
| Lean Meat | 3.5 |
| Vegetables | 0.5 |

## INGREDIENTS

12 ounces filet mignon in one piece

2 tablespoons canola oil

Pinch of coarse salt

Freshly ground black pepper

2 plum tomatoes, seeded and
   cut into thick slices

1 small red onion, cut into thick slices

4 low-carb wraps
   (10 inches in diameter)

2 tablespoons Dijon mustard

2 tablespoons prepared horseradish

4 ounces salt-free smoked mozzarella,
   cut into thin slices

2 cups loosely packed arugula

1. Build a fire in a charcoal grill, letting the coals burn down until covered with white ash or preheat a gas grill to medium. If using a grill pan, preheat the pan briefly over medium-high heat.

2. Rub the filet mignon with 1 tablespoon of the oil and season it with a pinch of salt and the pepper. Grill the filet mignon until nicely charred on both sides, 3 to 4 minutes per side for medium-rare. Let rest for 5 minutes. Leave the fire burning.

3. Meanwhile, rub the tomato and onion slices with the remaining oil and grill until nicely charred on both sides, about 2 minutes per side for the tomato and 3 minutes per side for the onion.

4. Slice the filet mignon in half the long way (through the thickness), then slice each half into thin slices. Place 1 wrap on a work surface. Spread it with one quarter of the mustard and horseradish. Arrange one quarter of the beef about 1 inch

from the edge closest to you. Arrange one quarter of the cheese in overlapping slices over the meat. Top with one quarter of the onion and tomato slices and the arugula. Folding in the outer edges, roll the wrap up tautly to make a fully encased, burritolike wrap. Repeat with the remaining wraps and ingredients. Cut the wraps in half crosswise and serve.

**A TIP FROM TOM**

**HOT ENOUGH?:** To determine if a charcoal grill is ready for cooking, use what's commonly referred to as the five-second test: Hold your hand about five inches over the grate. If you can keep it there for just five seconds before it becomes too hot, the grill is ready to go. If you can keep it there for only a few seconds, it's too hot and you should let the coals burn down a bit more and test again.

# in this chapter

*"They are emotional touchstones
that take me
back to a time and place."*

# pasta and risotto

ever since it first came into use, I've always felt a connection to the phrase comfort food, and was quite tickled when critics began using various adaptations of it, such as "elegant comfort food," to describe the style of my cooking at Ouest.

As far as I'm concerned, the ultimate comfort foods are pasta and risotto. Because I come from an Italian-American family, these dishes were part of the fabric of my everyday life growing up, and eating them as an adult always

meant more than physical nourishment: They are emotional touchstones that take me back to a time and a place. So when I was diagnosed with diabetes, pasta was at the forefront of my mind. How could it be that I couldn't touch these memories anymore? It's no understatement to say that I thought my life would be substantially diminished without them.

The answer to my quandary, as is the case with so many diabetes-related crossroads, was moderation. Instead of a heaping portion of pasta, I began to eat more modest amounts. The irony of course is that this is how pasta and risotto are consumed back in my ancestral home of Italy—serving sizes that would be considered paltry here are the norm over there, and pasta is most often served as a middle course, a bridge between the antipasti (literally, before pasta) and the main course.

Over time, I also began increasing the ratio of vegetables, seafood, and meat. Where there had previously been proportionately more pasta and rice, there was now more of the other stuff. It's not exactly what I was used to all my life, but I've come to love it just the same, and I hope you'll find that the following recipes meet any longings you might harbor in your own heart and appetite.

One last note: Because any amount of true pasta or rice carries with it an inescapable carbohydrate content, these recipes are scaled to serve six people rather than four. They are actually the perfect size for a pasta midcourse in a meal, and you might be surprised how filling they are paired with just a small salad or some steamed or sautéed green vegetables.

## did you know?

The mixture of bread crumbs, parsley, and lemon zest in this recipe is called a *gremolata,* and it's used to finish certain Italian dishes, especially rich, heavy ones that can really use the relief of fragrant citrus. You can also make *gremolata* with orange or lime zest. Use it to top braised meats or anything you feel would benefit from a fresh burst of flavor.

CARBOHYDRATE CHOICES: 2½

# rigatoni

## WITH CAULIFLOWER AND BLACK PEPPER

a pasta served by restaurateur Pino Luongo triggered this recipe. It was a clever dish of rigatoni sauced with cauliflower that had been cooked until it was falling apart, then combined with bread crumbs and black pepper. Here I cut down on the amount of pasta, include more cauliflower, and top it with a *gremolata,* a mix of bread crumbs, parsley, and lemon zest that perks up all the flavors (see this page).  SERVES 6

**INGREDIENTS**

¼ cup plus 2 teaspoons dry,
    unseasoned bread crumbs

2 teaspoons chopped fresh flat-leaf
    parsley leaves

1 teaspoon finely grated lemon zest

8 ounces rigatoni or mezzi rigatoni
    (½ of a 1-pound box)

1 teaspoon coarse salt

1 pound cauliflower, broken into
    medium-size florets

¼ cup olive oil

2 tablespoons minced garlic

¼ cup freshly grated Parmesan
    cheese

Pinch of crushed red pepper flakes

Pinch of freshly ground black pepper

1. Put the bread crumbs in a heavy-bottomed pan and toast over low heat, shaking the pan to prevent scorching, until lightly browned, 2 to 3 minutes. Let the bread crumbs cool, then transfer 2 teaspoons of them to a small bowl. Add the parsley and lemon zest and stir together to make a *gremolata*. Set the *gremolata* and the remaining ¼ cup of plain toasted bread crumbs aside separately.

2. Bring a large pot of water to a boil over high heat. Add the rigatoni, and let boil until al dente, about 12 minutes.

3. Meanwhile, put the cauliflower in a pot and add just enough water to almost cover the florets. Add the salt, bring to a simmer, and let simmer until the florets are tender when pierced with a knife, about 8 minutes. The rigatoni and cauliflower should finish cooking at about the same time.

4. Drain the rigatoni in a colander over the sink and set it aside. Drain the cauliflower over a pot and set aside the cooking liquid. Transfer about half of the cauliflower to a cutting board and finely chop it.

5. Heat the olive oil in a wide, deep, heavy-bottomed pan over medium-high heat. Add the garlic and cook until softened but not browned, about 2 minutes. Add the chopped and whole cauliflower florets to the pan and cook until the cauliflower just begins to brown at the edges, about 3 minutes. Pour in ½ cup of the reserved cooking liquid and cook, stirring, until the cauliflower begins to look like a loose sauce, about 2 minutes. Add the Parmesan cheese, the ¼ cup reserved toasted bread

## nutritional information
(PER SERVING)

| | |
|---|---|
| Calories | 294 |
| Fat | 12 g |
| Saturated Fat | 2 g |
| Trans Fat | 0 g |
| Total Carbohydrates | 36 g |
| Dietary Fiber | 3 g |
| Total Sugars | 3 g |
| Protein | 9 g |
| Cholesterol | 3 mg |
| Sodium | 467 mg |

## exchanges

| | |
|---|---|
| Fat | 2 |
| Starch | 2 |
| Lean Meat | 0.5 |
| Vegetables | 1 |

## shop right

**MEZZI RIGATONI:**
This is a smaller variety of rigatoni with the same ribbed surface and straight cut ends as its big brother.

crumbs, and the rigatoni and toss well. Season the rigatoni with the red pepper flakes and black pepper and toss again.

6. Divide the rigatoni among 6 shallow bowls and top each serving with some of the *gremolata*. Serve.

## nutritional information

**(PER SERVING)**

| | |
|---|---|
| Calories | 307 |
| Fat | 16 g |
| Saturated Fat | 3 g |
| Trans Fat | 0 g |
| Total Carbohydrates | 33 g |
| Dietary Fiber | 6 g |
| Total Sugars | 3 g |
| Protein | 10 g |
| Cholesterol | 4 mg |
| Sodium | 582 mg |

## exchanges

| | |
|---|---|
| Fat | 3 |
| Starch | 1.5 |
| Vegetables | 1 |

**CARBOHYDRATE CHOICES: 2**

# whole wheat spaghetti

## WITH MUSHROOMS AND THYME

i don't eat whole wheat pasta for the health benefits, but I do sometimes turn to it for its earthy flavor and alluring amber color. This distinctly autumnal dish is a case in point: The almost toasty quality of the spaghetti has so much natural affinity for the mushrooms that not much else is called for here. In fact, the "sauce" is created simply by cooking the mushrooms in some chicken stock.

**SERVES 6**

### INGREDIENTS

8 ounces whole wheat spaghetti
    (½ of a 1-pound box)
¼ cup plus 2 tablespoons extra-virgin
    olive oil
4 cloves garlic, minced
1 pound white button or cremini
    mushrooms, stems trimmed,
    thinly sliced

1 tablespoon plus 1 teaspoon fresh
    thyme leaves
2 teaspoons coarse salt
1 cup store-bought low-sodium
    chicken broth
¼ cup freshly grated Parmesan cheese
2 teaspoons Porcini Powder (page 325)
¼ cup torn fresh basil leaves

1. Bring a large pot of water to a boil over high heat. Add the spaghetti and let boil until al dente, about 8 minutes.

2. Meanwhile, heat the ¼ cup of extra-virgin olive oil in a wide, deep, heavy-bottomed pan over medium heat. Add the garlic and cook, with-

out browning, for 2 minutes. Add the mushrooms, thyme, and salt, stir, and cook for 1 minute. Add the chicken broth, increase the heat to high, and bring to a simmer. Lower the heat, and let the mushrooms simmer until slightly softened, about 5 minutes.

3. By now, the spaghetti should be done. Set aside ½ cup of the spaghetti cooking liquid in a heatproof container, then drain the spaghetti in a colander. Add the spaghetti to the pan with the mushrooms. Add the reserved spaghetti cooking liquid, Parmesan cheese, remaining 2 tablespoons of olive oil, and the Porcini Powder and basil. Toss well. Divide the spaghetti among 6 shallow bowls and serve.

variations and suggestions: You can use other kinds of mushrooms here, but remove them after they are just sautéed, then add them back at the end; they won't survive a long cooking process as well as button or cremini mushrooms.

CARBOHYDRATE CHOICE: 1

# fresh fettuccine

## WITH ASPARAGUS, PARMESAN, AND BLACK PEPPER

When you finish making this dish, you might think that something was wrong with the recipe: Surely a diabetic can't eat this much pasta? You'd be wrong—and right. A diabetic can't eat as much pasta as this seems to produce, but it's not as much pasta as it appears; in fact, there's less pasta here than in any other recipe in this chapter. The balance is made up by thinly shaved asparagus that's tossed with the fettuccine, Parmesan cheese, and black pepper. The result is a relatively light, healthful pasta dish and one of the ultimate character witnesses for the power of suggestion: Serve this to friends and family and they'll be as satisfied as if there actually were that much pasta. **SERVES 6**

## nutritional information
(PER SERVING)

| | |
|---|---|
| Calories | 137 |
| Fat | 5 g |
| Saturated Fat | 3 g |
| Trans Fat | 0 g |
| Total Carbohydrates | 18 g |
| Dietary Fiber | 2 g |
| Total Sugars | 1 g |
| Protein | 5 g |
| Cholesterol | 29 mg |
| Sodium | 126 mg |

## exchanges

| | |
|---|---|
| Fat | 1 |
| Starch | 1 |
| Vegetables | 0.5 |

## INGREDIENTS

12 spears jumbo asparagus
   (about 1 pound) ends trimmed
¼ teaspoon coarse salt
6 ounces fresh fettuccine
2 tablespoons unsalted butter
1 tablespoon freshly squeezed
   lemon juice

1 small clove garlic, minced
2 tablespoon freshly grated
   Parmesan cheese
1 teaspoon freshly ground black pepper
⅓ teaspoon finely grated lemon
   zest
1 tablespoon minced fresh chives

1. Trim the tips off the asparagus spears and set them aside for another use. Using a vegetable peeler, thinly shave the asparagus lengthwise into wide ribbons. Set the asparagus aside.

2. Bring a large pot of water to a boil over high heat. Add the salt, then the fettuccine, and let boil until done but still a little toothsome, about 3 minutes.

3. Meanwhile, heat ½ cup of water in a wide, deep, heavy-bottomed pan over medium-high heat. Swirl in the butter, to melt it, then add the lemon juice and garlic.

4. Drain the fettuccine and add it to the pan along with the asparagus, Parmesan cheese, black pepper, and lemon zest. Cook, stirring, for 1 minute. Add the chives and stir again. Divide the fettuccine and asparagus among 6 dinner plates or wide, shallow bowls and serve.

*Fresh Fettuccine with Asparagus, Parmesan & Black Pepper*

CARBOHYDRATE CHOICES: 2½

# spicy seafood pasta

I have a special fondness for dishes that transform as you eat them, and this is a perfect example. Once you've devoured some of the pasta, you're essentially left with a spicy seafood soup that—because the noodles are so small—can and should be eaten with a spoon. That means that this recipe is also very flexible; if you start with a bit less pasta, you can serve it as a soup right off the bat.

**SERVES 6**

## INGREDIENTS

3 tablespoons olive oil

4 cloves garlic, thinly sliced

1 small carrot, diced

½ medium-size Spanish onion, diced

⅓ cup tomato paste

⅔ cup dry white wine, plus ½ cup dry white wine

½ cup bottled clam juice

2 tablespoons distilled white vinegar

1 can (35 ounces) peeled whole tomatoes

½ teaspoon coarse salt

⅛ teaspoon freshly ground black pepper

1 teaspoon crushed red pepper flakes

Pinch of saffron

1 bay leaf, preferably fresh

8 ounces tubetti or other small tube pasta or shells (½ of a 1-pound box)

12 ounces mussels (about 12), scrubbed under cold running water and bearded (see Note)

8 ounces Manila clams (about 12), scrubbed under cold running water

4 large shrimp (about 1 ounce each) peeled, deveined, and cut in half lengthwise

4 ounces sea scallops (about 4) cut into quarters

¼ cup chopped fresh flat-leaf parsley leaves

¼ cup freshly grated Parmesan cheese

1. Heat 2 tablespoons of the olive oil in a large, heavy-bottomed saucepan over medium heat. Add half of the garlic, all of the carrot, and all of the onion to the pot and cook until softened but not browned, about 6 minutes. Add the tomato paste and cook, stirring to coat the other ingredients, for 2 to 3 minutes. Add the ⅔ cup of wine, the clam juice, and the vinegar. Bring to a simmer and cook until slightly reduced, 3 to 4 minutes.

2. Drain the tomatoes and put them in a bowl. Add the salt and pepper and crush the tomatoes by hand. Add the tomatoes to the pan and cook, stirring, for about 2 minutes. Add the red pepper flakes, saffron, and bay leaf. Lower the heat and let the sauce simmer until the tomatoes have broken down and the sauce thickens slightly, about 30 minutes.

3. Meanwhile bring a large pot of water to a boil over high heat. Add the pasta and let boil until al dente, 10 to 12 minutes.

4. While the pasta is cooking, heat the remaining 1 tablespoon of olive oil in a large, heavy-bottomed pan over medium-high heat. Add the remaining garlic and cook until it starts to sizzle, about 30 seconds. Add the

remaining ½ cup of white wine and let it come to a simmer, then add the mussels and clams. Cover the pan and cook the shellfish until the shells open, about 1 minute. Add the shrimp and scallops. Cover the pan and cook until the shrimp and scallops are cooked through, 2 minutes; then discard the bay leaf along with any clams or mussels that have not opened. Ladle 3 cups of the pasta sauce into the pan with the shellfish and toss gently, taking care not to crack the mussel or clam shells. Add the parsley and Parmesan cheese and toss again.

5. Drain the pasta in a colander and transfer it to a large serving bowl. Pour the sauce over the pasta and serve family style.

note: Don't beard the mussels until you are ready to cook the dish. Once bearded, if left too long, the mussels will spoil.

CARBOHYDRATE CHOICES: 2½

# creamy spaghetti
## WITH SCALLOPS AND BREAD CRUMBS

this recipe always reminds me of a classic bit from the original *Saturday Night Live*— the one about Shimmer, a new product that was both a floor wax *and* a dessert topping. Okay, maybe that's a bit of a stretch, but the scallops here are both a shellfish and a topping for the pasta. Rather than tossing the two together, sliced seared scallops are decoratively arranged over the spaghetti. It's quite a pretty presentation, especially when served family style from a large bowl, and really makes it easy to visualize the relatively high ratio of protein to pasta. There's not much spaghetti in each serving, but the scallops are filling enough that this could easily be a main course, or even a light meal on its own.

The scallops here are sliced thinly enough that searing them on only one side will fully cook them; don't cook them on both sides or they will become tough and chewy.

**SERVES 6**

## INGREDIENTS

6 tablespoons dry, unseasoned bread crumbs

1 tablespoon chopped fresh flat-leaf parsley leaves

1 teaspoon finely grated lemon zest

1 teaspoon chopped fresh dill

8 ounces dried spaghetti (½ of a 1-pound box)

1 teaspoon minced garlic

¼ cup plus 2 tablespoons heavy (whipping) cream

6 tablespoons (¾ stick) unsalted butter

Pinch of freshly ground black pepper

¼ cup freshly squeezed lemon juice, or more to taste

1 teaspoon Dijon mustard

12 ounces sea scallops (about 12)

2 tablespoons olive oil

1. Put the bread crumbs in a heavy-bottomed pan and toast over low heat, shaking the pan to prevent scorching, until lightly browned, about 3 minutes. Let the bread crumbs cool, then place them and the parsley, lemon zest, and dill in a bowl and stir together. Set aside.

2. Bring a large pot of water to a boil over high heat. Add the spaghetti and let boil until al dente, about 8 minutes.

3. Meanwhile, put the garlic and heavy cream in a small, heavy-bottomed saucepan and bring to a boil over medium-high heat. Whisk in the butter 1 tablespoon at a time until it is all incorporated. Stir the pepper, lemon juice, and mustard into the sauce. It's okay, even desirable, for the sauce to be lemony, so taste it and add more lemon juice if you like. Remove the sauce from the heat and keep it covered and warm.

4. Cut the scallops horizontally into ½ inch–thick rounds. Heat the olive oil in a nonstick pan over medium-high heat. When the oil begins to shimmer, working in batches, cook the scallops on one side only for 15 to 20 seconds. Set the cooked scallops aside on a plate and repeat until all the scallops are cooked on one side.

5. Drain the spaghetti in a colander and transfer it to a large bowl. Pour the sauce over the spaghetti and toss well. Divide the spaghetti among 6 pasta bowls. Arrange some of the scallops, seared side up, on top of the spaghetti in each bowl. Top each serving with some of the bread crumb mixture and serve.

## nutritional information
(PER SERVING)

| | |
|---|---|
| Calories | 419 |
| Fat | 23 g |
| Saturated Fat | 11 g |
| Trans Fat | 0 g |
| Total Carbohydrates | 36 g |
| Dietary Fiber | 2 g |
| Total Sugars | 2 g |
| Protein | 16 g |
| Cholesterol | 70 mg |
| Sodium | 174 mg |

## exchanges

| | |
|---|---|
| Fat | 4.5 |
| Starch | 2 |
| Lean Meat | 1 |

# linguine with clams

linguine with clams, like many shellfish dishes, has an element you don't see at the dinner table all that often—a direct reminder of where the food comes from. Often served with the clams still in their shells, this is a dish that makes you picture the ocean when you eat it. Those shells mean you have to pick the clams up out of the bowl and spear them with a fork, adding a dimension of playfulness. All of which verges on the superfluous: I, for one, don't need any extra prodding to turn to this dish a few times every summer; it's a delicious combination of pasta and clams (and butter, white wine, and parsley).

For a more substantial dish, don't add more pasta, add more clams—up to another half pound.

**SERVES 6**

## nutritional information
### (PER SERVING)

| | |
|---|---|
| Calories | 316 |
| Fat | 14 g |
| Saturated Fat | 5 g |
| Trans Fat | 0 g |
| Total Carbohydrates | 31 g |
| Dietary Fiber | 1 g |
| Total Sugars | 2 g |
| Protein | 13 g |
| Cholesterol | 45 mg |
| Sodium | 258 mg |

## exchanges

| | |
|---|---|
| Fat | 2 |
| Starch | 1.5 |
| Lean Meat | 0.5 |
| High Fat Meat | 0.5 |
| Vegetables | 0.5 |

## shop right

**CLAMS AND COCKLES:** Manila clams and New Zealand cockles, the latter recognizable by their green-tinted shells, are my varieties of choice for these mollusks. When shopping for them, seek out the ones that have no fishy odor, with an appropriate ratio of weight to size—those that seem surprisingly heavy might have mud trapped within. Clams and cockles should be tightly closed; if some aren't, often a squeeze of the shell will cause them to "clam up," in which case they are good to go.

## INGREDIENTS

8 ounces dried linguine
 (½ of a 1 pound box)
1 tablespoon extra-virgin olive oil
4 slices turkey bacon, cut into
 ¼-inch dice
3 tablespoons minced garlic
¼ cup dry white wine

¼ cup store-bought low-sodium
 chicken or vegetable broth
2 pounds clams or cockles, scrubbed
 under cold running water
3 tablespoons unsalted butter
2 tablespoons chopped fresh flat-leaf
 parsley leaves

1. Bring a large pot of water to a boil over high heat. Add the linguine and let boil until al dente, 7 to 8 minutes.

2. Meanwhile, heat the olive oil in a large, heavy-bottomed pan over medium heat. Add the turkey bacon and cook until browned and the fat has rendered, about 7 minutes. Add the garlic and cook for 30 seconds.

Transfer the bacon and garlic to a bowl.

3. Return the pan to the heat. Add the white wine and cook, stirring to scrape up any flavorful bits from the bottom of the pan. Bring the wine to a simmer and let simmer for 30 seconds. Add the broth and ¼ cup of water and bring to a boil, letting the liquid reduce slightly, about 2 min-

utes. Add the clams, cover the pan, and cook until the clams open, about 5 minutes; discard any clams that do not open after this time.

4. Stir in the butter and parsley. Return the bacon and garlic to the pan.

5. Drain the linguine in a colander, add it to the pan with the clams, and toss. Divide the linguine and clams among 6 wide, shallow bowls and serve.

# lobster pasta

## WITH RAW TOMATO SAUCE

a perfect summer dish, this pasta focuses on two of the hallmark ingredients of the season, lobster and tomatoes, and requires a minimum of time over a hot stove, just enough to poach the lobster and cook the pasta. The rest of the dish is based on the irresistible notion that hot pasta contains enough heat to unlock and soak up the flavors of a room temperature sauce, here made with the (cooled) lobster, tomatoes, olive oil, lemon, and herbs. To make this a more substantial main course, just add more lobster.

**SERVES 6**

## nutritional information
### (PER SERVING)

| | |
|---|---|
| Calories | 374 |
| Fat | 20 g |
| Saturated Fat | 3 g |
| Trans Fat | 0 g |
| Total Carbohydrates | 34 g |
| Dietary Fiber | 2 g |
| Total Sugars | 3 g |
| Protein | 15 g |
| Cholesterol | 45 mg |
| Sodium | 308 mg |

## exchanges

| | |
|---|---|
| Fat | 3.5 |
| Starch | 2 |
| Lean Meat | 1 |
| Vegetables | 0.5 |

## INGREDIENTS

2 live lobsters (1½ pounds each)

6 small plum tomatoes, cut into small dice, with their juice

6 large cloves garlic, minced

½ cup extra-virgin olive oil

2 tablespoons chopped fresh tarragon leaves

2 tablespoons chopped fresh flat-leaf parsley leaves

2 tablespoons freshly squeezed lemon juice, or more to taste

1 teaspoon grated lemon zest

½ teaspoon coarse salt

¼ teaspoon freshly ground black pepper

8 ounces dried small pasta shells (½ of a 1-pound box)

1 lemon, cut into wedges

1. Bring a large stockpot full of water to a boil over high heat. Add the lobsters to the boiling water and cook until the shells turn bright red, 6 minutes. Remove the pot from the heat and let the lobsters sit in the pot for about 90 seconds.

2. Fill a large bowl halfway with ice water. Using tongs, remove the lobsters from the pot and immerse them in the ice water. Once the lobsters have cooled, drain the water. Take the head of one lobster in one hand and the tail in the other and twist them in opposite directions until the upper and lower halves come apart. Using a large, heavy knife, split the lobster tail in half lengthwise. Remove and discard the gray-green tomalley (liver) and red roe (if any), along with the shells. Remove the meat from the body of the lobster. Crack the claws and remove the meat from within. Cut the lobster meat into 1-inch dice and set it aside. Repeat with the remaining lobster. (The lobster meat can be refrigerated in an airtight container for up to 24 hours. Let come to room temperature before proceeding.)

3. Put the tomatoes, garlic, olive oil, tarragon, parsley, lemon juice, lemon zest, salt, and pepper into a bowl. Stir and let sit for 10 to 15 minutes for the flavors of the sauce to develop.

4. Bring a large pot of water to a boil over high heat. Add the pasta and let boil until al dente, about 6 minutes. Drain the pasta in a colander and transfer it to a large pasta bowl. Pour the sauce over the pasta, add the lobster meat, and toss together. Divide the pasta among 6 bowls and serve with lemon wedges alongside for squeezing over the pasta.

## nutritional information
(PER SERVING)

| | |
|---|---|
| Calories | 381 |
| Fat | 13 g |
| Saturated Fat | 5 g |
| Trans Fat | 0 g |
| Total Carbohydrates | 37 g |
| Dietary Fiber | 2 g |
| Total Sugars | 3 g |
| Protein | 26 g |
| Cholesterol | 130 mg |
| Sodium | 170 mg |

## exchanges

| | |
|---|---|
| Fat | 2 |
| Starch | 2 |
| Lean Meat | 2 |
| Vegetables | 0.5 |
| Plant Protein | 0.5 |

CARBOHYDRATE CHOICES: 2½

# fettuccine
## WITH SHRIMP AND SHIITAKE MUSHROOMS

i don't know where I got the idea for this pasta that combines Italian fettuccine with distinctly Asian shiitake mushrooms and edamame (soybeans). All I can tell you is that it's a lovely and surprising dish that you won't find anyplace else, which makes it a natural for entertaining.   SERVES 6

## INGREDIENTS

1½ cups shelled fresh or frozen
  edamame (soybeans; about 6 ounces)
8 ounces dried fettuccine
  (½ of a 1-pound box)
2 tablespoons olive oil
2 large cloves garlic, very thinly
  sliced
6 large shiitake mushrooms,
  stems removed, caps cut into
  ¼ inch–thick slices
Pinch of coarse salt

1 pound large shrimp (about
  1 dozen), peeled, deveined,
  and cut in half lengthwise
3 tablespoons dry white wine
3 tablespoons unsalted butter
2 tablespoons freshly squeezed
  lemon juice
1 heaping tablespoon minced fresh
  chives
Pinch of freshly ground black
  pepper

1. Bring 2 large pots of water to a boil over high heat. Cook the edamame in one of the pots of boiling water until al dente, about 2 minutes.

2. Fill a large bowl halfway with ice water. Drain the edamame then transfer it to the ice water to stop the cooking and preserve the color. Drain the edamame again and set it aside.

3. Add the fettuccine to the other pot of boiling water and let boil until al dente, about 7 minutes.

4. Meanwhile, heat 1 tablespoon of the olive oil in a heavy-bottomed pan over medium-high heat. Add the garlic and when it begins to sizzle, after about 30 seconds, add the mushrooms and cook until slightly softened, about 1 minute. Season the mushrooms with the salt, then transfer them to a bowl.

5. Heat the remaining 1 tablespoon of olive oil in the pan. Add the shrimp and cook until they just begin to turn pink, about 30 seconds. Transfer the shrimp to the bowl with the mushrooms.

6. Return the pan to the heat and add the white wine. Using a wooden spoon, scrape up any flavorful bits stuck to the bottom of the pan. Add ¼ cup of water, bring to a boil, and cook until the liquid has reduced slightly, about 3 minutes. Whisk in the butter, then the lemon juice, chives, and pepper.

7. Drain the fettuccine in a colander.

8. Return the mushrooms and shrimp to the pan. Add the edamame and fettuccine and toss to evenly distribute. Divide the fettuccine and shrimp among 6 plates or wide, shallow bowls and serve.

### did you know?

Edamame (soybeans) are a popular starter at Japanese restaurants, served in salted pods from which diners squeeze or suck out the little individual beans. High in protein, edamame (the name means beans on branches) have many uses beyond this one: In Asia, they're a popular vegetable in their own right, found in all kinds of dishes and even pureed into drinks. As with green peas, it's perfectly fine to buy edamame frozen because the beans have been lightly cooked and flash frozen to preserve freshness.

# angel hair pasta

## WITH SHRIMP SCAMPI SAUCE

Shrimp scampi is something of a joke in a lot of kitchens because the name literally means "shrimp shrimp," which of course doesn't mean a thing. But the actual dish shrimp scampi deserves some affection for its straightforward blend of shrimp, olive oil, garlic, and spice. Here, the olive oil is infused with garlic and crushed red pepper flakes for a few minutes, then you add shrimp to the pan to soak up the big flavors. This is a perfect pasta sauce, and the shrimp can also be eaten on their own. **SERVES 6**

## nutritional information
### (PER SERVING)

| | |
|---|---|
| Calories | 389 |
| Fat | 19 g |
| Saturated Fat | 5 g |
| Trans Fat | 0 g |
| Total Carbohydrates | 30 g |
| Dietary Fiber | 1 g |
| Total Sugars | 1 g |
| Protein | 20 g |
| Cholesterol | 130 mg |
| Sodium | 115 mg |

## exchanges

| | |
|---|---|
| Fat | 3.5 |
| Starch | 1.5 |
| Lean Meat | 2 |
| Vegetables | 0.5 |

## INGREDIENTS

8 ounces dried angel hair pasta
   (½ of a 1-pound box)
¼ cup plus 1 tablespoon olive oil
8 large cloves garlic, very thinly sliced
⅛ teaspoon crushed red pepper flakes

¼ cup plus 2 tablespoons dry white wine
1 pound large shrimp (about 1 dozen),
   peeled and deveined
3 tablespoons unsalted butter
¼ cup chopped fresh flat-leaf parsley

1. Bring a large pot of water to boil over high heat. Add the angel hair and let boil until al dente, about 5 minutes.

2. While the angel hair is cooking, heat the olive oil in a wide, deep, heavy-bottomed pan over medium-low heat. Add the garlic and red pepper flakes and cook to gently infuse the olive oil with flavor but not brown the garlic, about 4 minutes. Add the white wine and cook until almost evaporated, about 5 minutes.

Add the shrimp to the pan and cook, stirring, until firm and pink, about 3 minutes. Swirl in the butter to thicken and enrich the sauce.

3. Set aside a few tablespoons of the angel hair cooking water, then drain the angel hair. Stir the angel hair cooking water into the pan with the shrimp to bind the sauce, then add the angel hair and toss to coat. Divide the angel hair among 6 bowls or plates. Scatter some parsley over each portion and serve.

# shrimp and tomato ravioli

Sauce these ravioli, made the easy way with purchased wonton wrappers, with whatever you like. Some of my favorite options are chicken or vegetable broth with butter and herbs swirled in or a light tomato sauce.

**SERVES 6**

## nutritional information

(PER 4 RAVIOLI SERVING WITHOUT BROTH OR SAUCE)

| | |
|---|---|
| Calories | 234 |
| Fat | 2 g |
| Saturated Fat | 0 g |
| Trans Fat | 0 g |
| Total Carbohydrates | 38 g |
| Dietary Fiber | 1 g |
| Total Sugars | 0 g |
| Protein | 15 g |
| Cholesterol | 63 mg |
| Sodium | 434 mg |

## exchanges

| | |
|---|---|
| Starch | 2.5 |
| Lean Meat | 1 |

## INGREDIENTS

8 ounces shrimp (about 8 large), peeled and deveined

1½ tablespoons chopped Roasted Plum Tomatoes (page 323)

½ teaspoon minced garlic

½ teaspoon fresh thyme leaves

⅛ teaspoon freshly ground black pepper

Pinch of cayenne pepper

1 large egg white

2 tablespoons whole milk

48 ravioli or wonton wrappers

⅓ cup store-bought low-sodium chicken or vegetable broth or light tomato sauce, for serving

1. Make sure all of the ingredients are cold. For the best results, also chill the food processor bowl and steel blade in the refrigerator or freezer briefly before using.

2. Put the shrimp, tomato, garlic, thyme, black pepper, and cayenne in the food processor. Process until well mixed. Add the egg white and milk and pulse until just incorporated.

3. Working in batches if necessary, place 24 ravioli or wonton wrappers in a single layer on your work surface. Put a small spoonful of the shrimp mixture in the center of each wrapper. Lightly moisten the outer edge of each wrapper with water using a small pastry brush or your index finger. Place a second wrapper on top of each filled wrapper and press them together with your finger to make the ravioli. (While many ravioli can be refrigerated or frozen, it's best to cook and serve these right away due to the delicate nature of the filling and the presence of egg and milk.)

4. Bring a large pot of water to a boil over high heat. Reduce the heat to a simmer and add the ravioli to the pot. Let the ravioli simmer until they begin to float, about 2 to 3 minutes. Drain and serve with your choice of broth or sauce.

CARBOHYDRATE CHOICES: 2½

# pad thai

this is one of two non-Italian pastas in this chapter, but I had to make room for pad thai, the stir-fried noodle dish that features egg and shrimp (and sometimes chicken) quickly cooked in a sizzling hot pan with a hit parade of Asian ingredients (fish sauce, soy sauce, and sesame oil) topped with crunchy bean sprouts and crushed peanuts. What's not to love?　　SERVES 6

## nutritional information

(PER SERVING)

| | |
|---|---|
| Calories | 340 |
| Fat | 14 g |
| Saturated Fat | 2 g |
| Trans Fat | 0 g |
| Total Carbohydrates | 38 g |
| Dietary Fiber | 1 g |
| Total Sugars | 2 g |
| Protein | 16 g |
| Cholesterol | 122 mg |
| Sodium | 595 mg |

## exchanges

| | |
|---|---|
| Fat | 2.5 |
| Starch | 2 |
| Lean Meat | 1.5 |
| Vegetables | 0.5 |

## INGREDIENTS

2 tablespoons canola oil

3 large cloves garlic, minced

1 medium-size shallot, minced

12 large shrimp, peeled, deveined, and coarsely chopped

2 tablespoons Asian fish sauce

2 tablespoons Asian (dark) sesame oil

1 large egg plus 1 large egg white, lightly beaten with 3 tablespoons cold water

2 tablespoons freshly squeezed lime juice

1 teaspoon low-sodium soy sauce

8 ounces rice noodles soaked in hot water for 15 to 20 minutes

About 1 cup bean sprouts

2 scallions, both white and green parts, thinly sliced, for garnish

¼ cup crushed unsalted peanuts

1. Heat the canola oil in a large, heavy-bottomed pan over medium-high heat. Add the garlic and shallot and cook for 1 minute. Add the shrimp and cook until they begin to turn firm and pink, about 30 seconds. Add the fish sauce and sesame oil and cook for 30 seconds. Add the eggs and cook, stirring, until the eggs form ribbons, about 30 seconds. Stir in the lime juice and soy sauce.

2. Drain the rice noodles and add them to the pan, along with ¼ cup of the bean sprouts. Stir well to mix everything together.

3. To serve, divide the pad thai among 6 plates or shallow bowls. Sprinkle some scallions over each portion and top each with 1 tablespoon of peanuts and the remaining sprouts.

**variations and suggestions:** You can have some fun with this dish, adding thinly sliced mint or Thai basil, or spicing it up with your choice of thinly sliced chiles or hot sauce.

# braised duck legs

## WITH EGG NOODLES

Slowly braising duck legs in wine, vinegar, and tomato makes them literally falling-apart tender and loaded with tangy flavor. I think of this very traditional, straightforward preparation as a bistro affair, so I favor serving the duck over a classic accompaniment of egg noodles.

The fat count is a bit misleading here because much of the duck legs' fat drains off as they cook.

**SERVES 6**

## nutritional information
(PER SERVING)

| | |
|---|---|
| Calories | 525 |
| Fat | 21 g |
| Saturated Fat | 5 g |
| Trans Fat | 0 g |
| Total Carbohydrates | 36 g |
| Dietary Fiber | 3 g |
| Total Sugars | 5 g |
| Protein | 34 g |
| Cholesterol | 154 mg |
| Sodium | 485 mg |

## exchanges

| | |
|---|---|
| Fat | 2 |
| Starch | 2 |
| Lean Meat | 3.5 |
| High Fat Meat | 0.5 |
| Vegetables | 1 |
| Alcohol | 0.5 |

### INGREDIENTS

3 plum tomatoes, seeded and
   cut into small dice
Pinch of coarse salt
Pinch of freshly ground black pepper
2 tablespoons olive oil
6 duck legs (about 8 ounces each)
4 slices turkey bacon, cut into small dice
1 medium-size Spanish onion,
   cut into ¼-inch dice

1 small carrot, cut crosswise into
   ¼-inch slices
2 cups medium-bodied red wine
¼ cup distilled white vinegar
⅓ cup tomato paste
8 ounces egg noodles
   (½ of a 1-pound package)

1. Put the tomatoes in a bowl and season them with the salt and pepper. Let the tomatoes marinate for 30 minutes.

2. Pour the olive oil in a large, heavy-bottomed saucepan and warm it over low heat. Add the duck legs to the pan, skin-side down. Cook gently, letting the

fat render, spooning it off and discarding it as it accumulates. After the fat stops rendering, 15 to 20 minutes, turn the legs over and brown them on the other side, about 4 minutes. Use tongs to transfer the duck legs to a plate.

**3.** Pour off all but a few tablespoons of fat from the pan. Add the turkey bacon and cook over medium-low heat, stirring, until browned and the fat is rendered, about 7 minutes. Add the marinated tomatoes, onion, carrot, red wine, and vinegar and cook, stirring, for 1 minute. Add the tomato paste and stir to coat all the ingredients with the paste.

**4.** Return the duck legs to the pan, increase the heat so that the liquid simmers, and braise the duck until it is tender and the meat is falling off the bone, about 1 hour 15 minutes. Using tongs to hold the legs, peel away and discard the skin, and remove the meat from the bones with a knife; it should come right off. Discard the bones. If not serving immediately, let the meat and sauce cool, then cover and refrigerate for a few days or freeze for up to 1 month. Let come to room temperature, then gently reheat before proceeding.

**5.** Bring a large pot of water to a boil over high heat. Add the egg noodles and let boil until just done, about 3 minutes. Drain the noodles and divide them among 4 dinner plates or wide, shallow bowls. Top each portion with some duck and sauce and serve.

## nutritional information
(PER SERVING)

| | |
|---|---|
| Calories | 395 |
| Fat | 18 g |
| Saturated Fat | 5 g |
| Trans Fat | 0 g |
| Total Carbohydrates | 56 g |
| Dietary Fiber | 13 g |
| Total Sugars | 17 g |
| Protein | 12 g |
| Cholesterol | 15 mg |
| Sodium | 540 mg |

## exchanges

| | |
|---|---|
| Fat | 3 |
| Starch | 2 |
| Lean Meat | 0.5 |
| Vegetables | 10.5 |

CARBOHYDRATE CHOICES: 4; 2 ADJUSTED FOR FIBER

# spaghetti squash spaghetti

## WITH A VEGETABLE TOMATO SAUCE

does this recipe really belong in the pasta chapter? Perhaps in most cookbooks the answer would be no, but in our case, I say it's a rousing yes, because it epitomizes the philosophy of satisfying cravings that's made eating with diabetes bearable to me. Serving the aptly named spaghetti squash as a pasta in its own right, is something I first saw done by my friend and fellow chef Rick Moonen. Here it is tossed with what is basically a garden tomato sauce, resulting in a tangy dish that may be one step removed from true pasta but that hits all the right buttons—and has the extra benefit of not leaving you feeling overstuffed.

**SERVES 6**

## INGREDIENTS

*2 medium-size spaghetti squash (about 4 pounds each)*

*4 teaspoons unsalted butter*

*¼ cup store-bought low-sodium chicken broth*

*3 tablespoons olive oil*

*1 medium-size Spanish onion, cut into small dice*

*4 large cloves garlic, minced*

*1 large carrot, cut into small dice*

*1 rib celery, cut into small dice*

*1 tablespoon tomato paste*

*5 cups canned crushed tomatoes, with their juices*

*¼ teaspoon crushed red pepper flakes*

*½ cup freshly grated Parmesan cheese, plus more for serving (optional)*

*¼ cup pine nuts*

*1 cup diced zucchini*

*1 cup diced red bell pepper*

*1 cup diced white button mushrooms*

*2 tablespoons thinly sliced fresh basil leaves*

1. Preheat the oven to 350°F.

2. Cut the spaghetti squash in half lengthwise. Scoop out and discard the seeds. Place the squash halves cut-side up on a baking sheet. Place 1 teaspoon of butter and 1 tablespoon of broth in each hollowed-out cavity and cover it with aluminum foil. Bake the squash until a knife-tip pierces it easily, about 1 hour.

3. Meanwhile, make the sauce: Heat 1½ tablespoons (4½ teaspoons) of the olive oil in a heavy-bottomed saucepan over medium heat. Add the onion, garlic, carrot, and celery and cook until softened but not browned,

about 5 minutes. Add the tomato paste and cook, stirring to coat the other ingredients, 2 to 3 minutes. Add the tomatoes and their juices, bring to a boil over medium-high heat, then lower the heat and let simmer very gently for 30 minutes. Stir in the red pepper flakes and Parmesan cheese.

4. Toast the pine nuts in a large pan over medium heat, shaking the pan frequently to prevent scorching, until golden brown and fragrant, about 3 minutes. Set the pine nuts aside.

5. Heat the remaining 1½ tablespoons (4½ teaspoons) of olive oil in a heavy-bottomed pan over medium

heat. Add the zucchini, bell pepper, and mushrooms and cook until al dente, about 4 minutes.

6. To serve, using a fork, scrape the flesh out of each squash half and transfer it to a large bowl. Add the sauce and cooked vegetables and toss to mix. Divide the spaghetti squash among 6 plates and top it with the toasted pine nuts, basil, and more Parmesan cheese, if desired.

**CARBOHYDRATE CHOICE: 1; ½ ADJUSTED FOR FIBER**

# vegetable lasagna

like the preceding recipe, there's no actual pasta in this dish—a variation of a recipe I've been making for years—but it really says "lasagna" to your taste buds, with the eggplant, zucchini, and yellow squash standing in for noodles and the tomatoes and oregano offering the same flavor notes as a sauce. In addition to serving this on its own, hot or cold, as a starter or main course, it's a wonderful side dish to grilled lamb and a surprising, guilt-free breakfast indulgence; serve it hot alongside eggs any way you like them.        **SERVES 6**

## nutritional information

(PER SERVING)

| | |
|---|---|
| Calories | 111 |
| Fat | 6 g |
| Saturated Fat | 1 g |
| Trans Fat | 0 g |
| Total Carbohydrates | 15 g |
| Dietary Fiber | 5 g |
| Total Sugars | 8 g |
| Protein | 3 g |
| Cholesterol | 2 mg |
| Sodium | 13 mg |

## exchanges

| | |
|---|---|
| Fat | 1 |
| Vegetables | 2.5 |

## INGREDIENTS

4 large, ripe beefsteak tomatoes, peeled (page 129) and coarsely chopped
1 teaspoon unsalted butter
2 large Spanish onions, cut in half lengthwise and very thinly sliced
Pinch of sugar
Nonstick cooking spray

½ medium-size eggplant, ends trimmed, peeled, and very thinly sliced lengthwise
1 medium-size zucchini, ends trimmed, very thinly sliced lengthwise
2 tablespoons chopped fresh oregano
1 medium-size yellow squash, ends trimmed, very thinly sliced lengthwise
2 tablespoons olive oil

1. Put the tomatoes in a strainer and set it over a bowl. Let the tomatoes drain as you prepare the rest of the dish.

2. Melt the butter in a wide, deep, nonstick pan over low heat. Add the onions and cook, stirring, until they begin to soften, about 5 minutes.

Sprinkle the sugar over the onions and cook, stirring periodically, until they are well caramelized and sweet, about 40 minutes. If they begin to scorch or stick to the pan, add a few drops of water occasionally, but only just enough to keep the onions from sticking.

3. Preheat the oven to 300°F.

4. Let the onions cool, then transfer them to a cutting board and coarsely chop them. Spray an 8 inch-square ovenproof glass baking dish with non-stick cooking spray. Put the onions in the bottom of the dish, and using a rubber spatula, press them down in an even layer.

5. Arrange the slices of eggplant over the onions, overlapping them slightly, so they cover the onions in a single layer. Top the eggplant with a layer of overlapping zucchini slices. Scatter the oregano over the zucchini, then top the oregano with a layer of overlapping yellow squash slices.

6. Press down on the tomatoes in the strainer with a kitchen spoon to extract any lingering moisture, then top the yellow squash with a layer of tomatoes, pressing down on them to create a nicely uniform top for the lasagna. Use a pastry brush to coat the tomatoes with the olive oil.

7. Bake the lasagna until the vegetables are nicely softened, about 4 hours. When done, a sharp, thin-bladed knife will easily pierce to the bottom. If the tomatoes begin to brown too much, lower the oven temperature to 275°F.

8. Remove the lasagna from the oven and let it rest for 10 minutes before slicing and serving. You can also let the lasagna cool completely and serve it cold. For the very best flavor and texture, cover the lasagna tightly with plastic wrap, weigh it down with cans or other heavy objects, and refrigerate it overnight to press out as much liquid as possible. Before serving, drain any liquid from the bottom of the baking dish. Serve the drained lasagna cold or reheat it in a 300°F oven for 12 to 15 minutes.

9. Cut the lasagna into 6 servings and serve.

### variations and suggestions:

❖ This lasagna invites improvisation: Serve it on a little puddle of your favorite tomato sauce and/or top it with some grated Parmesan or a dollop of ricotta cheese. Another alternative would be to drizzle some Parsley or Basil Puree (page 316) over each serving.

❖ For a quick herbed ricotta topping, put ¼ cup plus 2 tablespoons of ricotta cheese in a bowl (part-skim

Vegetable Lasagna

ricotta tastes good prepared this way). Add 1 tablespoon of grated Parmesan cheese, 2 teaspoons of chopped fresh basil, ½ teaspoon of minced garlic, and a pinch of pepper. Work everything together with a rubber spatula and top each serving of lasagna with a heaping tablespoon.

# asparagus and mushroom risotto

d o opposites attract in the kitchen the way they do in life? Based on the way asparagus—fresh, crunchy, and green—and mushrooms—earthy, woodsy, and soft—get on in this risotto, you'd have to answer yes. These two ingredients complement each other naturally, without calling attention to their union. There's nothing revolutionary here, but every mouthful is a study in perfect balance, and I haven't even mentioned the creamy rice yet. **SERVES 6**

## nutritional information
**(PER SERVING)**

| | |
|---|---|
| Calories | 233 |
| Fat | 14 g |
| Saturated Fat | 5 g |
| Trans Fat | 0 g |
| Total Carbohydrates | 21 g |
| Dietary Fiber | 1 g |
| Total Sugars | 2 g |
| Protein | 5 g |
| Cholesterol | 19 mg |
| Sodium | 135 mg |

## exchanges

| | |
|---|---|
| Fat | 2.5 |
| Starch | 1 |
| Vegetables | 0.5 |

## INGREDIENTS

3 tablespoons olive oil

8 ounces white button mushrooms, very thinly sliced

⅛ teaspoon coarse salt

6 spears jumbo asparagus, ends trimmed

3 tablespoons unsalted butter

½ medium-size Spanish onion, minced

⅔ cup risotto rice (see facing page)

¼ cup dry white wine

About 3 cups store-bought low-sodium chicken broth, simmering in a pot on a back burner

2 tablespoons freshly grated Parmesan cheese

1 tablespoon chopped fresh chives

1. Preheat the oven to 350°F.

2. Drizzle 1 tablespoon of the olive oil over the mushrooms and scatter the salt over them. Arrange the mushroom slices on a rimmed baking sheet without crowding and bake until slightly shriveled and darkened around the edges, 12 to 15 minutes. Transfer the mushrooms to a plate

and carefully pour off any liquid on the baking sheet into a small bowl and set aside.

3. Bring a large pot of water to a boil over high heat. Cook the asparagus in the boiling water until al dente, about 8 minutes.

4. Fill a large bowl halfway with ice water. Use tongs to remove the asparagus from the pot and transfer it to the ice water to stop the cooking and preserve the color. Once the asparagus has cooled, drain it and cut it into 1-inch, diagonal pieces. Set the asparagus aside.

5. Melt the butter in the remaining 2 tablespoons of oil in a large, heavy-bottomed pot over medium heat. Add the onion and cook until softened but not browned, about 4 minutes. Add the rice, stir to coat it with butter and oil, and cook for about 4 minutes. Add the white wine, bring it to a boil, and cook, stirring, until it evaporates nearly completely.

6. Ladle 1 cup of simmering chicken broth into the pot with the rice and cook, stirring, until it is nearly absorbed. Add the reserved mushroom liquid, if any, to the rice and stir. Continue to add broth in ½-cup increments, stirring the rice constantly. When you are down to the last cup or so, add the broth in smaller increments until the rice is softened but still a bit al dente (you may not need all of the broth or you may need to supplement it with more broth or water). This step should take about 18 minutes altogether.

7. Gently stir the asparagus, mushrooms, Parmesan cheese, and chives into the risotto. Divide the risotto among 6 dinner plates or wide, shallow bowls and serve.

**variations and suggestions:** To add another counterpoint of texture and flavor, scatter 1 tablespoon of toasted pine nuts over each serving of risotto.

## risotto rice

Many risotto recipes call interchangeably for Arborio, vialone nano, or carnaroli rice. But these varieties have important distinctions: Arborio is best suited for what Marcella Hazan calls the "more compact styles . . . popular in Lombardy, Piedmont, and Emilia-Romagna." Vialone nano, favored in the Veneto, is a better choice for seafood dishes, producing a wavy (*all'onda,* as the Italians say) result. And carnaroli, which didn't come along until 1945 is—get this—a hybrid of Italian and Japanese rice strains. It holds liquid very well and is good with vegetable risottos. In truth, you can use any of them in any risotto recipe, but use this information to select the best rice for each one.

**CARBOHYDRATE CHOICE: 1**

# creamy spinach risotto

Our intrepid Certified Diabetes Educator, Joy Pape, was a constant presence at the testing sessions for this book, and one of her oft-repeated refrains was, "Can we add more leafy greens to that?" The request was made so often that it occurred to me to load up a risotto, one of the starchier offerings in this book, with a fiber-full dose of spinach to offset the starch. The result was a delicious, texturally complex, and visually appealing risotto.

**SERVES 6**

### INGREDIENTS

2 tablespoons unsalted butter

2 tablespoons olive oil

½ medium-size Spanish onion, minced

⅔ cup risotto rice (see previous page)

¼ cup dry white wine

About 3 cups store-bought low-sodium chicken broth, simmering in a pot on a back burner

2 cups loosely packed baby spinach leaves or torn large spinach leaves

2 tablespoons freshly grated Parmesan cheese

1 tablespoon heavy (whipping) cream

1. Melt the butter in the oil in a large, heavy-bottomed pot over medium heat. Add the onion and cook until softened but not browned, about 4 minutes. Add the rice, stir to coat it with butter and oil, and cook for about 4 minutes. Add the white wine, bring it to a boil, and cook, stirring, until it evaporates nearly completely.

2. Ladle 1 cup of simmering chicken broth into the pot with the rice and cook, stirring, until it is nearly absorbed. Continue to add broth in ½-cup increments, stirring the rice constantly. When you are down to the last cup or so, add the broth in smaller increments until the rice is softened but still a bit al dente (you may not need all of the broth or you may need to supplement it with more broth or water). This step should take about 18 minutes altogether.

3. Stir the spinach into the risotto and allow it to wilt. Stir in the Parmesan cheese and cream. Divide the risotto among 6 dinner plates or wide, shallow bowls and serve.

variations and suggestions: To add a smoky note to this risotto, begin the dish by browning 2 diced slices of turkey bacon in the pot. Or, for a very different effect, add a teaspoon or two of lemon juice at the end to brighten the flavors.

CARBOHYDRATE CHOICES: 2

# mixed shellfish risotto

## WITH LEEKS AND PARSLEY

risotto is a perfect vehicle for just about anything, but it's even more perfect (if there is such a thing) for mixed shellfish; the creamy rice helps the different flavors and textures meld, while at the same time taking on a little something from each of them. This is a soupy but delicious risotto.

**SERVES 6**

### INGREDIENTS

1 medium-size plum tomato,
    seeded and cut into small dice
¼ teaspoon coarse salt
Pinch of freshly ground black pepper
2 tablespoons unsalted butter
2 tablespoons olive oil
½ medium-size Spanish onion, minced
3 large cloves garlic, thinly sliced
⅔ cup risotto rice (see page 175)
¼ cup dry white wine
About 3½ cups store-bought low-sodium
    chicken broth, simmering in a pot on
    a back burner

Tender centers of 2 small leeks,
    well rinsed, cut into ¼-inch
    diagonal slices
½ pound large shrimp, peeled,
    deveined, and halved lengthwise
6 ounces calamari (squid), cleaned
    (ask your fishmonger to do this) with
    tentacles, body cut into ¼-inch rings
2 tablespoons chopped fresh flat-leaf
    parsley leaves
1 teaspoon freshly grated Parmesan
    cheese

1. Season the tomato with the salt and pepper. Set the tomato aside.

2. Melt the butter in the oil in a large, heavy-bottomed pot over medium heat. Add the onion and garlic and cook until softened but not browned, about 4 minutes. Add the rice, stir to coat it with butter and oil, and cook for about 4 minutes. Add the white wine, bring it to a boil, and cook, stirring, until it evaporates nearly completely.

## making risotto in advance

Because of the long time it takes to patiently stir a risotto, it's a famously unhelpful choice for entertaining. But there is a way to make risotto almost entirely in advance: Prepare the risotto up until just before adding the last addition of stock, then transfer it to a rimmed baking sheet and let it cool. Transferred to an airtight container, the risotto can be refrigerated for up to 4 hours. When ready to serve, bring about ¼ cup stock to a simmer, add the rice and reheat. Stir in any additional stock needed in small increments (the stock can be cold). When the rice is ready, continue with the rest of the recipe.

## shop right

**OLIVES:** More and more markets have made room in their aisles for olive bars where you can mix and match your own house combination or purchase just one variety. This is where I get my olives, and I suggest you do the same—the freshness and quality will be superior to any mass-produced options. Whatever you do, stay far away from the flavorless canned black olives stored in water.

**3.** Set aside ½ cup of chicken broth for cooking the leeks and seafood. Ladle 1 cup of simmering chicken broth into the pot with the rice and cook, stirring, until it is nearly absorbed. Continue to add broth in ½-cup increments, stirring the rice constantly. When you are down to the last cup or so, add the broth in smaller increments until the rice is softened but still a bit al dente (you may not need all of the broth, or you may need to supplement it with more broth or water). This step should take about 18 minutes altogether. Stir in the seasoned tomato and then cover the risotto to keep it warm.

**4.** Pour the reserved ½ cup of chicken broth in a saucepan and bring to a simmer over low heat. Add the leeks to the pot and let simmer until they are tender, 3 to 4 minutes. Add the shrimp to the pot and cook for 45 seconds, then add the calamari to the pot and cook for an additional 30 seconds. Drain and discard the cooking liquid and stir the leeks and seafood into the risotto. Stir in the parsley and Parmesan cheese. Divide the risotto among 6 dinner plates or wide, shallow bowls and serve.

**CARBOHYDRATE CHOICE: 1**

# roasted tomato, black olive, and thyme risotto

**m**uch is made of the inherent beauty and deliciousness of late summer tomatoes, but I'd like to say a few words on behalf of the roasted tomato. Too often regarded as a means of salvaging out-of-season specimens in the fall and winter, there's actually good reason to roast tomatoes all year long: Without their charred flavor, intensified sweetness, and bite, this risotto would be a rather listless affair. But *with* roasted tomatoes, a sharp contrast is drawn between them and the olive and thyme, not to mention the rice, the flavor of which also comes to the fore when set off against this powerful foil.

**SERVES 6**

**INGREDIENTS**

2 tablespoons unsalted butter

2 tablespoons olive oil

½ medium-size Spanish onion, minced

⅔ cup risotto rice (see page 175)

¼ cup dry white wine

About 3 cups store-bought low-sodium chicken broth, simmering in a pot on a back burner

¼ cup chopped Roasted Plum Tomatoes (page 323)

2 tablespoons chopped kalamata olives

1 teaspoon fresh thyme leaves

nutritional information
(PER SERVING)

| | |
|---|---|
| Calories | 180 |
| Fat | 9 g |
| Saturated Fat | 3 g |
| Trans Fat | 0 g |
| Total Carbohydrates | 19 g |
| Dietary Fiber | 1 g |
| Total Sugars | 1 g |
| Protein | 3 g |
| Cholesterol | 12 mg |
| Sodium | 93 mg |

exchanges

| | |
|---|---|
| Fat | 1.5 |
| Starch | 1 |

1. Melt the butter in the oil in a large, heavy-bottomed pot over medium heat. Add the onion and cook until softened but not browned, about 4 minutes. Add the rice, stir to coat it with butter and oil, and cook for about 4 minutes. Add the white wine, bring it to a boil, and cook, stirring, until it evaporates nearly completely.

2. Ladle 1 cup of simmering chicken broth into the pot with the rice and cook, stirring, until it is nearly absorbed. Continue to add broth in ½-cup increments, stirring the rice constantly. When you are down to the last cup or so, add the broth in smaller increments until the rice is softened but still a bit al dente (you may not need all of the broth, or you may need to supplement it with more broth or water). This step should take about 18 minutes altogether.

3. Stir the roasted tomato, olives, and thyme into the risotto. Divide the risotto among 6 dinner plates or wide, shallow bowls and serve.

variations and suggestions:

❖ Scatter crumbled goat cheese over the risotto just before serving for a perfect, creamy counterpoint.

❖ Halve the recipe as a side dish to roast chicken or grilled or sautéed shrimp.

# in this chapter

*"Fish and shellfish
are more diabetes-friendly—
and more healthful overall."*

# fish and shellfish

this is easily the longest chapter of main courses in the book, and it's not just because I spend as much of my scandalously limited leisure time as possible knee-deep in a river, trying to catch something tasty for dinner. (Okay, not really: I always catch and release.)

No, the number of recipes on offer here is a tribute to the fact that, generally speaking, fish and shellfish are more diabetes-friendly— and more healthful overall—than poultry or meat. They're leaner, high in important nutri-ents like omega-3, and they lend themselves to lighter preparations, complementary ingredi-ents, and flavors.

Fish and shellfish are also wonderfully varied. In these pages you'll find flaky cod, rich and oily salmon, meaty tuna, and crisp soft-shelled crabs, to name just a few of the cast of characters. When shopping for any fish, look for clear, clean eyes and a distinctly fresh, *un*fishy smell. The best tip I know for pur-chasing fresh fish is to identify a dependable fishmonger and get it all from him or her.

Contrary to the popular myth, fish is easy to cook. Those who fear it tend to fear overcooking. Here's the key: You need to learn to trust carryover heat, the actual warmth retained by the fish itself that will continue to cook it once it comes out of the oven, or off the pan or grill. And when I say you need to learn to trust it, I mean you need to trust it the way Luke Skywalker learned to trust the Force. Most fish are lean and delicate and that carryover heat can do a lot of the actual cooking. If you need reassurance, use a paring knife to pry open the fish at the flake and sneak a peek inside after it's been off the heat for a minute or two; if it's not done, you can always cook it a little longer.

## nutritional information
(PER SERVING)

| | |
|---|---|
| Calories | 231 |
| Fat | 7 g |
| Saturated Fat | 3 g |
| Trans Fat | 0 g |
| Total Carbohydrates | 12 g |
| Dietary Fiber | 5 g |
| Total Sugars | 4 g |
| Protein | 29 g |
| Cholesterol | 122 mg |
| Sodium | 310 mg |

## exchanges

| | |
|---|---|
| Fat | 1 |
| Lean Meat | 3 |
| Vegetables | 2 |

**CARBOHYDRATE CHOICE: 1; ½ ADJUSTED FOR FIBER**

# baked striped bass
## WITH WILTED CABBAGE AND CHERVIL

baking delicate striped bass along with some white wine flavors and moistens the fish. After the bass is removed from its cooking vessel, the remaining liquid, enriched by some of the juices from the fish, is reduced and finished with lemon juice and butter. You serve the bass and sauce atop a bed of crunchy, wilted savoy cabbage, which cooks at the same time, resulting in a lean and clean meal that makes the cook (this means you) look good because it seems far more complicated on the plate than it was in the kitchen.    **SERVES 4**

### INGREDIENTS

½ cup store-bought low-sodium
    chicken broth
2 large cloves garlic, minced
Coarse salt
1 large head savoy cabbage,
    cored and coarsely chopped
4 striped bass fillets (5 ounces each)
    with the skin on

Pinch of freshly ground
    black pepper
Nonstick cooking spray
¼ cup dry white wine
1 tablespoon unsalted butter
Juice of ½ lemon
2 tablespoons chopped fresh chervil
    (see Note)

1. Preheat the oven to 350°F.

2. Pour the chicken broth into a large, heavy-bottomed pot and bring to a boil over high heat. Reduce the heat so the liquid is simmering and add the garlic. Season with ¼ teaspoon of salt. Add the cabbage and cook, stirring periodically, until the cabbage is nicely wilted but still al dente, 15 to 20 minutes.

3. Meanwhile, season the bass on the skin side with a pinch of salt and the pepper. Select a baking dish just large enough to hold the fish fillets in a single layer and spray it with nonstick cooking spray. Add the fish fillets to the prepared dish, skin side up, pour in the white wine, cover the dish with aluminum foil, and bake the bass until firm to the touch, 12 to 15 minutes.

4. Using a slotted spoon, spoon some cabbage into the center of each of 4 dinner plates, leaving its liquid behind in the pot. Using a spatula or slotted spoon, place a fish fillet over the cabbage on each plate.

5. Strain the juices from the baking dish with the fish into a small, heavy-bottomed saucepan and bring to a boil over high heat. To intensify the flavor, let boil until thickened and reduced, about 1 minute. Remove the pan from the heat and swirl in the butter and lemon juice. Strain a few tablespoons of the sauce over the fish on each plate, top with a scattering of chervil, and serve.

**note:** You can substitute fresh parsley or tarragon for the chervil.

---

CARBOHYDRATE CHOICE: 0

# grilled striped bass
## WITH PARSLEY PUREE AND PARSLEY ROOT

I developed this dish for one reason and one reason only: to showcase the unique attributes of parsley root, an admittedly hard to come by ingredient that blends an earthiness with the fresh green flavor of its namesake herb. When parsley root is available in the late spring and early summer I can't get enough of it, especially with fish. Here the parsley flavor is exponentially increased with a drizzling of parsley puree.          SERVES 4

## nutritional information
(PER SERVING)

| | |
|---|---|
| Calories | 266 |
| Fat | 19 g |
|    Saturated Fat | 4 g |
|    Trans Fat | 0 g |
| Total Carbohydrates | 4 g |
|    Dietary Fiber | 2 g |
|    Total Sugars | 0 g |
| Protein | 24 g |
| Cholesterol | 98 mg |
| Sodium | 230 mg |

## exchanges

| | |
|---|---|
| Fat | 3.5 |
| Lean Meat | 2.5 |
| Vegetables | 0.5 |

## INGREDIENTS

20 ounces parsley root (see Note), cut
 into 1-inch cubes (about 4 cups)
3 tablespoons extra-virgin olive oil
1 tablespoon unsalted butter
Pinch of coarse salt

Pinch of freshly ground black pepper
4 striped bass fillets
 (about 4 ounces each) with
 the skin on
½ cup Parsley Puree (page 316)

1. Put the parsley root in a medium-size, heavy-bottomed saucepan and add just enough cold water to cover. Bring to a simmer over medium-high heat and cook until the root is tender when pierced with a knife, about 20 minutes. Drain the parsley root in a colander.

2. Transfer the parsley root cubes to a food processor. Add 2 tablespoons of the olive oil, and the butter, and salt and pepper and process until smooth. Transfer the pureed parsley root back to the pan, cover it with aluminum foil, and keep warm.

3. Build a fire in a charcoal grill, letting the coals burn down until covered with white ash or preheat a gas grill to medium. If using a grill pan, briefly preheat the pan over medium-high heat.

4. Using a small sharp knife, lightly score the skin side of the bass to keep it from curling when cooked. Season the flesh side of the fish with a pinch of salt and pepper. Coat the skin side of the fish with the remaining 1 tablespoon of olive oil. Arrange the fish fillets on the grill, skin side down, and cook for 3 to 4 minutes, then turn them and cook until heated through and firm to the touch, about 2 more minutes.

5. Put a mound of parsley root puree in the center of each of 4 dinner plates. Place a fish fillet on top of the puree. Drizzle Parsley Puree over and around the fish and puree and serve.

note: If parsley root is not available, substitute celery root. If using celery root, remove the outer peel by carefully slicing it off with a paring knife.

# baked cod

## WITH PEPPER STEW

Y ou have to walk a fine line with white-fleshed fish like halibut and cod: They have the appealing ability to take on other flavors, but you don't want to overwhelm their own sweet, flaky qualities. By sautéing a stew of bell peppers and searing the fish separately, then briefly baking them together, this recipe gets the balance just right. A coating of bread crumbs helps ensure that the fish stays crunchy after its turn in the oven. I encourage you to use one red, one green, and one yellow pepper for a festive array of colors here. If you want to take some liberties and you like a little heat, incorporate a touch of serrano, Anaheim, or jalapeño as well. **SERVES 4**

## nutritional information
### (PER SERVING)

| | |
|---|---|
| Calories | 401 |
| Fat | 24 g |
| Saturated Fat | 7 g |
| Trans Fat | 0 g |
| Total Carbohydrates | 24 g |
| Dietary Fiber | 3 g |
| Total Sugars | 5 g |
| Protein | 25 g |
| Cholesterol | 65 mg |
| Sodium | 401 mg |

## exchanges

| | |
|---|---|
| Fat | 4.5 |
| Starch | 0.5 |
| Lean meat | 2 |
| Vegetables | 2 |

## INGREDIENTS

¼ cup olive oil

4 shallots, cut in half and thinly sliced lengthwise

1 medium-size clove garlic, thinly sliced

3 large bell peppers, preferably a mix of red, green, and yellow, stemmed, seeded and thinly sliced lengthwise

½ teaspoon fresh thyme leaves

Coarse salt

Pinch of freshly ground black pepper

4 cod fillets (4 ounces each)

2 tablespoons Dijon mustard

½ cup dry unseasoned bread crumbs

3 tablespoons unsalted butter

Juice of ½ medium-size lemon

1 tablespoon chopped fresh flat-leaf parsley or chives

1. Preheat the oven to 300°F.

2. Heat 1 tablespoon of the olive oil in a large, deep, heavy-bottomed pan over medium heat. Add the shallots and garlic and cook until softened but not browned, about 4 minutes. Add the bell peppers, reduce the heat to medium-low, and cook, stirring occasionally, until the peppers are wilted but not browned, 5 to 6 minutes.

**3.** Add a tablespoon or two of water to the pan to steam the peppers. Continue cooking the peppers, uncovered and stirring occasionally, until they soften and have "stewed down," 20 to 25 minutes. Use tongs to transfer the peppers to a baking dish just large enough to hold the fish in a single layer. Add the thyme and a pinch of salt to the baking dish and stir.

**4.** Spread the bread crumbs out on a plate. Season the cod with a pinch each of salt and pepper. Smear 1½ teaspoons of mustard on 1 side of each fish fillet and press the mustard-coated side into the bread crumbs just firmly enough for them to adhere to and coat the fish.

**5.** Carefully wipe out the pan that held the peppers, add the remain-ing 3 tablespoons of olive oil, and heat it over high heat. Add the cod, breaded-side down. Reduce the heat to medium and cook until the crumbs are golden, 2 to 3 minutes. Arrange the fish fillets on the pepper mixture, breaded-side up, and bake until the cod is cooked through, 7 to 8 minutes.

**6.** Wipe out the fish pan again and add ⅓ cup of cold water. Bring to a boil over high heat, then remove the pan from the heat and swirl in the butter, lemon juice, and a pinch of salt. Stir the parsley into the sauce.

**7.** Divide the pepper stew among 4 dinner plates, placing a cod fillet, breaded-side up, on top of each portion. Spoon sauce over and around the fish and serve.

## nutritional information
(PER SERVING)

| | |
|---|---|
| Calories | 314 |
| Fat | 17 g |
| Saturated Fat | 2 g |
| Trans Fat | 0 g |
| Total Carbohydrates | 14 g |
| Dietary Fiber | 0 g |
| Total Sugars | 1 g |
| Protein | 24 g |
| Cholesterol | 98 mg |
| Sodium | 228 mg |

## exchanges

| | |
|---|---|
| Fat | 3 |
| Starch | 0.5 |
| Lean Meat | 2 |

CARBOHYDRATE CHOICE: 1

# fish and chips–style cod

 ere's another recipe that I whipped up to satisfy a craving. Obviously, you're not supposed to eat a basketful of heavily battered, deep-fried cod on a diabetic diet. But you can enjoy all the flavor and crisp crust of this British pub staple by using a light, tempura-style batter and shallow frying

the fish in a small amount of oil. And you can by all means include the telltale finishing touch of any fish-and-chips feast: Sprinkle malt vinegar or aged sherry vinegar over the cod just before digging in.

If you like, go the chips route and pair this with the Baked Spicy Sweet Potato Fries on page 285. Or, go a different direction and serve the cod over shredded lettuce or mâche; the oil from the fish plus the vinegar you sprinkle on top will come together in a quick vinaigrette.   **SERVES 4**

## INGREDIENTS

½ cup all-purpose flour
¼ cup plus 2 tablespoons whole milk
¼ cup plus 2 tablespoons medium- to
  full-bodied ale
1 large egg
¼ teaspoon coarse salt

Pinch of freshly ground black pepper
1 pound cod fillet
½ cup canola oil, for frying
Malt vinegar or aged sherry vinegar,
  for serving

1. Put the flour, milk, ale, egg, salt, and pepper in a bowl and whisk them together. Cover the batter with plastic wrap and refrigerate it for 30 minutes.

2. Preheat the oven to 250°F.

3. Rinse the cod gently under cold running water and pat it dry with paper towels. Cut the fillets crosswise into eight ¾-inch-thick pieces.

4. Pour the oil into an 8-inch, non-stick pan to a depth of ½ inch and heat over medium to medium-high heat until shimmering, about 2 minutes.

5. Dip 4 pieces of cod in the batter, letting any excess run off and back into the bowl. Fry the fish pieces until golden, about 1 minute per side. Transfer the fried cod to a baking sheet and place in the oven to keep warm. Repeat with the remaining 4 pieces of cod.

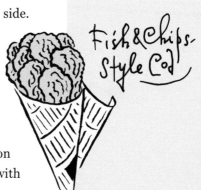

Fish & Chips-
Style Cod

6. Place two pieces of fish on each of 4 plates and serve with vinegar on the side.

## nutritional information
### (PER SERVING)

| | |
|---|---|
| Calories | 308 |
| Fat | 17 g |
| Saturated Fat | 5 g |
| Trans Fat | 0 g |
| Total Carbohydrates | 12 g |
| Dietary Fiber | 3 g |
| Total Sugars | 2 g |
| Protein | 26 g |
| Cholesterol | 98 mg |
| Sodium | 206 mg |

## exchanges

| | |
|---|---|
| Fat | 3 |
| Starch | 0.5 |
| Lean Meat | 2 |
| Vegetables | 1 |

CARBOHYDRATE CHOICE: 1

# almond-crusted mahimahi

## WITH SPRING VEGETABLES

this very efficient recipe, making fine use of the season's vegetables, is just the kind of thing I love to cook when spring arrives. It doesn't keep me cooped up in the kitchen any longer than I need to be. I bake fish and vegetables together, then take the fish out of the pan and create a quick sauce by pouring a lemon and garlic mixture over the vegetables.  **SERVES 4**

### INGREDIENTS

¼ cup ground almonds

¼ cup dry unseasoned bread crumbs

1 large egg white

4 mahimahi fillets (4 ounces each; 1 to 1½ inches thick), with the skin on

Coarse salt and freshly ground black pepper

2 tablespoons olive oil

12 spears pencil-thin asparagus (about ¾ pound), ends trimmed, cut in 2-inch pieces

4 shiitake mushrooms, stems removed, caps very thinly sliced

4 scallions, white and light green parts only, trimmed and cut into 1-inch pieces

¼ cup dry white wine

1 large garlic clove, crushed and peeled

2 tablespoons unsalted butter

1 teaspoon freshly squeezed lemon juice

1. Preheat the oven to 350°F.

2. Put the almonds and bread crumbs in a heavy-bottomed pan and toast over low heat, shaking the pan frequently to prevent scorching, until golden brown, about 3 minutes. Transfer the bread crumb mixture to a bowl and let cool.

3. Put the egg white in a wide, shallow bowl. Season the mahimahi with a pinch each of salt and pepper. Dip the skin side of the fish fillets in the egg white, then in the bread crumb mixture, pressing down just firmly enough for the mixture to adhere to the fish.

4. Heat the olive oil in a wide, deep, heavy-bottomed, ovenproof pan over medium heat. Add the mahimahi, breaded-side down, and cook until lightly browned, about 3 minutes. Turn the fillets and cook on the second side for 30 to 40 seconds. Transfer the fish to a plate and wipe out the pan. Return the fish fillets, bread crumb–side up, to the pan. Scatter the asparagus pieces, mushrooms, and scallions around the fish. Pour in the white wine. Bake the fish, uncovered, until the wine is reduced, the fish is firm, and the vegetables are hot, 8 to 10 minutes.

5. Meanwhile, put ⅓ cup of water, the garlic, and a pinch each of salt and pepper in a small, heavy-bottomed saucepan and bring to a boil over medium-high heat. Swirl in the butter and lemon juice to make a sauce.

6. Remove the pan from the oven and, using tongs, place 1 fillet in the center of each of 4 dinner plates. Pour the sauce over the vegetables in the pan. Set the pan over medium-high heat and bring to a simmer, stirring the vegetables and sauce together. Ladle some sauce and vegetables over and around each fish fillet and serve.

**CARBOHYDRATE CHOICES: 1½; 1 ADJUSTED FOR FIBER**

# seared halibut

## WITH SPINACH AND LEMON

by adding lemon juice and zest to a creamed spinach recipe, the steak house staple becomes a perfect accompaniment to halibut, about as different from red meat as you can get. Purists might find the inclusion of Parmesan cheese in a fish dish unusual, but I'll let you in on a little secret: Every chef I know puts the two together on at least one plate in their repertoire, even if it's not instantly apparent. This is a looser creamed spinach than you might be used to, functioning as a sauce as much as a vegetable.

**SERVES 4**

## nutritional information
### (PER SERVING)

| | |
|---|---|
| Calories | 339 |
| Fat | 14 g |
| Saturated Fat | 5 g |
| Trans Fat | 0 g |
| Total Carbohydrates | 23 g |
| Dietary Fiber | 5 g |
| Total Sugars | 7 g |
| Protein | 32 g |
| Cholesterol | 61 mg |
| Sodium | 577 mg |

## exchanges

| | |
|---|---|
| Fat | 2 |
| Nonfat Milk | 0.5 |
| Lean Meat | 3 |
| Vegetables | 2 |

## halibut

The most common halibut in the United States is Atlantic halibut; there is a Pacific halibut but it is less plentiful as it is fished during a very short season. In recipes, halibut may be replaced with other flatfish such as sole and flounder, although cooking times must be adjusted for differences in thickness.

### INGREDIENTS

1 pound fresh spinach, well-rinsed, tough stems discarded

2 tablespoons unsalted butter

2 tablespoons all-purpose flour

2⅓ cups low-fat (1 percent) milk

1 medium-size garlic clove, crushed and peeled

Pinch of freshly ground black pepper

Finely grated zest and juice from ½ lemon, or more to taste

2 teaspoons freshly grated Parmesan cheese

1 teaspoon extra-virgin olive oil

½ teaspoon coarse salt

2 teaspoons canola oil

4 halibut fillets (about 4 ounces each)

1. Working over the sink, squeeze any excess liquid out of the spinach by hand. Coarsely chop the spinach and set it aside.

2. Heat a large, heavy-bottomed pan over medium heat. Add the butter and let it melt, then sprinkle the flour over the butter and cook, stirring, for 3 to 4 minutes, taking care to not let the mixture brown. Remove the pan from the heat and let the butter and flour mixture cool.

3. Place the milk and garlic in a small, heavy-bottomed saucepan and bring to a boil over medium-high heat. Immediately remove the pot from the heat. Add pepper and stir. Whisk the hot milk into the butter and flour mixture and return the pan to the stove over medium-low heat. Cook, stirring, until thickened, 4 to 5 minutes.

4. Stir the spinach into the pan with the milk and flour mixture and cook until heated through, 2 to 3 minutes. Sprinkle the lemon juice and zest, Parmesan cheese, olive oil, and salt over the spinach and stir. Taste and add more lemon juice if necessary. Remove the pan from the heat and cover to keep warm.

5. Heat the canola oil in a large, heavy-bottomed, nonstick pan over medium-high heat. Add the halibut fillets and sear on both sides, 4 to 5 minutes per side.

6. Place a mound of spinach in the center of each of 4 dinner plates. Arrange a halibut fillet on each mound of spinach and serve.

variations and suggestions: In place of the halibut, use cod, fluke, flounder, or sole. All would be delicious here; adjust the cooking time, as the thickness and size of the fillets will vary greatly.

CARBOHYDRATE CHOICES: 1½

# milk-poached halibut

## WITH MUSHROOM PUREE AND BRAISED LETTUCE

this dish features three unusual preparations, but it's by no means experimental or avant-garde. Pureeing the mushrooms makes them a smooth and creamy component; garlic and truffle oil punch up their flavor. The lettuce is simply braised in a quantity of chicken broth and water, resulting in a uniquely luscious take on this vegetable. And the halibut is poached in milk to emphasize its natural sweetness. Put everything together and you've got something that friends and family won't soon forget, especially the final moments when the last bits meld together on the plate. **SERVES 4**

## nutritional information
### (PER SERVING)

Calories......................413
Fat..............................20 g
   Saturated Fat...........7 g
   Trans Fat..................0 g
Total Carbohydrates....21 g
   Dietary Fiber............2 g
   Total Sugars...........17 g
Protein.........................38 g
Cholesterol..............68 mg
Sodium..................592 mg

## exchanges

Fat.................................3
Nonfat Milk ....................1
Lean Meat......................3
Vegetables.................1.5

## INGREDIENTS

2 tablespoons extra-virgin
   olive oil

2 tablespoons unsalted butter

3 medium-size cloves garlic, thinly
   sliced, plus 2 medium-size cloves,
   crushed and peeled

12 ounces white button mushrooms,
   trimmed and thinly sliced

¾ teaspoon coarse salt

Freshly ground black pepper

1 teaspoon white truffle oil

4 small heads Bibb or Boston lettuce,
   trimmed

⅔ cup store-bought low-sodium
   chicken broth

4¼ cups low-fat (1 percent) milk

4 halibut fillets (about 4 ounces each;
   ideally 1-inch thick), at room
   temperature

1 tablespoon chopped fresh chives

2 teaspoons freshly squeezed lemon
   juice

1. Heat the olive oil and 1 tablespoon of the butter in a medium-size, heavy-bottomed saucepan over medium heat. Add the sliced garlic. When it sizzles, after about 30 seconds, add the mushrooms and season with ¼ teaspoon of the salt and a pinch of pepper. Cook the mushrooms until just cooked, 5 to 6 minutes.

2. Transfer the mushrooms to a food processor. Add the truffle oil and puree to a smooth consistency. Cover the mushroom puree and keep warm.

3. Preheat the oven to 350°F.

4. Arrange the heads of lettuce in a single layer in a medium-size shallow baking dish.

5. Put the chicken broth, ⅓ cup of water, 1 crushed garlic clove, ¼ teaspoon of the salt, and a pinch of pepper in a small, heavy-bottomed saucepan and bring to a boil over high heat. Pour the broth mixture over the lettuce. Cover the baking dish with aluminum foil and bake until the lettuce is tender, 25 to 30 minutes.

6. Meanwhile, put 4 cups of the milk, the remaining crushed garlic clove, the remaining ¼ teaspoon of salt, and a pinch of pepper in a wide, heavy-bottomed pot and bring to a simmer over medium heat. Carefully

add the halibut fillets and let simmer until the fish is opaque and flakes easily when lightly pressed, 5 to 6 minutes.

7. Make a quick sauce by bringing the remaining ¼ cup of milk to a simmer in a small, heavy-bottomed saucepan over medium heat and cook until slightly thickened, about 2 minutes. Swirl in the remaining 1 tablespoon of butter and the chives and lemon juice.

8. Mound some mushroom puree in the center of each of 4 dinner plates. Using a slotted spoon, remove the halibut fillets from their cooking liquid and lean 1 fillet against the mushroom puree on each plate. Spoon some sauce over the fish on each plate, set a head of braised lettuce alongside, and serve.

## nutritional information

(PER SERVING)

| | |
|---|---|
| Calories | 198 |
| Fat | 8 g |
| Saturated Fat | 1 g |
| Trans Fat | 0 g |
| Total Carbohydrates | 4 g |
| Dietary Fiber | 2 g |
| Total Sugars | 1 g |
| Protein | 28 g |
| Cholesterol | 42 mg |
| Sodium | 267 mg |

## exchanges

| | |
|---|---|
| Fat | 1 |
| Lean Meat | 3 |
| Vegetables | 0.5 |

CARBOHYDRATE CHOICE: 0

# prosciutto-wrapped halibut

## WITH ASPARAGUS AND CHERVIL

In my cooking, I strive for harmony (things that meld seamlessly on the plate and palate) but also for the less obvious ideal of contrast, things that are, for lack of a better word, opposites—in flavor, temperature, and texture. Case in point: Simply wrapping halibut in prosciutto and crisping the meat around the fish puts a little salt and crunch in every bite. The prosciutto really grounds this dish, which also features asparagus that has been cooked and cooled and diced egg whites. It would be too one-note without the prosciutto, but with it, a simple balance is achieved. **SERVES 4**

## INGREDIENTS

*12 spears large or jumbo asparagus (about 1 pound), peeled with ends trimmed*
*½ tablespoon extra-virgin olive oil*
*½ tablespoon freshly squeezed lemon juice*
*1 hard-cooked egg, white part only, finely diced*

*4 halibut fillets (about 4 ounces each)*
*Pinch of freshly ground black pepper*
*4 thin slices of prosciutto (about 1 ounce total)*
*2 teaspoons canola oil*
*2 tablespoons chopped fresh chervil*

1. Bring a large pot of water to a boil. Cook the asparagus in the boiling water until al dente, about 8 minutes.

2. Fill a large bowl halfway with ice water. Use tongs to remove the asparagus from the pot and transfer it to the ice water to stop the cooking and preserve the color. Once the asparagus has cooled, drain it and pat dry with paper towels. Set the asparagus aside.

3. Make a vinaigrette by whisking the olive oil and lemon juice together in a bowl, then whisking in the diced egg white.

4. Preheat the oven to 350°F.

5. Season each halibut fillet with pepper and then wrap each with a slice of prosciutto.

6. Heat the canola oil in a large, heavy-bottomed, ovenproof, non-stick pan over medium-high heat. Add the prosciutto-wrapped halibut fillets, seam side down, and sear on both sides until the prosciutto is crisp, about 2 minutes per side. Turn the wrapped halibut over one more time, so that the seam sides are down and bake until the fish is cooked through, 3 to 4 minutes.

7. Arrange 3 asparagus spears on each of 4 dinner plates and spoon the vinaigrette over them. Lean a halibut fillet against the asparagus on each plate. Scatter the chervil over the fish and asparagus and serve.

## nutritional information
(PER SERVING)

Calories.....................380*
Fat..............................26 g*
   Saturated Fat.........4 g
   Trans Fat.................0 g
Total Carbohydrates....6 g
   Dietary Fiber............1 g
   Total Sugars............2 g
Protein.......................23 g
Cholesterol..........67 mg*
Sodium................106 mg

## exchanges

Fat.............................4
Lean Meat....................3
Vegetables....................1

*These values are deceptively high because when you remove the skin it lowers them a bit, but the lower value amounts cannot be accurately calculated.

**CARBOHYDRATE CHOICE: ½**

# cold poached salmon

## WITH HERB COULIS

the beauty of poaching salmon, if you do it right, is that by cooking it very gently you end up with a moist, plump piece of fish that's still salmon colored. This is where that carryover heat I was talking about in the introduction to this chapter really comes into play: Get the salmon out of the pot before it's completely done and let it finish cooking as it rests. Classically, cold poached salmon is topped with or accompanied by mayonnaise, but an herb coulis is much lighter and proves an even better foil for the fish.   **SERVES 4**

### INGREDIENTS

1 leek, both white and green parts, trimmed and cut crosswise into 3 or 4 large pieces and well rinsed

½ medium-size Spanish onion, quartered

½ cup dry white wine

1 teaspoon distilled white vinegar

10 black peppercorns

2 bay leaves, preferably fresh

½ cup Herb Coulis (page 317)

4 pieces of salmon (4 ounces each) with the skin on

1. Pour 2 quarts of water into a large, heavy-bottomed pot. Add the leek, onion, white wine, vinegar, peppercorns, and bay leaves. Bring to a simmer over medium heat.

2. Add the pieces of salmon and let poach until it's almost cooked through, 10 to 12 minutes. Using tongs, very carefully transfer the salmon to a plate and let it cool (discard the poaching liquid and solids). Once cool, cover the salmon loosely with plastic wrap and refrigerate until cold, at least 2 hours, or overnight.

3. When ready to serve, carefully remove and discard the skin from each piece of salmon. Set 1 piece on each of 4 plates, top with some Herb Coulis, and serve.

# salmon

## WITH LEEKS AND CAVIAR

Caviar has a lot of famous partners: blinis, smoked salmon, vodka, and Champagne. I may be alone in this sentiment, but I'd also put leeks high on a list of perfect matches for caviar. Something wonderful happens when the gentle sweetness and meltingly tender texture of the leek is juxtaposed with the tiny pearls of briny caviar. That combination is the basis of this dish, and I hope you find this unheralded twosome as much of a winner as I do. **SERVES 4**

## nutritional information
### (PER SERVING)

Calories......................452
Fat.................................27 g
    Saturated Fat..........6 g
    Trans Fat...................0 g
Total Carbohydrates...27 g
    Dietary Fiber............3 g
    Total Sugars.............5 g
Protein............................27 g
Cholesterol..............90 mg
Sodium....................157 mg

## exchanges

Fat...................................4.5
Starch..........................0.5
Lean Meat.....................3
Vegetables..................2.5

### INGREDIENTS

*2 medium-size Yukon Gold potatoes (4 or 5 ounces each)*

*Coarse salt*

*4 cups leeks, white part only, trimmed well rinsed, and finely chopped*

*2 large cloves garlic, crushed and peeled*

*¼ cup freshly squeezed lemon juice*

*1 tablespoon unsalted butter*

*3 tablespoons extra-virgin olive oil, plus more for serving*

*4 salmon fillets (4 ounces each; preferably cut in squares)*

*Freshly ground black pepper*

*¼ cup chopped fresh chives*

*2 teaspoons caviar (preferably American sturgeon)*

*2 teaspoons crème fraîche*

1. Preheat the oven to 350°F.

2. Peel the potatoes and cut them in half lengthwise. Put the potatoes in a small, heavy-bottomed saucepan just large enough to hold them in a single layer. Cover the potatoes with cold water and add ½ teaspoon of salt, and bring to a simmer over medium-high heat. Cook the potatoes until they can be easily pierced with a small, sharp knife, 10 to 12 minutes.

3. Put the leeks in a medium-size, heavy-bottomed saucepan and add 1½ cups of water, the garlic, and a pinch

of salt. Bring to a boil over medium-high heat and cook until tender, 15 to 18 minutes, stirring occasionally.

4. Transfer the leek mixture to a food processor and puree until smooth. Add the lemon juice, 2 tablespoons of the olive oil, and the butter. Puree the leek mixture until all of the ingredients are thoroughly incorporated, then pass it through a fine-mesh strainer set over a bowl, pressing down on the mixture with a spatula to extract as much flavorful puree as possible. Return the leek puree to the pan and cover it.

5. Heat the remaining 1 tablespoon of olive oil in a large, heavy-bottomed, ovenproof pan over high heat. Season the salmon with a pinch each of salt and pepper. Put the salmon in the pan and cook for 1 to 2 minutes per side. Transfer the pan to the oven and bake the fish until it has finished cooking, 3 to 4 minutes.

6. Meanwhile, reheat the leek puree briefly over medium heat. Put 1 piece of potato in the center of each of 4 plates and lightly crush the potatoes with a fork. Season the potatoes with a pinch each of salt and pepper, a few drops of extra-virgin olive oil, and 1 tablespoon of chopped chives. Ladle some leek puree over the potato on each plate and top it with a piece of salmon. Spoon ½ teaspoon of caviar and ½ teaspoon of crème fraîche over each piece of salmon and serve.

## nutritional information
### (PER SERVING)

| | |
|---|---:|
| Calories | 260 |
| Fat | 6 g |
| Saturated Fat | 1 g |
| Trans Fat | 0 g |
| Total Carbohydrates | 9 g |
| Dietary Fiber | 2 g |
| Total Sugars | 3 g |
| Protein | 39 g |
| Cholesterol | 2 mg |
| Sodium | 280 mg |

## exchanges

| | |
|---|---:|
| Fat | 0.5 |
| Lean Meat | 4.5 |
| Vegetables | 1.5 |

CARBOHYDRATE CHOICE: ½

# poached skate

## WITH TOMATO-SAFFRON BROTH

Skate is one of the more unusual fish one can cook, as indicated by the way it's sold: Because of skate's raylike shape, the meat is referred to as "wings," although it actually comes from the enlarged pectoral fin of the fish. Pleasantly ridged and very delicate and flaky, skate wings lend themselves to gentle cooking techniques, which is what led me to poach them right in the broth they're served with rather than searing them in a hot pan. Be sure to serve the skate as soon as you've cooked it; it has a high gelatin content that threatens to ruin its texture as it chills. **SERVES 4**

## INGREDIENTS

1 tablespoon olive oil

½ medium-size onion,
   cut into small dice

½ medium-size fennel bulb,
   cut into small dice

2 cloves garlic, very thinly sliced

2 teaspoons tomato paste

5 medium-size plum tomatoes,
   coarsely chopped

½ cup dry white wine

2 teaspoons distilled white vinegar

Pinch of crushed red pepper flakes

¼ teaspoon crumbled saffron
   threads

Pinch of coarse salt

Pinch of freshly ground black pepper

2 cups store-bought low-sodium
   chicken broth

4 skate wings (about 6 ounces each)

1 tablespoon fresh thyme leaves

1. Heat the olive oil in a medium-size, heavy-bottomed pot over medium heat. Add the onion, fennel, and garlic and cook until softened but not browned, about 4 minutes. Add the tomato paste and cook, stirring to coat the other ingredients with the paste, for 2 minutes. Add the tomatoes, white wine, vinegar, red pepper flakes, saffron, salt, and black pepper. Bring to a simmer and cook, stirring occasionally, until the tomatoes break down, 8 to 10 minutes. Stir in the chicken broth and bring the mixture to a simmer.

2. Carefully lower the skate wings into the broth and poach until cooked through, 3 to 4 minutes.

3. Carefully remove the wings with a fish or other large spatula and set 1 wing in each of 4 wide, shallow bowls. Ladle the broth over and around the fish. Garnish with the thyme leaves and serve.

variations and suggestions: You can add poached mussels to the broth after removing the skate (follow the instructions in Steps 2 and 3 on page 221 for poaching the mussels). Or make this dish with mussels in place of the skate.

## shop right

**SKATE:** When shopping for skate, beware of any ammoniated smell, which is a sure sign of spoilage. Skate is highly perishable, so be sure to cook it the same day you purchase it.

## nutritional information
### (PER SERVING)

Calories......................309
Fat.................................20 g
   Saturated Fat........2 g
   Trans Fat.................0 g
Total Carbohydrates....7 g
   Dietary Fiber.............1 g
   Total Sugars.............2 g
Protein........................30 g
Cholesterol...............52 mg
Sodium...................371 mg

## exchanges

Fat.................................3
Lean Meat.....................3
Vegetables....................1

**CARBOHYDRATE CHOICE: ½**

# pan-seared snapper
## WITH A QUICK OLIVE RELISH

Pan searing snapper over very high heat turns the skin crisp and toothsome, a perfect contrast to the delicate flesh. Another perfect contrast—olive relish is made by simply combining olives, olive oil, and parsley with shallots and celery that have been cooked in a vinegary solution. You can sear the fish in the time it takes the shallots and celery to cool, meaning you can cook this dish from beginning to end in about ten minutes. Go for it.

**SERVES 4**

## INGREDIENTS

¼ cup distilled white vinegar

4 small shallots, finely diced

4 ribs celery, finely diced

¾ cup pitted, chopped green olives

1 lemon, divided into sections,
   sections peeled (see page 211)

3 tablespoons olive oil

1 tablespoon minced fresh parsley

1 tablespoon canola oil

4 snapper fillets (5 ounces each)
   with the skin on

Pinch of freshly ground black pepper

1. Put the vinegar and 1 cup of cold water in a medium-size pot and bring to a boil over high heat. Add the shallots and celery and cook until slightly softened, about 1 minute. Drain the shallots and celery and let cool.

2. Put the cooled shallots and celery in a bowl. Add the olives, lemon sections, olive oil, and parsley and stir to mix. Set the olive relish aside.

3. Heat the canola oil in a large, heavy-bottomed, nonstick pan over medium-high heat. Add the snapper fillets, skin side down, and sear until the skin is very crisp, about 5 minutes. Turn the fish over and cook for 1 to 2 minutes to heat it through.

4. Put a snapper fillet in the center of each of 4 plates. Using a slotted spoon, top the fish with the olive relish. Add the pepper to the olive oil left in the relish bowl and decoratively drizzle the oil around the fish, then serve.

# roast snapper

## WITH SCALLION PUREE

Picture flaky, white snapper atop a puree of scallions loaded with fresh, sweet onion flavor. This elemental combination—as stark visually as it is on the palate—works because the fish, usually the focal point of a dish, curiously enough here offers relief from the intense scallion puree. **SERVES 4**

## nutritional information
### (PER SERVING)

| | |
|---|---|
| Calories | 266 |
| Fat | 14 g |
| Saturated Fat | 2 g |
| Trans Fat | 0 g |
| Total Carbohydrates | 3 g |
| Dietary Fiber | 1 g |
| Total Sugars | 1 g |
| Protein | 30 g |
| Cholesterol | 52 mg |
| Sodium | 341 mg |

## exchanges

| | |
|---|---|
| Fat | 2.5 |
| Lean Meat | 3 |
| Vegetables | 0.5 |

## INGREDIENTS

1½ bunches scallions, ends trimmed

½ bunch fresh flat-leaf parsley

3 small ice cubes

1½ tablespoons extra-virgin olive oil

1 small clove garlic

½ teaspoon coarse salt

½ teaspoon freshly ground black pepper

2 tablespoons canola oil

4 snapper fillets (about 5 ounces each), with the skin on

1. Bring a medium-size pot of water to a boil over high heat. Fill a large bowl halfway with ice water.

2. Blanch the scallions in the boiling water for 10 seconds. Use tongs to remove the scallions from the pot and transfer them to the ice water to stop the cooking and set the color. Repeat with the parsley, adding it to the bowl of ice water with the scallions. Drain the scallions and parsley and coarsely chop them. You should have about 1½ cups of chopped herbs.

3. Transfer the herbs to a food processor and add 2 tablespoons of cold water and the ice cubes, olive oil, garlic, salt, and pepper. Process until smooth and well incorporated, about 1 minute. You should have about 2 cups of scallion puree. (You can refrigerate the puree in an airtight container overnight; just be sure to first chill it by placing it in a stainless-steel bowl set atop another bowl half full of ice water and stirring it until cold. This will keep the scallion puree from turning brown. Let the puree

come to room temperature before proceeding.)

4. Preheat the oven to 350°F.

5. Heat the canola oil in a wide, deep, heavy-bottomed, ovenproof pan over medium-high heat. Add the snapper, skin side down, and cook, pressing down on the fish with a spatula to keep it from curling, for 3 to 4 minutes. Turn the fish over and bake it until cooked through, 7 to 8 minutes, depending on its thickness.

6. To serve, spoon some scallion puree into the center of each of 4 dinner plates and top with a fillet.

## nutritional information
(PER SERVING)

| | |
|---|---|
| Calories | 426 |
| Fat | 27 g |
| Saturated Fat | 10 g |
| Trans Fat | 0 g |
| Total Carbohydrates | 9 g |
| Dietary Fiber | 1 g |
| Total Sugars | 1 g |
| Protein | 31 g |
| Cholesterol | 83 mg |
| Sodium | 236 mg |

## exchanges

| | |
|---|---|
| Fat | 5 |
| Starch | 0.5 |
| Lean Meat | 3 |

**CARBOHYDRATE CHOICE: ½**

# snapper piccata

One of my first big jobs in New York City was working as sous chef to Alfred Portale at the legendary Gotham Bar and Grill. One of the dishes on our early menu was a quickly floured and sautéed fish sauced with a beurre blanc and finished with capers and scallions. I've long since forgone such complicated sauce making in my own kitchen, especially at home, but I've never lost my affection for the combination of snapper and the gentle acidity of white wine. Here, the combination is achieved by slicing and quickly cooking the fish, then topping it with a simple pan sauce: Because the pieces of snapper are so thin, the flavors penetrate effortlessly.   **SERVES 4**

## INGREDIENTS

¼ cup all-purpose flour

¼ cup olive oil

4 snapper fillets (about 5 ounces each) with the skin, cut on the diagonal into thirds

½ cup dry white wine

½ cup store-bought low-sodium chicken broth

4 tablespoons (½ stick) unsalted butter

4 scallions, white part only, trimmed and thinly sliced diagonally

2 tablespoons chopped fresh chives

2 tablespoons plus 2 teaspoons freshly squeezed lemon juice

2 tablespoons drained capers

Pinch of freshly ground black pepper

1. Spread the flour out in a wide, shallow bowl. Heat the olive oil in a large, deep pan over medium-high heat.

2. Dredge the snapper fillets in the flour, shaking off any excess. Put the fish in the pan, skin side down, and cook until the skin is crisp, about 2 minutes. Turn the fillets and cook until just cooked through, about 2 minutes longer. Transfer the fillets to a platter, skin side up.

3. Return the pan to the heat, add the white wine, and cook until the wine is almost evaporated, about 3 minutes, stirring to loosen any flavorful bits cooked onto the bottom of the pan. Add the chicken broth, bring to a simmer, and let simmer until reduced by about half, about 4 minutes. Swirl in the butter until it melts, then stir in the scallions and chives.

4. Remove the pan from the heat and add the lemon juice, capers, and pepper. Pour the sauce over the fish and serve family style from the center of the table.

how low can you go?

You can omit dredging the fish in the flour and use half the amount of olive oil; the fish won't be as crisp, but the flavors will be more or less the same.

CARBOHYDRATE CHOICE: 0

# whole roasted snapper

One of the most dramatic things you can bring to a dinner table is also one of the easiest to prepare. A whole roast fish makes a big impact, but you want to make sure to cook the fish properly. Doing this depends on understanding something fundamental: When dealing with a whole fish you're contending with a little universe of textures, including skin, flesh, and bone. Just as you would when grilling a thick steak, it's best to let the fish spend some time at room temperature before cooking it, which will help all those disparate elements get along during their time together in the oven. With this in mind, be sure to purchase an impeccably fresh fish with clear eyes, a firm body, and a clean (unfishy) smell.

If you've never roasted a whole fish, it might sound daunting, but the worst that can happen is that you slightly overcook it, in which case you can shift gears and make a salad: Fillet and flake the fish and toss it with chopped celery, chopped onion, and lemon juice.

## nutritional information
(PER SERVING)

| | |
|---|---|
| Calories | 215 |
| Fat | 6 g |
| Saturated Fat | 1 g |
| Trans Fat | 0 g |
| Total Carbohydrates | 3 g |
| Dietary Fiber | 1 g |
| Total Sugars | 1 g |
| Protein | 35 g |
| Cholesterol | 63 mg |
| Sodium | 350 mg |

## exchanges

| | |
|---|---|
| Fat | 0.5 |
| Lean Meat | 4 |
| Vegetables | 0.5 |

Whole Roasted Snapper

You can also roast whole fish other than snapper, including striped bass, branzino (the most popular whole-roasted fish in Italian restaurants), and pompano.

**SERVES 4**

## INGREDIENTS

*1 whole snapper (about 3 pounds),*
  *gilled, gutted, and scaled*
  *(ask your fishmonger to do this)*
*½ teaspoon coarse salt*
*Pinch of freshly ground black pepper*
*10 sprigs fresh tarragon*

*1 lemon, very thinly sliced*
*½ red onion, very thinly sliced*
*2 cloves garlic, very thinly sliced*
*1 tablespoon olive oil*
*Nonstick cooking spray*

1. Preheat the oven to 450°F. When preheated, put a rack in a roasting pan and preheat it in the oven for 10 to 15 minutes.

2. Rinse the fish inside and out under gently running cold water and pat dry with paper towels. Season the inside of the snapper with the salt and pepper. Stuff it with the tarragon, lemon, onion, and garlic. Score the fish's skin, preferably with a razor blade, making 2-inch-long diagonal slashes about 2 inches apart and taking care not to cut into the flesh. Rub the olive oil over the outside of the fish.

3. Remove the roasting pan from the oven and spray the rack with nonstick cooking spray. Set the fish on the rack and return the pan to the oven.

4. Bake the fish until the flesh in its center—midway between the head and tail—is opaque, 25 to 30 minutes. (Use a paring knife to pry apart the skin at one of the scores in the skin so you can peek.)

5. Transfer the snapper to a serving platter and present it to the table. Then, using 2 tablespoons, start just behind the collar of the fish (below the head, just behind the gills) and draw one of the spoons right down the center, breaking through the skin. (Don't worry if the fish breaks into pieces; you've already wowed everybody with the whole fish itself.) Pry the skin away from the flesh of the fish and use the spoons to remove and serve portions of the fish on 4 plates. (Gently flip the fish over and repeat the process on the second side.)

# swordfish

## WITH LENTILS AND BACON

Lentils are sort of a forgotten legume in contemporary American kitchens, which I've always thought was a shame because they have such a gentle yet earthy flavor and a wonderful texture. I use lentils all the time in my restaurant, often cooking them long enough that they just barely hold their shape. I recommend using the French green lentils called *lentilles du Puy*, which are sweeter and more flavorful than other lentils. They are also more forgiving to cook with, holding their shape longer than other varieties, which tend to turn to mush rather quickly. Here they're complemented by turkey bacon and set off against two perfect foils: swordfish and a vinaigrette made with coarse grain mustard and white balsamic vinegar. **SERVES 4**

## nutritional information
### (PER SERVING)

Calories ....................... 471
Fat .............................. 23 g
   Saturated Fat ........... 4 g
   Trans Fat ................. 0 g
Total Carbohydrates ... 32 g
   Dietary Fiber ........... 12 g
   Total Sugars ............. 7 g
Protein ........................ 34 g
Cholesterol .............. 51 mg
Sodium ................. 553 mg

## exchanges

Fat ............................... 4
Starch ......................... 1.5
Lean Meat .................... 3
Vegetables ................... 1

---

## INGREDIENTS

¼ cup plus ½ tablespoon
   extra-virgin olive oil

1 cup diced celery

1 cup diced onion

⅔ cup diced carrot

2 cloves garlic, minced

3 cups store-bought low-sodium
   chicken or vegetable broth

⅔ cup lentils, preferably French
   lentilles du Puy

1 teaspoon fresh thyme leaves

½ teaspoon coarse salt

⅛ teaspoon freshly ground
   black pepper

3 tablespoons freshly squeezed
   lemon juice

1 tablespoon distilled white vinegar

1 tablespoon white balsamic vinegar

2 tablespoons coarse grain mustard

Nonstick cooking spray

2 slices turkey bacon, cut into ½-inch
   pieces

4 swordfish fillets (4 ounces each;
   preferably cut in 3-inch squares)

¼ cup microgreens (next page)

---

1. Heat 1½ tablespoons of the olive oil in a large, heavy-bottomed pot over medium heat. Add the cel-ery, onion, carrot, and garlic and cook, stirring, until softened but not browned, about 8 minutes. Add the

## shop right

**MICROGREENS:**
Microgreens are a mixture of smaller delicate varieties of everything from salad greens to herbs. They are available in many specialty food markets, but if you can't find them, substitute frisée.

chicken broth, lentils, thyme, salt, and a pinch of pepper and bring to a simmer. Let simmer until the lentils are soft, about 30 minutes.

2. Meanwhile, make the vinaigrette: Put the lemon juice, white vinegar, white balsamic vinegar, mustard, the remaining 3 tablespoons of the olive oil, and a few grinds of pepper in a bowl and whisk them together.

3. After the lentils have cooked for about 30 minutes, spray a heavy-bottomed nonstick pan with cooking spray and heat it over medium heat. Add the turkey bacon and cook until

browned and the fat is rendered, about 7 minutes. Using a slotted spoon, transfer the bacon to paper towels, leaving the fat in the pan.

4. Heat the pan with the bacon fat over medium-high heat. Add the swordfish fillets to the pan and sear until just cooked through, 4 to 5 minutes per side.

5. To serve, divide the lentils among 4 wide, shallow bowls. Top each with a swordfish fillet and drizzle the vinaigrette over and around the fish. Sprinkle the bacon over the fish and garnish with the microgreens.

**CARBOHYDRATE CHOICE: 0**

# grilled tuna

## WITH TONNATO SAUCE AND A RADISH SALAD

based on the Italian dish *vitello tonnato,* in which slices of cooked, cooled veal are layered, lasagna like, with a rich sauce made from preserved tuna, this main course dish might also be dubbed "tuna, two ways" because it dresses the fresh fish with *tonnato* sauce. To keep the fat count down, the sauce is made with domestic tuna packed in water, but there's just enough extra-virgin olive oil to give it a richness that recalls the classic. A radish salad adds some peppery crunch.                    **SERVES 4**

## INGREDIENTS

2 large egg yolks (see Note)

3 ounces canned tuna in water
(½ of a 6-ounce can), drained

2 large cloves garlic, minced

2 to 4 tablespoons plus 1 teaspoon
freshly squeezed lemon juice

⅓ cup plus 1 teaspoon extra-virgin
olive oil

Pinch of coarse salt

Freshly ground black pepper

4 ribs celery, cut diagonally
into ¼-inch-thick slices,
plus 2 tablespoons of the prettiest
leaves from the bunch

2 large radishes, very thinly sliced

1 tablespoon chopped fresh flat-leaf
parsley leaves

1 pound sushi-grade tuna steaks

1 tablespoon canola oil

1. Make the *tonnato* sauce: Put the egg yolks in a food processor and process just to emulsify them. Add the tuna, garlic, and 1 tablespoon of the lemon juice and pulse to combine. With the motor running, slowly add the ⅓ cup of olive oil in a thin stream to make a thick, creamy emulsion. Add a pinch each of salt and pepper. Taste the sauce; if it seems too thick or intense, blend in another tablespoon or two of lemon juice.

2. Build a fire in a charcoal grill, letting the coals burn down until covered with white ash or preheat a gas grill to medium-high.

3. Meanwhile, make the radish salad: Put the celery, radishes, 1 teaspoon of lemon juice, and the remaining 1 teaspoon of olive oil in a small bowl and toss them together. Scatter the parsley over the top.

4. Rub the canola oil over the tuna and season it with a pinch of pepper. Grill the tuna until nicely charred on both sides but still rare in the center, about 4 minutes per side.

5. To serve, pool some *tonnato* sauce in the center of each of 4 dinner plates. Put a piece of tuna on top and mound some radish salad over the tuna.

note: The *tonnato* sauce contains two raw egg yolks. Be sure to use very fresh eggs of the best quality and that have been stored in the refrigerator.

## nutritional information
(PER SERVING)

Calories....................438
Fat.............................31 g
   Saturated Fat...........5 g
   Trans Fat..................0 g
Total Carbohydrates.....3 g
   Dietary Fiber.............1 g
   Total Sugars.............1 g
Protein......................34 g
Cholesterol............159 mg
Sodium..................199 mg

## exchanges

Fat.............................5.5
Lean Meat....................4
Vegetables.................0.5

## nutritional information
(PER SERVING)

| | |
|---|---|
| Calories | 526 |
| Fat | 32 g |
| Saturated Fat | 5 g |
| Trans Fat | 0 g |
| Total Carbohydrates | 18 g |
| Dietary Fiber | 3 g |
| Total Sugars | 3 g |
| Protein | 39 g |
| Cholesterol | 147 mg |
| Sodium | 380 mg |

## exchanges

| | |
|---|---|
| Fat | 6 |
| Starch | 0.5 |
| Lean Meat | 5 |
| Medium Fat Meat | 0.5 |
| Vegetables | 0.5 |

CARBOHYDRATE CHOICE: 1

# niçoise-style tuna

## WITH BEANS, POTATO, AND OLIVES

all the telltale components of a niçoise salad—tiny green beans, eggs, olives, and so on—are present in this new take on that classic, with the important swap of fresh, seared tuna for the preserved. After the salad is tossed and plated alongside the warm fish, you drizzle the remaining dressing around it like a sauce. The fat content of this dish is relatively high, but bear in mind that this really is a meal in itself, featuring protein and salad on the same plate, with a very low carbohydrate count, especially considering the presence of the potato.

**SERVES 4**

## INGREDIENTS

4 ounces haricots verts, ends trimmed

2 small Yukon Gold potatoes, peeled and cut into 1-inch dice

4 tuna fillets (5 ounces each)

¼ cup plus 2 tablespoons extra-virgin olive oil

Pinch of coarse salt

⅓ teaspoon freshly ground black pepper

2 soft-boiled eggs

2 tablespoons Dijon mustard

2 cups frisée lettuce

¼ cup chopped fresh flat-leaf parsley leaves

8 niçoise olives, pitted and slivered

1. Build a fire in a charcoal grill, letting the coals burn down until covered with white ash. If using a gas grill, preheat it to medium-high after the beans and potatoes have been cooked. If using a grill pan, briefly preheat the pan over medium-high heat.

2. Bring a medium-size pot of water to a boil over high heat. Fill a large bowl halfway with ice water.

3. Cook the haricots verts in the boiling water until tender, about 2 minutes. Drain the beans and transfer them to

the ice water to stop the cooking and preserve the color. Once the beans have cooled, drain them again and pat them dry with paper towels.

**4.** Rinse out the pot and fill it halfway with water. Bring the water to a boil and add the potatoes. Boil the potatoes until the pieces are tender when pierced with a knife, but still hold their shape, about 5 minutes. Drain the potatoes and set them aside to cool.

**5.** Rub the tuna fillets with 2 tablespoons of the olive oil and season them with the salt and ¼ teaspoon of the pepper. Grill the tuna for 3 to 4 minutes per side for medium-rare or a bit longer for more well-done. Put 1 piece of tuna in the center of each of 4 dinner plates.

**6.** Make the dressing and salad: Put the eggs and mustard in a large bowl and whisk, breaking up the eggs and creating an emulsion. Slowly whisk in the ¼ cup of olive oil, then ¼ cup plus 1 tablespoon of hot water. Season the dressing with the remaining ¼ teaspoon of pepper. Add the frisée, haricots verts, potatoes, and parsley to the bowl and gently toss.

**7.** To serve, mound some salad alongside the tuna on each plate. Top each serving with a few olive slivers.

*Niçoise-Style Tuna*

CARBOHYDRATE CHOICES: 2; 1½ ADJUSTED FOR FIBER

# grilled tuna

## WITH RED PEPPER PUREE, BLACK OLIVE RELISH, AND WHITE BEAN PUREE

*a*t my restaurant Ouest, this dish with its vibrant colors, balance of sweetness and acidity, and smooth purees, is so popular, that it's been on the menu almost nonstop since we first opened our doors nearly ten years ago. I tried swapping it out a few times but was always met with such resistance from our regulars that I think I'll stop trying. **SERVES 4**

## nutritional information
(PER SERVING)

| | |
|---|---|
| Calories | 501 |
| Fat | 26 g |
| Saturated Fat | 4 g |
| Trans Fat | 0 g |
| Total Carbohydrates | 30 g |
| Dietary Fiber | 8 g |
| Total Sugars | 4 g |
| Protein | 36 g |
| Cholesterol | 43 mg |
| Sodium | 193 mg |

## exchanges

| | |
|---|---|
| Fat | 4.5 |
| Starch | 1.5 |
| Lean Meat | 3.5 |
| Vegetables | 1 |

## INGREDIENTS

2 roasted red peppers (page 324),
   1 seeded and coarsely chopped,
   1 seeded and cut into fine dice
1 tablespoon tomato paste
1 tablespoon plus 1 teaspoon
   sherry vinegar
¼ teaspoon minced garlic
⅛ teaspoon fresh thyme leaves
Coarse salt
Pinch of crushed red pepper flakes
5 tablespoons extra-virgin olive oil

8 kalamata olives, pitted and
   finely diced
1 tablespoon finely grated
   lemon zest
2 teaspoons chopped fresh flat-leaf
   parsley leaves
1 can (15 or 16 ounces) organic,
   low-sodium white beans,
   rinsed and drained
4 tuna fillets (about 4 ounces each)
Pinch of freshly ground black pepper

1. Make the red pepper puree: Put the coarsely chopped roasted pepper, tomato paste, sherry vinegar, garlic, thyme, ⅛ teaspoon of salt, red pepper flakes, and 2 tablespoons of water in a food processor. Process until liquid, stopping the motor once or twice to scrape down the side of the bowl with a rubber spatula. With the motor running, drizzle in 2 tablespoons of the olive oil and process until the mixture is smooth. You should have a generous ½ cup of pepper puree. Transfer the pepper puree to a bowl and clean out the processor before making the bean puree.

2. Make the olive relish: Put the olives, finely diced roasted pepper, lemon zest, 1 tablespoon of the olive oil, and the parsley in a bowl. Toss them together and set aside.

3. Make the bean puree: Put the beans in the food processor with ⅛ teaspoon of salt, and the remaining 2 tablespoons of olive oil. Puree until smooth. If the mixture looks too stiff, blend in a few tablespoons of hot water. Set the bean puree aside.

4. Build a fire in a charcoal grill, letting the coals burn down until covered with white ash or preheat a gas grill to medium-high.

5. Season the tuna fillets with a pinch of black pepper and a pinch of salt. Grill the tuna for 3 to 4 minutes per side for medium-rare or a bit longer for more well-done.

6. Quickly warm the bean puree in a small, heavy-bottomed pot over medium heat or by setting the pot right on the grill.

7. To serve, mound some bean puree on each of 4 dinner plates. Lean a tuna fillet against the puree. Top the tuna with some olive relish and drizzle some red pepper puree around the tuna and bean puree on each plate.

CARBOHYDRATE CHOICES: 2

# pan-seared tuna

## WITH POTATO PUREE, MUSHROOM BROTH, AND MUSHROOM SALAD

Sometimes main courses are deceptive. They seem to be about the protein—in this case, tuna—but often they're really about what's going on around it. That's certainly the case here, where when you get right down to it, the tuna is supporting, rounding out, and giving weight to the mushroom-themed elements of the dish: the broth and the salad. The finished dish is so pretty and delicious that your friends and family might not notice its economy: It uses inexpensive button mushrooms and utilizes every part of them. The stems flavor the broth and the caps are the foundation of the salad. **SERVES 4**

## INGREDIENTS

8 white button mushrooms, stems trimmed, removed, and set aside; caps very thinly sliced

¼ cup dry white wine

1 medium-size clove garlic, crushed and peeled

1 tablespoon Porcini Powder (page 325)

1¼ teaspoons coarse salt

1¼ pounds Idaho or russet potatoes, peeled and cut into large dice

2 cups loosely packed fresh flat-leaf parsley leaves

¼ cup freshly squeezed lemon juice

2 tablespoons extra-virgin olive oil

A few drops white truffle oil

¼ cup plus 2 tablespoons low-fat milk

1 tablespoon olive oil

1 tablespoon unsalted butter

2 tablespoons canola oil

4 tuna fillets (4 ounces each)

## nutritional information
(PER SERVING)

Calories ..................... 491
Fat ................................ 27 g
   Saturated Fat .......... 5 g
   Trans Fat ................. 0 g
Total Carbohydrates ... 26 g
   Dietary Fiber ............ 4 g
   Total Sugars ............. 3 g
Protein ........................ 33 g
Cholesterol ............... 52 mg
Sodium ................. 681 mg

## exchanges

Fat ................................... 4.5
Starch ................................. 1
Lean Meat ...................... 3.5
Vegetables ........................ 1

1. Make the mushroom broth: Put the mushroom stems, the white wine, garlic, Porcini Powder, ¼ teaspoon of the salt and 2 cups of water, in a small heavy-bottomed saucepan and bring to a simmer over medium-high heat. Reduce the heat and let simmer until the broth is flavorful, about 40 minutes. Strain the broth through a fine-mesh strainer set over a small pot and keep warm. Discard the solids.

2. Put the potatoes and 8 cups of water in a medium-size, heavy-bottomed saucepan and set it over high heat. Add the remaining 1 teaspoon of salt to the water and bring to a boil. Boil the potatoes until tender when pierced with a knife, about 10 minutes.

3. While the potatoes are cooking, put the mushroom caps, parsley, lemon juice, extra-virgin olive oil, and truffle oil in a bowl and toss to mix. Set the mushroom salad aside.

4. Drain the potatoes into a colander and return the potatoes to the pot. Place the pot over low heat and cook, stirring, until any lingering moisture evaporates, 1 to 2 minutes. Transfer the potatoes to a bowl and mash them with a potato masher. Add the milk, regular olive oil, and butter and continue mashing until all of the ingredients are incorporated and the potatoes are smooth.

5. Heat the canola oil in a large pan over medium-high heat. Put the tuna in the pan and sear the fish 3 to 4 minutes per side for medium-rare or a bit longer for more well-done.

6. To serve, spoon some potato puree in 4 wide, shallow bowls and top each with a piece of tuna. Spoon some mushroom salad alongside each piece of tuna. Ladle some broth around the fish and potatoes.

## nutritional information
(PER SERVING)

| | |
|---|---|
| Calories | 224 |
| Fat | 11 g |
| Saturated Fat | 3 g |
| Trans Fat | 0 g |
| Total Carbohydrates | 5 g |
| Dietary Fiber | 1 g |
| Total Sugars | 2 g |
| Protein | 21 g |
| Cholesterol | 49 mg |
| Sodium | 327 mg |

## exchanges

| | |
|---|---|
| Fat | 2 |
| Lean Meat | 2 |
| Vegetables | 0.5 |

CARBOHYDRATE CHOICE: 0

# white fish en papillote

I know what you're thinking: "What's this fancy French term, *en papillote*, doing in this supposedly accessible book?" Relax, this is actually one of the easiest techniques in the entire tome. *En papillote* simply refers to cooking ingredients, usually fish, vegetables, and aromatics, in a sealed parchment paper bundle. As they bake together, the controlled environment causes the fish to steam to a tender flakiness, while absorbing the flavors that surround it. An extra benefit is that the presentation is a crowd-pleaser: You just plop the packets on plates and let everybody cut into his or her own at the table.

As if this weren't all easy and appealing enough, sometime in the past few generations somebody realized that you can use aluminum foil and get the same result, so you don't even need to run out and buy some parchment paper, which I'm guessing there's only a fifty-fifty chance you have lying around the kitchen. Of course, if you do, go ahead and use it.　　**SERVES 4**

## INGREDIENTS

1 tablespoon unsalted butter

1 lemon, divided into sections, sections peeled (see this page)

4 white fish fillets, such as cod (4 ounces each)

4 plum tomatoes, seeded and thickly sliced crosswise

¼ cup fresh flat-leaf parsley leaves

8 fresh tarragon leaves (optional)

2 small shallots, minced

½ teaspoon coarse salt

¼ teaspoon freshly ground black pepper

½ cup dry white wine

2 tablespoons extra-virgin olive oil

1. Preheat the oven to 325°F.

2. Cut 4 pieces of aluminum foil (or parchment paper), each about 18 inches square. Smear butter on each piece and top each with a fish fillet. Neatly pile the tomatoes, lemon sections, parsley, tarragon, if using, and shallots on top of each fillet and season them with the salt and pepper. Sprinkle each fillet with ⅛ cup of the wine and 1½ teaspoons of the olive oil.

3. Fold the foil up over each fillet and crimp the edges together to create a packet. Put the fish packets on a baking sheet and set the baking sheet over medium heat on a stovetop burner until you hear a sizzling sound, about 45 seconds. Transfer the baking sheet to the oven and bake the fish until cooked through, about 7 minutes.

4. Carefully put a foil packet on each of 4 plates and serve. Remind diners to cut the packets open cautiously, being mindful of the steam that will escape.

## sectioning citrus

To section a lemon or orange, cut off the top and bottom of the fruit to expose the flesh. Stand it upright on a cutting board and, working from top to bottom and following the curve of the fruit, cut away the skin and pith (the bitter white stuff between the skin and flesh) in wide strips. If any pith remains, carefully trim it away. Separate the sections. Working with one section at a time, hold it over a bowl and use the tip of a sharp knife to make a slit in the membrane of the section, loosening the fruit within. Push the fruit out into the bowl and repeat with the remaining sections.

## nutritional information
(PER SERVING)

| | |
|---|---|
| Calories | 147 |
| Fat | 2 g |
| Saturated Fat | 0 g |
| Trans Fat | 0 g |
| Total Carbohydrates | 2 g |
| Dietary Fiber | 1 g |
| Total Sugars | 1 g |
| Protein | 29 g |
| Cholesterol | 52 mg |
| Sodium | 571 mg |

## exchanges

| | |
|---|---|
| Lean Meat | 3 |

CARBOHYDRATE CHOICE: 0

# grilled whole fish

I find grilling a whole fish irresistible—both in terms of presentation and taste. Many home cooks find managing a whole fish on the grill to be somewhat daunting, but it's actually quite simple. Just make sure the grate is nice and clean, brush the fish skin lightly with oil, and once the fish is on the grill, leave it alone and let the fire do its thing. Rather than use a basket to facilitate the turning of the fish, try this simple technique: Start the fish near the edge of the grill closest to you, with the cavity facing you. When the time comes to turn the fish, simply use a spatula to gingerly flip the fish away from you toward the center of the grill.

I've used tarragon in this recipe, but you should by all means experiment with different herbs; each one perfumes the fish in its own distinct way. **SERVES 4**

## INGREDIENTS

*1 whole, white-fleshed fish such as snapper, striped sea bass, or orata (2½ to 3 pounds), gilled, gutted, and scaled (ask your fishmonger to do this)*

*1 large lemon, thinly sliced*
*4 fresh sprigs fresh tarragon*
*1 teaspoon coarse salt*
*1 teaspoon freshly ground black pepper*

1. Build a fire in a charcoal grill, letting the coals burn down until covered with white ash or preheat a gas grill to medium-high.

2. Rinse the fish inside and out under gently running cold water and pat it dry with paper towels. Score the fish's skin, preferably with a razor, making 2-inch-long diagonal slashes about 2 inches apart and taking care not to cut into the flesh.

3. Put the fish on the grill grate and grill until the flesh is opaque in the center, 5 minutes per side. (Use a paring knife to pry apart the skin at one of the scores in the skin so you can peek).

4. Using a large spatula, carefully remove the fish from the grill and set it on a platter. Using 2 tablespoons, start just behind the collar of the fish (below the head, just behind the gills) and draw one of the spoons right

down the center, breaking through the skin. Pry the skin away from the flesh of the fish and use the spoons to divide the flesh among 2 plates. (Gently flip the fish over and repeat the process with the second side.)

CARBOHYDRATE CHOICES: 2

# asian shrimp sauté

When the character Bubba Blue goes off on his ode to shrimp in *Forrest Gump*, audiences couldn't stop laughing, but I just sat there nodding: "Yep, love that one. And that one. That's good, too. Oh, I love pepper shrimp," and on and on and on. Bubba Blue knew what he was talking about when it came to shrimp. Since coming to New York City, I've grown to really enjoy shrimp in Chinese restaurants, and this recipe approximates the effect of a wok for a quick accumulation of flavors that comes pretty close to Chinese: Garlic, ginger, rice vinegar, and soy come together around shrimp, mushrooms, bok choy, and scallions. If you have enough room in your carb count for the day, serve it over white or brown rice, or with rice noodles.

**SERVES 4**

## nutritional information
### (PER SERVING)

| | |
|---|---|
| Calories | 362 |
| Fat | 15 g |
| Saturated Fat | 2 g |
| Trans Fat | 0 g |
| Total Carbohydrates | 27 g |
| Dietary Fiber | 3 g |
| Total Sugars | 3 g |
| Protein | 22 g |
| Cholesterol | 129 mg |
| Sodium | 461 mg |

## exchanges

| | |
|---|---|
| Fat | 2.5 |
| Lean Meat | 2 |
| Vegetables | 2 |

### INGREDIENTS

12 large shrimp (about 1 ounce each), peeled, deveined, and cut in half lengthwise

½ cup cornstarch

2 tablespoons canola oil

2 tablespoons minced garlic

1 tablespoon minced peeled fresh ginger

½ cup dry white wine

2 tablespoons rice wine vinegar, or 1 tablespoon distilled white vinegar

2 tablespoons low-sodium soy sauce

2 tablespoons white sesame seeds

Pinch of crushed red pepper flakes

4 large shiitake mushrooms, stems removed, caps very thinly sliced

⅓ cup roasted unsalted peanuts (optional)

2 scallions, both white and green parts, trimmed and chopped

1 baby bok choy, or 4 stalks regular bok choy, cut into ¼-inch slices

1 tablespoon Asian (dark) sesame oil

**1.** Place the shrimp in a large bowl, and toss with ¼ cup plus 1 tablespoon of the cornstarch.

**2.** Heat the canola oil in a wide, deep, heavy-bottomed, nonstick pan over medium-high heat. Add the garlic and ginger and cook, stirring, until sizzling, but not browned, about 1 minute. Add the shrimp and quickly cook until firm, pink, and just starting to brown, about 4 minutes. Return the shrimp to their bowl (wash it out first).

**3.** Return the pan to the heat and add the wine, vinegar, soy sauce, and ½ cup water. Cook, stirring, to scrape up any flavorful bits from the bottom of the pan. Add the sesame seeds, red pepper flakes, and the remaining 3 tablespoons of cornstarch, stir until the sauce thickens, and cook for about 1 minute. If the sauce starts to become too syrupy, add a tablespoon or 2 more water.

**4.** Add the shrimp, mushrooms, peanuts, if using, scallions, and bok choy to the pan and cook stirring, until warmed through, about 45 seconds.

**5.** Transfer the shrimp and sauce to a bowl, drizzle the sesame oil over them, and serve family style from the center of the table.

## nutritional information
**(PER SERVING)**

| | |
|---|---|
| Calories | 373 |
| Fat | 19 g |
| Saturated Fat | 6 g |
| Trans Fat | 0 g |
| Total Carbohydrates | 18 g |
| Dietary Fiber | 4 g |
| Total Sugars | 73 g |
| Protein | 30 g |
| Cholesterol | 198 mg |
| Sodium | 586 mg |

## exchanges

| | |
|---|---|
| Fat | 3 |
| Lean Meat | 2.5 |
| Medium Fat Meat | 0.5 |
| Vegetables | 2.5 |

CARBOHYDRATE CHOICE: 1

# sizzled shrimp

## WITH TOMATO AND FETA CHEESE

Years ago, I was drafted to serve as the chef of a Greek-leaning Mediterranean restaurant on New York's Upper East Side. I decided to brush up on my knowledge of Greek cuisine and was browsing through a cookbook when I happened upon a version of this dish. My first response was distaste: shrimp with feta cheese and fennel-flavored ouzo? How could it possibly be any good? But I became mildly obsessed with the idea until, finally, I succumbed to my interest and whipped up a version of it. It was better than I ever imagined it could be, and while I've long since moved on from that restaurant, I still have a soft spot for the way this dish finds harmony among these seemingly disparate ingredients. It's delicious even without the ouzo, so much so that I've made the liqueur optional. **SERVES 4**

## INGREDIENTS

1 pound medium-size shrimp
(about 20 shrimp), peeled and
deveined

2 tablespoons freshly squeezed
lemon juice

3 tablespoons olive oil

4 cloves garlic, thinly sliced,
plus 1 clove, minced

1 small fennel bulb, thinly sliced

½ medium-size Spanish onion,
diced

½ cup dry white wine

2 tablespoons distilled white
vinegar

2 tablespoons ouzo (optional)

4 beefsteak tomatoes, coarsely
chopped and drained of liquid

⅛ teaspoon coarse salt

Pinch of crushed red pepper flakes

1 teaspoon chopped fresh oregano

4 ounces feta cheese, crumbled
(about 1 cup)

1 tablespoon chopped fresh flat-leaf
parsley leaves

1. Preheat the oven to 350°F.

2. Put the shrimp in a medium-size bowl, pour the lemon juice over them, stir to coat, and let marinate while you begin making the tomato sauce.

3. Heat 2 tablespoons of the olive oil in a heavy-bottomed pan over medium-high heat. Add the sliced garlic, fennel, and onion and cook until softened but not browned, 5 to 6 minutes. Add the white wine, vinegar, and ouzo, if using, and cook, stirring, to scrape up any flavorful bits from the bottom of the pan.

4. Add the tomatoes, salt, red pepper flakes, and oregano, stir, and cook gently over low heat until the tomatoes soften but still hold their shape, 10 to 15 minutes.

5. Meanwhile, heat the remaining 1 tablespoon of olive oil in another, heavy-bottomed, ovenproof pan over medium-high heat. Add the minced garlic and cook until it sizzles, about 30 seconds. Add the shrimp and cook, stirring, until they turn firm and pink, 35 to 45 seconds. Remove the pan from the heat and top the shrimp with the tomato sauce. Scatter the feta cheese over the shrimp and tomatoes and bake until the tomatoes are bubbly and the cheese is melted, 8 to 10 minutes.

6. Divide the shrimp, tomatoes, and feta cheese among 4 plates or bowls. Scatter parsley over each portion and serve.

Sizzled Shrimp

## nutritional information
### (PER SERVING)

Calories.....................244
Fat..............................7 g
  Saturated Fat............1 g
  Trans Fat.................0 g
Total Carbohydrates...28 g
  Dietary Fiber............2 g
  Total Sugars.............3 g
Protein......................17 g
Cholesterol.............28 mg
Sodium.................384 mg

## exchanges

Fat...............................1
Starch............................1
Lean Meat...................1.5
Vegetables......................1

CARBOHYDRATE CHOICES: 2

# bay scallops provençal

One of the many charms of Provençal-style cooking is that its main-stays, such as saffron, tomatoes, and red peppers, are so pure and elemental that they satisfy with minimal complication. This dish could not be simpler to prepare: You whip up a quick, piquant tomato sauce, toss it with tiny, sweet bay scallops, and serve the scallops over saffron rice. It's a perfect fall dish that will get you in and out of the kitchen in no time, and its flavors match the mood of the season. **SERVES 4**

## INGREDIENTS

*1 tablespoon plus 2 teaspoons extra-virgin olive oil*

*1 large shallot, minced*

*1 large clove garlic, minced*

*4 very ripe plum tomatoes, peeled (see page 129) and coarsely chopped, with their juice*

*½ teaspoon coarse salt*

*¼ teaspoon fresh thyme leaves*

*¼ teaspoon crumbled saffron threads*

*Pinch of crushed red pepper flakes*

*½ small Spanish onion, minced*

*½ red bell pepper, stem and seeds removed, diced*

*½ cup white rice*

*¾ pound bay scallops*

*¼ teaspoon freshly ground black pepper*

*¼ cup coarsely chopped fresh flat-leaf parsley leaves*

**1.** Heat 1 teaspoon of the olive oil in a wide, deep, nonstick pan over medium-high heat. Add the shallot and garlic and cook, stirring, until softened but not browned, about 2 minutes. Add the tomatoes, salt, thyme, ⅛ teaspoon of the saffron, and the red pepper flakes and cook, stirring, until and the tomatoes have begun to give off their liquid and break down, about 5 minutes.

**2.** Transfer the tomato mixture to a blender or food processor (see page 102 for a safety note on blending hot liquids) and puree until it is smooth and has the consistency of a thin tomato sauce. Add a tablespoon or two of cold water to thin the tomato mixture if necessary, bearing in mind that it will thicken a bit more as it is tossed with the scallops. (The tomato mixture can be cooled and refrigerated in an airtight container for up to 4 hours. Let come to room temperature before proceeding.)

3. When ready to continue, make the saffron rice: Heat 2 teaspoons of the olive oil in a small, heavy-bottomed saucepan over medium heat. Add the onion and bell pepper and cook, stirring occasionally, until the vegetables are softened but not browned, about 4 minutes. Add the rice and remaining ⅛ teaspoon of saffron and stir to mix. Add 1 cup of cold water, stir, bring to a simmer, and let simmer until the rice has absorbed the water and is al dente, about 20 minutes.

4. Meanwhile, using the same nonstick pan as you did for the tomato mixture, wipe out the pan and heat the remaining 2 teaspoons of olive oil over medium-high heat until nice and hot. Season the scallops with the black pepper, add them to the pan, and cook until opaque and just faintly golden, 1½ to 2 minutes. Remove the pan from the heat, add the tomato sauce, and toss well to heat the sauce and incorporate the flavors. Some of the sauce should just cling to the scallops, the way it does in a well-made gnocchi dish.

5. Spoon some saffron rice into the center of each of 4 dinner plates. Spoon the scallops and sauce over the rice, scatter the parsley over the top, and serve.

variations and suggestions: You can make this dish with other shellfish, or a mix of shellfish. One nice variation would be 4 large shrimp, peeled and cut in half lengthwise, 4 ounces of bay scallops, and 4 small calamari bodies, cut into ringlets (no tentacles). Follow the recipe, cooking the shrimp for 30 seconds, then add the scallops and cook for 30 seconds, then add the calamari and cook for a final 15 to 20 seconds.

CARBOHYDRATE CHOICE: 0

# grilled scallops

## WITH A CELERY SALAD

for most home cooks, celery is the *un*vegetable, by which I mean that everybody knows it's a vegetable, but most would never serve it as one in its own right, instead opting to eat it raw or making it part of the base for

## plan ahead

If you are preparing Grilled Scallops in advance and you're making the optional Herb Coulis, you can blanch the celery for the salad and the parsley for the coulis using the same pot of boiling water.

## nutritional information

(PER SERVING)

| | |
|---|---|
| Calories | 207 |
| Fat | 14 g |
| Saturated Fat | 2 g |
| Trans Fat | 0 g |
| Total Carbohydrates | 5 g |
| Dietary Fiber | 1 g |
| Total Sugars | 1 g |
| Protein | 15 g |
| Cholesterol | 28 mg |
| Sodium | 207 mg |

## exchanges

| | |
|---|---|
| Fat | 2.5 |
| Lean Meat | 1.5 |
| Vegetables | 0.5 |

### A TIP FROM TOM

**PEELING CELERY:**
When serving large pieces of celery, be sure to peel the back of the rib. This might seem like a "restaurant" thing to do, but removing the vegetable's outermost layer makes it much less fibrous—even elegant.

soups, stews, sauces, and so on. I love the flavor of celery, and braise it for accompaniment to fish or meats, or make it the focus of a salad, like this one paired with grilled sea scallops.

**SERVES 4**

## INGREDIENTS

*4 ribs celery, peeled (see this page) and cut into 1-inch-wide diagonal pieces, plus ½ cup of the most delicate, attractive celery leaves from the bunch*

*2 cups frisée lettuce*

*¼ cup loosely packed fresh parsley leaves (see Note)*

*¼ cup olive oil*

*2 teaspoons freshly squeezed lemon juice*

*Coarse salt and freshly ground black pepper*

*12 sea scallops (about 1 ounce each; see facing page)*

*Herb Coulis (page 317; optional)*

1.  Bring a large pot of water to a boil over high heat. Fill a large bowl halfway with ice water.

2.  Cook the celery pieces in the boiling water until just tender, about 2 minutes. Use a slotted spoon to remove the celery from the pot and transfer it to the ice water to stop the cooking and preserve the color. Once the celery has cooled, drain it and pat dry with paper towels.

3.  Empty the bowl of ice water and wipe the bowl dry. Add the celery, celery leaves, frisée, and parsley. Drizzle 3 tablespoons of the olive oil and the lemon juice over the greens. Season them with a pinch each of salt and pepper and gently toss.

4.  Build a fire in a charcoal grill, letting the coals burn down until covered with white ash or preheat a gas grill to medium. If using a grill pan, briefly preheat the pan over medium-high heat.

5.  Rub the scallops with the remaining 1 tablespoon of olive oil and season them with a pinch each of salt and pepper, if desired. Grill the scallops until cooked through and light grill marks have formed, about 2 minutes per side.

6.  To serve, arrange 3 scallops in the center of each of 4 dinner plates. Mound some celery salad alongside the scallops and drizzle some Herb Coulis, if using, over the scallops and around the plate.

note: If you plan to serve the scallops with the Herb Coulis, set aside ¼ cup of parsley leaves from one of the bunches of parsley before you make the coulis.

CARBOHYDRATE CHOICES: 1½

# sautéed sea scallops

## WITH PUREED CELERIAC AND A BALSAMIC REDUCTION

I've included this recipe in the book to illustrate the dramatically different effects that can be produced by pairing the same flavors, in this case scallops and celery. In the previous recipe grilled scallops are paired with a light celery stalk salad; these scallops are seared and set atop a puree of celeriac—celery root—a celery family member. The drizzle of a balsamic vinegar and veal stock reduction (veal glace) here adds another layer of refinement and sophistication.

**SERVES 4**

---

### INGREDIENTS

*1 tablespoon unsalted butter*

*1 small leek, white part only, trimmed,
    well rinsed, and coarsely chopped*

*½ medium-size Spanish onion,
    coarsely chopped*

*1 rib celery, coarsely chopped, nicest
    yellow leaves reserved for garnish*

*2 cloves garlic, thinly sliced*

*1½ cups peeled, diced celeriac (celery root)*

*2 cups store-bought low-sodium
    chicken broth*

*2 tablespoons low-fat milk*

*⅔ cup balsamic vinegar*

*1 small container (1½ ounces)
    store-bought veal glace (see Note),
    diluted with 1 tablespoon hot water*

*2 teaspoons olive oil*

*12 large sea scallops
    (about 2 ounces each; see this page),
    preferably diver harvested*

*Pinch of coarse salt*

*Pinch of freshly ground black pepper*

---

1. Melt the butter in a medium-size, heavy-bottomed pot set over low heat. Add the leek, onion, celery, and garlic and cook until softened but not browned, about 4 minutes. Add the celeriac and chicken broth, bring to a boil, then reduce the heat and let simmer until the celeriac is tender when pierced with a knife, about 20 minutes.

2. Strain the contents of the pot over a bowl, setting aside the liquid. Place the strained celeriac mixture in a food processor. Add 2 tablespoons of the liquid and puree until smooth (see

## nutritional information
(PER SERVING)

| | |
|---|---|
| Calories | 358 |
| Fat | 7 g |
| Saturated Fat | 3 g |
| Trans Fat | 0 g |
| Total Carbohydrates | 29 g |
| Dietary Fiber | 3 g |
| Total Sugars | 11 g |
| Protein | 41 g |
| Cholesterol | 66 mg |
| Sodium | 822 mg |

## exchanges

| | |
|---|---|
| Fat | 1 |
| Lean Meat | 3.5 |
| Vegetables | 3 |

## shop right

**SCALLOPS:** When purchasing sea scallops (as opposed to bay scallops) try to purchase diver-harvested ones, which are the freshest available. Whatever you do, don't purchase scallops that are shipped in a milky preserving solution, because the scallops absorb the liquid, which adversely affects their flavor. Even if the scallops look fresh, ask your fishmonger if they were stored in a preservative before arriving at the store.

page 102 for a safety note on pureeing hot liquids) adding more of the liquid as necessary to produce a mashed potato–like consistency. Then blend in the milk. Set the celeriac puree aside, covered, and keep warm.

3. Put the balsamic vinegar in a small, heavy-bottomed saucepan and bring to a simmer over medium heat. Reduce the heat so the vinegar is barely simmering and continue to simmer until reduced to about 2 tablespoons, about 20 minutes. Stir in the diluted veal glace, remove the pan from the heat, and set aside. (Do not make the vinegar and veal glace reduction in advance because it will become tacky if it sits too long.)

4. Heat the olive oil in a wide, deep, heavy-bottomed nonstick pan over high heat. Season the scallops on both sides with a pinch each of salt and pepper. Add the scallops to the pan and cook until golden, about 1 minute, then turn them and cook just to sear the other side, about 20 seconds.

5. Remove the pan from the heat, but leave the scallops in the pan while you spoon the celeriac puree onto 4 serving plates, dividing it evenly among them. Decoratively arrange 3 scallops on top of the puree on each plate.

6. Quickly reheat the vinegar and veal glace reduction, then drizzle it over and around the scallops on each plate. Garnish the scallops with the celery leaves and serve.

note: Veal glace—*glace de veau*—is veal stock that has been highly reduced to concentrate its flavor. You can find veal glace at the meat or butcher counter and from specialty food stores.

**plan ahead**

If you want to make the mussels in advance you can steam them in white wine and garlic and shuck them. Chill the mussels in a stainless-steel bowl set over a bowl of ice water and refrigerate them in an airtight container for a few hours.

# poached mussels

## WITH THREE VARIATIONS

most mussel recipes call for steaming the mussels open in a mixture of white wine and garlic, or something along those lines, and that's how I used to cook them myself. But I recently discovered a new and staggeringly simple way to cook mussels by poaching them in a large pot of simmering water. This might not sound revolutionary, but the process results in mussels as sweet and delicious as any I've ever tasted. The only downside is that you need to serve the mussels right away with whatever sauce you have in mind. Here are three recipes using this poaching technique.

Most of the mussels sold in the United States today are cultivated, but if you can find the slightly more expensive green-lipped New Zealand variety, I think they're worth every penny for their sublime sweetness.

**CARBOHYDRATE CHOICE: 0**

# mussels

### WITH LEMON, GARLIC, AND PARSLEY

It doesn't get more classical than mussels with garlic and parsley. For some reason, lemon isn't part of the traditional recipe, but it's a logical, nutritionally harmless addition that brings welcome acidity to the bowl.  **SERVES 4**

### INGREDIENTS

⅓ cup store-bought low-sodium
    chicken broth

2 tablespoons unsalted butter

1 small clove garlic, minced

Juice of 1 lemon

2 pounds mussels, scrubbed under
    cold running water and bearded

2 tablespoons chopped fresh
    flat-leaf parsley leaves

1. Heat the chicken broth in a medium-size saucepan over medium heat. Whisk in the butter, garlic, and lemon juice and cook for 1 minute. Remove the pan from the heat and set it aside while you cook the mussels.

2. Fill a large pot two thirds full with water and bring to a boil over high heat.

3. Working in 2 batches, add the mussels and gently stir them around with a slotted spoon, taking care not to break the shells. After the mussels open, about 1 minute, continue to stir them for another 5 to 10 seconds, then use the spoon to transfer them to a heatproof bowl and keep them covered, being sure to shake out as much liquid as possible. Repeat until all of the mussels are cooked. Discard any mussels that do not open.

4. When the mussels are cool enough to handle, remove them from their shells, if desired. Pour the sauce over the mussels, add the parsley, and toss them gently. Divide the mussels among 4 bowls and serve.

## nutritional information
(PER SERVING)

| | |
|---|---|
| Calories | 99 |
| Fat | 7 g |
| Saturated Fat | 4 g |
| Trans Fat | 0 g |
| Total Carbohydrates | 3 g |
| Dietary Fiber | 0 g |
| Total Sugars | 0 g |
| Protein | 6 g |
| Cholesterol | 29 mg |
| Sodium | 153 mg |

## exchanges

| | |
|---|---|
| Fat | 1 |
| Lean Meat | 1 |

**A TIP FROM TOM**

**MUSSEL LIQUOR:**
When the cooked mussels are resting, they will give off some very flavorful juice. Add this to any of these mussel sauces, or whatever recipes you make with the mussels.

## nutritional information

Calories....................164
Fat................................7 g
    Saturated Fat...........4 g
    Trans Fat..................0 g
Total Carbohydrates....18 g
    Dietary Fiber............8 g
    Total Sugars.............4 g
Protein........................10 g
Cholesterol................29 mg
Sodium...................264 mg

## exchanges

Fat.................................1
Lean Meat.........................1
Vegetables....................2.5

# mussels

### WITH ARTICHOKE HEARTS AND CHERVIL

I've always found that mussels and artichokes have a great affinity for one another—both in terms of taste and texture. The chervil pulls all of the flavors together and gives the dish a subtle but important lift. **SERVES 4**

### INGREDIENTS

*2 lemons, cut in half*

*1 teaspoon whole black peppercorns*

*4 medium-size artichokes*

*2 pounds mussels, scrubbed under cold running water and bearded*

*2 tablespoons unsalted butter*

*1 small clove garlic, minced*

*2 tablespoons chopped fresh chervil (see Note)*

1. Fill a large pot halfway with water. Squeeze the juice of 2 lemon halves into the pot, catching the seeds in your hand, add the peppercorns, and bring the water to a boil over high heat.

2. Meanwhile, prepare the artichokes for cooking: Fill a large bowl halfway with cold water and squeeze the juice from the remaining two lemons into the bowl, catching the seeds in your hand.

3. Working with one at a time, trim the artichokes by slicing 1 inch off the top of each and trimming the outer, dark green portion off the stem. Snap off and discard the tough outer leaves. As you finish trimming each artichoke, put it in the cold lemon water.

4. Add the artichokes to the boiling water and cover the pot. Reduce the heat so the liquid is simmering and let the artichokes simmer until they are tender, about 40 minutes. Drain the artichokes in a colander and let them cool.

5. When the artichokes are cool enough to handle, pull off the leaves, discarding all but the most tender, light-colored ones. Remove the chokes from the artichokes by pulling out and discarding the pale innermost conically arranged leaves. Use a tablespoon to scrape off and discard the fuzzy choke over the hearts. Cut the hearts into quarters.

6. Fill a large pot two thirds full with water and bring to a boil over high heat.

7. Working in 2 batches, add the

mussels and gently stir them around with a slotted spoon, taking care to not break the shells. After the mussels open, about 1 minute, continue to stir them for another 5 to 10 seconds, then use the spoon to transfer them to a heatproof bowl and keep them covered, being sure to shake out as much liquid as possible. Repeat until all of the mussels are cooked. Discard any mussels that do not open.

8. When the mussels are cool enough to handle, remove them from their shells, if desired.

9. Melt the butter in a heavy-bottomed pan over medium heat. Add the garlic and cook until just slightly softened, about 1 minute. Add the artichoke hearts and cook, stirring, just until warmed through, then add the mussels and toss.

10. Divide the mussels, artichoke hearts, and sauce among 4 wide, shallow bowls. Top with a scattering of chervil. Arrange some of the tender artichoke leaves around the bowls, for dipping into the sauce, and serve.

note: If chervil is not available, you can substitute chives or parsley.

---

CARBOHYDRATE CHOICE: 0

# poached mussels
### WITH GREEN CURRY

The curry paste and coconut milk in this recipe result in a broth that's delicious enough to stand on its own as a soup. With the mussels it becomes a complete and complex meal. **SERVES 4**

---

## INGREDIENTS

*2 teaspoons canola oil*

*1 clove garlic, minced*

*2 teaspoons minced peeled fresh ginger*

*1 tablespoon Thai green curry paste (see Note)*

*¼ cup unsweetened coconut milk*

*1 cup store-bought low-sodium chicken broth*

*Juice and finely grated zest of 1 lime*

*2 pounds mussels, scrubbed under cold running water and bearded*

*¼ cup coarsely chopped fresh cilantro leaves*

---

1. Heat the oil in a wide, heavy-bottomed pot over medium heat. Add the garlic and ginger and cook until just slightly softened, about 1 minute. Add the curry paste, stir to coat the garlic and ginger, and cook about

## nutritional information
(PER SERVING)

| | |
|---|---|
| Calories | 107 |
| Fat | 7 g |
| Saturated Fat | 3 g |
| Trans Fat | 0 g |
| Total Carbohydrates | 5 g |
| Dietary Fiber | 1 g |
| Total Sugars | 1 g |
| Protein | 7 g |
| Cholesterol | 15 mg |
| Sodium | 269 mg |

## exchanges

| | |
|---|---|
| Fat | 1 |
| Lean Meat | 1 |

1 minute. Stir in the coconut milk and chicken broth. Bring to a simmer and let simmer until the flavors develop, 4 to 5 minutes.

**2.** Fill a large pot two thirds with water and bring to a boil over high heat. Add the lime juice and zest.

**3.** Working in 2 batches, add the mussels and gently stir them around with a slotted spoon, taking care not to break the shells. After the mussels open, about 1 minute, continue to stir them for another 5 to 10 seconds, then use the spoon to transfer them to a heatproof bowl and keep them

covered, being sure to shake out as much liquid as possible. Repeat until all of the mussels are cooked. Discard any mussels that do not open.

**4.** When the mussels are cool enough to handle, remove them from their shells, if desired. Add the mussels to the pot with the sauce and toss them gently. Divide the mussels among 4 bowls, garnish them with the cilantro, and serve.

**note:** Thai green curry paste is available in the international section of supermarkets and in Asian groceries.

## nutritional information

**(PER SERVING)**

| | |
|---|---|
| Calories | 344 |
| Fat | 15 g |
| Saturated Fat | 3 g |
| Trans Fat | 0 g |
| Total Carbohydrates | 18 g |
| Dietary Fiber | 3 g |
| Total Sugars | 7 g |
| Protein | 23 g |
| Cholesterol | 279 mg |
| Sodium | 650 mg |

## exchanges

| | |
|---|---|
| Fat | 2.5 |
| Lean Meat | 2.5 |
| High Fat Meat | 0.5 |
| Vegetables | 2.5 |

**CARBOHYDRATE CHOICE: 1**

# quick sauté of calamari

## WITH A GARLICKY CLAM BROTH

It's been said of calamari that you can only enjoy it after it's been cooked really fast (fried or sautéed) or really slow (braised). This is a fast calamari recipe that offsets its oceanic flavor with browned turkey bacon, tomato, herbs, and hot red pepper flakes. The calamari can be eaten on its own or tossed with one or two ounces of cavatelli for a quick pasta dish that's even quicker if you make the calamari and sauce in advance.    **SERVES 4**

## INGREDIENTS

4 slices turkey bacon, finely diced

1 medium-size Spanish onion,
　finely diced

4 cloves garlic, thinly sliced,
　plus 3 cloves, minced

2 tablespoons tomato paste

Pinch of sugar

1 cup dry white wine

1 tablespoon distilled white
　vinegar

14 ounces (half of a 28-ounce can)
　Italian plum tomatoes, drained
　of their juice and crushed by
　hand

½ cup bottled clam juice

¾ cup store-bought low-sodium
　chicken broth

½ teaspoon crushed red
　pepper flakes

Pinch of coarse salt

Pinch of freshly ground black
　pepper

1 tablespoon chopped fresh
　oregano

1 bay leaf, preferably fresh

3 pounds calamari (squid),
　cleaned (ask your fishmonger
　to do this), tentacles discarded
　or saved for another use

3 tablespoons olive oil

## plan ahead

The calamari and sauce can be cooled and refrigerated in an airtight container for up to 2 days. Reheat gently before serving.

1. Cook the bacon in a medium-size, heavy-bottomed saucepan set over medium-high heat until it is crisp and renders its fat, about 7 minutes. Add the onion and sliced garlic to the pan and cook, stirring, until softened but not browned, about 4 minutes. Add the tomato paste and sugar and stir to coat the other ingredients with the paste. Add the white wine and vinegar and cook, stirring, for 2 minutes. Stir in the tomatoes, clam juice, chicken broth, red pepper flakes, a pinch each of salt and pepper, and ½ cup of water. Increase the heat to high, bring to a boil, then reduce the heat so the liquid is simmering. Stir in the oregano and bay leaf and let continue to simmer, uncovered, for 25 minutes.

2. Split the calamari bodies open lengthwise and cut them into ¼-inch-wide strips.

3. Heat the olive oil in large, heavy-bottomed pan over medium-high heat. Add the minced garlic and the calamari strips and cook, stirring, until the calamari just begins to curl, about 30 seconds. Add the sauce to the pan and stir well. Use tongs or a wooden spoon to fish out and discard the bay leaf. To serve, divide the calamari and sauce among 4 wide, shallow bowls.

**CARBOHYDRATE CHOICE: ½**

# grilled calamari

## WITH GRILLED RADICCHIO, GREENS, AND BASIL PUREE

When most people hear the word *calamari* (squid), they picture crisp fried rings and tentacles served up in a paper cone with some kind of dipping sauce alongside. I love that classic bar snack as much as the next guy, but calamari also lends itself to other cooking techniques. Here, I give it a summery shellfish treatment by grilling marinated squid and serving them alongside bitter radicchio, also grilled. The basil puree adds a decorative burst of color and also freshens the charred flavors. **SERVES 4**

## INGREDIENTS

8 ounces calamari (squid), cleaned (ask your fishmonger to do this)

¼ cup plus ½ teaspoon extra-virgin olive oil

½ cup freshly squeezed lemon juice

4 medium-size cloves garlic, minced

1 head radicchio, cut into 4 pieces with the root end intact

1 ounce watercress

½ teaspoon coarse salt

Pinch of freshly ground black pepper

¼ cup Basil Puree (page 316)

1. Butterfly the body of a calamari by sliding a knife into the cavity and making a single cut to open it up. Repeat with the remaining calamari. Leave the tentacles whole. Set the calamari pieces aside.

2. Build a fire in a charcoal grill, letting the coals burn down until covered with white ash or preheat a gas grill to high. If using a grill pan, preheat the pan briefly over medium-high heat.

3. Make a marinade by putting ¼ cup of the olive oil, the lemon juice, and garlic in a wide-mouthed bowl and whisking them together.

4. One at a time, dip the radicchio quarters into the marinade, holding them by the root end and letting any excess marinade drip back into the bowl, then arrange them on the grill. Grill the radicchio, turning with tongs, until nicely charred all over, about 10 minutes in total.

**5.** As soon as the radicchio is on the grill, add the pieces of calamari to the marinade and let marinate for 10 minutes. Put the watercress in a separate bowl, drizzle the remaining ½ teaspoon of olive oil over it, and gently toss.

**6.** Remove the pieces of calamari from the marinade, season them with the salt and pepper, and grill until they are opaque and light grill marks have formed, about 1 minute on each side.

**7.** Artfully arrange the calamari, radicchio, and watercress on each of 4 dinner plates. Drizzle some basil puree over all and serve.

**variations and suggestions:** If you can't find radicchio or find it too bitter, you can substitute grilled Belgian endive.

**how low can you go?**

You can lower the fat in this dish substantially by omitting the Basil Puree and scattering torn fresh basil over the calamari instead.

CARBOHYDRATE CHOICE: 1

# soft-shell crabs

## WITH SCALLION COUSCOUS AND CURRY VINAIGRETTE

i don't eat or cook much Indian food, but some of my favorite Indian dishes are made with crab, a predilection that led me to concoct this vaguely Indian dish featuring soft-shell crabs, seared to a crisp and paired with a simple scallion couscous and a curry vinaigrette enlivened with lime juice. This is an easy dish to cook, but the potent flavors and fun textures are deeply satisfying. **SERVES 4**

### INGREDIENTS

1½ teaspoons curry powder

6 tablespoons canola oil

1 tablespoon freshly squeezed lime juice

½ teaspoon finely grated lime zest

½ cup dry couscous

8 soft-shell crabs (about 3 ounces each) cleaned, legs pricked with a pin (see page 229)

1 scallion, both white and green parts, trimmed and very thinly sliced

## nutritional information
### (PER SERVING)

| | |
|---|---|
| Calories | 427 |
| Fat | 23 g |
| Saturated Fat | 2 g |
| Trans Fat | 0 g |
| Total Carbohydrates | 19 g |
| Dietary Fiber | 2 g |
| Total Sugars | 0 g |
| Protein | 34 g |
| Cholesterol | 133 mg |
| Sodium | 503 mg |

## exchanges

| | |
|---|---|
| Fat | 4 |
| Starch | 1 |
| Lean Meat | 3.5 |

1. Put the curry powder in a bowl and pour 1 tablespoon of hot water over it. Let the curry steep for 5 minutes, then stir to make a paste. Whisk in 2 tablespoons of the oil, the lime juice, and the zest. Let the vinaigrette sit for 30 minutes for the flavor to develop, then strain it, discarding the solids.

2. Put the couscous in a medium-size, heatproof bowl. Bring 1 cup of water to a boil in a small pot and pour it over the couscous. Cover the bowl tightly with plastic wrap and let the couscous steep.

3. Meanwhile, heat 2 tablespoons of the remaining oil in a wide, deep, heavy-bottomed nonstick pan over medium-high heat. Add 2 to 4 crabs, depending on their size, and cook until nicely browned on 1 side, about 5 minutes. Turn the crabs over and cook until browned on the second side, about 5 minutes longer. Transfer the cooked crabs to a dinner plate and repeat until all of the crabs are cooked. At some point, the pan will become dry; add the remaining 2 tablespoons of oil and let warm before adding the next batch of crabs.

4. To serve, remove the plastic wrap from the couscous and fluff it with a fork. Stir in the scallion. Mound some couscous in the center of each of the plates. Lean 2 crabs against the couscous on each plate. Drizzle some curry vinaigrette over the crabs and spoon the rest decoratively around the plate.

**CARBOHYDRATE CHOICE: 0**

# soft-shell crabs
## WITH TOMATOES AND A TOMATO-BASIL VINAIGRETTE

the cool thing about a soft-shell crab is that you can eat the whole thing, meaning you don't have to do the work of removing the meat. If you don't know, soft-shells are crabs that are caught within hours of when they molt, or shed their tough outer shell. Cook them over high heat and the soft undershell becomes nicely crisp and crunchy, giving way to the sweet, succulent meat within. Because the molting process takes place in the spring and summer, soft-shell crabs are one of the quintessential ingredients of those seasons, and they get on great with their contemporaries, such as tomato and basil, featured here in a chunky vinaigrette that doubles as an accompaniment.

**SERVES 4**

## INGREDIENTS

*4 medium-size plum tomatoes, cut into ¼-inch dice*

*1 small garlic clove, minced*

*2 tablespoons extra-virgin olive oil*

*1½ tablespoons freshly squeezed lemon juice*

*1 tablespoon minced shallot or white onion*

*2 teaspoons minced fresh basil leaves (see Note)*

*¼ teaspoon coarse salt*

*¼ teaspoon freshly ground black pepper*

*¼ cup canola oil*

*2 cups loosely packed mixed salad greens*

*8 soft-shell crabs (about 3 ounces each) cleaned, legs pricked with a pin (see this page)*

1. Put the tomatoes in a bowl. Add the garlic, olive oil, lemon juice, shallot, basil, salt, and pepper. Toss the tomatoes and set them aside.

2. Heat 2 tablespoons of the canola oil in a wide, deep, heavy-bottomed nonstick pan over medium-high heat. Add 2 to 4 crabs, depending on their size, shell side down, and cook until nicely browned on 1 side, about 5 minutes. Turn the crabs over and cook until browned on the second side, about 5 minutes. Transfer the cooked crabs to dinner plates and repeat until all the crabs are cooked.

At some point, the pan will become dry; add the remaining 2 tablespoons of canola oil and let warm before adding the next batch of crabs.

3. Serve 2 crabs on each of 4 dinner plates, mounding some of the salad greens between them. Using a slotted spoon, spoon some tomatoes over the crabs, then use a regular kitchen spoon to drizzle some vinaigrette over the greens and around the plate.

note: You can substitute fresh chives or flat-leaf parsley.

**A TIP FROM TOM**

**SOFT-SHELL CRAB LEGS:** There's a hidden danger when cooking soft-shell crabs: The legs can fill up with hot air, and even explode, spraying molten crab goo all over the place. To keep this from happening, use a clean safety pin or sewing needle to perforate the legs prior to cooking, which will allow steam to escape.

# in this chapter

*"When you're entertaining,*
*or just in the mood for something special."*

# poultry
# and meat

i think of this as the "going out to dinner" chapter because on some level many poultry and meat dishes represent a degree of indulgence for people with diabetes, not necessarily on the carbohydrate front—the Carbohydrate Choices in the following recipes are consistent with those in the rest of the book—but because of the level of calories, fat, and cholesterol. For example, no matter how virtuous the other ingredients on the plate, dishes that feature duck and lamb will always be relatively high in fat because duck and lamb themselves are high in fat. Nevertheless, if you're like me you allow yourself these minor transgressions at restaurants, and there's no reason not to make similar exceptions at home, when you're entertaining, or just in the mood for something special. In other words, there's a time and place for these choices as well.

Because I expect these recipes will be the exception rather than the norm in your diet, poultry and meat have been grouped into one chapter that represents a broad sampling of the two categories, everything from turkey burgers and meat loaf to multicomponent, restaurant-style dishes featuring a meat, vegetable, and sauces. In the case of the latter, the nutritional analyses can be deceptively high because many of these dishes constitute a full meal—so they might not be as decadent as you thought they were.

## nutritional information
### (PER SERVING)

| | |
|---|---|
| Calories | 464 |
| Fat | 22 g |
| Saturated Fat | 6 g |
| Trans Fat | 0 g |
| Total Carbohydrates | 23 g |
| Dietary Fiber | 1 g |
| Total Sugars | 1 g |
| Protein | 34 g |
| Cholesterol | 81 mg |
| Sodium | 618 mg |

## exchanges

| | |
|---|---|
| Fat | 4 |
| Starch | 1.5 |
| Lean Meat | 3 |

**CARBOHYDRATE CHOICES: 1½**

# chicken paillard

## WITH LEMON AND CAPERS

Oh, how I miss fried chicken! Whether it came from Colonel Sanders or was part of my own restaurant's staff meal, I used to love pigging out on this quintessentially American indulgence whenever I had the chance. Fortunately, I've hit on a way of quenching the same hankering in a slightly different manner: Breaded, sautéed chicken offers enough crunch to suggest fried chicken. It's not nearly as decadent, but the difference is made up by the presence of lemon, which to me is a natural pairing for chicken and puts this dish over the top with flavor rather than texture.    SERVES 4

### INGREDIENTS

4 small skinless, boneless chicken breasts (about 4 ounces each)

4 large egg whites

2 tablespoons Dijon mustard

Pinch of coarse salt

1 cup toasted bread crumbs

¼ cup olive oil

⅔ cup dry white wine

2 tablespoons freshly squeezed lemon juice

2 tablespoons unsalted butter

2 tablespoons store-bought low-sodium chicken broth

1 tablespoon capers, drained

2 tablespoons chopped fresh flat-leaf parsley leaves

1. Preheat the oven to 400°F.

2. Working with 1 piece of chicken at a time, put it between 2 pieces of plastic wrap and gently pound it with a meat mallet or the bottom of a small, heavy-bottomed pan to a thickness of about ¼ inch.

3. Put the egg whites and mustard in a small bowl and whisk to mix. Add the salt. Spread the bread crumbs out on a plate. Dip the pounded chicken in the egg and mustard mixture, then press it into the bread crumbs, pressing down just firmly enough that the bread crumbs adhere to both sides.

4. Heat the olive oil in a wide, deep, heavy-bottomed skillet. Add the chicken and cook until lightly browned on 1 side, about 5 minutes. Transfer the chicken to a baking sheet, uncooked side up. Put the baking sheet in the oven and bake the chicken until it is firm to the touch, about 10 minutes.

5. Add the white wine to the pan used to brown the chicken, bring it to a simmer over high heat, and continue simmering until slightly reduced, about 5 minutes. Add the lemon juice, bring to a boil, and let boil until reduced, about 2 minutes. Remove the pan from the heat and swirl in the butter, then add the chicken broth, capers, and parsley.

6. Put 1 piece of chicken on each of 4 serving plates. Spoon some sauce over the chicken and serve.

CARBOHYDRATE CHOICE: 1

# grilled chicken

## WITH GRILLED RADICCHIO, BLUE CHEESE, AND WALNUTS

When my wife, Abigail, and I blow town and escape to the happy obscurity of upstate New York where we spend our free time, we don't just leave behind the traffic, the high prices, and the stress, we also simplify our (that is, *my*) time in the kitchen. There's no more than one course at our lunches and dinners up there for the simple reason that once we plant ourselves at the table on our riverfront deck, we don't want to get up again for as long as possible.

Over the years, we've devised a number of house favorites to suit this predilection. This is one of our frequent quick go-to dinners. Basically, it's a salad and

## nutritional information
### (PER SERVING)

| | |
|---|---|
| Calories | 568 |
| Fat | 38 g |
| Saturated Fat | 7 g |
| Trans Fat | 0 g |
| Total Carbohydrates | 15 g |
| Dietary Fiber | 3 g |
| Total Sugars | 8 g |
| Protein | 43 g |
| Cholesterol | 105 mg |
| Sodium | 292 g |

## exchanges

| | |
|---|---|
| Fat | 6 |
| Starch | 0.5 |
| Lean Meat | 4 |
| High Fat Meat | 0.5 |
| Vegetables | 0.5 |
| Plant Protein | 0.5 |

a grilled chicken, but instead of one preceding the other, they both are served at the same time. The combination of their flavors and, more important, temperatures is satisfying in a very primal way; we never tire of this dish.     **SERVES 4**

## INGREDIENTS

⅔ cup balsamic vinegar

1 cup walnut pieces

¼ cup plus 2 tablespoons extra-virgin olive oil

4 medium-size cloves garlic, chopped

¼ cup freshly squeezed lemon juice

1 teaspoon chopped fresh flat-leaf parsley leaves

1 teaspoon chopped fresh chives

½ teaspoon fresh thyme leaves

1 large head radicchio, quartered with the root end left intact

2 Belgian endives, cut in half lengthwise

4 skinless, boneless chicken breast halves (about 6 ounces each), cut in half lengthwise (for a total of 8 pieces)

2 ounces blue cheese, crumbled (about ½ cup)

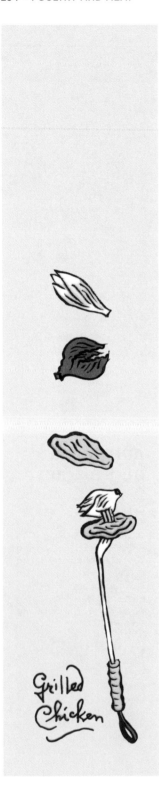

Grilled Chicken

1. Put the balsamic vinegar in a small, heavy-bottomed saucepan set over medium-high heat, bring to a simmer, and let simmer until reduced by half, about 5 minutes. Set the pan aside and let the vinegar cool to room temperature.

2. Meanwhile, put the walnuts in a nonstick pan and toast over medium heat, stirring frequently to prevent scorching, until lightly browned and fragrant, about 4 minutes. Set the walnuts aside to cool.

3. Make the marinade: Put the olive oil, garlic, lemon juice, parsley, chives, and thyme in a large bowl and stir them together. Set aside 2 tablespoons of the marinade for the radicchio and

endives, then add the chicken to the bowl and turn the pieces to coat. Let the chicken marinate in the refrigerator for about 45 minutes.

4. Meanwhile, build a fire in a charcoal grill, letting the coals burn down until covered with white ash. If using a gas grill, preheat it to medium-high near the end of the marinating time.

5. Drizzle the reserved marinade over the radicchio and endive. Arrange the radicchio and endive on the grill and grill, turning once, until slightly softened and nicely charred all over, 10 to 12 minutes. Transfer the radicchio and endive to a bowl and tent them with aluminum foil to keep warm.

**6.** Remove the chicken from the marinade and discard the marinade. Arrange the chicken pieces on the grill and grill until the juices run clear when pierced with a knife, 3 to 4 minutes per side.

**7.** To serve, put 2 pieces of chicken on each of 4 dinner plates. Set 1 piece of radicchio and an endive half alongside. Drizzle the reduced balsamic vinegar and scatter the blue cheese and toasted walnuts over each serving.

CARBOHYDRATE CHOICE: 1

# sautéed chicken

## WITH TANGY MUSHROOM SAUCE

as much as I love chicken, the real star of this dish is the hearty sauce of mushrooms, tomatoes, and red wine. It's a versatile stew that you can also use as a sauce for pasta or polenta. Or even omit the chicken and enjoy the sauce on its own as a vegetarian main course.     **SERVES 4**

### INGREDIENTS

1 tablespoon unsalted butter

1 tablespoon plus 1 teaspoon olive oil

12 ounces white button mushrooms, stems removed, large mushrooms quartered, smaller ones cut in half or left whole

Pinch of coarse salt

Pinch of freshly ground black pepper

1 rib celery, cut into small dice

1 large carrot, peeled and cut into small dice

½ medium-size Spanish onion, cut into small dice

Pinch of Porcini Powder (optional; page 325)

1 tablespoon all-purpose flour

¾ cup red wine

2 plum tomatoes, peeled (see page 129) and finely chopped

1 bay leaf, preferably fresh

1 quart store-bought low-sodium vegetable broth

4 skinless, boneless chicken breast halves (about 6 ounces each)

½ tablespoon chopped fresh flat-leaf parsley leaves

½ tablespoon fresh thyme leaves

## nutritional information
(PER SERVING)

| | |
|---|---|
| Calories | 290 |
| Fat | 9 g |
| Saturated Fat | 3 g |
| Trans Fat | 0 g |
| Total Carbohydrates | 13 g |
| Dietary Fiber | 1 g |
| Total Sugars | 5 g |
| Protein | 28 g |
| Cholesterol | 72 mg |
| Sodium | 273 mg |

## exchanges

| | |
|---|---|
| Fat | 1.5 |
| Lean Meat | 2.5 |
| Vegetables | 1.5 |

## mushrooms

In this and other recipes featuring button mushrooms, the easiest way to add more sophistication and flavor is to call on the range of available mushrooms, from true wild varieties such as chanterelles and black trumpet to cultivated ones such as oyster and hen of the woods. Cremini mushrooms would be an especially tasty alternative here.

1. Melt ½ tablespoon of the butter in 1½ teaspoons of the olive oil in a large, heavy-bottomed pot over medium-high heat. Increase the heat to high, add the mushrooms, season them with the salt and pepper, and cook, stirring, until nicely browned all over, about 5 minutes. Transfer the mushrooms to a bowl and set aside.

2. Add 1½ teaspoons of the olive oil and the remaining ½ tablespoon of butter to the pot and heat over medium-high heat. Add the celery, carrot, onion, and Porcini Powder, if using, and cook, stirring, until the vegetables are softened and lightly browned, about 8 minutes. Sprinkle the flour over the vegetables and cook, stirring, until the rawness cooks out of the flour, about 2 minutes.

3. Pour in the red wine, increase the heat to high, and bring to a boil, stirring to scrape up any flavorful bits stuck to the bottom of the pot. Cook until the wine has almost completely evaporated, about 4 minutes.

4. Add the tomatoes, bay leaf, and vegetable broth to the pot and bring to a boil over high heat, then reduce the heat and let simmer until the sauce is nicely thickened and the vegetables and tomatoes have broken down, about 30 minutes.

5. Return the mushrooms to the pot along with any liquid they have given off while resting. Increase the heat to high, bring to a boil, and let boil for 8 minutes. Turn off the heat and let the mushroom and tomato sauce rest for 30 minutes. Use tongs or a slotted spoon to fish out and discard the bay leaf. (The sauce can be cooled, covered, and refrigerated in an airtight container for up to 2 days or frozen for up to 1 month. Reheat gently before proceeding.)

6. When ready to serve, heat the remaining 1 teaspoon of olive oil in a large, heavy-bottomed, nonstick pan over medium-high heat. Add the chicken breasts to the pan and cook on both sides until nicely golden brown and the meat is white at the center, about 5 minutes per side.

7. Stir the parsley and thyme into the mushroom and tomato sauce. Put 1 chicken breast on each of 4 dinner plates. Spoon the sauce over and around the chicken and serve.

# stuffed chicken breasts

## WITH BASIL, GOAT CHEESE, AND SUN-DRIED TOMATO

this is a fun, flavorful meal to have on tap: You pound out a chicken breast, fill it with goat cheese, basil, and sun-dried tomatoes, then roll it up and wrap it in plastic. The prepared chicken can be refrigerated or frozen until you're ready to gently poach it in boiling water, slice it, and serve. It's as right for an everyday meal as it is for a dinner party, and its convenience is compounded by the fact that after the chicken has been cooked and sliced, you can enjoy any leftovers cold the next day.

This recipe calls for cooking plastic-wrapped chicken in simmering water. Be assured that the wet heat of the poaching liquid will not melt the plastic or cause it to taint the chicken.  **SERVES 4**

## nutritional information
### (PER SERVING)

| | |
|---|---|
| Calories | 294 |
| Fat | 11 g |
|    Saturated Fat | 6 g |
|    Trans Fat | 0 g |
| Total Carbohydrates | 2 g |
|    Dietary Fiber | 0 g |
|    Total Sugars | 1 g |
| Protein | 46 g |
| Cholesterol | 121 mg |
| Sodium | 318 mg |

## exchanges

| | |
|---|---|
| Fat | 0.5 |
| Lean Meat | 4 |
| High Fat Meat | 1 |

### INGREDIENTS

4 ounces goat cheese,
   at room temperature

3 dry-packed sun-dried tomatoes
   (about 1 ounce), finely chopped

8 large fresh basil leaves,
   coarsely chopped

Pinch of coarse salt

Pinch of freshly ground black
   pepper

4 skinless, boneless chicken breast
   halves (about 6 ounces each)

1. Put the goat cheese, sun-dried tomatoes, and basil in a bowl, season with the salt and pepper, and stir together with a rubber spatula just until well combined.

2. Sandwich 1 chicken breast half between 2 sheets of plastic wrap and use a meat mallet or the bottom of a heavy pot or pan to gently pound it to a thickness of about ½ inch. Repeat until all of the chicken breast halves have been pounded, then discard the used plastic wrap.

3. Place a clean 12 by 18–inch piece

of plastic wrap in the center of a work surface. Arrange 1 pounded chicken breast half in the center. Spoon one quarter of the goat cheese filling in the center of the chicken and roll the meat up around it. Wrap the plastic tightly around the chicken and wind the ends of the plastic wrap over and over, as though wringing out a towel, until the chicken breast forms a cylinder and the ends of the plastic wrap don't come undone when you release them. Repeat with the remaining pieces of chicken and filling. (The filled chicken can be refrigerated for up to 24 hours or frozen for up to 3 days. If frozen, thaw in the refrigerator overnight. Let come to room temperature before proceeding, but do not let uncooked chicken rest at room temperature for an extended period of time.)

4. When you're ready to cook the chicken, fill a large pot three quarters full with water and bring to a simmer over medium-high heat. Poach the wrapped breasts in the water until the chicken turns opaque and is firm to the touch and any juices in the packet are clear, about 15 minutes. (To ensure doneness, check for an internal temperature of 165°F with an instant-read thermometer.) Remove the breasts from the water with tongs or a slotted spoon and let rest for 5 minutes before unwrapping.

5. Use a sharp knife or kitchen shears to remove the plastic from the stuffed chicken, taking care not to cut into the meat. Slice each chicken breast diagonally into ½-inch-thick slices, arrange the slices of each breast on its own plate, and serve.

## nutritional information
(PER SERVING)

| | |
|---|---|
| Calories | 447 |
| Fat | 27 g |
| Saturated Fat | 3 g |
| Trans Fat | 0 g |
| Total Carbohydrates | 22 g |
| Dietary Fiber | 4 g |
| Total Sugars | 4 g |
| Protein | 28 g |
| Cholesterol | 63 mg |
| Sodium | 847 mg |

## exchanges

| | |
|---|---|
| Fat | 5 |
| Lean Meat | 2.5 |
| Vegetables | 2 |

CARBOHYDRATE CHOICES: 1½

# chinese chicken and vegetables

have you ever eaten at a Chinese restaurant with an open kitchen or witnessed a professional wok-meister ply his trade? It's something to behold when somebody gifted in this type of cookery really lets it fly, adding hot oil, vegetables, and meat to a smoking-hot vessel with what looks like abandon but is really a very careful precision.

Well, when you cook this dish, even though you won't be using a wok, I want you to pretend that you are that cook: Get your pan very hot and have all your ingredients lined up in the order for which they're called. Then, go to work, adding them to the pan and taking them out as soon as they're ready, meaning cooked through, but still crunchy.

Relative to most of the dishes in this book, there's a fair bit of sodium and fat here but far less than you'll find in similar offerings at your average American Chinese restaurant.

**SERVES 4**

## INGREDIENTS

3 tablespoons cornstarch

3 tablespoons sesame seeds

½ cup low-sodium soy sauce

5 large cloves garlic

2 tablespoons rice wine vinegar

1½ tablespoons grated peeled fresh ginger

¼ cup canola oil

1 red bell pepper, stemmed, seeded, and cut into 1-inch squares

1 green bell pepper, stemmed, seeded, and cut into 1-inch squares

½ Spanish onion, cut into 1-inch dice

Florets from 2 stalks broccoli, peeled and cut diagonally (about 4 cups)

5 shiitake mushrooms, stems removed, caps thinly sliced

1 pound skinless, boneless chicken breast, diced

2 teaspoons Asian (dark) sesame oil

1 bunch scallions, both white and green parts, trimmed and coarsely chopped

½ cup crushed cashews or unsalted, roasted peanuts (optional)

1. Whisk the cornstarch into ½ cup of cold water and set aside.

2. Heat a dry nonstick pan over low heat. Add the sesame seeds and toast, stirring to prevent scorching, until lightly toasted, 2 to 3 minutes.

3. Put the soy sauce, garlic, rice vinegar, ginger, and toasted sesame seeds in a blender and pulse until well blended. Set the soy sauce mixture aside.

4. Heat a large pan over high heat. Add 1 tablespoon of canola oil to the pan. Once the oil is hot but not smoking, add the bell peppers and onion and cook, stirring, for 30 to 40 seconds. Transfer the bell peppers to

a large bowl. Return the pan to the stove and heat 1 tablespoon more of canola oil in it. Add the broccoli, and cook, stirring, for 45 seconds to 1 minute. Transfer the broccoli to the bowl with the peppers. Return the pan to the stove and heat 1 tablespoon more of canola oil in it. Cook the mushrooms, stirring, for 20 to 30 seconds, then transfer them to the bowl with the peppers and broccoli. Return the pan to the stove and get the pan really hot. Add the remaining 1 tablespoon of oil to the pan. Add the chicken to the pan and cook, stirring, until cooked through, 1 to 2 minutes. Transfer the chicken to the bowl with the vegetables.

**5.** Add 1 cup of water and the soy sauce mixture to the pan and bring to a boil. Whisk in the cornstarch mixture and let the sauce reduce and thicken for about 45 seconds. Return the chicken and vegetables to the pan and toss with the sauce.

**6.** Divide the chicken among 4 plates. Drizzle some sesame oil over each, then scatter the scallions and nuts, if desired, over the top and serve.

**variations and suggestions:** You can adapt this dish to include other vegetables; bamboo shoots and snap peas would be especially appropriate and tasty.

## nutritional information
(PER SERVING)

Calories......................216
Fat..............................11 g
   Saturated Fat............1 g
   Trans Fat...................0 g
Total Carbohydrates.....9 g
   Dietary Fiber.............3 g
   Total Sugars.............2 g
Protein........................19 g
Cholesterol.............68 mg
Sodium....................99 mg

## exchanges

Fat..............................1.5
Lean Meat...................2.5
Vegetables......................1

CARBOHYDRATE CHOICE: ½

# chicken curry

**WITH ONIONS**

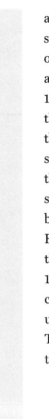 don't spend a lot of time thinking about the science of food—I'll leave that to the Harold McGees of the world—but I do know that smell accounts for about 90 percent of taste, which is why I positively love curry. Is there a more pleasingly potent, fragrant, almost transporting scent in the world of food?

Based on a couldn't-be-simpler staple of New York City Chinese—yes, Chinese—restaurants, this chicken curry with onions is a wonderfully complex one-pan affair that builds layer after layer of texture and flavors in a series of easy, logical steps. You slowly sweat down onions until they are meltingly tender. Then you add thinly sliced chicken and cook it in a matter of seconds. Curry flavors the other ingredients, and a few spoonfuls of water create an instant sauce. A squeeze of lime juice at the table ups the ante by bringing all the other flavors even more to life with its acidity.  **SERVES 4**

## INGREDIENTS

2 tablespoons canola oil

1 large Spanish onion, cut in half
   lengthwise and thickly sliced
   crosswise

2 cloves garlic, minced

¼ cup dry white wine

12 ounces skinless dark-meat chicken
   (legs and thighs), thinly sliced
   (see this page)

4 ounces spinach, well rinsed in
   several changes of cold water,
   tough stems discarded

2 tablespoons curry powder

Pinch of freshly ground black
   pepper

1 large lime, cut into 4 wedges

1. Heat the oil in a large, deep pan over low heat. Add the onion and garlic and cook, covered, until the onion is very soft, about 15 minutes. Add a tablespoon of cold water if necessary to help keep the onion from browning.

2. Remove the cover, increase the heat to high, add the white wine, and cook until the wine evaporates, about 3 minutes.

3. Add the chicken and cook until it begins to turn white, about 2 minutes, then stir in the spinach and cook until it wilts and turns dark green, about 3 minutes. Scatter the curry powder and pepper over the chicken and spinach and cook, stirring, until the curry powder blends in and a sauce forms, 2 minutes. Add a tablespoon or two of water if necessary.

4. Divide the chicken, onion, and spinach among 4 dinner plates and serve with a lime wedge alongside for squeezing over the chicken.

**variations and suggestions:** If you like, serve the chicken curry with a small amount of rice or your favorite rice noodles. You can also make it with white meat chicken if you prefer.

---

**A TIP FROM TOM**

**BONING CHICKEN LEGS:** Purchase chicken legs with the thigh attached. Working with one at a time, set the leg on a cutting board with the skin side up and score the ankle all around with a very sharp knife. Working from the drumstick "ankle" to the thigh joint to the end of the thigh, use the tip of the knife to very carefully push the meat away from the bone. Once the bone has been removed, for the neatest, most uniform pieces, slice the meat perpendicular to where the bone was.

## nutritional information

(PER SERVING—
1 DRUMSTICK AND THIGH)

| | |
|---|---|
| Calories | 478 |
| Fat | 14 g |
| Saturated Fat | 3 g |
| Trans Fat | 0 g |
| Total Carbohydrates | 34 g |
| Dietary Fiber | 5 g |
| Total Sugars | 9 g |
| Protein | 34 g |
| Cholesterol | 109 mg |
| Sodium | 644 mg |

## exchanges

| | |
|---|---|
| Fat | 1.5 |
| Starch | 0.5 |
| Lean Meat | 4 |
| Vegetables | 3 |

**CARBOHYDRATE CHOICES: 2; 1½ ADJUSTED FOR FIBER**

# chicken cacciatore

Okay, pop quiz: Do you like chicken cacciatore? Of course you do. Everybody does. How could you not? The name alone is cause for adoration.

Now, here's the extra credit question: What is chicken cacciatore? It's a bit of a trick question, actually, because while we all feel we know this dish, most of us (me included, until I just pulled the food dictionaries off my shelf) really don't. *Cacciatore* means hunter, but as Marcella Hazan points out in one of her books, every hunter makes his own version. All people really agree on is that most cacciatore recipes feature rabbit or chicken, tomatoes, onions, and other vegetables. So here is this hunter's version of the stew, made with lots of garlic and tomato, with fresh thyme giving it an evocative, woodsy quality. **SERVES 4**

### INGREDIENTS

½ cup all-purpose flour

4 skinless chicken legs
(about 6 ounces each), separated
into thighs and drumsticks

½ teaspoon coarse salt

⅛ teaspoon freshly ground black pepper

2 tablespoons olive oil

1 medium-size Spanish onion,
coarsely chopped

4 small-size carrots, peeled and
cut crosswise into thirds

3 ribs celery, cut crosswise into quarters

15 cloves garlic, crushed and peeled

3 tablespoons tomato paste

2½ cups store-bought low-sodium
chicken broth

2 cups medium-bodied red wine

⅓ cup distilled white vinegar

6 medium-size plum tomatoes,
coarsely chopped, with their juice

2 bay leaves, preferably fresh

1 tablespoon fresh thyme leaves

Pinch of crushed red pepper flakes

Pinch of ground cumin

Pinch of ground coriander

2 tablespoons freshly grated
Parmesan cheese

2 tablespoons chopped fresh flat-leaf
parsley leaves

Extra-virgin olive oil (optional),
for serving

1. Spread the flour out on a plate. Season the chicken legs and thighs with the salt and pepper and dredge them in the flour, shaking off any excess.

2. Heat the olive oil in a wide, deep, heavy-bottomed pot or Dutch oven over medium-high heat. Add the chicken legs and thighs and lightly brown them, turning until nicely golden, about 6 minutes total cooking time.

3. Transfer the chicken pieces to a plate and set aside. Pour off all but 2 tablespoons of fat from the pot. Add the onion, carrots, celery, and garlic and cook until the onions and celery are softened but not browned, about 4 minutes.

4. Add the tomato paste and cook, stirring to coat the vegetables, 2 to 3 minutes. Pour in the chicken broth, red wine, and vinegar, bring to a simmer, and let simmer for 3 to 4 minutes. Add the tomatoes, bay leaves, thyme, red pepper flakes, cumin, and coriander. Return the chicken to the pot and let simmer until it is quite tender and easily pulls away from the bone when pressed, about 1 hour and 20 minutes.

5. To serve, remove and discard the bay leaves. Divide the chicken and vegetables among 4 plates and top with a scattering of Parmesan and parsley and a drizzle of extra-virgin olive oil, if desired.

## how low can you go?

There are eight pieces of chicken in this dish, so it can serve six to eight people if some or all diners are dependably one drumstick or thigh eaters.

CARBOHYDRATE CHOICE: 0

# butterflied broiled chicken

**WITH A QUICK PAN SAUCE**

if you roast or braise a lot of chicken then you are intimately familiar with one of the great annoyances of this otherwise user-friendly bird: The breast cooks before the legs are finished. So you need to yank the breasts out of the oven, tent them with aluminum foil, or perform some other preventative task to avoid overcooking a portion of your dinner.

## nutritional information
### (PER SERVING)

| | |
|---|---|
| Calories | 671 |
| Fat | 47 g |
| Saturated Fat | 12 g |
| Trans Fat | 0 g |
| Total Carbohydrates | 3 g |
| Dietary Fiber | 0 g |
| Total Sugars | 1 g |
| Protein | 46 g |
| Cholesterol | 183 mg |
| Sodium | 441 mg |

## exchanges

| | |
|---|---|
| Fat | 3 |
| Medium Fat Meat | 6.5 |

This recipe, for reasons I don't really understand, eliminates that hassle. All I can tell you is that by removing the chicken's backbone and flattening the bird out, it cooks evenly and just right. You also get a nice, crisp skin and, thanks to the bed of vegetables under the butterflied chicken, the meat is full-flavored and succulent.

**SERVES 4**

## INGREDIENTS

4 large cloves garlic, minced

2 tablespoons chopped fresh flat-leaf parsley

Finely grated zest of 1 lemon

½ teaspoon coarse salt

Pinch of freshly ground black pepper

3 tablespoons olive oil

1 chicken (3 to 3½ pounds), backbone removed (see this page)

1 Spanish onion, cut into 8 pieces through the root end

2 large carrots, cut into 1-inch diagonal slices

2 ribs celery, cut into thirds diagonally

1 cup medium-bodied red wine

1 cup store-bought low-sodium chicken broth

1. Preheat the broiler and position an oven rack 6 to 8 inches below the heating element.

2. Put the garlic, parsley, lemon zest, salt, and pepper in a bowl. Add the olive oil and stir to make a paste.

3. Cut off any skin extending beyond the meat of the chicken. Using your fingers or a spoon, insert the herb paste under the skin of the thighs and breasts.

4. Put the onion, carrots, and celery in a roasting pan in a single layer. Put the chicken on top of the vegetables, skin side up, and broil until the skin is nicely crisp and browned, 12 to 14 minutes. Using tongs, carefully turn the chicken over and broil until an instant-read meat thermometer inserted in the top of the thigh reads 165°F, 12 to 14 minutes longer.

5. Transfer the chicken to a cutting board. Using a slotted spoon, remove and discard the vegetables, then skim off and discard any fat from the pan. Put the roasting pan over 2 burners on the stove top over high heat. Pour in the red wine, bring to a boil, and continue to boil until reduced by three quarters, about 4 minutes. Pour in the chicken broth, bring to a boil, and continue to boil until reduced by one half, about 3 minutes.

6. To serve, cut the chicken into pieces, separating the drumstick and the thigh and cutting the breast in half. Pass the sauce alongside in a sauceboat or spoon some over each serving.

CARBOHYDRATE CHOICE: 0

# basic steamed chicken

this is a very handy recipe to have in your repertoire. It's a simply steamed chicken gently seasoned with garlic, rosemary, and lemon. The chicken meat can be used in any number of dishes, such as the salad on page 93, or for making other salads, wraps, sandwiches, and soups. You can also snack on the chicken or serve it on its own or with a sauce. And, the broth produced by cooking the chicken this way is a useful by-product that you can freeze and use to enrich sauces or soups. **SERVES 4**

## nutritional information
(PER SERVING)

Calories....................203
Fat..............................5 g
　　Saturated Fat............1 g
　　Trans Fat...................0 g
Total Carbohydrates.....2 g
　　Dietary Fiber.............1 g
　　Total Sugars...............1 g
Protein.........................35 g
Cholesterol.............114 mg
Sodium..................606 mg

## exchanges

Lean Meat....................4.3

## INGREDIENTS

1 chicken (about 3 pounds),
　skin removed
1 teaspoon coarse salt
Freshly ground black pepper

2 sprigs fresh rosemary
1 lemon, cut in half
4 cloves garlic, crushed and
　peeled

1. Rinse the chicken under cold running water and pat it dry with paper towels. Season the chicken inside and out with the salt and some pepper. Stuff the cavity of the chicken with the rosemary, lemon, and garlic and tie the chicken legs together with kitchen string.

2. Pour water to a depth of 1 to 2 inches into a large, heavy-bottomed pot and bring to a simmer over medium heat.

3. Place the chicken in a steamer basket and set it over the simmering water without letting the basket touch the water. Cover the pot and steam the chicken until it is plump all over and the meat juices run clear when pierced at the thigh with a sharp knife, 45 minutes to 1 hour.

**4.** Using tongs or a meat fork (insert the fork into the cavity), transfer the chicken to a cutting board. Snip off and discard the kitchen string. Remove and discard the rosemary, lemon, and garlic. (If you like, you can also use the broth that's in the pot; strain it, let it cool, then refrigerate it in an airtight container for up to 3 days or freeze it for up to 2 months.)

**5.** If not serving the chicken immediately, carve it and wrap the individual pieces in plastic wrap, then refrigerate them for up to 2 days.

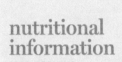

## nutritional information
**(PER SERVING)**

| | |
|---|---|
| Calories | 335 |
| Fat | 16 g |
| Saturated Fat | 4 g |
| Trans Fat | 0 g |
| Total Carbohydrates | 13 g |
| Dietary Fiber | 1 g |
| Total Sugars | 1 g |
| Protein | 32 g |
| Cholesterol | 165 mg |
| Sodium | 709 mg |

## exchanges

| | |
|---|---|
| Fat | 1.5 |
| Starch | 0.5 |
| Lean Meat | 4 |

**CARBOHYDRATE CHOICE: ½**

# turkey and bacon loaf

turkey has been a successful, lighter stand-in for beef in burgers for years now, and it's even more successful as an understudy in this variation on meat loaf, where the slow baking of the ground turkey, mixed with egg, onion, and mustard, leads to a moist, flavorful result. Turkey bacon that's mixed in before baking provides a smoky baseline. **SERVES 6**

## INGREDIENTS

2 slices turkey bacon, coarsely chopped

1 small-size Spanish onion, minced

1 large egg, beaten

¾ cup dry unseasoned bread crumbs

2½ tablespoons Dijon mustard

2 tablespoons freshly grated Parmesan
 cheese

½ teaspoon coarse salt

1 teaspoon freshly ground
 black pepper

1 teaspoon fresh thyme leaves

1 teaspoon chopped fresh tarragon

2 pounds lean ground turkey

**1.** Preheat the oven to 350° F.

**2.** Heat a small, heavy-bottomed nonstick pan over medium-high heat. Add the turkey bacon and cook until browned and the fat is rendered, about 7 minutes. Add the onion and cook until softened but not browned, about 4 minutes. Transfer the onion and bacon to a large mixing bowl and let cool.

**3.** Once the onion and bacon are cool, add the egg, bread crumbs, mustard, Parmesan cheese, salt, pepper, thyme, and tarragon. Stir together well, add the turkey and knead with immaculately clean hands.

**4.** Transfer the turkey mixture to a loaf pan and bake until an instant-read meat thermometer inserted in the center of the loaf reads 165°F, 50 to 55 minutes. Remove the turkey loaf from the oven and let stand for 5 minutes before slicing and serving.

**CARBOHYDRATE CHOICES: 2; 1½ ADJUSTED FOR FIBER**

# turkey-stuffed peppers

an American spin on an Italian-American classic; sausage and peppers are recast here in the form of a quick-to-make turkey sausage that's stuffed into green bell peppers and baked. The thing I love about this dish, and any stuffed pepper dish, is that the juice of the peppers melds so very well with the filling. You can experiment with different types of peppers, such as Italian frying peppers. Anaheim peppers are especially tasty here; they're harder to fill but if you have a taste for heat, it's worth trying at least once.   **SERVES 4**

## nutritional information
### (PER SERVING)

| | |
|---|---|
| Calories | 335 |
| Fat | 16 g |
| Saturated Fat | 4 g |
| Trans Fat | 0 g |
| Total Carbohydrates | 13 g |
| Dietary Fiber | 1 g |
| Total Sugars | 1 g |
| Protein | 32 g |
| Cholesterol | 165 mg |
| Sodium | 709 mg |

## exchanges

| | |
|---|---|
| Fat | 1.5 |
| Starch | 0.5 |
| Lean Meat | 4 |

## INGREDIENTS

2 teaspoons fennel seeds

1 teaspoon olive oil

1 pound lean ground turkey

1 cup diced Spanish onion

3 large cloves garlic, minced

1½ cups cooked brown rice

¼ cup freshly grated Parmesan cheese

1 teaspoon coarse salt

¼ teaspoon sugar

¼ teaspoon crushed red pepper flakes

⅛ teaspoon freshly ground black pepper

⅛ teaspoon ground coriander

4 large green bell peppers

1. Preheat the oven to 350°F.

2. Put the fennel seeds in a heavy-bottomed pan and toast over medium heat, stirring frequently to avoid scorching, until fragrant, about 3 minutes. Transfer to a large bowl and set aside to cool.

3. Heat the olive oil in a pan over medium heat. Add the ground turkey and brown it as you would ground beef, breaking up the pieces with a fork or a wooden spoon, until browned all over, 5 to 6 minutes. Transfer the turkey to the bowl with the fennel seeds.

4. Add the onion and garlic to the pan and cook over medium until softened but not browned, about 4 minutes. Transfer the onion and garlic to the bowl with the turkey and fennel seeds and let cool.

5. Add the brown rice, 2 tablespoons of the Parmesan cheese, and the salt, sugar, red pepper flakes, black pepper, and corian-der to the bowl with the turkey and stir well.

6. Cut the top ½ inch off the bell peppers and seed the peppers. Trim off the very bottom of each pepper so it can stand upright (but do not cut into the inside of the peppers). Soften them by sticking them on a meat fork and holding them over a gas flame until warmed but not blackened. You can also soften the peppers by placing them on a baking sheet under the broiler, turning them every 45 seconds, about 3 minutes total. When cool enough to handle, fill the peppers with the turkey mixture. Arrange the stuffed peppers in a baking dish without crowding and top them with a sprinkling of the remaining 2 tablespoons of Parmesan. Cover the dish loosely with aluminum foil, and bake the peppers until they are softened and the filling is cooked through, about 45 minutes.

7. Remove the foil and bake another 5 minutes to brown the top. Put 1 pepper on each of 4 plates and serve.

Turkey-Stuffed Peppers

CARBOHYDRATE CHOICE: 0

# whole roasted turkey

This is probably a recipe unlike any other you've ever used for roasting a whole turkey. I myself was always taught that the rule of thumb was twenty minutes per pound, and I've also seen techniques that put water or stock in the pan with the bird, tent the breast with aluminum foil, and of course, call for lots of basting. If you have a tried-and-true method that has served you well every Thanksgiving, then by all means stick to it. But my method is much simpler than the traditional ones, and I highly recommend it. Basically, I treat the turkey like a big chicken, using a modified version of the technique I'd use to roast a whole chicken, starting it in a very hot oven and lowering the temperature as soon as the bird starts to brown. At that point, I cook the turkey for fifteen minutes per pound, letting it coast to doneness for fifteen minutes after I've turned the oven off.

I normally season turkeys inside and out, but in order to keep the sodium down here, I have seasoned only the cavity. Using an instant-read meat thermometer to determine doneness is crucial; be sure to insert it at the top of a thigh. **SERVES 30**

## nutritional information

(PER SERVING 4 OUNCES OF MIXED WHITE AND DARK MEAT WITHOUT SKIN)

| | |
|---|---|
| Calories | 193 |
| Fat | 5 g |
| Saturated Fat | 2 g |
| Trans Fat | 0 g |
| Total Carbohydrates | 0 g |
| Dietary Fiber | 0 g |
| Total Sugars | 0 g |
| Protein | 35 g |
| Cholesterol | 105 mg |
| Sodium | 178 mg |

## exchanges

| | |
|---|---|
| Lean Meat | 4.5 |

### INGREDIENTS

1 turkey (about 16 pounds)

1 teaspoon coarse salt

1 tablespoon freshly ground
    black pepper

1. Take the turkey out of the refrigerator about 1 hour before you plan to cook it. This will help it cook more quickly and evenly. (You can speed the thawing process of a frozen turkey by running lukewarm water over it.)

2. Preheat the oven to 425°F.

3. Rinse the turkey inside and out with gently running cold water and pat it dry with paper towels. Season the cavity with the salt and pepper.

4. Set a roasting rack in a roasting pan and place the turkey, breast side

up, on the rack. Bake the turkey until the skin over the breast begins to take on a nice golden, almost burnished color, about 30 minutes. Reduce the temperature to 300°F and continue to roast the turkey until almost done, about 3½ more hours. Turn off the oven and let the turkey sit in the oven until an instant-read meat thermometer inserted into the thickest part of a thigh reads 175°F, about 15 minutes longer.

**5.** Carefully transfer the turkey to a cutting board, tent it with aluminum foil, and let it rest for 20 to 30 minutes before carving and serving.

## nutritional information

(PER SERVING)

| | |
|---|---|
| Calories | 147 |
| Fat | 4 g |
| Saturated Fat | 1 g |
| Trans Fat | 0 g |
| Total Carbohydrates | 8 g |
| Dietary Fiber | 2 g |
| Total Sugars | 5 g |
| Protein | 19 g |
| Cholesterol | 71 mg |
| Sodium | 89 mg |

## exchanges

| | |
|---|---|
| Fat | 0.5 |
| Lean Meat | 2.5 |
| Fruit | 0.5 |
| Vegetables | 0.5 |

CARBOHYDRATE CHOICE: ½

# grilled duck breast paillard

## WITH ORANGE, ONION, AND MINT

duck *à l'orange* taught cooks a lesson that has reverberated through the ages: When serving duck, there's nothing like some sweetness on the plate to counterbalance its rich, almost livery flavor. Usually that sweetness, at least where oranges are concerned, is achieved with a syrupy sauce made with Grand Marnier to intensify the citrus quality. But in this case, where thin slices of duck are cooked on the grill, a simple orange salad does the trick, especially with sharp red onion and fragrant mint in the mix. **SERVES 4**

### INGREDIENTS

4 skinless duck breast halves (about 6 ounces each)
Pinch of coarse salt
Pinch of freshly ground black pepper
2 cups loosely packed frisée lettuce

2 small-size oranges, sectioned with the sections peeled
1 small-size red onion, thinly sliced
1 teaspoon thinly sliced fresh mint leaves
Squirt of freshly squeezed lemon juice

1. Preheat a gas grill to medium-high or build a fire in a charcoal grill, letting the coals burn down until covered with white ash. If using a grill pan, briefly preheat the pan over medium-high heat.

2. Place the duck breasts on a cutting board and, working very carefully and using a very sharp, long knife, slice them in half horizontally. Place one piece of duck between 2 pieces of plastic wrap and, using a meat mallet or the bottom of a heavy pan, pound it as thinly as possible. Repeat with the remaining pieces of duck. Season the duck with the salt and pepper. Place the duck on the grill and grill until just pink inside, 3 to 4 minutes per side.

3. Put the frisée, orange sections, onion, mint, and lemon juice in a bowl and toss together. Put 2 slices of duck breast on each of 4 plates, overlapping them slightly. Top each with some salad and serve.

variations and suggestions: To make this into a main course salad, use twice as much salad and half as much duck.

---

CARBOHYDRATE CHOICES: 2½

# duck schnitzel

## WITH CELERY ROOT "REMOULADE"

this dish is all about the contrast between the pounded, breaded slices of duck breast and the creamy celery root "rémoulade," a coleslaw-like salad made from thin slices of the vegetable (rather than cabbage) tossed with a mayonnaise-like dressing. The slivered cornichons add an important, briny counterpoint that lifts the otherwise heavy flavors and textures.

The recipe calls for magret duck breast (*magret de canard*). Magrets are crossbred from Muscovy and Pekin (Long Island) ducks. Their breasts are unusually large but are the perfect size for dividing into two portions, as they are here. They're also exceptionally meaty, so they hold together well when split horizontally.

SERVES 4

## nutritional information
(PER SERVING)

| | |
|---|---|
| Calories | 450 |
| Fat | 21 g |
| Saturated Fat | 3 g |
| Trans Fat | 0 g |
| Total Carbohydrates | 38 g |
| Dietary Fiber | 3 g |
| Total Sugars | 3 g |
| Protein | 25 g |
| Cholesterol | 71 mg |
| Sodium | 533 mg |

## exchanges

| | |
|---|---|
| Fat | 4 |
| Starch | 1.5 |
| Other Carbohydrates | 0.5 |
| Lean Meat | 2.5 |
| Vegetables | 2 |

## INGREDIENTS

1½ tablespoons Dijon mustard

2 teaspoons olive oil

1½ teaspoons freshly squeezed lemon
  juice

1 teaspoon minced fresh flat-leaf
  parsley leaves

Pinch of freshly ground black pepper

1 pound celery root, trimmed and
  cut into matchsticks

2 skinless magret duck breasts
  (about 12 ounces each)

½ cup all-purpose flour

2 large egg whites

½ cup dry unseasoned bread
  crumbs

¼ cup canola oil

4 cornichons, cut lengthwise into
  thin slivers

1. Make the "rémoulade": Put the mustard, olive oil, and lemon juice in a bowl and whisk until blended. Whisk in about 2 teaspoons of hot water, a few drops at a time, to emulsify the mixture. Stir in the parsley and season with the pepper. Fold in the celery root and set the "rémoulade" aside.

2. Place the duck breasts on a cutting board and, working very carefully and using a very sharp, long knife, slice them in half horizontally.

3. Spread the flour out on a plate. Put the egg whites in a wide bowl, add 2 tablespoons of cold water, and beat. Spread the bread crumbs out on another plate.

4. Working with 1 piece of duck at a time, dredge the breasts in the flour, dip them in the egg mixture, letting any excess run back into the bowl, then coat them with bread crumbs, pressing down just enough for the crumbs to adhere.

5. Heat the canola oil in a large, deep pan over medium heat. Add the duck, working in batches if necessary, and cook until the crumbs are golden and the meat is cooked through, about 4 minutes per side.

6. To serve, divide the "rémoulade" among 4 dinner plates, topping it with some slivered cornichon. Arrange a duck schnitzel alongside. Drizzle the dressing remaining in the bowl around the duck and "rémoulade" on each plate.

# rabbit stew

"tastes like chicken" has long been a humorous way of describing rabbit, but it happens to be apt. Rabbit is like a more flavorful answer to chicken and it's especially appropriate for a diabetes diet because it's very lean and you cook it without the skin. If you've never tried rabbit, this recipe is a very user-friendly way to introduce yourself to one of the most underappreciated meats in American kitchens. If you already have a fondness for it, here's a very traditional, rustic rabbit stew to add to your repertoire. If you're so inclined, toss a small quantity of orzo or pappardelle in with this. It's also delicious alongside simply roasted root vegetables. **SERVES 4**

## nutritional information
**(PER SERVING)**

Calories.....................251
Fat...............................6 g
    Saturated Fat..........2 g
    Trans Fat...............0 g
Total Carbohydrates....16 g
    Dietary Fiber............3 g
    Total Sugars............7 g
Protein.........................13 g
Cholesterol.............33 mg
Sodium.................203 mg

## exchanges

Fat.............................0.5
Lean Meat...................1.5
Vegetables....................2

## INGREDIENTS

2 teaspoons unsalted butter

1 teaspoon canola oil

4 rabbit fryer legs
    (about 5 ounces each)

1 large Spanish onion, cut in half
    crosswise and thinly sliced
    lengthwise

3 small carrots, cut diagonally into
    ½-inch pieces

2 tablespoons tomato paste

Pinch of coarse salt

Pinch of freshly ground black pepper

4 plum tomatoes, cut into 1-inch dice,
    with their juice

2 cups red wine

2 cups store-bought low-sodium
    chicken broth

¼ cup white wine vinegar

6 cloves garlic, thinly sliced

1 teaspoon chopped fresh marjoram
    leaves

1 teaspoon fresh thyme leaves

1 bay leaf, preferably fresh

1. Preheat the oven to 300°F.

2. Melt the butter in the oil in a heavy-bottomed, ovenproof Dutch oven over medium-high heat and cook until the butter begins to brown. Add the rabbit legs, skinned side down, and cook until nicely browned, about 2 minutes per side.

3. Remove the rabbit from the Dutch oven and discard all but 2 tablespoons of fat. Add the onion and carrots and cook over medium

heat for 3 to 4 minutes. Add the tomato paste and cook, stirring to coat the vegetables with the paste, for about 3 minutes. Season the vegetables with the salt and pepper and add the tomatoes, red wine, chicken broth, vinegar, garlic, marjoram, thyme, bay leaf, and ½ cup of water. Increase the heat to bring to a boil. Return the rabbit to the Dutch oven, bring to a boil again, then cover, and quickly transfer the pot to the oven. Bake the rabbit at a gentle simmer until it is tender to the touch, about 30 minutes.

**4.** Remove the pot from the oven. Using tongs or a slotted spoon, transfer the rabbit legs to a cutting board and let them cool. Skim any residual fat from the sauce. As soon as the legs are cool enough to handle, remove all of the meat from the bones and return it to the stew, and discard the bones. Reheat the stew briefly, then divide it among 4 shallow bowls and serve.

## nutritional information
### (PER SERVING)

Calories......................260
Fat.................................14 g
  Saturated Fat...........5 g
  Trans Fat...................0 g
Total Carbohydrates.....0 g
  Dietary Fiber.............0 g
  Total Sugars..............0 g
Protein........................31 g
Cholesterol..............95 mg
Sodium...................160 mg

## exchanges

Fat..................................1.5
Lean Meat...................4.5

CARBOHYDRATE CHOICE: 0

# grilled beef tenderloin

if you're serving beef to a big crowd and plan to grill, monitoring the doneness of a large number of steaks can be a daunting task for even the most accomplished backyard grill master. As an alternative, think about grilling a whole tenderloin of beef, which can serve up to ten people. You won't have the same, marbled quality as with a rib eye or New York strip, but grilling and slicing a whole tenderloin makes a big impact, and one tenderloin yields different levels of doneness, as the ends tend to be more well-done than the center, so you can accommodate varying tastes at the table. This is a fairly basic recipe, but you can dress it up with a coating of pureed garlic, or cracked pepper, or serve it with one or more of the many side dishes from the chapter that begins on page 273.

**SERVES 10**

## INGREDIENTS

*1 beef tenderloin (about 2½ pounds), trimmed of any excess fat*
*1 tablespoon extra-virgin olive oil*

*½ teaspoon coarse salt*
*½ teaspoon freshly ground black pepper*

1. Build a fire in a charcoal grill, letting the coals burn down until covered with white ash or preheat a gas grill to medium.

2. Rub the beef with the olive oil and season it with the salt and pepper.

3. Grill the beef, turning frequently to ensure even cooking, until nicely charred all over and an instant-read meat thermometer inserted in the center of the tenderloin reads 120° to 125°F for rare, about 18 minutes, or longer for more well-done.

4. Transfer the tenderloin to a cutting board and let rest for 10 minutes, then slice it crosswise into 10 pieces and serve.

CARBOHYDRATE CHOICE: 0

# filets mignons

## WITH BLACK AND GREEN PEPPERCORN SAUCE

this is my riff on the classic steak au poivre, or steak with peppercorns, which traditionally features loads of brandy and cream. My version uses just enough of both to make their presence felt but adds a healthy dose of Dijon mustard, which gets on great with the other ingredients and gives the sauce its body. One of the things I love most about this dish is actually cooking it, making a pan sauce based on the flavor left behind after the filets have been seared. **SERVES 4**

### nutritional information
(PER SERVING)

| | |
|---|---|
| Calories | 328 |
| Fat | 18 g |
| Saturated Fat | 5 g |
| Trans Fat | 0 g |
| Total Carbohydrates | 4 g |
| Dietary Fiber | 1 g |
| Total Sugars | 0 g |
| Protein | 33 g |
| Cholesterol | 98 mg |
| Sodium | 231 mg |

### exchanges

| | |
|---|---|
| Fat | 2 |
| Lean Meat | 4.5 |

### INGREDIENTS

2 tablespoons canola oil

4 filets mignons (about 5 ounces each), tied around the "equator" with kitchen string

1 small shallot, minced

2 tablespoons Cognac

1 cup store-bought low-sodium beef broth

1 teaspoon cracked black pepper

1 tablespoon brined whole green peppercorns, rinsed and drained

1 tablespoon Dijon mustard

2 teaspoons heavy (whipping) cream

2 tablespoons chopped fresh flat-leaf parsley leaves

1. Preheat the broiler.

2. Heat the oil in a wide, deep, heavy-bottomed pan over medium-high heat. Add the filets and sear them well on both sides, about 3 minutes per side, then transfer them to a baking sheet or baking dish and set aside.

3. Add the shallot to the pan and cook until softened but not browned, about 2 minutes, stirring to loosen any flavorful bits stuck to the bottom of the pan. Carefully pour in the Cognac and let simmer until it is nearly evaporated, about 2 minutes. Add the beef broth, increase the heat

to high, and boil until reduced to about ½ cup, about 5 minutes. Stir in the cracked black pepper and the green peppercorns, then the mustard and cream, stirring until the sauce thickens, 2 to 3 minutes. Remove the pan from the heat, and cover the sauce to keep it warm.

4. Broil the filets without turning until sizzling, 2 to 3 minutes for medium-rare or a bit longer for more well-done.

5. Put 1 filet on each of 4 dinner plates. Stir the parsley into the sauce, spoon some sauce over each piece of meat, and serve.

## nutritional information
(PER SERVING)

| | |
|---|---|
| Calories | 419 |
| Fat | 27 g |
| Saturated Fat | 8 g |
| Trans Fat | 0 g |
| Total Carbohydrates | 8 g |
| Dietary Fiber | 2 g |
| Total Sugars | 4 g |
| Protein | 35 g |
| Cholesterol | 105 mg |
| Sodium | 257 mg |

## exchanges

| | |
|---|---|
| Fat | 3.5 |
| Lean Meat | 4.5 |
| High Fat Meat | 0.5 |
| Vegetables | 1.5 |

CARBOHYDRATE CHOICE: ½

# grilled filets mignons
## WITH WATERCRESS AND GORGONZOLA SALAD

meat connoisseurs will tell you that when it comes to steak there's no substitute for the marbled quality of a New York strip, rib eye, or porterhouse. If I'm being honest, I can't say that I disagree. But I also have a soft spot for meltingly tender filet mignon, which of course has a significantly lower fat content. Peppery watercress is a classic accompaniment, and a little Gorgonzola cheese brings it all home. **SERVES 4**

## INGREDIENTS

*4 filets mignons (about 5 ounces each),
    cut in half crosswise*
*2 tablespoons olive oil*
*Pinch of coarse salt*
*Pinch of freshly ground black pepper*
*2 small bunches watercress, tough
    stems trimmed*

*2 roasted red peppers (page 324),
    thinly sliced*
*½ medium-size red onion, thinly sliced*
*¼ cup crumbled Gorgonzola, or other
    blue cheese (about 1 ounce)*
*2 tablespoons extra-virgin olive oil*
*1 tablespoon freshly squeezed lemon juice*

1. Build a fire in a charcoal grill, letting the coals burn down until covered with white ash or preheat a gas grill to high. If using a grill pan, briefly preheat the pan over high heat.

2. Rub the slices of filet with the regular olive oil and season them with the salt and pepper. Grill the filets until charred on both sides, 3 to 4 minutes per side for medium rare.

3. Put the watercress, red peppers, onion, and Gorgonzola in a bowl. Drizzle the extra-virgin olive oil and lemon juice over the salad and toss.

4. To serve, put 2 slices of grilled filet on each of 4 dinner plates and mound some salad alongside, slightly overlapping the beef.

CARBOHYDRATE CHOICE: 1

# veal scaloppine

**C**ertain dishes can hit you like an old song, surprising you with how well they stand up after all these years and how much you still love them. That's certainly the way I feel about this dish of pounded-out, breaded veal medallions seared in a pan and finished with a lemony, buttery sauce. It's not flashy or groundbreaking, but a few times a year, there's nothing I'd rather eat.

SERVES 4

## nutritional information
(PER SERVING)

| | |
|---|---|
| Calories | 443 |
| Fat | 23 g |
| Saturated Fat | 7 g |
| Trans Fat | 0 g |
| Total Carbohydrates | 21 g |
| Dietary Fiber | 1 g |
| Total Sugars | 4 g |
| Protein | 23 g |
| Cholesterol | 111 mg |
| Sodium | 297 mg |

## exchanges

| | |
|---|---|
| Fat | 4 |
| Starch | 1 |
| Lean Meat | 3 |

## INGREDIENTS

4 veal cutlets (about 4 ounces each)

½ cup all-purpose flour

1 cup skim milk

½ cup dry unseasoned bread crumbs

¼ cup olive oil

2 tablespoons minced shallot

⅔ cup dry white wine

⅔ cup store-bought low-sodium chicken broth

2 tablespoons freshly squeezed lemon juice

2 tablespoons unsalted butter

2 teaspoons capers, rinsed and drained

2 tablespoons minced fresh flat-leaf parsley leaves

**1.** Sandwich 1 piece of veal at a time between 2 pieces of plastic wrap and, using a meat mallet or the bottom of a heavy pot or pan, gently pound it to a thickness of ¼ inch. Pound out all 4 pieces of veal before proceeding.

**2.** Spread the flour out on a plate, pour the milk into a wide, shallow bowl, and spread the bread crumbs out on another plate.

**3.** Dredge the veal scaloppine in the flour, then dip them in the milk, letting any excess drip off back into the bowl. Press the scaloppine in the bread crumbs just firmly enough for the crumbs to adhere.

**4.** Heat 2 tablespoons of the olive oil in a heavy-bottomed pan over medium-high heat. Add the breaded veal and cook until nicely golden on both sides, about 4 minutes per side. Transfer each scaloppine to a serving plate and keep warm.

**5.** To make the sauce, carefully wipe out the pan and heat the remaining 2 tablespoons of olive oil over medium-high heat. Add the shallot and cook until softened but not browned, about 2 minutes. Add the white wine and let simmer until almost completely evaporated, about 4 minutes. Add the chicken broth and let simmer until nicely thickened, about 2 minutes. Swirl in the lemon juice and butter and add the capers and parsley.

**6.** Spoon some sauce over each veal scaloppine and serve.

# seared calf's liver

## WITH A MUSTARD-TARRAGON SAUCE

I've loved calf's liver since I was a little kid, when my grandmother served me small amounts of liver between huge slices of bread. In time, the bread got thinner and the liver got thicker, until I was hooked for life. Here, sautéed liver is topped with a room-temperature mustard-tarragon sauce that starts with a puree of one of liver's natural complements, onions. It might sound like every child's worst culinary nightmare, but I recommend serving this with the Bacony Brussels Sprouts (page 275). **SERVES 4**

### nutritional information
(PER SERVING)

Calories.....................189
Fat...................................4 g
  Saturated Fat............1 g
  Trans Fat.................0 g
Total Carbohydrates....12 g
  Dietary Fiber.............1 g
  Total Sugars............1.5 g
Protein.........................24 g
Cholesterol............312 mg
Sodium..................471 mg

### exchanges

Lean Meat.................3.5
Vegetables................0.5

## INGREDIENTS

1 large Spanish onion, coarsely chopped

¼ cup Dijon mustard

1 teaspoon chopped fresh tarragon

1 teaspoon chopped fresh flat-leaf parsley leaves

8 pieces calf's liver (½-inch thick; 1 pound total)

Pinch of coarse salt

2 teaspoons freshly ground black pepper

Nonstick cooking spray

1. Put the onion in a small, heavy-bottomed saucepan and add enough cold water just to cover it by 1 inch. Bring to a simmer over medium-high heat and let simmer until the onion is tender, about 5 minutes. Using a slotted spoon, transfer the onion to a blender, setting aside the cooking liquid. Add the mustard, tarragon, and parsley to the blender and puree until smooth. If the mixture is so dense the blender seizes, add a tablespoon or two of the reserved cooking liquid to free it. Set the mustard-tarragon sauce aside. (Do not make this sauce ahead of time; the herbs will turn it a nasty, khaki color.)

2. Season the liver with the salt and pepper. Heat a wide, heavy-bottomed, nonstick pan over medium heat. Spray the pan with nonstick cooking spray and heat the pan to high. Add the liver and sear it quickly on one side, about 1 minute, then turn it over,

reduce the heat to medium, and sear on the other side for about 1 minute for medium-rare, or a bit longer for more well-done.

3. Put 2 pieces of liver on each of 4 dinner plates. Spoon some mustard-tarragon sauce over and around the liver and serve.

## nutritional information
### (PER SERVING)

| | |
|---|---|
| Calories | 383 |
| Fat | 21 g |
| Saturated Fat | 7 g |
| Trans Fat | 0 g |
| Total Carbohydrates | 13 g |
| Dietary Fiber | 1 g |
| Total Sugars | 3 g |
| Protein | 33 g |
| Cholesterol | 179 mg |
| Sodium | 486 mg |

## exchanges

| | |
|---|---|
| Fat | 1 |
| Starch | 0.5 |
| Lean Meat | 2.5 |
| Medium Fat Meat | 0.5 |
| Vegetables | 0.5 |

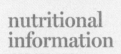

**CARBOHYDRATE CHOICE: 1**

# meat loaf

I never tire of this meat loaf. It's based on a recipe that a few of my cooks shared with me years ago. In order to keep the level of sodium down, I make it with no salt other than what's present in the crushed saltines. If you miss it, I suggest sprinkling a pinch of salt over your portion and inviting others to do the same.

**SERVES 6**

## INGREDIENTS

1 tablespoon olive oil

1 medium-size Spanish onion, finely chopped

3 cloves garlic, minced

2 large eggs, beaten

½ teaspoon fresh thyme leaves

3 tablespoons plus 1 teaspoon Dijon mustard

2 tablespoons Worcestershire sauce

½ teaspoon Tabasco sauce

1 cup whole milk

2 pounds ground meat (ideally equal parts beef, pork, and veal)

⅔ cup crushed salt-free saltine crackers

¼ cup minced fresh flat-leaf parsley leaves

1 teaspoon freshly ground black pepper

1. Preheat the oven to 350°F.

2. Heat the olive oil in a small, heavy-bottomed pan over medium-high heat. Add the onion and garlic and cook until softened but not browned,

about 4 minutes. Transfer the onion and garlic to a mixing bowl and let cool.

3. Once the onion and garlic are cool, add the eggs, thyme, mustard,

Worcestershire sauce, Tabasco sauce, and milk. Stir together well.

**4.** Put the meat in another bowl and pour the egg mixture over it. Add the saltines, parsley, and pepper and knead together with immaculately clean hands.

**5.** Transfer the meat mixture to a loaf pan and bake until an instant-read meat thermometer inserted into the center of the loaf reads 160°F, about 1 hour. Let the meat loaf stand for 5 minutes before slicing and serving.

**variations and suggestions:** If you're looking for something new to do with meat loaf, believe it or not, you can grill leftover slices: Just make sure the grill is good and hot, and oil the meat loaf (not the grate) lightly before cooking to keep the slices from sticking. Grill the meat loaf until it is warmed through and the slices have slight grill marks.

CARBOHYDRATE CHOICE: 0

# garlic-roasted pork loin

## WITH SALSA VERDE

This vaguely Latin dish features slow-roasted pork that's been larded with garlic. As the meat cooks, the garlic "melts" and transmits its flavor throughout the loin. The result is a succulent, aromatic meat achieved with very little work. The slightly spicy *salsa verde*, made with cilantro, serrano pepper, and lemon juice, is the perfect complement for the intensity of the pork. If you have leftovers, very thin slices make one of the best sandwiches.

**SERVES 4**

### INGREDIENTS

1½ pounds boneless pork loin
4 cloves garlic, peeled and cut into
    thin slivers
1 tablespoon olive oil

1 teaspoon coarse salt
½ teaspoon freshly ground
    black pepper
¾ cup Salsa Verde (page 319)

## nutritional information
(PER SERVING)

Calories ..................... 341
Fat ............................ 23 g
    Saturated Fat ........... 4 g
    Trans Fat ................. 0 g
Total Carbohydrates ..... 2 g
    Dietary Fiber ............ 0 g
    Total Sugars ............. 0 g
Protein ...................... 32 g
Cholesterol ............. 100 mg
Sodium .................. 609 mg

## exchanges

Fat ............................. 3
Lean Meat ................. 4.5
Vegetables ................ 0.5

1. Preheat the oven to 425°F.

2. Using the tip of a sharp, thin-bladed knife, make small ½ inch–deep slits all over the pork loin. Using the blade of the knife as a guide, slide a garlic sliver into each slit. Rub the olive oil all over the pork and season it with the salt and pepper.

3. Preheat a roasting pan or large, heavy-bottomed ovenproof skillet in the oven for 10 minutes.

4. Put the pork in the hot roasting pan and roast until an instant-read meat thermometer inserted into the center of the loin reads 140°F, 35 to 40 minutes. Every 10 minutes or so give the loin a quarter turn to ensure even browning.

5. Transfer the pork to a cutting board, cover it with aluminum foil, and let rest for 10 minutes. Carve the loin crosswise into 8 slices and put 2 slices on each of 4 dinner plates. Spoon 3 tablespoons of the Salsa Verde over the pork on each plate and serve.

## nutritional information
### (PER SERVING)

| | |
|---|---|
| Calories | 196 |
| Fat | 10 g |
| Saturated Fat | 2 g |
| Trans Fat | 0 g |
| Total Carbohydrates | 8 g |
| Dietary Fiber | 1 g |
| Total Sugars | 1 g |
| Protein | 15 g |
| Cholesterol | 37 mg |
| Sodium | 167 mg |

## exchanges

| | |
|---|---|
| Fat | 1.5 |
| Starch | 0.5 |
| Lean Meat | 2 |

CARBOHYDRATE CHOICE: ½

# pork pepperoncini

two varieties of peppers that come in jars—small, slender green pepperoncini and red-hot cherry peppers—are rarely seen anywhere other than in salad bars and on pizzas. I've harnessed them in a surprising dish, bringing their uniquely sweet heat to a quick stew that's served atop sautéed pork cutlets. I think of this as a deconstructed spicy salami, with pork and pepper coming together in a new and very compelling way. **SERVES 4**

## INGREDIENTS

2 tablespoons canola oil

4 thin pork cutlets (about 4 ounces each)

½ cup all-purpose flour

½ cup thinly sliced pepperoncini, seeds rinsed out, drained

½ cup thinly sliced hot cherry peppers, seeds rinsed out, drained

¼ cup dry white wine

½ cup store-bought low-sodium chicken broth

1. Heat the oil in a wide, heavy-bottomed pan set over medium-high heat.

2. Dredge the pork cutlets in the flour, shaking off any excess, and add them to the pan. Cook the cutlets until they turn white and are firm to the touch, about 3 minutes on each side, then transfer each cutlet to a dinner plate.

3. Add the pepperoncini and cherry peppers to the pan and cook, stirring, until slightly softened, about 2 minutes. Pour in the wine, increase the heat to high, and boil until the liquid is almost completely evaporated, about 4 minutes. Pour in the chicken broth, bring to a boil, and continue boiling until the liquid is reduced by about half and the mixture appears nicely stewlike, about 3 minutes. Pour the pepper stew over the pork and serve.

CARBOHYDRATE CHOICE: 1

# bacon-wrapped pork tenderloin

## WITH A SWEET PEA STEW

i'm such a fan of pork, in all its forms, that there used to be a game in my restaurant kitchen: each line cook would take turns trying to conceive the most outlandishly porcine dish he could imagine. (Pork Fat Noodles in a Ham Broth Garnished with Bacon Bits was one memorable improv. Another was Fat Back Alfredo.) The game was played in jest, but I couldn't be more serious about my deep and abiding affection for all things pork, even when the bacon is represented by the turkey variety. This dish adapts one of my most pork-centric imaginings, bacon-wrapped pork tenderloin, substituting that turkey bacon for the real thing and depositing the pork on a pea stew that brings some welcome sweetness and color to the plate.  **SERVES 4**

## nutritional information
(PER SERVING)

| | |
|---|---|
| Calories | 364 |
| Fat | 17 g |
| Saturated Fat | 5 g |
| Trans Fat | 0 g |
| Total Carbohydrates | 16 g |
| Dietary Fiber | 4 g |
| Total Sugars | 7 g |
| Protein | 36 g |
| Cholesterol | 121 mg |
| Sodium | 706 mg |

## exchanges

| | |
|---|---|
| Fat | 1.5 |
| Starch | 0.5 |
| Lean Meat | 2.5 |
| High Fat Meat | 1 |
| Vegetables | 1 |

## INGREDIENTS

2 cups (one 10-ounce package)
  frozen peas
1½ tablespoons olive oil
1 large Spanish onion, cut into
  small dice
4 large cloves garlic, thinly sliced
2 cups store-bought low-sodium
  chicken broth

1 tablespoon unsalted butter
Freshly ground black pepper
1 pound pork tenderloin,
  trimmed to a cylindrical shape
Pinch of ground coriander
Pinch of garlic powder
12 slices turkey bacon
1 teaspoon canola oil

1. Put the peas in a small pot. Add just enough water to cover and cook over medium-high heat until the water simmers and the peas are soft, 2 to 3 minutes after the water has come to a simmer. Meanwhile, fill a large bowl halfway with ice water. When the peas are done, reserve a few tablespoons of the pea cooking liquid, then drain the peas and transfer them to the ice water. Drain the peas again and set aside.

2. Heat the olive oil in a wide, deep, heavy-bottomed pan over medium heat. Add the onion and garlic and cook until softened but not browned, about 4 minutes. Add 2 tablespoons of the reserved pea cooking liquid and cook until it evaporates, about 1 minute. Add 1 cup of the chicken broth and cook until it is almost completely evaporated, about 5 minutes.

3. Add the remaining 1 cup of chicken broth and cook until it's

almost completely evaporated but the onion is still moist, about 3 minutes. Add the drained peas and stir to mix.

4. Spoon the pea mixture onto a rimmed baking sheet and mash it with the back of a fork. Return the mashed pea mixture to the pan, place it over medium-low heat, and add the butter and a few grinds of pepper. Stir until the butter melts. Remove the pea stew from the heat and cover it to keep warm.

5. Preheat the oven to 400°F.

6. Season the pork with a pinch of pepper and the coriander and garlic powder. Arrange the slices of turkey bacon next to each other on a cutting board so that the long sides overlap slightly. Position the pork tenderloin crosswise at the top of the bacon. Wrap the tenderloin up in the bacon.

7. Rub the canola oil over the surface of a wide, deep, nonstick pan. Place the pan over medium-high heat. Sear the wrapped pork tenderloin, seam side down, to seal the bacon, 3 to 4 minutes. Turn the wrapped pork and cook all over until the bacon is uniformly crisp, about 10 minutes.

8. Place the wrapped pork in a small roasting pan and roast it until an instant-read meat thermometer inserted in the thickest part reads 160°F, 8 to 10 minutes, turning it every 3 to 4 minutes.

9. When the bacon-wrapped pork is done, transfer it to a cutting board, cover it loosely with aluminum foil, and let rest for 5 minutes.

10. To serve, reheat the pea stew, if necessary, over medium-low heat. Slice the pork tenderloin into 4 equal portions. Spoon equal amounts of the pea stew into the center of each of 4 plates. Place one piece of bacon-wrapped pork on top of each portion of stew and serve.

CARBOHYDRATE CHOICE: 1

# grilled lamb patties

## WITH CUCUMBER AND ONION SALAD

You need look no further than my last name to know that I'm of Italian, not Greek, descent. So I make no claims as to authentic Greek roots for this dish. All I can tell you is that once in a while I get into a Greek state of mind, and lamb is one of the things that presses that button for me. So, when I decided to make lamb patties for this book, it wasn't long before I was scouring the pantry and fridge for the oregano, cucumbers, mint, and feta cheese. Here's the result: a light, summery main course.

It's worth noting that this recipe has a relatively high fat and calorie count, but the carbohydrate tally was low enough that I decided to include it.

**SERVES 4**

## nutritional information
### (PER SERVING)

| | |
|---|---|
| Calories | 542 |
| Fat | 42 g |
| Saturated Fat | 17 g |
| Trans Fat | 0 g |
| Total Carbohydrates | 12 g |
| Dietary Fiber | 2 g |
| Total Sugars | 3 g |
| Protein | 28 g |
| Cholesterol | 166 mg |
| Sodium | 848 mg |

## exchanges

| | |
|---|---|
| Fat | 3.5 |
| Starch | 0.5 |
| Lean Meat | 0.5 |
| Medium Fat Meat | 0.5 |
| High Fat Meat | 2.5 |
| Vegetables | 1 |

## INGREDIENTS

*1 pound ground lamb*

*2 large cloves garlic, minced*

*1 large egg*

*⅓ cup diced Spanish onion*

*1 heaping tablespoon Dijon mustard*

*½ teaspoon coarse salt*

*¼ teaspoon freshly ground black pepper*

*¼ cup dry unseasoned bread crumbs*

*¼ cup freshly grated Parmesan cheese (about 1 ounce)*

*¼ teaspoon ground cumin*

*¼ teaspoon ground coriander*

*¼ teaspoon dried oregano*

*Pinch of cayenne pepper*

*1 English (seedless) cucumber, thinly sliced crosswise*

*½ small-size red onion, thinly sliced*

*2 tablespoons extra-virgin olive oil*

*3 tablespoons freshly squeezed lemon juice*

*1 tablespoon chopped fresh mint leaves*

*3 ounces feta cheese, crumbled (about ¾ cup)*

1. Put the lamb, garlic, egg, Spanish onion, mustard, salt, pepper, bread crumbs, Parmesan cheese, cumin, coriander, oregano, and cayenne pepper in a bowl and knead them together. Form into 4 patties, cover, and refrigerate for at least 20 minutes and up to 2 hours.

2. Build a fire in a charcoal grill, letting the coals burn down until covered with white ash or preheat a gas grill to high. If using a grill pan, briefly preheat the pan over high heat.

3. Put the cucumber and red onion in a bowl and drizzle the olive oil and lemon juice over them. Add the mint and feta cheese and toss to mix.

4. Grill the lamb patties until lightly charred and cooked through, 4 to 5 minutes per side.

5. Divide the cucumber and onion salad among 4 plates. Place a lamb patty on each plate and serve.

Grilled Lamb Patties

# grilled lamb chops

## WITH CAULIFLOWER STEW

W e serve a version of this dish at my restaurant, Ouest, where customers love the interplay of charred, grilled lamb and the almost sweet-and-sour cauliflower stew. The secret ingredient here is the vinegar, which really lifts the other flavors. If at all possible, make the stew the day before you plan to serve it so the vinegar has a chance to really become integrated; it can be a little harsh when it's first stirred in but mellows with just a few hours of refrigeration. **SERVES 4**

### nutritional information
**(PER SERVING)**

| | |
|---|---|
| Calories | 326 |
| Fat | 15 g |
| Saturated Fat | 4 g |
| Trans Fat | 0 g |
| Total Carbohydrates | 15 g |
| Dietary Fiber | 5 g |
| Total Sugars | 7 g |
| Protein | 33 g |
| Cholesterol | 87 mg |
| Sodium | 280 mg |

### exchanges

| | |
|---|---|
| Fat | 1.5 |
| Lean Meat | 4 |
| Vegetables | 3 |

## INGREDIENTS

2 tablespoons olive oil

1 head of cauliflower, stems trimmed,
   broken into florets

8 medium-size plum tomatoes,
   cut into sixths

6 cloves garlic, very thinly sliced

1 tablespoon tomato paste

Pinch of sugar

2 tablespoons distilled white
   vinegar

3 cups store-bought low-sodium
   chicken broth

8 loin lamb chops (about 1 inch
   thick and 12 ounces each)

Pinch of coarse salt

Pinch of freshly ground black pepper

1. Heat 1 tablespoon of the olive oil in a large, heavy-bottomed pot over high heat. Add the cauliflower and cook, stirring occasionally, until browned all over, about 8 minutes. Transfer the cauliflower to a plate and set it aside.

2. Add the tomatoes and garlic to the pot, reduce the heat to medium, and cook, stirring, until the tomatoes begin to break down, about 10 minutes. Stir in the tomato paste and sugar and cook, stirring, for 4 minutes. Pour in the vinegar, and increase the heat to bring to a simmer. Let the tomato mixture simmer until almost all of the liquid has evaporated, about 3 minutes. Return the cauliflower to the pot and add the chicken broth. Bring to a simmer and let simmer until the cauliflower

is soft when pierced with a knife, about 6 minutes. If possible, let the cauliflower stew cool and refrigerate it overnight in an airtight container to give the flavors a chance to integrate. Let the stew come to room temperature before continuing with the recipe.

**3.** Build a fire in a charcoal grill, letting the coals burn down until covered with white ash or preheat a gas grill to medium-high. If using a grill pan, preheat the pan over medium-high heat.

**4.** Rub the lamb chops with the remaining 1 tablespoon of olive oil and season with the salt and pepper. Grill the lamb chops until medium-rare, 3 to 4 minutes per side, or longer for more well-done.

**5.** Gently reheat the cauliflower stew. Spoon some stew on one side of each of 4 dinner plates, set 2 chops next to the stew on each plate and serve.

## nutritional information
**(PER SERVING)**

| | |
|---|---|
| Calories | 530 |
| Fat | 37 g |
| Saturated Fat | 13 g |
| Trans Fat | 0 g |
| Total Carbohydrates | 24 g |
| Dietary Fiber | 4 g |
| Total Sugars | 3 g |
| Protein | 22 g |
| Cholesterol | 85 mg |
| Sodium | 455 mg |

## exchanges

| | |
|---|---|
| Fat | 3 |
| Starch | 1 |
| High Fat Meat | 2.5 |
| Vegetables | 0.5 |

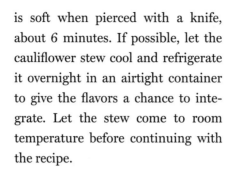

**CARBOHYDRATE CHOICES: 1½**

# lamb sausage
## WITH WARM POTATO SALAD

**m**any home cooks have confided in me that they have never made sausage because they're intimidated by the idea of stuffing it into casings. I've always thought this was a shame because the casings are really incidental, a way for producers to sell sausage but that has nothing to do with its texture or flavor. So, I encourage one and all to try this recipe for lamb sausage, which is shaped into patties, and discover how easy sausage making can be. It's paired with a vinegary potato salad that nicely counterbalances the gamy quality of the meat.

**SERVES 4**

## INGREDIENTS

1 pound Idaho potatoes
   (1 large potato), diced
1 tablespoon chopped fresh flat-leaf
   parsley leaves
2 teaspoons extra-virgin olive oil
1 teaspoon distilled white vinegar
¾ teaspoon coarse salt
2 teaspoons fennel seeds
1 pound ground lamb
1 tablespoon minced garlic,
   plus 2 teaspoons garlic mashed to
   a paste with the side of a knife

1 teaspoon ground coriander
½ teaspoon ground cumin
½ teaspoon freshly ground black
   pepper
Pinch of crushed red pepper flakes
2 tablespoons canola oil
¼ cup whole, thick yogurt,
   preferably Greek
2 teaspoons freshly squeezed
   lemon juice
2 cups loosely packed salad
   greens

**how low can you go?**

Fingerling potatoes are also well-suited to potato salad and are relatively low in starch compared with other varieties.

1. Bring a small pot of water to a boil, add the potatoes, and cook until tender when pierced with a knife, about 5 minutes. Drain the potato.

2. Put the parsley, olive oil, vinegar, and ¼ teaspoon of salt in a bowl and stir together. Add the potatoes to the bowl and toss to coat the potatoes. Cover the potatoes and set them aside.

3. Toast the fennel seeds in a small pan over low heat, stirring frequently to prevent scorching, until fragrant, about 3 minutes. Transfer the seeds to a bowl and let cool. Add the lamb, minced garlic, coriander, cumin, black pepper, red pepper flakes, and the remaining ½ teaspoon of salt to

the bowl and knead together with immaculately clean hands. Shape the sausage into 4 patties.

4. Heat the canola oil in a large, heavy-bottomed pan over medium-high heat. Add the lamb patties and cook until cooked through, about 4 minutes per side.

5. While the lamb sausage is cooking, make a dressing by placing the yogurt, lemon juice, mashed garlic, and a pinch of black pepper in a bowl and stirring them together. Add the greens and toss to coat.

6. Put a sausage patty on each of 4 plates. Mound some potato salad and dressed greens alongside and serve.

## nutritional information
(PER SERVING)

Calories.....................154
Fat...............................6 g
   Saturated Fat...........2 g
   Trans Fat.................0 g
Total Carbohydrates.....0 g
   Dietary Fiber............0 g
   Total Sugars............0 g
Protein.......................23 g
Cholesterol..............73 mg
Sodium...................109 mg

## exchanges

Lean Meat.....................3

**CARBOHYDRATE CHOICE: 0**

# roasted leg of lamb

## WITH ROASTED GARLIC AND ROSEMARY

much like the beef tenderloin on page 254, this recipe is included for those times when you're hosting a large group and want a crowd-pleasing, cook-friendly main course. In this classic preparation of leg of lamb you spread roasted garlic puree and chopped rosemary inside the boned leg, then roll, tie, and roast it. In addition to the nearly foolproof results, it will fill your home with appetite-arousing aromas. **SERVES 24**

## INGREDIENTS

6 cloves Roasted Garlic (page 321), pureed

1 leg of lamb (about 6 pounds), boned (ask your butcher to do this)

1 tablespoon chopped fresh rosemary leaves

2 tablespoons extra-virgin olive oil

½ teaspoon coarse salt

½ teaspoon freshly ground black pepper

1. Preheat the oven to 375°F. Put a large roasting pan in the oven and preheat it for 10 minutes.

2. Smear the garlic puree over the inside of the leg of lamb and scatter the rosemary over the garlic. Roll up the lamb as tautly and evenly as possible and tie it with kitchen string at 1-inch intervals. Rub the outside of the lamb with the olive oil and season it all over with the salt and pepper.

3. Put the lamb in the hot roasting pan and roast it until an instant-read meat thermometer inserted in the thickest part of the leg reads 130°F for medium-rare, about 90 minutes, or a bit longer for more well-done. Periodically give the lamb a quarter turn to ensure even browning.

4. Transfer the leg of lamb to a cutting board, cover it with aluminum foil, and let rest for 30 minutes. Carve the lamb into 24 pieces and serve.

# stuffed red peppers

## WITH LAMB, ORZO, AND FETA CHEESE

t he bright flavors of Mediterranean cooking are on full display in this dish, which looks very much like the ground beef stuffed peppers of America but features lamb, feta cheese, orzo, and thyme packed into a red pepper that infuses those ingredients with flavor and moisture as they cook. Any good-quality feta cheese presents a bit of a challenge for people with diabetes because it's sold in brine; fortunately a little goes a very long way.

**SERVES 4**

## nutritional information
(PER SERVING)

Calories......................415
Fat.............................27 g
   Saturated Fat..........11 g
   Trans Fat.................0 g
Total Carbohydrates...20 g
   Dietary Fiber............4 g
   Total Sugars............8 g
Protein......................21 g
Cholesterol..............74 mg
Sodium..................310 mg

## exchanges

Fat..............................2
Starch......................0.5
High Fat Meat................2
Vegetables...................2

---

### INGREDIENTS

12 ounces ground lamb

¼ cup plus 2 tablespoons cooked, drained orzo

¼ cup dry unseasoned bread crumbs

1 ounce feta cheese, crumbled (about ¼ cup)

2 tablespoons finely grated Parmesan cheese

1 tablespoon fresh thyme leaves

4 large red bell peppers

About 1½ cups store-bought low-sodium chicken broth

1 tablespoon olive oil

---

1. Preheat the oven to 325°F.

2. Put the lamb, orzo, bread crumbs, feta and Parmesan cheeses, and the thyme in a bowl and stir them together.

3. Cut the top ½ inch off the bell peppers and seed the peppers. Trim the very bottom off each pepper so it can stand upright (but do not cut into the inside of the peppers). Spoon the lamb mixture into the bell peppers, dividing it evenly among them and gently packing it down. Stand the peppers in a small baking dish and pour the chicken broth and olive oil around them. Cover the dish with aluminum foil and bake the peppers until they are soft and the lamb mixture is cooked through, about 30 minutes, or longer for more well-done.

4. Place 1 pepper on each of 4 plates and serve.

# in this chapter

*"Use what's here
to dress up the most simple recipes."*

# side dishes and accompaniments

Y ou need look no further than the popularity of steak houses, which are enjoying a steady and seemingly limitless trajectory of success, to know that many Americans love eating a grilled or broiled piece of meat (or fish or fowl) with a side dish or two alongside. Even at my restaurant, Ouest, some of the most frequently ordered selections are what we call Simple Grills, which are just what the name says: a piece of protein seasoned, oiled, and cooked over an open flame, with a selection of sides, like the ones in this chapter, offered à la carte.

Believe it or not, it's my opinion that the recipes in this seemingly incidental chapter are actually among the most useful dishes in this book. They provide a way to augment everyday cooking by inviting you to mix and match selections from my repertoire with favorites from your own, or even other books, or by pairing them with your own straightforward preparations of fish, poultry, and meat.

If you have diabetes, these recipes offer greater control of your diet, letting you select the protein of your choice—not to mention the portion size, type and degree of seasoning, and cooking method—using what's here to dress up the most simple of recipes and bring something special to any meal.

**CARBOHYDRATE CHOICE: ½**

# broccoli rabe

## WITH OLIVE OIL AND RED PEPPER

bitter broccoli rabe, also know as rapini, is a variety of broccoli that has an almost turniplike bitterness. When blanched, then sautéed with garlic and crushed red pepper, this is a quintessential side dish for grilled and roast beef or pork. Leftovers are delicious cold or at room temperature and can be added to sandwiches or chopped up and tossed with pasta. The classic combination would be orecchiette (ear-shaped pasta) with broccoli rabe and sausage.

**SERVES 4 AS A SIDE DISH**

### INGREDIENTS

*1½ pounds (about 2 small bunches) broccoli rabe, stems trimmed*

*2 tablespoons olive oil*

*2 large cloves garlic, very thinly sliced*

*¼ teaspoon crushed red pepper flakes*

1. Bring a large pot of water to a boil over high heat. Fill a large bowl halfway with ice water.

2. Cook the broccoli rabe in the boiling water for 1 minute. Use tongs or a slotted spoon to remove the broccoli rabe from the pot and transfer it to the ice water to stop the cooking and preserve the color. Drain the broccoli rabe and pat it dry with paper towels.

3. Heat the olive oil in a wide, deep, heavy-bottomed pan over medium-high heat. Add the broccoli rabe, garlic, and red pepper flakes and cook, stirring, until the broccoli rabe is cooked through but still al dente, about 2 minutes.

4. Transfer the broccoli rabe to a serving bowl or serve it alongside fish or meat.

# bacony brussels sprouts

i've done a lot of original things with bacon in my time, but I cannot claim credit for the combination of bacon and brussels sprouts. Nonetheless, I had to include it in this book because I never tire of it, and the dish loses very little when made with diabetes-friendly turkey bacon. These brussels sprouts go well with just about anything and are a must at Thanksgiving dinner.

**SERVES 4 AS A SIDE DISH**

## nutritional information
(PER SERVING)

Calories ........................ 165
Fat ................................ 10 g
    Saturated Fat ........... 5 g
    Trans Fat .................. 0 g
Total Carbohydrates .... 13 g
    Dietary Fiber ............. 5 g
    Total Sugars ............. 4 g
Protein ......................... 9 g
Cholesterol ............... 33 mg
Sodium .................. 366 mg

## exchanges

Fat ................................. 1
High Fat Meat ............. 0.5
Vegetables ................. 2.5

## INGREDIENTS

4 slices turkey bacon, finely diced

3 large cloves garlic, thinly sliced

½ large Spanish onion,
    cut into small dice

1 cup store-bought low-sodium
    chicken broth

1 pound large brussels sprouts,
    trimmed and quartered

1½ tablespoons unsalted butter

1 ounce Pecorino Romano cheese,
    finely grated (about ¼ cup)

1. Bring a large pot of water to a boil over high heat.

2. Meanwhile, cook the turkey bacon in a large, deep, nonstick pan over medium heat until browned and the fat is rendered, about 7 minutes.

3. Add the garlic and onion to the pan with the bacon and cook until softened but not browned, about 4 minutes. Add the chicken broth, increase the heat to high and bring to a boil. Let the broth boil until it is reduced by about two thirds, about

7 minutes. Remove the pan from the heat and set it aside.

4. Add the brussels sprouts to the boiling water. Boil until tender when pierced with a knife, 6 to 7 minutes. Drain the sprouts and add them to the pan with the bacon mixture. Add the butter and Pecorino Romano and stir over medium-high heat until the butter and cheese melt and the flavors are incorporated. Serve the brussels sprouts family style from the center of the table or a buffet.

## nutritional information
### (PER SERVING)

Calories.....................127
Fat...............................11 g
   Saturated Fat..........2 g
   Trans Fat...................0 g
Total Carbohydrates.....7 g
   Dietary Fiber............3 g
   Total Sugars............3 g
Protein.........................2 g
Cholesterol...............0 mg
Sodium...................155 mg

## exchanges

Fat.................................2
Vegetables......................1

## plan ahead

The cauliflower can be refrigerated in an airtight container for up to 2 days. Do *not* let it come to room temperature before serving.

---

CARBOHYDRATE CHOICE: 1/2

# cauliflower

## WITH LEMON AND PARSLEY

m y grandmother made this side dish on hot summer days when I was growing up. I'd never prepared it myself, but the flavor was so etched into my taste memory that when we were testing recipes for this book, I nailed it on the first try. This cauliflower is the ultimate summer picnic or snack food: quick to cook and best served cold. Serve it with cold poached fish or grilled chicken. **SERVES 4 AS A SIDE DISH**

### INGREDIENTS

*1 pound cauliflower, broken into uniform-size small florets*
*3 tablespoons extra-virgin olive oil*
*2 small cloves garlic, minced*
*2 tablespoons freshly squeezed lemon juice*

*⅛ teaspoon grated lemon zest*
*¼ teaspoon coarse salt*
*1 tablespoon chopped fresh flat-leaf parsley leaves*

---

1. Put the cauliflower in a pot and add just enough water to almost cover the florets. Bring to a simmer and let simmer until the florets are tender when pierced with a knife, about 8 minutes.

2. Meanwhile, make a lemon vinaigrette: Put the olive oil, garlic, and lemon juice and zest in a large bowl and whisk them together.

3. When the cauliflower is done, drain it and transfer it to the bowl with the vinaigrette. Season it with the salt and toss well. Let cool, then add the parsley, toss again, and serve.

CARBOHYDRATE CHOICES: 1½; 1 ADJUSTED FOR FIBER

# curried cauliflower

What is there *not* to love about curried cauliflower? It's easy to prepare, has a lovely golden hue, and is addictively delicious, both for its exotic flavor and comfort-food texture. The most important step in this recipe is extracting as much moisture as possible from the pureed cauliflower; keep working it in the nonstick pan to really cook out any lingering water. This will intensify the flavor of both the cauliflower and the curry in the finished dish. Serve the cauliflower with grilled or roast lamb, and a simple salad. **SERVES 4 AS A SIDE DISH**

## nutritional information
(PER SERVING)

| | |
|---|---|
| Calories | 129 |
| Fat | 3 g |
| Saturated Fat | 2 g |
| Trans Fat | 0 g |
| Total Carbohydrates | 22 g |
| Dietary Fiber | 10 g |
| Total Sugars | 10 g |
| Protein | 8 g |
| Cholesterol | 8 mg |
| Sodium | 240 mg |

## exchanges

| | |
|---|---|
| Fat | 0.5 |
| Vegetables | 4 |

## INGREDIENTS

1 head cauliflower (about 3½ pounds), broken into uniform-size small florets
¼ teaspoon coarse salt
2 cloves garlic, crushed with the side of a knife

1 tablespoon unsalted butter
1 teaspoon curry powder
Pinch of freshly ground black pepper

1. Put the cauliflower and garlic in a medium-size, heavy-bottomed pot. Add just enough cold water to cover and stir in ⅛ teaspoon of the salt. Set the pot over high heat and bring to a boil, then reduce the heat and let simmer just until the florets are tender when pierced with a knife, 15 to 20 minutes.

2. Drain the cauliflower well, transfer it and the garlic to a food processor, and puree to the consistency of loose mashed potatoes.

3. Transfer the pureed cauliflower to a large nonstick pan and cook over low heat to evaporate as much moisture as possible, scraping and stirring it with a rubber spatula to keep it from burning, 6 to 8 minutes. Fold in the butter, the remaining ⅛ teaspoon of salt, and the curry powder. Season the cauliflower with the black pepper and serve.

## plan ahead

The cauliflower puree can be kept warm for up to 2 hours in a double boiler set over simmering water.

**variations and suggestions:** Omit the curry for plain cauliflower puree, a fine alternative to mashed potatoes. You can also make this into a cauliflower soup with the addition of milk, stock, or a combination of the two; the amount to add depends on how thick or thin you want the soup to be.

## nutritional information
(PER SERVING)

| | |
|---|---|
| Calories | 144 |
| Fat | 5 g |
| Saturated Fat | 1 g |
| Trans Fat | 0 g |
| Total Carbohydrates | 23 g |
| Dietary Fiber | 5 g |
| Total Sugars | 0 g |
| Protein | 8 g |
| Cholesterol | 0 mg |
| Sodium | 130 mg |

## exchanges

| | |
|---|---|
| Fat | 0.5 |
| Vegetables | 4.5 |

## plan ahead

If you are not serving the kale at once, spread it out on a baking sheet to cool, then refrigerate it in an airtight container for up to 24 hours. Reheat the kale gently in a pan over low heat before serving or serve it at room temperature.

CARBOHYDRATE CHOICES: 1½; 1 ADJUSTED FOR FIBER

# garlicky wilted kale

more toothsome than spinach, less bulky than broccoli, kale is unique among leafy greens: a sturdy vegetable that's both bitter and gently peppery. My preferred method of cooking kale is to leave it a bit damp after rinsing it; the moisture causes the kale to steam when sautéed. Kale is a natural alongside almost any fish and also wonderful with roast pork, and grilled steak.

SERVES 4 AS A SIDE DISH

## INGREDIENTS

*1 tablespoon olive oil*
*1 large clove garlic, very thinly sliced*
*2 pounds green kale, stems and center stalks removed, well rinsed and left a little damp*

*Pinch of coarse salt*
*Pinch of freshly ground black pepper*

Heat the olive oil in a heavy-bottomed pan over medium-high heat. Add the garlic and cook until softened but not browned, about 2 minutes. Add the kale (it will sizzle and steam on contact with the hot oil), season it with a pinch of salt and pepper, and cook, stirring, until wilted, tender, and bright green, about 5 minutes. Serve.

CARBOHYDRATE CHOICE: 1

# stewed leeks

raw leeks have a delicate flavor, and stewing gives them a tender texture to match. The leeks are best served with grilled or roast fish.

**SERVES 4 AS A SIDE DISH**

## INGREDIENTS

*1 pound leeks (about 6 medium-size leeks), white and light green parts, trimmed, well rinsed and cut diagonally into ¼-inch pieces*

*3 tablespoons store-bought low-sodium chicken broth*
*1 tablespoon unsalted butter*
*1 large clove garlic, minced*
*Pinch of coarse salt*

Put the leeks, chicken broth, butter, garlic, and salt in a wide, deep, heavy-bottomed pan and bring to a simmer over low heat. Let simmer, stirring occasionally, until the leeks are tender and the liquid has almost completely evaporated, 10 to 15 minutes.

## nutritional information
(PER SERVING)

| | |
|---|---|
| Calories | 97 |
| Fat | 3 g |
| Saturated Fat | 2 g |
| Trans Fat | 0 g |
| Total Carbohydrates | 16 g |
| Dietary Fiber | 2 g |
| Total Sugars | 4 g |
| Protein | 2 g |
| Cholesterol | 8 mg |
| Sodium | 58 mg |

## exchanges

| | |
|---|---|
| Fat | 0.5 |
| Vegetables | 3 |

## plan ahead

The leeks can be cooled and refrigerated in an airtight container for up to 48 hours. Gently reheat them in a pan over low heat, stirring occasionally, before serving.

## nutritional information
**(PER SERVING)**

| | |
|---|---|
| Calories | 185 |
| Fat | 2 g |
| Saturated Fat | 0 g |
| Trans Fat | 0 g |
| Total Carbohydrates | 34 g |
| Dietary Fiber | 2 g |
| Total Sugars | 3 g |
| Protein | 8 g |
| Cholesterol | 0 mg |
| Sodium | 279 mg |

## exchanges

| | |
|---|---|
| Starch | 2 |
| Vegetables | 0.5 |

CARBOHYDRATE CHOICES: 2

# broiled onion rings

i used to think that a degree of greasiness was essential to great onion rings, but these changed my mind: They have the requisite crunch and sweetness, and broiling is so much easier than deep-frying that, at the end of the day, as both cook and diner, I actually prefer these. Serve them with sandwiches, steaks, and just about anything else you might be eating when you find yourself craving onion rings.

**SERVES 6 AS A SIDE DISH (4 ONION RINGS PER PERSON)**

## INGREDIENTS

*1 large Spanish onion, cut into ⅛ inch-thick slices and separated into about 24 rings*

*¾ cup all-purpose flour*

*3 large egg whites, lightly beaten*

*1½ cups dry unseasoned bread crumbs*

*½ teaspoon onion powder*

*⅛ teaspoon coarse salt*

1. Bring a pot of water to a boil over high heat. Add the onion rings and cook until tender, 3 to 4 minutes. Drain the onion rings well and set them aside to cool.

2. Meanwhile, preheat the broiler and position a rack about 8 inches beneath the heating element.

3. Spread the flour out on a plate. Place the egg whites into a wide, shallow bowl. Put the bread crumbs, onion powder, and salt in another wide, shallow bowl and stir them together. One by one, dredge the onion rings in the flour, shaking off any excess, then dip the rings in the egg white,

Onion Rings

followed by the bread crumb mixture. As they are breaded, arrange the onion rings on a baking sheet.

**4.** Put the baking sheet under the broiler and broil the onion rings until nicely golden, turning them once, 2 to 3 minutes per side.

**5.** Transfer the broiled onion rings to a bowl or plate or serve them alongside a main course.

CARBOHYDRATE CHOICES: 0

# roasted cippolini onions

Cooking sweet cippolini onions with balsamic vinegar until the vinegar is reduced produces an irresistible sweet-and-sour effect. These are delicious with calf's liver and other full-flavored meats, poultry, and game.                    **SERVES 4 AS A SIDE DISH**

## INGREDIENTS

2 tablespoons canola oil

1½ pounds cippolini onions (about 24 onions), peeled (see this page)

⅔ cup balsamic vinegar

Pinch of coarse salt

Pinch of freshly ground black pepper

**1.** Preheat the oven to 400°F.

**2.** Heat the oil in a wide, deep, heavy-bottomed, ovenproof pan over medium heat. Add the onions and cook, stirring, just until they begin to turn golden all over, about 5 minutes. Pour in the balsamic vinegar, season the onions with the salt and pepper, and bring to a boil.

**3.** Transfer the pan to the oven and bake the onions, stirring them periodically to prevent scorching and ensure even cooking, until the vinegar is reduced to a syrupy glaze and the onions are meltingly soft, about 5 minutes. Serve the onions hot.

## nutritional information
(PER SERVING)

| | |
|---|---|
| Calories | 160 |
| Fat | 7 g |
| Saturated Fat | 1 g |
| Trans Fat | 0 g |
| Total Carbohydrates | 21 g |
| Dietary Fiber | 4 g |
| Total Sugars | 16 g |
| Protein | 2 g |
| Cholesterol | 0 mg |
| Sodium | 40 mg |

## exchanges

| | |
|---|---|
| Fat | 1.5 |
| Vegetables | 2.5 |

### A TIP FROM TOM

**PEELING CIPPOLINI ONIONS:** To peel cippolini onions, bring a small pot of water to a boil and add the onions. Cook them for just two or three seconds, then drain the onions in a colander. As soon as the cippolini are cool enough to handle, peel them; the skins will be loosened and come off easily with the aid of a small, sharp knife.

## nutritional information
(PER SERVING)

Calories .......................... 68
Fat .................................. 3 g
   Saturated Fat ........... 0 g
   Trans Fat ................... 0 g
Total Carbohydrates ..... 9 g
   Dietary Fiber ............. 0 g
   Total Sugars ............. 2 g
Protein ........................... 2 g
Cholesterol ................ 0 mg
Sodium .................... 30 mg

## exchanges

Fat ................................. 0.5
Vegetables ................... 1.5

**CARBOHYDRATE CHOICE: 1/2**

# whole roasted shallots

b e warned: once you roast whole shallots, you might find yourself serving them over and over again. With a minimum of work—you just toss them with olive oil, water, salt, and pepper and pop them in the oven—the unpeeled shallots take on an elegant burnished color and become meltingly tender. Serve these with roast beef, pork, and lamb, or with an assertively flavored meaty fish such as swordfish or tuna. **SERVES 4 AS A SIDE DISH**

## INGREDIENTS

*8 large shallots, root ends trimmed,*
   *skins left on*
*1 tablespoon olive oil*

*Pinch of coarse salt*
*Pinch of freshly ground black*
   *pepper*

1. Preheat the oven to 350°F.

2. Put the shallots in a small baking dish. Drizzle the olive oil and 1 tablespoon of water over them and season them with the salt and pepper. Cover the dish with aluminum foil, crimping it along the edges of the dish, and bake the shallots until tender when pierced with a knife, 30 to 35 minutes.

3. Serve the shallots straight from the oven in their skins or set them aside covered with the foil to keep warm, for up to 2 hours. Before serving reheat the shallots gently in an oven preheated to 200°F. To eat the shallots you pop them out of their skins.

CARBOHYDRATE CHOICE: 0

# ouest spinach

t his is another recipe from Jorge Carrera, the madly talented sous chef I've mentioned a few times in this book. He turned me on to this spinach recipe, which includes chives, nutmeg, and most important dill. It never would have occurred to me to combine that herb with spinach, but the alchemy it produces is wonderful: Neither your eye nor your taste buds will place the taste, but the dill adds a beguiling extra something. It makes a delicious filling for omelets or souffles, or increase the quantities and serve it, hot or cold, as a side dish.

**MAKES ABOUT 1 CUP; SERVES 4 AS A LIGHT SIDE DISH**

### INGREDIENTS

*1 tablespoon olive oil*

*½ small shallot, minced*

*1 large clove garlic, minced*

*1 pound spinach, well rinsed and left a little damp, tough stems discarded*

*Pinch of ground nutmeg*

*1 teaspoon minced fresh chives*

*1 tablespoon minced fresh dill*

1. Heat the olive oil in a wide, deep, heavy-bottomed pan over medium-high heat. Add the shallot and garlic and cook until softened but not browned, about 2 minutes.

2. Add the spinach and cook, stirring, until it cooks down and turns dark green, about 3 minutes. Stir in the nutmeg, chives, and dill, and remove the pan from the heat.

3. Serve hot or spread the spinach out on a plate or baking sheet to cool as quickly as possible. The spinach can be refrigerated in an airtight container for up to 24 hours.

## nutritional information
(PER ¼ CUP SERVING)

Calories............................61
Fat.......................................4 g
   Saturated Fat............1 g
   Trans Fat...................0 g
Total Carbohydrates.....5 g
   Dietary Fiber................3 g
   Total Sugars...............1 g
Protein................................3 g
Cholesterol.................0 mg
Sodium....................90 mg

## exchanges

Fat...................................0.5
Vegetables........................1

**CARBOHYDRATE CHOICE: 1**

# creamed spinach

## WITH PARMESAN CHEESE

a direct descendent of the steak house culture, creamed spinach is one of the dishes that people love when ordering food à la carte. My version includes some Parmesan cheese, which helps bind the spinach. Serve the spinach with steak or with grilled or roast pork and meaty fish like tuna or swordfish.

**SERVES 4 AS A SIDE DISH**

### INGREDIENTS

2 tablespoons unsalted butter

2 tablespoons all-purpose flour

2⅓ cups 1 percent milk

1 clove garlic, peeled and crushed

Pinch of freshly ground black pepper

1 pound spinach, well rinsed in several changes of cold water, tough stems discarded

2 tablespoons freshly grated Parmesan cheese

1 teaspoon extra-virgin olive oil

¼ teaspoon coarse salt

1. Heat a large pan over low heat. Add the butter and let it melt. Sprinkle the flour over the butter, then stir it and cook for 3 to 4 minutes without browning. Remove the pan from the heat and let the flour and butter mixture cool.

2. Place the milk and garlic in a small pot and bring to a boil. Remove the pot from the heat. Remove and discard the garlic. Add the pepper and stir. Whisk the warm milk into the flour and butter mixture. Return the pan to the stove over medium-low heat and cook, stirring, until thickened, 4 to 5 minutes.

3. Squeeze any remaining water out of the spinach. Coarsely chop the spinach and stir it into the pan with the milk and flour mixture. Cook the spinach until it is bright green and the sauce has reduced slightly and begins to cling to the leaves, 2 to 3 minutes. Sprinkle the Parmesan cheese, olive oil, and salt on top, stir well and serve.

CARBOHYDRATE CHOICE: 1

# baked spicy sweet potato fries

d on't get *too* excited: You can't eat too many of these. But when you've just got to have a French fry–like side, these will more than do the trick—baked rather than fried, the sweet potatoes are quite good and the heat of cayenne makes up for the relatively low amount of salt.

SERVES 4

## nutritional information
(PER SERVING)

Calories........................140
Fat................................7 g
  Saturated Fat............1 g
  Trans Fat.................0 g
Total Carbohydrates....18 g
  Dietary Fiber............3 g
  Total Sugars.............6 g
Protein.........................2 g
Cholesterol................0 mg
Sodium...................151 mg

## exchanges

Fat................................1.5
Starch............................1

## INGREDIENTS

2 large sweet potatoes
   (about 1¼ pounds total)
2 tablespoons canola oil

¼ teaspoon cayenne pepper
¼ teaspoon coarse salt

1. Preheat the oven to 400°F.

2. Cut the sweet potatoes into roughly ½ inch-thick wedges and place them in a large bowl. Drizzle the oil over the wedges and sprinkle the cayenne and salt on top. Toss the potatoes to evenly distribute the seasoning, then spread them out on a rimmed baking sheet in a single layer without crowding.

3. Bake the potato wedges, shaking the baking sheet occasionally to prevent scorching and ensure even cooking, until the potatoes are cooked through and slightly crisp, about 30 minutes.

4. Divide the potatoes among 4 plates or serve them family style from the center of the table.

Sweet Potato Fries

# pickled vegetables

Pickling is a very simple technique that imparts enough vinegary goodness to vegetables that they become an enjoyable snack in their own right and don't require a dressing or dip. I don't bother putting pickled vegetables in jars: The sterilizing process is, for lack of a better word, a pain, and the actual pickling is so easy that I think the three-day shelf life in the refrigerator offers plenty of convenience. These pickled vegetables are a ready-made accompaniment to various proteins for a quick, complete meal.

## nutritional information
**(PER SERVING)**

| | |
|---|---|
| Calories | 33 |
| Fat | 0 g |
| Saturated Fat | 0 g |
| Trans Fat | 0 g |
| Total Carbohydrates | 6 g |
| Dietary Fiber | 2 g |
| Total Sugars | 5 g |
| Protein | 2 g |
| Cholesterol | 0 mg |
| Sodium | 1,445 mg |
| (see Note, page 288) | |

## exchanges

| | |
|---|---|
| Vegetables | 0.5 |

**CARBOHYDRATE CHOICE: ½**

## pickled asparagus
### SERVES 4 AS A SIDE DISH

Pickled asparagus offers a tangy contrast to cold poached salmon, adds a kick to vegetable wraps, makes a wonderful garnish for martinis, and is delicious to snack on.

### INGREDIENTS

*2 cups distilled white vinegar*

*1 tablespoon sugar*

*1 tablespoon coarse salt*

*12 spears pencil-thin asparagus (about ¾ pound), ends trimmed*

1. Put the vinegar, sugar, salt, and 2 cups of water in a nonreactive medium-size saucepan and bring to a boil, stirring, to dissolve the sugar and salt.

2. Arrange the asparagus in a single layer in a shallow, heatproof pan. Pour the boiling liquid over the asparagus. Let cool slightly at room temperature, about 15 minutes. Cover the pan with plastic wrap and refrigerate the asparagus until cold, or for up to 3 days.

CARBOHYDRATE CHOICE: 1

# pickled red onions

**SERVES 4 AS A SIDE DISH**

Serve these pickled onions as a topping for grilled or roast fish, poultry, or meat; layer them into sandwiches and quesadillas; or chop and scatter them over spicy foods, especially Mexican dishes.

## INGREDIENTS

*1 pound red onions (about 2 large or*
  *4 small onions), sliced ¼-inch thick*
  *and separated into rings*
*5 cups distilled white vinegar*
*2 whole star anise*
*1 tablespoon black peppercorns*
*1 teaspoon coriander seed*
*1 teaspoon sugar*
*1 bay leaf, preferably fresh*

1. Put the onions in a large stainless-steel bowl.

2. Put the vinegar in a nonreactive pot and add 2½ cups of water, the star anise, peppercorns, coriander, sugar, and bay leaf. Bring to a boil and boil for 2 minutes.

3. Strain the pickling liquid through a fine-mesh strainer set over the onions. Discard the solids. Let the onions cool, then cover the bowl and refrigerate the onions for 24 hours, or for up to 1 week, to let the flavors develop.

## nutritional information
(PER SERVING)

| | |
|---|---|
| Calories | 53 |
| Fat | 0 g |
| Saturated Fat | 0 g |
| Trans Fat | 0 g |
| Total Carbohydrates | 12 g |
| Dietary Fiber | 2 g |
| Total Sugars | 6 g |
| Protein | 1 g |
| Cholesterol | 0 mg |
| Sodium | 5 mg |

## exchanges

| | |
|---|---|
| Vegetables | 2 |

---

CARBOHYDRATE CHOICE: 1

# pickled cauliflower

**SERVES 4 AS A SIDE DISH**

Pickled cauliflower makes a high-impact addition to tossed salads, is a perfect accompaniment for roast chicken, and provides a nice foil for Indian food, especially spicy dishes.

## INGREDIENTS

*1 head (about 1½ pounds)*
  *cauliflower, broken into*
  *small florets*
*2 cups distilled white vinegar*
*1 tablespoon plus 1 teaspoon sugar*
*1 tablespoon plus 1 teaspoon*
  *coarse salt*
*¼ teaspoon dry mustard*
*Pinch of crushed red pepper flakes*

## nutritional information
(PER SERVING)

| | |
|---|---|
| Calories | 60 |
| Fat | 0 g |
| Saturated Fat | 0 g |
| Trans Fat | 0 g |
| Total Carbohydrates | 13 g |
| Dietary Fiber | 4 g |
| Total Sugars | 8 g |
| Protein | 3 g |
| Cholesterol | 0 mg |
| Sodium | 1,975 mg |
| (see Note, page 288) | |

## exchanges

| | |
|---|---|
| Vegetables | 1.5 |

1. Bring a large pot of water to a boil over high heat. Fill a large bowl halfway with ice water.

2. Cook the cauliflower in the boiling water until al dente, about 4 minutes. Drain the cauliflower and transfer it to the ice water to stop the cooking. Drain the cauliflower again and transfer the florets to a shallow, heatproof baking dish.

3. Put 2½ cups of water and the vinegar, sugar, salt, mustard, and red pepper flakes in a nonreactive pot and bring to a boil over high heat, stirring to dissolve the sugar and salt. Remove the pot from heat and let the liquid cool for 20 to 30 minutes.

4. Pour the pickling liquid over the cauliflower. Cover the dish and refrigerate the cauliflower overnight, or for up to 3 days to let the flavors develop.

note: The sodium level of the asparagus and cauliflower pickles is deceptively high because it includes the pickling liquid itself. Since you won't be drinking that liquid, the true amount of sodium consumed in the vegetables is actually significantly lower but impossible to compute. To lower the sodium even further, rinse and/or wipe off the pickling liquid with a clean paper towel before serving.

## nutritional information
(PER SERVING)

| | |
|---|---|
| Calories | 235 |
| Fat | 22 g |
| Saturated Fat | 4 g |
| Trans Fat | 0 g |
| Total Carbohydrates | 6 g |
| Dietary Fiber | 1 g |
| Total Sugars | 1 g |
| Protein | 4 g |
| Cholesterol | 8 mg |
| Sodium | 182 mg |

## exchanges

| | |
|---|---|
| Fat | 4.5 |
| Starch | 0.5 |

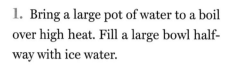

CARBOHYDRATE CHOICE: ½

# pesto risotto

a t the Italian table risotto is a first course. At American tables it does double duty as either a starter or a main dish. I also find that certain risottos, especially those that don't feature fish or meat themselves, make perfect side dishes, a welcome alternative to more conventional starches, such as potatoes. The basil and garlic in this pesto risotto make it a natural to serve alongside white-fleshed fish. **SERVES 6 AS A SIDE DISH**

## INGREDIENTS

About 1½ cups store-bought
    low-sodium chicken broth

1 tablespoon olive oil

1 tablespoon unsalted butter

¼ medium-size Spanish onion, minced

⅓ cup risotto rice (see page 175)

2 tablespoons dry white wine

⅔ cup Homemade Pesto (page 317)

1. Pour the chicken broth into a small pot and bring it to a simmer over low heat.

2. Heat the olive oil and butter in a large, heavy-bottomed pot over medium heat. Add the onion and cook until softened but not browned, about 4 minutes. Add the rice, stir to coat it with butter and oil, and cook for about 4 minutes. Add the wine, bring to a boil, and cook, stirring, until it is nearly completely evaporated.

3. Ladle ½ cup of simmering broth into the pot with the rice and cook, stirring, until it is nearly absorbed by the rice. Continue to add broth in ½ cup increments, stirring the rice constantly, until the rice is softened but still a bit al dente. (You may not need all of the broth, or you may need to supplement it with more broth or some water.) This step should take about 18 minutes altogether.

4. Stir in the pesto and serve the risotto family style or spoon it alongside other foods.

CARBOHYDRATE CHOICE: 1

# thanksgiving stuffing
## WITH OYSTERS AND SAUSAGE

**i**'ve been making a version of this stuffing for years, and it's one of the things I love and look forward to most when Thanksgiving rolls around. One of the stuffing's many appealing attributes is that it will fill your home with the smells of good cooking—first the toasted pine nuts and then the sausage,

## nutritional information
(PER SERVING)

| | |
|---|---|
| Calories | 222 |
| Fat | 12 g |
| Saturated Fat | 2 g |
| Trans Fat | 0 g |
| Total Carbohydrates | 12 g |
| Dietary Fiber | 1 g |
| Total Sugars | 2 g |
| Protein | 12 g |
| Cholesterol | 38 mg |
| Sodium | 363 mg |

## exchanges

| | |
|---|---|
| Fat | 2 |
| Starch | 0.5 |
| Lean Meat | 1.5 |
| Vegetables | 0.5 |

A TIP FROM TOM

**CROUTONS:** To make croutons, slice a baguette or country bread into ¼-inch to ½-inch-thick slices and then crosswise into cubes. (You can freeze the bread to make it easier to slice neatly.) Arrange in a single layer on a baking tray and bake in an oven preheated to 300°F, shaking the tray occasionally to ensure even cooking, until golden-brown and slightly hardened, 15 to 20 minutes. Remove from the oven and let cool, or serve warm. (The croutons can be held in an airtight container at room temperature for a day or two.)

vegetables, white wine, and herbs. Once the stuffing is in the oven, your senses and those of the people watching the ball game in the next room will be utterly, fully engaged. Of course, given our reason for being here together, I have to skimp on the bread a bit, but never fear: Mushrooms do a good job of making up for volume, while adding another flavor to the mix. **SERVES 8**

## INGREDIENTS

½ cup pine nuts

1 tablespoon canola oil

4 ounces white button mushrooms, cut into large dice

12 ounces chicken sausage, preferably Italian style (fennel and garlic), casings removed and discarded, sausage crumbled into small pieces

6 large cloves garlic, very thinly sliced

3 ribs celery, cut crosswise into ¼ -inch slices

1 large Spanish onion, diced

1½ to 2 cups dry croutons, cut from day-old country bread or whole wheat bread (see this page)

1 cup dry white wine

12 oysters, such as bluepoint or Malpeque, shucked and coarsely chopped

1 cup store-bought low-sodium chicken broth

1 tablespoon chopped fresh marjoram leaves

1 teaspoon fresh thyme leaves

1. Preheat the oven to 350°F.

2. Put the pine nuts in a heavy-bottomed pan and toast over medium heat, shaking the pan to prevent scorching, until lightly toasted, about 3 minutes. Transfer the pine nuts to a large bowl and set aside.

3. Carefully wipe out the pan and set it over medium-high heat. Add the oil and let it get nice and hot. Add the mushrooms and cook them until they begin to give off their liquid, about 5 minutes. Transfer the mushrooms to the bowl with the pine nuts.

4. Add the sausage to the pan and cook over medium heat until the fat is rendered and the sausage browns, about 8 minutes. Add the garlic, celery, and onion to the pan and cook until softened but not browned, about 4 minutes. Transfer the sausage and vegetables to the bowl. Add the croutons to the bowl.

**5.** Return the pan to the stove top over medium heat. Add the white wine and cook, stirring to loosen any flavorful bits stuck to the bottom of the pan. Add the oysters and cook gently, about 2 minutes. Stir in the chicken broth and bring to a boil, then immediately pour the oysters and liquid over the contents of the bowl. Add the marjoram and thyme and, using 2 wooden spoons or latex-gloved hands, work everything together. (If you are using your hands, let the mixture cool slightly before delving in.) Transfer the stuffing to a casserole dish.

**6.** Bake the stuffing until crusty on top and heated through, 35 to 40 minutes. Serve the stuffing hot.

# in this chapter

*"The lion's share of my desserts
are fruit based."*

# desserts

i have to confess that even before I developed diabetes, I didn't have much of a sweet tooth, but I did always enjoy a little something from that realm to punctuate my day, or put a button on a meal. This might have been the one and only way in which my dining habits were perfectly suited to my condition, and they form the basis for this chapter. Most of the recipes that follow are based not on sugar substitutes, whole wheat flour, or other stand-ins but on creating and consuming a small but satisfying amount of something with the true flavor, texture, and character of dessert.

That said, where possible, I lean on natural rather than refined sugars, meaning that the lion's share of my desserts are fruit based. I also try to avoid going too heavy on pastry, scattering dabs of it over a crumble, or putting a scant quarter inch of it in the bottom of a single-serve ramekin or foil cup, rather than going for an all-out pie or tart shell.

# granitas

a *granita* is a homemade Italian ice that requires no special equipment to produce. You make the base, freeze it on a shallow tray, and periodically scrape it with a fork, causing little ice crystals to form, which make for an elegant dessert. Here are a few of my favorites; you can adapt the formulas for other *granitas*, using the lemon recipe for lime or orange, and the watermelon for cantaloupe or honeydew.

For festive occasions, or to enhance an everyday meal, serve the *granita* in martini glasses.

## nutritional information
(PER SERVING)

| | |
|---|---|
| Calories | 40 |
| Fat | 0 g |
| Saturated Fat | 0 g |
| Trans Fat | 0 g |
| Total Carbohydrates | 11 g |
| Dietary Fiber | 0 g |
| Total Sugars | 9 g |
| Protein | 0 g |
| Cholesterol | 0 mg |
| Sodium | 0 mg |

## exchanges

Other Carbohydrates ... 0.5

CARBOHYDRATE CHOICE: ½

## lemon granita
**MAKES ABOUT 3 CUPS; SERVES 8**

### INGREDIENTS
*⅓ cup sugar*
*1 cup freshly squeezed lemon juice*
*¼ teaspoon finely grated lemon zest*

1. Put the sugar and 2 cups of water in a small, heavy-bottomed saucepan and bring to a boil over high heat. Let boil, whisking to dissolve the sugar, for 5 minutes. Remove the pan from the heat and let the sugar water cool.

2. Stir the lemon juice and zest into the sugar water. Pour the mixture into a 13 by 9–inch baking dish and freeze it for at least 4 hours, scraping it every 45 minutes to 1 hour with a fork to form ice crystals.

3. Spoon the *granita* into small glasses or bowls and serve.

Granita

CARBOHYDRATE CHOICE: ½

# watermelon granita

**MAKES ABOUT 3 CUPS; SERVES 8**

## INGREDIENTS

*3 tablespoons sugar*

*2 cups pureed seedless watermelon*

*¼ teaspoon finely grated lemon zest*

1. Put the sugar and 1 cup of water in a small, heavy-bottomed sauce-pan and bring to a boil over high heat. Let boil, whisking to dissolve the sugar, for 5 minutes. Remove the pan from the heat and let the sugar water cool.

2. Stir the watermelon and lemon zest into the sugar water. Pour the mixture into a 13 by 9-inch bak-ing dish and freeze it for at least 4 hours, scraping it every 45 minutes to 1 hour with a fork to form ice crystals.

3. Spoon the *granita* into small glasses or bowls and serve.

CARBOHYDRATE CHOICE: 0

# coffee granita

**MAKES ABOUT 3 CUPS; SERVES 8**

## INGREDIENTS

*2 tablespoons sugar*

*2 cups strong, brewed coffee or espresso*

1. Put the sugar and 1 cup of water in a small, heavy-bottomed sauce-pan and bring to a boil over high heat. Let boil, whisking to dissolve the sugar, for 5 minutes. Remove the pan from the heat and let the sugar water cool.

2. Stir the coffee into the sugar water. Pour the mixture into a 13 by 9-inch baking dish and freeze it for at least 4 hours, scraping it every 45 minutes to 1 hour with a fork to form ice crystals.

3. Spoon the *granita* into small glasses or bowls and serve.

## watermelon granita nutritional information
(PER SERVING)

| | |
|---|---|
| Calories | 35 |
| Fat | 0 g |
| Saturated Fat | 0 g |
| Trans Fat | 0 g |
| Total Carbohydrates | 9 g |
| Dietary Fiber | 0 g |
| Total Sugars | 8 g |
| Protein | 0 g |
| Cholesterol | 0 mg |
| Sodium | 1 mg |

## exchanges

| | |
|---|---|
| Fruit | 0.5 |
| Other Carbohydrates | 0.5 |

## coffee granita nutritional information
(PER SERVING)

| | |
|---|---|
| Calories | 12 |
| Fat | 0 g |
| Saturated Fat | 0 g |
| Trans Fat | 0 g |
| Total Carbohydrates | 3 g |
| Dietary Fiber | 0 g |
| Total Sugars | 3 g |
| Protein | 0 g |
| Cholesterol | 0 mg |
| Sodium | 9 mg |

## exchanges

None

Calories........................66
Fat................................1 g
   Saturated Fat...........0 g
   Trans Fat..................0 g
Total Carbohydrates....15 g
   Dietary Fiber..............1 g
   Total Sugars............13 g
Protein..........................2 g
Cholesterol.................1 mg
Sodium....................53 mg

## exchanges

Fruit................................1

**CARBOHYDRATE CHOICE: 1**

# melon soup

## WITH FRUIT

One dessert that I find most appealing is fruit soup, which takes a format we all associate with the savory part of a meal and adapts it to something sweet. The key to this soup is the buttermilk, which adds body and a gently tangy counterpoint to the assorted melons. **SERVES 4**

### INGREDIENTS

1½ cups diced cantaloupe

1½ cups diced honeydew

½ cup 1 percent buttermilk

½ cup small ice cubes

2 tablespoons orange juice

1½ tablespoons freshly squeezed
   lemon juice

Few drops of freshly squeezed
   lime juice

½ small orange, separated into
   sections, membranes removed
   (see page 211), or ¼ cup plus
   2 tablespoons raspberries or
   blueberries

Put the cantaloupe, honeydew, buttermilk, ice cubes, orange juice, lemon juice, and lime juice in a blender and blend until pureed. Divide the soup among 4 shallow bowls and garnish with the orange sections.

# pots de crème

plain and simple, these are sophisticated, decadent answers to pudding, rendered here in orange, chocolate-mint, and mocha.

## orange pots de crème

you will need four 4- to 5-ounce ramekins or foil cups (see Note, page 299).     **SERVES 4**

### INGREDIENTS

*⅔ cup heavy (whipping) cream*
*⅓ cup whole milk*
*3 tablespoons Grand Marnier*
*¼ cup freshly squeezed orange juice*
*1 teaspoon finely grated orange zest*
*4 large egg yolks*
*2 teaspoons sugar*

1. Preheat the oven to 300°F.

2. Heat the cream and milk in a small saucepan over medium-low heat until just simmering.

3. Meanwhile, pour the Grand Marnier into a small saucepan, bring it to a boil over medium-high heat, and cook it for 3 to 4 minutes to burn off the alcohol. Stir in the orange juice and zest. Let the liquid return to a boil and continue to boil until reduced by about half, 4 minutes. Whisk the orange mixture into the pan with the cream and milk.

4. Whisk the egg yolks and sugar together in a bowl. Whisk the orange-cream mixture into the yolks, a little at a time to avoid cooking the eggs. Pour the resulting mixture through a fine-mesh strainer into a small pitcher or measuring cup. Set it aside and let cool for about 15 minutes.

5. Divide the mixture among 4 ramekins and place them in a roasting pan. Pour hot water into the pan until it comes halfway up the sides of the ramekins. Cover the pan with aluminum foil and bake the pots de crème until set but still a little wobbly when you gently shake them, 30 to 35 minutes.

6. Remove the ramekins from the roasting pan with tongs or pot holder and let them cool for about an hour at room temperature. Refrigerate the pots de crème for at least 2 hours or overnight before serving.

## nutritional information
### (PER SERVING)

| | |
|---|---|
| Calories | 157 |
| Fat | 13 g |
| Saturated Fat | 7 g |
| Trans Fat | 0 g |
| Total Carbohydrates | 5 g |
| Dietary Fiber | 0 g |
| Total Sugars | 3 g |
| Protein | 3 g |
| Cholesterol | 174 mg |
| Sodium | 23 mg |

## exchanges

| | |
|---|---|
| Fat | 2.5 |
| Medium Fat Meat | 0.5 |

## nutritional information
(PER SERVING)

Calories......................303
Fat...............................28 g
   Saturated Fat..........15 g
   Trans Fat...................0 g
Total Carbohydrates....16 g
   Dietary Fiber.............2 g
   Total Sugars.............11 g
Protein...........................5 g
Cholesterol.............213 mg
Sodium.....................63 mg

## exchanges

Fat..............................4.5
Other Carbohydrates.......1
Medium Fat Meat..........0.5

# mint chocolate pots de crème

You will need four 4- to 5-ounce ramekins or foil cups (see Note, facing page). **SERVES 4**

---

### INGREDIENTS

*3 ounces bittersweet chocolate,*
   *coarsely chopped (about ¾ cup)*
*⅓ cup whole milk*
*¼ cup loosely packed fresh mint leaves*
*⅔ cup heavy (whipping) cream*
*1 teaspoon brewed espresso or*
   *strong brewed coffee*
*Pinch of coarse salt*
*3 large egg yolks*
*2 teaspoons sugar*

---

1. Preheat the oven to 300°F.

2. Put the chocolate in a heatproof bowl and set it aside.

3. Heat the milk in a medium-size saucepan over low heat until just simmering. Remove the pan from the heat, add the mint leaves and let them steep for 15 minutes. Strain the mint leaves from the milk and discard the leaves.

4. Return the milk to the saucepan and add the cream, espresso, and salt. Cook over medium-low heat, stirring occasionally, until the mixture just comes to a simmer. Pour the milk mixture over the chocolate and whisk until the chocolate melts and is incorporated.

5. Whisk the egg yolks and sugar together in another bowl. Whisk in the hot chocolate mixture, a little at a time to avoid cooking the eggs. Pour the resulting mixture through a fine-mesh strainer into a small pitcher or measuring cup. Set it aside and let cool for about 15 minutes.

6. Divide the mixture among 4 ramekins and place them in a roasting pan. Pour hot water into the pan until it comes halfway up the sides of the ramekins. Cover the pan with aluminum foil and bake the pots de crème until set but still a little wobbly when you gently shake them, 30 to 35 minutes.

7. Remove the ramekins from the roasting pan with tongs or pot holder and let them cool for about an hour at room temperature. Refrigerate the pots de crème for at least 2 hours or overnight before serving.

**variations and suggestions:** You can skip Step 3 (infusing the milk with the mint leaves), and instead add ¼ teaspoon of peppermint extract to the milk along with the cream, espresso, and salt.

# mocha
# pots de crème

You will need four 4- to 5-ounce ramekins or foil cups (see Note). **SERVES 4**

## INGREDIENTS

*3 ounces bittersweet chocolate,*
*coarsely chopped*

*⅔ cup heavy (whipping) cream*

*⅓ cup whole milk*

*2 tablespoons strong brewed coffee*

*Pinch of coarse salt*

*3 large egg yolks*

*2 teaspoons sugar*

1. Preheat the oven to 300°F.

2. Put the chocolate in a heatproof bowl and set it aside.

3. Put the cream, milk, coffee, and salt in a medium-size saucepan and cook over medium-low heat, stirring occasionally, until the mixture just comes to a simmer. Pour the cream mixture over the chocolate and whisk until the chocolate melts and is incorporated.

4. Whisk the egg yolks and sugar together in another bowl. Whisk in the hot chocolate mixture, a little at a time to avoid cooking the eggs. Pour the resulting mixture through a fine-mesh strainer into a small pitcher or measuring cup. Set it aside and let cool for about 15 minutes.

5. Divide the mixture among 4 ramekins and place them in a roasting pan. Pour hot water into the pan until it comes halfway up the sides of the ramekins. Cover the pan with aluminum foil and bake the pots de crème until set but still a little wobbly when you gently shake them, 30 to 35 minutes.

6. Remove the ramekins from the roasting pan with tongs or pot holder and let them cool for about an hour at room temperature. Refrigerate the pots de crème for at least 2 hours or overnight before serving.

note: Ramekins and aluminum foil cups are available at baking supply stores and well-stocked gourmet shops.

## nutritional information
(PER SERVING)

| | |
|---|---|
| Calories | 302 |
| Fat | 28 g |
| Saturated Fat | 15 g |
| Trans Fat | 0 g |
| Total Carbohydrates | 15 g |
| Dietary Fiber | 2 g |
| Total Sugars | 11 g |
| Protein | 5 g |
| Cholesterol | 213 mg |
| Sodium | 62 mg |

## exchanges

| | |
|---|---|
| Fat | 4.5 |
| Other Carbohydrates | 1 |
| Medium Fat Meat | 0.5 |

## nutritional information
### (PER SERVING)

| | |
|---|---|
| Calories | 145 |
| Fat | 3 g |
| Saturated Fat | 1 g |
| Trans Fat | 0 g |
| Total Carbohydrates | 29 g |
| Dietary Fiber | 3 g |
| Total Sugars | 17 g |
| Protein | 3 g |
| Cholesterol | 1 mg |
| Sodium | 54 mg |

## exchanges

| | |
|---|---|
| Fat | 0.5 |
| Fruit | 1.5 |

CARBOHYDRATE CHOICES: 2

# banana mousse

no, this doesn't approach the decadence of a banana cream pie, but that obscenely indulgent recipe inspired this one: All of the expected flavors and textures are here, from sliced bananas to a sweet and creamy blend of bananas and cream (okay, yogurt). Still, it's delicious.

**SERVES 4**

## INGREDIENTS

*3 large bananas*

*3 tablespoons 1 percent milk*

*2 teaspoons sugar*

*¼ teaspoon pure vanilla extract*

*Pinch of coarse salt*

*1 teaspoon freshly squeezed lemon juice*

*½ cup plain nonfat yogurt*

*2 tablespoons macadamia nuts, chopped*

1. Put 2 of the bananas and the milk, sugar, vanilla, salt, lemon juice, and yogurt in a blender and blend to make a thick mousse, but do not overprocess.

2. Slice the remaining banana and divide the slices among 4 small bowls. Spoon the banana mousse over the banana slices and top each serving with some crumbled macadamia nuts.

# bananas foster

Similar to the famous dessert that originated at Brennan's restaurant in New Orleans, this fusion of bananas, rum, and butter is delicious on its own or with a creamy topping.

**SERVES 4**

## INGREDIENTS

2 tablespoons (¼ stick) unsalted butter

¼ cup light brown sugar

1 teaspoon freshly squeezed lemon juice

½ teaspoon ground cinnamon

Pinch of coarse salt

3 large bananas, cut in half lengthwise, then cut in half crosswise

2 tablespoons light or dark rum

Whipped cream, vanilla ice cream, or frozen yogurt, for serving

1. Heat a nonstick pan over medium heat. Add 1 tablespoon of the butter to the pan and let it melt. Add the brown sugar, lemon juice, cinnamon, salt, and 2 tablespoons of water and swirl them together. Add the bananas and cook until they soften, 1 or 2 minutes.

2. Add the rum and remove the pan from the heat. Working away from anything flammable, light the rum using a long kitchen match. Let the alcohol burn off for a few seconds, then stir in the remaining tablespoon of butter until it melts.

3. Divide the bananas and sauce among 4 small bowls or plates and serve with whipped cream, low-fat ice cream, or frozen yogurt.

## nutritional information

(PER SERVING WITHOUT THE CREAMY TOPPING

| | |
|---|---|
| Calories | 204 |
| Fat | 6 g |
| Saturated Fat | 4 g |
| Trans Fat | 0 g |
| Total Carbohydrates | 36 g |
| Dietary Fiber | 3 g |
| Total Sugars | 25 g |
| Protein | 1 g |
| Cholesterol | 15 mg |
| Sodium | 32 mg |

## exchanges

| | |
|---|---|
| Fat | 1 |
| Other Carbohydrates | 0.5 |
| Fruit | 1.5 |

## nutritional information

Calories ........................ 70
Fat ................................. 3 g
   Saturated Fat ........... 2 g
   Trans Fat .................. 0 g
Total Carbohydrates .... 13 g
   Dietary Fiber ............ 2 g
   Total Sugars ........... 10 g
Protein ........................... 0 g
Cholesterol ................ 8 mg
Sodium ........................ 1 mg

## exchanges

Fat ................................ 0.5
Fruit .............................. 0.5

**CARBOHYDRATE CHOICE: 1**

# apple pie filling

i was trying to come up with a less doughy way of making apple pie when it occurred to me that what I really love about the Great American Dessert isn't the pie, but the filling. So here you go: my recipe for apple pie filling. You can use it to fill a pie, of course, but some more diabetes-friendly applications might be to serve it over low-fat ice cream or frozen yogurt as I suggest here or to puree it into a spread.

**SERVES 4**

### INGREDIENTS

2 Granny Smith apples, peeled, cored, and cut into ¼ inch-thick slices
Juice of 1 lemon
1 tablespoon unsalted butter
1 tablespoon light brown sugar

¼ teaspoon ground cinnamon
¼ teaspoon ground ginger
1 tablespoon Pernod (optional)
Low-fat ice cream or frozen yogurt, for serving

1. Put the apples in a bowl, toss them with the lemon juice, and set them aside.

2. Heat a 10-inch pan over medium-high heat. Add the butter and when it begins to sizzle and turn brown add 3 tablespoons of water and reduce the heat to low. Add the brown sugar, cinnamon, and ginger, stir and let cook for 30 to 40 seconds.

3. Add the apples to the pan and cook them, stirring, until they begin to soften, 2 to 3 minutes. Transfer the apples to a plate and spread them out in a single layer to cool.

4. Return the pan to the medium heat and add 2 tablespoons of water and the Pernod, if using, or an additional tablespoon of water. Bring to a boil, stirring to release any particles of apple cooked onto the bottom of the pan, then let simmer over low heat until reduced to a syrup, about 3 minutes.

5. Drizzle the syrup over the apples and stir to coat. Divide the filling among 4 plates or bowls and serve with the accompaniment of your choice, such as low-fat ice cream or frozen yogurt.

# apple turnovers

## WITH WALNUTS AND CINNAMON

the unbeatable trio of apples, cinnamon, and walnuts comes together in a little phyllo triangle that proves to be the perfect parcel for them. Be sure to use a soft apple variety, such as McIntosh or winesap; other crisper varieties won't break down properly when cooked and pureed.    **SERVES 6**

### INGREDIENTS

6 soft, red apples, peeled, cored,
   and thinly sliced

3 tablespoons sugar

2 tablespoons cold unsalted butter
   cut into cubes, plus 4 tablespoons
   melted unsalted butter

2 teaspoons freshly squeezed
   lemon juice

1 teaspoon peeled, finely grated
   fresh ginger

1 cup walnuts, coarsely ground

6 sheets phyllo dough, thawed if frozen

1. Put the apple slices in a heavy-bottomed pan and set it over medium heat. Sprinkle 2 tablespoons of the sugar, the 2 tablespoons of cold butter, and the lemon juice and ginger over the apples. Cook, stirring periodically, until the apples are softened and the other ingredients have melted into a syrupy glaze, 12 to 15 minutes.

2. Let the apples and glaze cool, then transfer them to a food processor and process to a thick paste.

3. Stir the walnuts and the remaining 1 tablespoon of sugar together in a bowl.

4. Preheat the oven to 350°F.

5. To assemble the turnovers, place a sheet of phyllo on a work surface. Using a pastry brush and working along one of the long edges, brush some of the melted butter length-wise over half of the sheet of phyllo, then fold it in half over the buttered side, pressing down to make one

## nutritional information
### (PER SERVING)

| | |
|---|---|
| Calories | 389 |
| Fat | 25 g |
| Saturated Fat | 9 g |
| Trans Fat | 0 g |
| Total Carbohydrates | 40 g |
| Dietary Fiber | 5 g |
| Total Sugars | 23 g |
| Protein | 5 g |
| Cholesterol | 30 mg |
| Sodium | 95 mg |

## exchanges

| | |
|---|---|
| Fat | 5 |
| Starch | 1 |
| Other Carbohydrates | 1 |
| Very Lean Meat | 0.5 |
| Fruit | 1 |

thick sheet. Mound some apple puree about an inch from the short edge closest to you. Starting from the lower left corner, fold the phyllo diagonally up over the filling so that the corner touches the right edge of the phyllo; it will form a triangle. Keep folding the triangle upward, as though folding a flag, until you have about an inch of phyllo remaining at the top. Brush the exposed phyllo with some melted butter and fold it over to seal. Repeat with the remaining sheets of phyllo and filling. Arrange the turnovers in a single layer on a nonstick or aluminum foil-lined baking sheet. Brush the tops of the phyllo turnovers with the remaining butter and scatter the walnut-sugar mixture over the butter.

6. Bake the turnovers until they are lightly browned and the nuts are fragrant, 12 to 15 minutes. Remove the baking sheet from the oven and let the turnovers rest for 5 minutes, then put one turnover on each of 6 plates and serve.

**variations and suggestions:** For an optional sauce, put 2 cups of apple cider, 1 tablespoon of lemon juice, and ⅛ teaspoon of ground cinnamon in a small, heavy-bottomed saucepan. Bring to a simmer and let simmer until reduced to about ¼ cup. Drizzle the sauce over the turnovers, and serve.

CARBOHYDRATE CHOICES: 2

# blueberry buckle

a blueberry buckle brings to mind a dessert version of a berry pancake, with the fruit embedded in the batter rather than layered on or under it. When baked, the berries soften and their juices flavor the surrounding cake. The buckle can also be made with other small, juicy berries such as raspberries or boysenberries. **SERVES 10**

## INGREDIENTS

*1⅔ cups all-purpose flour*

*¼ cup sugar*

*4 tablespoons (½ stick) cold unsalted
   butter, cut into cubes, plus
   6 tablespoons butter, at room
   temperature*

*½ teaspoon ground cinnamon*

*½ teaspoon grated nutmeg*

*¼ teaspoon double-acting baking
   powder*

*½ teaspoon coarse salt*

*1 teaspoon pure vanilla extract*

*½ teaspoon finely grated lemon zest*

*3 large eggs*

*18 ounces blueberries (about 3 cups)*

*Nonstick cooking spray*

1. Put ⅓ cup of the flour, 2 tablespoons of the sugar, the 4 tablespoons of cold butter, and the cinnamon and nutmeg in a food processor. Pulse until the mixture resembles coarse cornmeal. This will be the topping for the buckle. Transfer it to a small bowl, using a rubber spatula to remove as much as possible from the processor bowl, and chill it in the refrigerator for 30 minutes.

2. Put the remaining 1⅓ cups of flour and the baking powder and salt in a small bowl and stir them together.

3. Preheat the oven to 350°F.

4. Put the 6 tablespoons of softened butter and the remaining 2 tablespoons of sugar in the bowl of a stand mixer fitted with a paddle attachment and cream them. Add the vanilla and lemon zest and mix until incorporated. Add the flour mixture to the bowl and blend it into the butter mixture. Add the eggs to the batter one at a time, adding the next egg only after the previous one has been incorporated. Remove the bowl from the mixer and gently fold in the blueberries with a rubber spatula, taking care not to burst them.

5. Spray a 12 or 14–inch-square baking dish with cooking spray. Pour the batter into the dish, spreading it out evenly with the spatula. Scatter the topping over the batter.

6. Bake the buckle until lightly golden brown and a toothpick inserted in the center comes out clean, 25 to 30 minutes. Let the buckle cool, then slice and serve it.

## nutritional information
(PER SERVING)

| | |
|---|---|
| Calories | 249 |
| Fat | 13 g |
| Saturated Fat | 8 g |
| Trans Fat | 0 g |
| Total Carbohydrates | 29 g |
| Dietary Fiber | 2 g |
| Total Sugars | 10 g |
| Protein | 4 g |
| Cholesterol | 95 mg |
| Sodium | 130 mg |

## exchanges

| | |
|---|---|
| Fat | 2.5 |
| Starch | 1 |
| Other Carbohydrates | 0.5 |
| Fruit | 0.5 |

## variations and suggestions

One of my favorite variations to this recipe replaces the strawberries with peaches: Use enough medium-size peaches, peeled and cut into 1-inch dice (to make 3 cups dice). Add ¼ cup of sugar, 1 tablespoon of freshly squeezed lemon juice, and 1 tablespoon of cornstarch to make the filling and follow the rest of the directions for the cobbler as written.

CARBOHYDRATE CHOICE: 1

# strawberry cobbler

this is a quintessential summer dessert that takes fresh, seasonal fruit and does something simple and delicious with it. You can adapt this recipe to use other fruits such as peaches (see the Variations and Suggestions). Bear in mind that sweetness varies from batch to batch of strawberries, so you may be able to use less sugar if the ones you have are particularly sweet. By the same token, if the fruit is especially juicy, you might need to use a bit more cornstarch to bind the filling.

This recipe calls for almond flour, available at specialty food shops, which lends body and flavor to the topping. **SERVES 10**

## INGREDIENTS

3 cups strawberries, hulled, larger berries cut in half

⅓ cup plus 2 tablespoons sugar

2 teaspoons finely grated orange zest

2 teaspoons cornstarch

2 tablespoons (¼ stick) unsalted butter

2 tablespoons almond flour

2 tablespoons all-purpose flour

Nonstick cooking spray

1. Preheat the oven to 375°F.

2. Put the strawberries, ⅓ cup of the sugar, and the orange zest and cornstarch in a bowl and toss to combine. Let the berries stand while you make the crumble topping.

3. Put the butter, almond flour, all-purpose flour, and remaining 2 tablespoons of sugar in a bowl, toss them together, and work the mixture with your fingers until it comes together in a loose dough.

4. Spray a 9 by 13–inch baking dish with nonstick cooking spray. Put the strawberries in the dish, using a rubber spatula to gently pat them down into an even layer. Sprinkle the crumble topping evenly over the strawberries.

5. Bake the cobbler until the topping is golden and the fruit is bubbling, about 45 minutes. Let cool slightly and serve warm.

# miniature pumpkin pies

## WITH GRAHAM CRACKER CRUSTS

these little single-serving pies show how satisfying a few bites of the real thing can be: They're made with a quick graham-cracker crust pressed into the bottom of a tin into which pumpkin pie filling is spooned. Once the miniature pies are baked and chilled, the result is enough to make even the most ardent sweet tooths feel fulfilled.

You will need ten 4-ounce aluminum foil ramekins or foil cups (see Note, page 299). **SERVES 10**

see Note, page 299

## nutritional information
### (PER SERVING)

Calories........................171
Fat.................................12 g
   Saturated Fat...........7 g
   Trans Fat.................0 g
Total Carbohydrates....12 g
   Dietary Fiber.............1 g
   Total Sugars.............8 g
Protein............................3 g
Cholesterol...............93 mg
Sodium....................135 mg

## exchanges

Fat....................................2
Starch..........................0.5
Other Carbohydrates...0.5

## INGREDIENTS

1 can (15 ounces) 100% pure pumpkin

6 ounces cream cheese, at room temperature

4 tablespoons (½ stick) unsalted butter, melted, plus 1 tablespoon at room temperature

¼ cup sugar

1 large egg, plus 2 large egg yolks, lightly beaten

1 teaspoon pure vanilla extract

½ teaspoon ground cinnamon

¼ teaspoon coarse salt

½ cup graham cracker crumbs

1. Put the pumpkin in a mixing bowl and mash it up with a fork. Add the cream cheese, melted butter, sugar, egg and egg yolks, vanilla, cinnamon, and salt and blend with a hand mixer until well incorporated.

2. Put the softened butter and graham cracker crumbs in a bowl and mix them together with a fork. Press the crumb mixture into the bottoms of ten foil ramekins. Put the tins in the refrigerator and chill them for 10 minutes.

3. Preheat oven to 350°F.

4. Divide the pumpkin filling among the tins. Set the tins in a roasting pan and pour warm water into the

roasting pan until it comes halfway up the sides of the tins. Bake until the miniature pies are set (a toothpick inserted into the center of a pie will come out clean), 20 to 25 minutes.

5. Remove the roasting pan from the oven. Carefully remove the tins from the pan with tongs or pot holder and let cool, then refrigerate the pies until set, about 2 hours or up to overnight. Serve the pies cold.

## nutritional information
### (PER SERVING)

| | |
|---|---|
| Calories | 299 |
| Fat | 22 g |
| Saturated Fat | 13 g |
| Trans Fat | 1 g |
| Total Carbohydrates | 22 g |
| Dietary Fiber | 0 g |
| Total Sugars | 9 g |
| Protein | 5 g |
| Cholesterol | 169 mg |
| Sodium | 65 mg |

## exchanges

| | |
|---|---|
| Fat | 4 |
| Starch | 0.5 |
| Other Carbohydrates | 0.5 |
| Medium Fat Meat | 0.5 |

**CARBOHYDRATE CHOICES: 1½**

# citrus curd "pie"

Citrus and cream are a match made in heaven, the acid of the citrus lightens the richness of the cream. Citrus curd makes a perfect, user-friendly pie filling, but to cut down on carbs, I have another proposition for you; bake strips of pie crust dough and use them as little edible spoons to dip into the curd. Bonus feature: Kids love this.

This curd is made with lime juice, but you can use the same recipe to make lemon curd or a combination of the two for a more balanced flavor.

You will need six 4-ounce foil ramekins or foil cups (see Note, page 299).

**SERVES 6**

## INGREDIENTS

½ cup plus 2 tablespoons all-purpose flour, plus more for dusting
Pinch of coarse salt
5 tablespoons cold unsalted butter
About 2 tablespoons ice water

⅔ cup strained freshly squeezed lime juice
1 tablespoon finely grated lime zest
¼ cup sugar
3 large eggs
⅔ cup heavy (whipping) cream

1. Make the pastry "spoons": Put the flour and salt in a large bowl and mix them together. Cut in 3 tablespoons of the butter until pea-size crumbs form. Add the ice water in 1 tablespoon increments, mixing it

in until the dough holds together. Form the dough into a disk, wrap it in plastic wrap, and refrigerate it for 30 minutes.

2. Preheat the oven to 350°F.

3. Roll the dough out to a thickness of ⅛ inch (it will be approximately 6 by 10 inches). Cut the pastry dough into 12 strips, each about 10 inches long and ½ inch wide. Transfer the strips of pastry to a baking sheet and bake until lightly golden, 15 to 20 minutes. Remove the baking sheet from the oven and let the pastry cool for 20 minutes.

4. Meanwhile, make the citrus curd: Fill a large bowl halfway with ice water and set it aside. Set aside a large stainless-steel bowl for making the citrus curd. Fill a saucepan that is just slightly smaller than the bottom of that stainless-steel bowl halfway with water and bring it to a simmer over medium-high heat.

5. Meanwhile, put the lime juice, zest, and sugar in a small, heavy-bottomed saucepan and whisk them together. Set the pot over medium heat and cook, whisking, until the sugar dissolves, about 3 minutes.

6. Break the eggs into the large, stainless-steel bowl and beat them lightly. Whisk the hot lime mixture, a little at a time, into the eggs, taking care not to let them cook or scramble.

7. Set the bowl with the lime mixture over the simmering water and whisk until the mixture is thick enough to coat the back of a wooden spoon, 6 to 7 minutes, moving the bowl on and off the heat to keep the lime mixture warm but prevent it from actually cooking. Whisk in the remaining 2 tablespoons of butter. Remove the bowl from the heat.

8. Place the bowl with the lime mixture in the bowl of ice water and continue whisking to cool.

9. Put the cream in a bowl and whisk vigorously or beat with a mixer until soft peaks form. Fold the whipped cream into the lime mixture. Divide the citrus curd evenly among the 6 foil ramekins. (The ramekins can be refrigerated, covered with aluminum foil, for up to 6 hours.)

10. Serve the ramekins of citrus curd with the pastry "spoons" alongside for dipping.

# goat cheese cake

t his is a low-sugar version of a cake we've served in my restaurants for years. The goat cheese behaves very well in this recipe, providing the essential creamy texture along with a surprising tanginess.

**MAKES ONE 9-INCH CAKE; SERVES 16**

## nutritional information
(PER SERVING)

| | |
|---|---|
| Calories | 294 |
| Fat | 24 g |
| Saturated Fat | 15 g |
| Trans Fat | 0 g |
| Total Carbohydrates | 10 g |
| Dietary Fiber | 0 g |
| Total Sugars | 9 g |
| Protein | 8 g |
| Cholesterol | 139 mg |
| Sodium | 178 mg |

## exchanges

| | |
|---|---|
| Fat | 4 |
| Other Carbohydrates | 0.5 |
| Medium Fat Meat | 0.5 |

## INGREDIENTS

12 ounces cream cheese, at room
    temperature
4 ounces goat cheese (1 small log), at
    room temperature
⅓ cup sugar

1 teaspoon pure vanilla extract
1 teaspoon pure anise extract
2 cups full-fat sour cream
3 large eggs

1. Preheat the oven to 325°F

2. Put the cream cheese and goat cheese in a bowl and work them together with a rubber spatula until completely mixed, then work in the sugar, vanilla extract, anise extract, and sour cream. Add the eggs one at a time, adding the next egg only after the previous one has been well incorporated.

3. Wrap the bottom of a 9-inch springform pan snugly with aluminum foil and pour the cheese cake mixture into it. Set the pan in a roasting pan or other wide, deep pan and pour warm water into the pan until it comes half-way up the side of the springform pan.

4. Bake the cheesecake until it is set (a toothpick inserted in the center will come out clean), 45 to 50 minutes.

5. Remove the roasting pan from the oven, then carefully remove the springform pan from the roasting pan. Let the cheese cake cool to room temperature before releasing it from the pan and slicing and serving it, or cover it with plastic wrap and refrigerate it for up to 2 days.

# snickerdoodles

here's a relatively low-sugar version of the popular sugar and cinnamon dusted cookie with the irresistible name They keep well enough that you could also pack, wrap, and give them out as a gift during the holidays.

**MAKES ABOUT 30 COOKIES**

## nutritional information
**(PER COOKIE)**

| | |
|---|---|
| Calories | 63 |
| Fat | 3 g |
| Saturated Fat | 2 g |
| Trans Fat | 0 g |
| Total Carbohydrates | 8 g |
| Dietary Fiber | 0 g |
| Total Sugars | 3 g |
| Protein | 1 g |
| Cholesterol | 15 mg |
| Sodium | 15 mg |

## exchanges

| | |
|---|---|
| Fat | 0.5 |
| Starch | 0.5 |

## INGREDIENTS

1¼ cups plus 2 tablespoons
   all-purpose flour

¼ cup plus 3 tablespoons sugar

1 teaspoon cream of tartar

½ teaspoon baking powder

Pinch of coarse salt

8 tablespoons (1 stick) unsalted
   butter, at room temperature

1 large egg

Nonstick cooking spray

1 tablespoon ground cinnamon

1. Preheat the oven to 350°F.

2. Put the flour, ¼ cup plus 2 table-spoons of the sugar, and the cream of tartar, baking powder, and salt in a bowl and mix them together.

3. Put the butter in a large bowl and beat on high with an electric mixer until the butter is light in color and fluffy. Reduce the speed of the mixer, add the egg, and beat until incorporated. Add the dry ingredients to the bowl and beat on medium speed until a dough forms.

4. Spray a large baking sheet with nonstick spray. Shape the dough into balls about the size of a chestnut and arrange them on the baking sheet about 1 inch apart.

5. Mix the remaining 1 tablespoon of sugar and the cinnamon together in a small bowl. Lightly sprinkle the sugar mixture over the balls of dough. Bake the cookies until the balls flatten a bit and turn nicely golden, about 20 minutes.

6. Using a spatula, transfer the cookies to a wire rack to cool. The cookies can be enjoyed right away or stored in an airtight container at room temperature for up to 4 days.

# in this chapter

*"Appealing options for dressing up
just about anything."*

# condiments
# and basics

i've paired up the two categories of recipes in this chapter because they offer an
opportunity to add an extra level of finesse
to your cooking—both at the beginning and end
of the process.

The condiments featured here run the
gamut from sandwich spreads and a vinaigrette
to a compound butter and finishing touches that
borrow from a number of Western cuisines. My
hope is that the range of flavors and influences
will provide you with appealing options for
dressing up just about anything you like.

There are also a handful of kitchen basics
that will keep some oft-called-on flavors just a
grab away, and in the most user-friendly form:
roasting garlic mellows its sharp flavor; roasting
tomatoes intensifies them for year-round use;
and Porcini Powder will knock your socks off
with its potent and versatile intensity. Finally,
the stocks and broths that follow are better than
all but the very best store-bought versions, and
are almost certainly lower in sodium. I urge you
to try making your own stock at least once: it's
the easiest way I know to improve the quality
of a wide range of foods. It's also a great way
to use up leftover meats, vegetables, and herbs
that, if you're like me, sometimes accumulate in
the kitchen faster than I can use them up.

## nutritional information

(PER ¼ CUP SERVING)

| | |
|---|---|
| Calories | 313 |
| Fat | 32 g |
| Saturated Fat | 4 g |
| Trans Fat | 0 g |
| Total Carbohydrates | 10 g |
| Dietary Fiber | 7 g |
| Total Sugars | 1 g |
| Protein | 2 g |
| Cholesterol | 0 mg |
| Sodium | 37 mg |

## exchanges

| | |
|---|---|
| Fat | 6.5 |

**A TIP FROM TOM**

**REFRIGERATING AVOCADO MOUSSE:** As anybody who's ever cooked with avocados knows, the challenge is that oxidation causes the flesh to discolor quickly. To save the Avocado Mousse for several hours, use a rubber spatula to transfer it to a resealable plastic bag, seal the bag almost all the way, then gently squeeze out all of the air before closing the bag completely. The mousse can be refrigerated for three or four hours before serving.

**CARBOHYDRATE CHOICE: ½; 0 ADJUSTED FOR FIBER**

# avocado mousse

Use this creamy avocado preparation as a vegetable dip or sandwich spread. It's also a perfect accompaniment for grilled prawns.

**MAKES ABOUT 1 CUP; SERVES 4**

### INGREDIENTS

*2 large ripe Hass avocados, cut in half, pitted, and peeled*

*¼ cup plus 1 tablespoon olive oil*

*3 tablespoons freshly squeezed lemon juice*

*Pinch of coarse salt*

Put the avocados in a food processor. With the motor running, add the olive oil, followed by the lemon juice, and process until a thick and creamy mousse forms. Add the salt and pulse the motor to incorporate it. Serve the mousse as a dip, spread, or condiment.

**CARBOHYDRATE CHOICE: 0**

# tahini dressing

In addition to being a crucial ingredient in the Swiss, Avocado, and Sprouts Sandwiches on page 139, this dressing is wonderful for making tuna salad or for dressing chicken and turkey sandwiches. Use Tahini Dressing sparingly; it has a high fat content, but even just a tablespoon packs a lot of flavor.

**MAKES ABOUT ½ CUP; SERVES 8**

## INGREDIENTS

¼ cup plus 2 tablespoons tahini

2 tablespoons plus 1½ teaspoons
low-sodium soy sauce

1 tablespoon plus 1½ teaspoons freshly
squeezed lemon juice

1½ teaspoons minced garlic

¾ teaspoon minced fresh parsley

¾ teaspoon white sesame seeds

Put the tahini, soy sauce, lemon juice, garlic, parsley, sesame seeds, and 1½ teaspoons of hot water in a bowl and whisk them together. Use immediately or store as described in the Tip at right.

CARBOHYDRATE CHOICE: 0

# red wine vinaigrette

this is a good everyday salad dressing. It's especially delicious with tomatoes, thanks to the relatively high ratio of vinegar to olive oil.

MAKES ABOUT ½ CUP; SERVES 4

## INGREDIENTS

⅓ cup olive oil

3 tablespoons red wine vinegar

½ small clove garlic, minced

¼ teaspoon dried thyme

¼ teaspoon dried oregano

Pinch of sugar

Pinch of coarse salt

Pinch of freshly ground black pepper

Put the olive oil, wine vinegar, garlic, thyme, oregano, sugar, and a pinch of salt, and pepper in a bowl and whisk them together. You can use the vinaigrette right away or store in an airtight container in the refrigerator for up to 3 days. Shake the vinaigrette well or whisk again just before using.

## plan ahead

If you are storing the Parsley Puree for more than a few hours, pour a thin layer of olive oil over the top to seal the puree and keep it from discoloring; be sure to spoon the oil off before using the puree. Placed in an airtight container, the puree can be refrigerated for up to 3 days.

CARBOHYDRATE CHOICE: 0

# parsley puree

Chopped fresh parsley is scattered over more dishes with less thought than any other garnish, as a way of adding a burst of color and mild herb flavor just before serving. But when you concentrate the parsley in this puree, it reveals itself to be a potent ingredient to be used just as selectively and judiciously as any other condiment or sauce. I recommend the puree as a finishing touch for fresh tomatoes and vegetables, white-fleshed fish, and chicken. **MAKES ABOUT 1 CUP; SERVES 8**

## INGREDIENTS

*2 small ice cubes, plus more ice for the water bath in Step 1*
*1 large bunch fresh flat-leaf parsley*
*1 large clove garlic, minced*
*Pinch of coarse salt*
*Pinch of freshly ground black pepper*
*¼ cup plus 2 tablespoons extra-virgin olive oil*

1. Bring a large pot of water to a boil over high heat. Fill a large bowl halfway with ice water.

2. Hold the bunch of parsley by the stems, dip the leaves in the boiling water for 10 seconds, then dip them in the ice water to stop the cooking and preserve the color. Pat the parsley dry with paper towels and cut off and discard the stems.

3. Put the parsley, and the 2 ice cubes, garlic, a pinch of salt and pepper, and 3 tablespoons of cold water in a blender and puree until smooth.

With the motor running, slowly drizzle in the olive oil to make a thick, emulsified mixture. Use immediately or store as described at left.

## variations and suggestions:

❖ This same recipe can be used to make Basil Puree; just substitute a bunch of basil for the parsley.

❖ You can also have some fun with this Parsley Puree by adding pine nuts or walnuts and grated Parmesan cheese to make a winter version of pesto. Or add grated lemon zest to go the other direction and lighten it up.

CARBOHYDRATE CHOICE: 0

# homemade pesto

**t**his is my pretty straightforward take on one of the best uses I know for fresh basil, the Italian condiment that blends it with pine nuts, Parmesan cheese, and garlic. Toss pesto with pasta, stir a tablespoonful into soups, or spread it on cooked fish, chicken, or beef. It has a relatively high fat count, but a little goes a long way. **MAKES ABOUT 1 CUP; SERVES 8**

## INGREDIENTS

½ cup pine nuts

2 cups loosely packed fresh basil leaves
(about 1 bunch)

¼ cup freshly grated Parmesan cheese

1 large clove garlic

½ cup olive oil

Pinch of coarse salt

Pinch of freshly ground black pepper

**1.** Put the pine nuts in a heavy-bottomed pan and toast them over medium heat, shaking the pan frequently to prevent scorching, until the pine nuts are golden and fragrant, about 2 minutes. Transfer the pine nuts to a blender and let cool.

**2.** Once the pine nuts are cool, add the basil, Parmesan cheese, garlic, olive oil, and a pinch of salt, and pepper to the blender and puree to a thick paste, stopping the motor occasionally to scrape down the side if necessary. Use within 3 hours.

CARBOHYDRATE CHOICE: 0

# herb coulis

**t**his fragrant, fresh-tasting herb garnish is a quick way to bring color and flavor to fish and shellfish, chicken, and even sliced, grilled steak. **MAKES ABOUT 1 CUP; SERVES 8**

## nutritional information
(PER 2 TABLESPOON SERVING)

Calories.........................97
Fat.................................10 g
   Saturated Fat............1 g
   Trans Fat...................0 g
Total Carbohydrates......1 g
   Dietary Fiber.............0 g
   Total Sugars.............0 g
Protein............................1 g
Cholesterol...................1 mg
Sodium.....................36 mg

## exchanges

Fat....................................2

**A TIP FROM TOM**

**KEEPING HERB PUREES GREEN:** If you're wondering what the ice cubes in the Herb Coulis and the Parsley Puree (facing page) accomplish, they are there to keep the heat of the blender blade from "cooking" the delicate parsley leaves, turning them an unappealing khaki color. Keep this in mind whenever blending herbs and use an ice cube or two in place, or in addition to, a portion of the water or other liquid called for in the recipe.

## nutritional information

| | |
|---|---|
| Calories | 130 |
| Fat | 14 g |
| Saturated Fat | 2 g |
| Trans Fat | 0 g |
| Total Carbohydrates | 1 g |
| Dietary Fiber | 0 g |
| Total Sugars | 0 g |
| Protein | 0 g |
| Cholesterol | 0 mg |
| Sodium | 34 mg |

## exchanges

| | |
|---|---|
| Fat | 3 |

## plan ahead

**The coulis can be refrigerated for up to 4 hours. Let come to room temperature before serving.**

### INGREDIENTS

2 small ice cubes, plus more ice for the water bath in Step 1

2 bunches fresh flat-leaf parsley leaves

½ cup olive oil

2 teaspoons fresh chervil

2 teaspoons fresh tarragon leaves

⅛ teaspoon coarse salt

1. Bring a large pot of water to a boil over high heat. Fill a large bowl halfway with ice water.

2. Holding the bunches of parsley by the stems, dip the leaves in the boiling water for 10 seconds, then dip them in the ice water to stop the cooking and preserve the color. Cut off and discard the stems.

3. Put the parsley leaves, olive oil, the 2 ice cubes, chervil, tarragon, salt, and 1 tablespoon of cold water in a blender and puree until smooth (the mixture will still be a little coarse). If necessary, add more cold water, ½ teaspoon at a time, to thin the coulis to a pourable consistency. Use immediately or store as described at left.

CARBOHYDRATE CHOICE: 0

# tomato salsa

here's my fairly classic recipe for salsa, one of the greatest, guilt-free condiments you will ever come across. Some of my favorite uses for it are on eggs, poultry, and of course as a dip, but its applications are virtually endless. **MAKES ABOUT 1 ½ CUPS; SERVES 6**

## nutritional information

| | |
|---|---|
| Calories | 12 |
| Fat | 0 g |
| Saturated Fat | 0 g |
| Trans Fat | 0 g |
| Total Carbohydrates | 3 g |
| Dietary Fiber | 1 g |
| Total Sugars | 2 g |
| Protein | 1 g |
| Cholesterol | 0 mg |
| Sodium | 23 mg |

## exchanges

| | |
|---|---|
| Vegetables | 0.5 |

### INGREDIENTS

½ small Spanish onion, cut into 3 or 4 large pieces

½ jalapeño pepper, seeded and coarsely chopped

4 medium-size plum tomatoes, seeded and quartered

½ cup loosely packed fresh cilantro leaves

Juice of 1 large lime

Pinch of coarse salt

Put the onion and jalapeño in a food processor and pulse just until minced. Add the tomatoes and pulse just until chunky and incorporated. Add the cilantro, lime juice, and salt and pulse just until the cilantro is chopped and well distributed. Transfer the salsa to an airtight container and refrigerate it for at least 2 hours to chill it and let the flavors develop. It will keep for up to 2 days.

CARBOHYDRATE CHOICE: 0

# salsa verde

another recipe from Ouest's prep kitchen guru Jorge Carrera, this *salsa verde* (literally green sauce) brings a spicy, garlicky burst of herbaceous flavor to anything it touches. To ensure a pleasingly grainy texture, you mince individual ingredients by hand, then stir them together. Spoon the *salsa verde* over roast pork or poached fish and chicken, or use it as a condiment with grilled steak. **MAKES 1 ½ CUPS; SERVES 4**

## INGREDIENTS

¼ cup plus 2 tablespoons olive oil

⅓ cup loosely packed fresh flat-leaf parsley, minced

3 tablespoons fresh cilantro leaves, minced

1½ tablespoons minced serrano pepper (leave the seeds in for a hotter salsa)

1½ tablespoons freshly squeezed lemon juice

1 teaspoon grated lemon zest

2 large cloves garlic, minced

¼ teaspoon coarse salt

Pinch of crushed red pepper flakes

Put the olive oil, parsley, cilantro, srrano pepper, lemon juice and zest, garlic, salt, red pepper flakes, and ½ cup of cold water in a bowl and stir them together. Let the *salsa verde* sit at room temperature for 10 minutes before serving.

## nutritional information
(PER 6 TABLESPOON SERVING )

Calories......................186
Fat..............................20 g
  Saturated Fat.........3 g
  Trans Fat.................0 g
Total Carbohydrates....2 g
  Dietary Fiber............0 g
  Total Sugars.............0 g
Protein.........................0 g
Cholesterol..............0 mg
Sodium...................124 mg

## exchanges
Fat...................................4

## plan ahead

To make the *salsa verde* in advance, prepare it without adding the lemon zest or juice. It can be refrigerated in an airtight container for up to 3 days. Stir in the lemon juice and zest just before serving.

## nutritional information
### (PER 1/2 CUP SERVING)

| | |
|---|---|
| Calories | 103 |
| Fat | 4 g |
| Saturated Fat | 0 g |
| Trans Fat | 0 g |
| Total Carbohydrates | 16 g |
| Dietary Fiber | 3 g |
| Total Sugars | 6 g |
| Protein | 2 g |
| Cholesterol | 0 mg |
| Sodium | 10 mg |

## exchanges

| | |
|---|---|
| Fat | 0.5 |
| Starch | 0.5 |
| Vegetables | 1 |

CARBOHYDRATE CHOICE: 1

# onion relish

Serve this tangy onion and vegetable relish alongside relatively fatty meats or fish cooked with the skin on; the acid of the vinegar and natural sweetness of the onion will help offset their richness.

MAKES ABOUT 2 CUPS

## INGREDIENTS

2 cups distilled white vinegar

2 whole star anise

1½ teaspoons sugar

¼ teaspoon ground allspice

1 tablespoon canola oil

1 large Spanish onion, finely diced (about 2½ cups)

1 red bell pepper, stemmed, seeded, and finely diced (about 1½ cups)

Kernels from 1 ear of corn (about 1 cup)

1 tablespoon minced serrano or jalapeño pepper (leave all or some of the seeds in for a hotter relish)

2 scallions, both white and green parts, thinly sliced (about ⅔ cup)

¼ cup coarsely chopped fresh cilantro leaves

½ large lime

1. Put the vinegar in a heavy-bottomed nonreactive saucepan and add the star anise, sugar, and allspice. Bring to a boil over high heat and boil until reduced by about half, about 8 minutes. Remove from the heat and, using tongs or a slotted spoon, remove and discard the star anise. Let the vinegar mixture cool.

2. Meanwhile, heat the oil in a heavy-bottomed pan over medium heat. Add the onion, bell pepper, corn, and serrano pepper and cook just until the vegetables are cooked through but still al dente, 3 to 4 minutes (you want the vegetables to have a little bite).

3. Transfer the onion mixture to a mixing bowl and let cool. Add the scallions to the bowl. Pour the cooled vinegar mixture over the vegetables. Add the cilantro and squeeze a few drops of lime juice over the bowl. Stir the relish to mix, then taste for seasoning, adding more lime juice if desired. Refrigerate the relish in an airtight container for at least 2 hours, or overnight, to let the flavors develop.

# grilled red onions

**g**rilling red onions delivers a combination of sweet and charred flavors and, of course, crunch. The onions are especially welcome in many sandwiches and as a topping to meat and meatless burgers.

**SERVES 4 (½ ONION PER SERVING)**

## INGREDIENTS

2 medium-size red onions,
    cut into ¼-inch slices

Nonstick cooking spray

1. Build a fire in a charcoal grill, letting the coals burn down until covered with white ash or preheat a gas grill to medium. If using a grill pan, briefly preheat the pan over medium-high heat.

2. Spray the onion slices lightly with cooking spray. Arrange the onion slices on the grill grate and grill, turning once, until lightly charred and slightly softened, about 3 minutes per side. The onions can be used hot or cooled to room temperature.

## nutritional information
**(PER SERVING)**

| | |
|---|---|
| Calories | 25 |
| Fat | 0 g |
| Saturated Fat | 0 g |
| Trans Fat | 0 g |
| Total Carbohydrates | 5 g |
| Dietary Fiber | 1 g |
| Total Sugars | 2 g |
| Protein | 1 g |
| Cholesterol | 0 mg |
| Sodium | 6 mg |

## exchanges

| | |
|---|---|
| Vegetables | 1 |

# roasted garlic

**r**oast garlic cloves can be tossed into salads or used as a garnish for fish and meat dishes, pureed and stirred into soups and sauces, or spread on everything from a leg of lamb bound for the oven to sandwich bread as an alternative to mustard or mayonnaise. They're a fun ingredient to play with and there's almost no end to their use.

**MAKES ABOUT 1 CUP; SERVES 4**

## nutritional information
**(PER SERVING OF 3 TO 4 GARLIC CLOVES)**

| | |
|---|---|
| Calories | 26 |
| Fat | 0 g |
| Saturated Fat | 0 g |
| Trans Fat | 0 g |
| Total Carbohydrates | 3 g |
| Dietary Fiber | 0 g |
| Total Sugars | 0 g |
| Protein | 1 g |
| Cholesterol | 0 mg |
| Sodium | 32 mg |

## exchanges

| | |
|---|---|
| Vegetables | 0.5 |

## INGREDIENTS

*1 head of garlic, separated into unpeeled cloves*

*1 teaspoon olive oil*

*Pinch of coarse salt*

*Pinch of freshly ground black pepper*

1. Preheat the oven to 350°F.

2. Put the garlic cloves in a small baking dish, ideally one that's just large enough to hold them in a single layer. Drizzle the olive oil and 1 tablespoon of water over the garlic and season it with a pinch of salt and pepper. Stir or shake the baking dish to coat the cloves all over with the oil and seasoning.

3. Cover the baking dish with aluminum foil and bake the garlic until the cloves are tender when pierced with a knife, 30 to 40 minutes.

4. Let the garlic cloves cool, push the garlic cloves out of their papery skins, and discard the skins. The garlic can be refrigerated in an airtight container for up to 3 days.

## nutritional information

(PER 1 TEASPOON SERVING)

| | |
|---|---|
| Calories | 34 |
| Fat | 4 g |
| Saturated Fat | 2 g |
| Trans Fat | 0 g |
| Total Carbohydrates | 0 g |
| Dietary Fiber | 0 g |
| Total Sugars | 0 g |
| Protein | 0 g |
| Cholesterol | 10 mg |
| Sodium | 41 mg |

## exchanges

| | |
|---|---|
| Fat | 1 |

CARBOHYDRATE CHOICE: 0

# garlic butter

One of the great conveniences of the classic French kitchen is compound butter, flavored with garlic, herbs, wine, and/or other ingredients, then sliced and served on top of meats, fish, and fowl. This garlic butter can be melted over grilled steak or grilled fish, or tossed with broccoli, asparagus, or haricots verts. You can also adapt it for specific dishs, adding chopped mint for lamb or some grated lemon zest to make it more fish friendly.

Just a teaspoon of this butter per serving of meat, fish, or vegetable is enough to make an impact.

**MAKES ABOUT ½ CUP, ENOUGH FOR 24 SERVINGS**

## INGREDIENTS

8 tablespoons (1 stick) unsalted butter, at room temperature

1 small clove garlic, minced

1 teaspoon minced shallot

2 teaspoons minced fresh flat-leaf parsley

½ teaspoon minced fresh tarragon

½ teaspoon coarse salt

⅛ teaspoon freshly ground black pepper

Put the butter, garlic, shallot, parsley, tarragon, salt, and pepper in a bowl and, using a rubber spatula, work them together, making sure the herbs are evenly distributed. Place a piece of parchment paper, about 12-inches square, on a work surface and turn the butter out onto the parchment paper, scraping down the side of the bowl with the spatula. Roll the parchment paper around the butter, shaping it into a 12-inch-long cylinder. Keeping the parchment around the butter, wrap the cylinder in plastic wrap. Tighten the plastic around the cylinder by twisting the ends over and over as though wringing a towel. Store as described at right.

### plan ahead

**The butter can be refrigerated for up to 3 days or frozen for up to 2 months. There's no need to thaw it before using.**

CARBOHYDRATE CHOICE: 0

# roasted plum tomatoes

roasting tomatoes intensifies their sweetness without requiring the addition of sugar. It also provides a way to use this summer ingredient all year long because it coaxes the flavor from out-of-season tomatoes. Use these tomatoes in salads and sandwiches or chop them up as a flavoring agent for anything from soups to stews to sauces and risottos.

SERVES 4 (4 TOMATO HALVES PER PERSON)

### nutritional information
(PER SERVING)

| | |
|---|---|
| Calories | 23 |
| Fat | 0 g |
| Saturated Fat | 0 g |
| Trans Fat | 0 g |
| Total Carbohydrates | 5 g |
| Dietary Fiber | 2 g |
| Total Sugars | 3 g |
| Protein | 1 g |
| Cholesterol | 0 mg |
| Sodium | 6 mg |

### exchanges

| | |
|---|---|
| Vegetables | 1 |

## INGREDIENTS

*Nonstick cooking spray*

*8 plum tomatoes, cut in half lengthwise and seeded*

*¼ teaspoon freshly ground black pepper*

1. Preheat the oven to 250°F.

2. Line a cookie sheet with aluminum foil. Spray the foil with cooking spray. Put the tomatoes, cut side down, on the foil, and season them with the pepper.

3. Roast the tomatoes until shrunken and just starting to shrivel around the edges and at the ends, about 90 minutes; the time will vary based on the size and ripeness of the tomatoes.

4. Let the tomatoes cool. They can be refrigerated, whole or chopped, in an airtight container for up to 2 days or chopped and frozen for up to 2 months.

## nutritional information
### (PER SERVING)

| | |
|---|---|
| Calories | 35 |
| Fat | 1 g |
| Saturated Fat | 0 g |
| Trans Fat | 0 g |
| Total Carbohydrates | 5 g |
| Dietary Fiber | 2 g |
| Total Sugars | 3 g |
| Protein | 1 g |
| Cholesterol | 0 mg |
| Sodium | 3 mg |

## exchanges

| | |
|---|---|
| Vegetables | 1 |

CARBOHYDRATE CHOICE: ½

# roasted bell peppers

Instead of purchasing store-bought roast peppers stored in that watery brine, it's easy to make your own freshly roasted red peppers, which will have more flavor and texture. Use the peppers in sandwiches, sliced in salads, or chopped up and added to soups, stews, sauces, pastas, and risottos.

SERVES 4 (½ PEPPER PER PERSON)

## INGREDIENTS

*2 large red bell peppers*

*1 tablespoon olive oil*

1. Lightly coat the bell peppers with olive oil, stick them on a meat fork, and roast them over a gas burner set to medium flame until the skins start

to blacken and blister, turning the peppers to cook them evenly all over, about 10 to 12 minutes total cooking time. (This can also be done on a baking dish under the broiler.)

2. Put the peppers in a heatproof bowl, cover it tautly with plastic wrap, and let the peppers steam in their own heat for about 10 minutes.

Remove the peppers from the bowl and, using a paring knife, remove their skins. Discard the skins.

3. Cut off the tops of the peppers, seed them, and cut them into sections or chop them as needed for individual recipes. The roast peppers can be refrigerated, whole or chopped, in an airtight container for up to 2 days.

CARBOHYDRATE CHOICES: 1½; 1 ADJUSTED FOR FIBER

# porcini powder

i don't know a better way of amping up the mushroom flavor in a dish than by using this intense powder, made by baking already dried porcini to the point that when you grind them, they turn into a powder so fine that it rises like smoke when you lift the top off the grinder. Use this to coat fish and meats before searing them, or stir the powder into mushroom sauces, soups, pastas, and risottos. **MAKES ABOUT 3 TABLESPOONS**

### INGREDIENTS

*1 package (1½ ounces) dried porcini mushrooms*

1. Preheat the oven to 275°F.

2. Spread the mushrooms in a single layer on a baking sheet. Bake them until completely dried, about 12 minutes.

3. Let the mushrooms cool, then transfer them to a clean coffee grinder or spice mill and grind them until pulverized, just a few seconds. The mushroom powder can be used right away or stored in an airtight container in a cool, dry place for up to 6 months.

## nutritional information
(PER 3 TABLESPOON SERVING)

| | |
|---|---|
| Calories | 151 |
| Fat | 2 g |
| Saturated Fat | 0 g |
| Trans Fat | 0 g |
| Total Carbohydrates | 21 g |
| Dietary Fiber | 7 g |
| Total Sugars | 1 g |
| Protein | 13 g |
| Cholesterol | 0 mg |
| Sodium | 16 mg |

## exchanges

| | |
|---|---|
| Vegetables | 4 |

## nutritional information
### (PER SERVING)

| | |
|---|---|
| Calories | 99 |
| Fat | 8 g |
| Saturated Fat | 1 g |
| Trans Fat | 0 g |
| Total Carbohydrates | 5 g |
| Dietary Fiber | 1 g |
| Total Sugars | 2 g |
| Protein | 2 g |
| Cholesterol | 0 mg |
| Sodium | 245 mg |

## exchanges

| | |
|---|---|
| Fat | 1.5 |
| Vegetables | 1 |

CARBOHYDRATE CHOICE: 0

# mushroom duxelles

mushroom duxelles are a mainstay of French cooking, a hash made by sautéing mushrooms with shallots and seasoning. My version uses sliced mushroom caps rather than the traditional diced mushrooms and calls upon Porcini Powder as a secret weapon. (Save the stems for the Mushroom Broth, on the facing page.) This versatile mixture can be stirred into broths to make a quick soup or sauce or spread over cooked fish or chicken. It can also be stirred into plain risotto or the mushroom and farro salad on page 74 or tossed with pasta and a pinch of Parmesan cheese.

**MAKES ABOUT 1 CUP; SERVES 4**

## INGREDIENTS

*2 tablespoons extra-virgin olive oil*

*1 medium-size shallot, thinly sliced*

*1 medium-size clove garlic, very thinly sliced*

*½ pound white button mushrooms, stems removed and discarded or set aside for another use, caps thinly sliced*

*1 tablespoon Porcini Powder (previous page)*

*½ teaspoon coarse salt*

*Pinch of freshly ground black pepper*

*½ teaspoon white truffle oil*

Heat the olive oil in a large, heavy-bottomed pan over medium heat. Add the shallot and garlic and cook until softened but not browned, 2 to 3 minutes. Add the mushrooms, Porcini Powder, salt, and pepper, and cook, stirring, until the mushrooms soften, about 3 minutes. Stir in the truffle oil and 1 tablespoon of water. Use the duxelles right away or let it cool and refrigerate it in an airtight container for up to 2 days.

CARBOHYDRATE CHOICE: 0

# mushroom broth

there's nothing like a mushroom broth to really drive home the flavor of mushroom-themed dishes, of which there are many in this book. You can also call on it when cooking mushroom-based recipes from other sources, using it as an alternative to vegetable or chicken stock.

**MAKES ABOUT 1 QUART; SERVES 4**

## INGREDIENTS

2 tablespoons canola oil

2 ribs celery, coarsely chopped

1 large Spanish onion,
    coarsely chopped

1 large carrot, coarsely chopped

2 cloves garlic, peeled and crushed

2 sprigs fresh thyme

1 bay leaf, preferably fresh

1 tablespoon whole black peppercorns

⅓ cup dry white wine

1 tablespoon distilled white
    vinegar

1 pound white button mushrooms

1 teaspoon coarse salt

3 or 4 pieces dried porcini
    mushrooms (optional)

1. Heat the oil in a large, heavy-bottomed saucepan over medium heat. Add the celery, onion, and carrot and cook, stirring, for 1 minute. Add the garlic, thyme, bay leaf, and peppercorns and cook, stirring, for 2 minutes. Add the white wine, vinegar, mushrooms, salt, and dried porcini, if using. Cook, stirring occasionally, until the mushrooms give off their liquid, about 8 minutes.

2. Pour in 4½ cups of cold water, increase the heat to high, and bring to a boil. Then, reduce the heat so the liquid is simmering and let simmer, uncovered, for 40 minutes.

3. Strain the mushroom broth through a fine-mesh strainer set over a large bowl, pressing down on the solids with a spoon or the back of a ladle to extract as much flavorful liquid as possible. Discard the solids. You can use the broth immediately or let it cool and refrigerate it in an airtight container for up to 3 days or freeze it for up to 2 months.

## nutritional information
(PER 1 CUP SERVING; SEE NOTE)

| | |
|---|---|
| Calories | 90 |
| Fat | 7 g |
| Saturated Fat | 1 g |
| Trans Fat | 0 g |
| Total Carbohydrates | 2 g |
| Dietary Fiber | 0 g |
| Total Sugars | 1 g |
| Protein | 1 g |
| Cholesterol | 0 mg |
| Sodium | 492 mg |

## Exchanges

| | |
|---|---|
| Fat | 1.5 |
| Vegetables | 0.5 |

Note: Since the solids are strained out, some vegetables were not counted in this analysis. Carbohydrate values may be slightly higher than indicated.

## nutritional information

Calories.............................9
Fat......................................0 g
    Saturated Fat............0 g
    Trans Fat...................0 g
Total Carbohydrates.....2 g
    Dietary Fiber..............0 g
    Total Sugars................1 g
Protein...............................0 g
Cholesterol.................0 mg
Sodium.....................12 mg

## exchanges

Vegetables...................0.5

Note: Since the solids are strained out, some vegetables were not counted in this analysis. Carbohydrate values may be slightly higher than indicated.

CARBOHYDRATE CHOICE: 0 (SEE NOTE)

# vegetable broth

Of all the broths and stocks one can make, vegetable broth is the one I've always believed home cooks *should* make, because there's no good reason not to. If you're like most people who cook on a regular basis, then you probably find yourself discarding a fair amount of vegetables and herbs, the remnants of bunches that wilted before they got used up. Those vegetables can be used to make a stock; in fact, this recipe needn't be followed to the letter: You can use more or less of some vegetables, or substitute similar vegetables (more leek can replace onion, and vice versa; tomatoes can be left out; and so on).

**MAKES ABOUT 1 QUART; SERVES 4**

### INGREDIENTS

2 large ribs celery, cut crosswise
    into 3 or 4 pieces each
½ large Spanish onion,
    cut into large dice
5 large cloves garlic,
    crushed and peeled
1 medium-size plum tomato,
    cut in half lengthwise and seeded

1 medium-size leek, white and light
    green parts only, cut into 1-inch
    pieces and well rinsed
6 fresh herb sprigs (your choice of
    parsley, oregano, and/or thyme) or
    6 bay leaves
1 tablespoon whole black peppercorns

1. Put the celery, onion, garlic, tomato, leek, herbs, and peppercorns in a heavy-bottomed stockpot. Pour in just 6 cups of water to cover and bring to a boil over high heat. Reduce the heat so the liquid is simmering and let simmer, uncovered, for 1 hour.

2. Strain the vegetable broth through a fine-mesh strainer set over a large bowl, pressing down on the solids with a spoon or the back of a ladle to extract as much flavorful liquid as possible. Discard the solids. You can use the broth right away or let it cool and refrigerate it in an airtight container for up to 3 days or freeze for up to 2 months.

# clam broth

t his homemade clam broth is a pure, lower-sodium alternative to bottled clam juice. You can chop and freeze the cooked clams for use in soups and stews. **MAKES ABOUT 1 QUART; SERVES 4**

## nutritional information
(PER 1 CUP SERVING)

| | |
|---|---|
| Calories | 69 |
| Fat | 0 g |
| Saturated Fat | 0 g |
| Trans Fat | 0 g |
| Total Carbohydrates | 3 g |
| Dietary Fiber | 0 g |
| Total Sugars | 0 g |
| Protein | 3 g |
| Cholesterol | 7 mg |
| Sodium | 13 mg |

## exchanges

Very lean meat .......... 0.5

### INGREDIENTS

*6 chowder clams*
*4 large cloves garlic, crushed and peeled*

*1 cup dry white wine*

1. Put the clams, garlic, and white wine in a large, heavy-bottomed non-reactive pot. Pour in just enough cold water to cover the clams. Cover the pot and set it over high heat. Cook until the clams open, about 7 minutes. (Discard any clams that have not opened.)

2. Strain the clam broth through a fine-mesh strainer set over a large bowl. Discard the clams and garlic or set them aside for another use. You can use the broth immediately or let it cool and refrigerate it in an airtight container for up to 3 days or freeze it for up to 2 months.

**A TIP FROM TOM**

**FREEZING STOCKS AND BROTHS:** You can freeze the vegetable broth and other broths and stocks in ice cube trays rather than in cup, pint, or quart containers. Store the frozen cubes in freezer bags and remove only as much as you need for a given recipe, or stir the frozen cubes into sauces, soups, and stews for a little extra flavor. This will help you avoid one of the great annoyances of cooking—the "use it or lose it" scenario that arises when you have leftover opened stock on hand.

# chicken stock

t o lower the sodium content of any recipe in this book that uses store-bought chicken broth, make your own chicken stock instead. What you lose in salt, you more than make up for with the essence of chicken and pleasing viscosity of a homemade stock. To help make it as easy as possible to make your own, I break with the tradition of six or more hours of simmering; one hour does the trick. **MAKES ABOUT 1 QUART; SERVES 4**

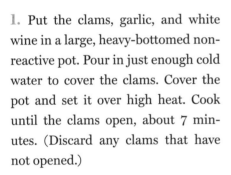

## nutritional information

(PER 1 CUP SERVING; SEE NOTE)

| | |
|---|---|
| Calories | 40 |
| Fat | 2 g |
| Saturated Fat | 1 g |
| Trans Fat | 0 g |
| Total Carbohydrates | 0 g |
| Dietary Fiber | 0 g |
| Total Sugars | 0 g |
| Protein | 3 g |
| Cholesterol | 13 mg |
| Sodium | 29 mg |

## exchanges

| | |
|---|---|
| Medium Fat Meat | 0.5 |

Note: Since the solids are strained out, some vegetables were not counted in this analysis. Carbohydrate values may be slightly higher than indicated.

## INGREDIENTS

2½ pounds chicken bones (see Note)

1 large rib celery, cut crosswise into 3 or 4 large pieces

1 large carrot, unpeeled, cut crosswise into 3 or 4 pieces

1 small Spanish onion, cut into large dice

3 medium-size cloves garlic, crushed and peeled

2 sprigs fresh thyme

2 bay leaves, preferably fresh

1 tablespoon whole black peppercorns

1. Put the chicken bones, celery, carrot, onion, garlic, thyme, bay leaves, and peppercorns in a heavy-bottomed stockpot. Pour in just enough water to cover the chicken bones; it should take about 5 cups. Bring to a boil over high heat, then reduce the heat so the liquid is simmering and let simmer, uncovered, for 1 hour. During this time, use a kitchen spoon or the edge of a fine mesh strainer to skim off any scum that rises to the surface.

2. Using tongs or a slotted spoon, remove and discard the chicken bones, then strain the chicken stock through a fine-mesh strainer set over a large bowl. Discard the solids. Let the stock cool, then spoon off any fat that has risen to the surface. (To speed the cooling process, you can stir a few ice cubes into the stock, or set the bowl in the refrigerator or freezer.) The stock can be refrigerated in an airtight container for up to 3 days or frozen for up to 2 months.

note: You can substitute chicken parts, preferably thighs and wings, for the chicken bones.

CARBOHYDRATE CHOICE: 0 (SEE NOTE)

# beef stock

making your own beef stock, with a relatively small ratio of water to bones, vegetables, and aromatics, produces a more powerful flavor than you will ever find in a mass-produced, store-bought broth. Best of all, the greater flavor comes with even less sodium, a true win-win proposition that's well worth the small effort it takes to make this stock.

MAKES ABOUT 1 QUART; SERVES 4

## INGREDIENTS

2 pounds beef bones, preferably shank or shin, with some meat on them

1 medium-size onion, unpeeled, quartered through the root

1 medium-size carrot, unpeeled, cut into 3 or 4 large pieces

1 rib celery, cut into 3 or 4 large pieces

5 sprigs fresh flat-leaf parsley

3 sprigs fresh thyme

1 bay leaf, preferably fresh

1 teaspoon whole black peppercorns

1. Preheat the oven to 425°F.

2. Preheat a roasting pan in the oven for 10 to 15 minutes. Add the beef bones to the pan in a single layer and roast for 35 to 40 minutes, shaking the pan every few minutes to turn the bones and ensure even roasting. Remove the pan from the oven and let the beef bones cool.

3. Put the beef bones, onion, carrot, celery, parsley, thyme, bay leaf, and peppercorns in a heavy-bottomed stockpot. Pour in just enough water to cover the beef bones; it should take about 7 cups. Bring to a boil over high heat, then lower the heat so the liquid is simmering and let simmer, uncovered, for 2 hours. During this time, use a kitchen spoon or the edge of a fine-mesh strainer to skim off any scum that rises to the surface.

4. Using tongs or a slotted spoon, remove and discard the beef bones, then strain the beef stock through a fine-mesh strainer set over a large bowl. Discard the solids. Let the stock cool, then spoon off any fat that has risen to the surface. (To speed the cooling process, you can stir a few ice cubes into the stock, or set the bowl in the refrigerator or freezer.) The stock can be refrigerated in an airtight container for up to 3 days or frozen for up to 2 months.

## nutritional information

(PER 1 CUP SERVING; SEE NOTE)

| | |
|---|---|
| Calories | 102 |
| Fat | 6 g |
| Saturated Fat | 2 g |
| Trans Fat | 0 g |
| Total Carbohydrates | 0 g |
| Dietary Fiber | 0 g |
| Total Sugars | 0 g |
| Protein | 12 g |
| Cholesterol | 25 mg |
| Sodium | 47 mg |

## Exchanges

| | |
|---|---|
| Fat | 0.5 |
| Lean Meat | 1.5 |

Note: Since the solids are strained out, some vegetables were not counted in this analysis. Carbohydrate values may be slightly higher than indicated.

# conversion tables

## approximate equivalents

1 STICK BUTTER = 8 TBS = 4 OZ = ½ CUP

1 CUP ALL-PURPOSE PRESIFTED FLOUR OR DRIED BREAD CRUMBS = 5 OZ

1 CUP GRANULATED SUGAR = 8 OZ

1 CUP (PACKED) BROWN SUGAR = 6 OZ

1 CUP CONFECTIONERS' SUGAR = 4½ OZ

1 CUP HONEY OR SYRUP = 12 OZ

1 CUP GRATED CHEESE = 4 OZ

1 CUP DRIED BEANS = 6 OZ

1 LARGE EGG = ABOUT 2 OZ OR ABOUT 3 TBS

1 EGG YOLK = ABOUT 1 TBS

1 EGG WHITE = ABOUT 2 TBS

Please note that all conversions are approximate but close enough to be useful when converting from one system to another.

## weight conversions

| U.S./U.K | METRIC | U.S./U.K | METRIC |
|---|---|---|---|
| ½ OZ | 15 G | 7 OZ | 200 G |
| 1 OZ | 30 G | 8 OZ | 250 G |
| 1½ OZ | 45 G | 9 OZ | 275 G |
| 2 OZ | 60 G | 10 OZ | 300 G |
| 2½ OZ | 75 G | 11 OZ | 325 G |
| 3 OZ | 90 G | 12 OZ | 350 G |
| 3½ OZ | 100 G | 13 OZ | 375 G |
| 4 OZ | 125 G | 14 OZ | 400 G |
| 5 OZ | 150 G | 15 OZ | 450 G |
| 6 OZ | 175 G | 1 LB. | 500 G |

## liquid conversions

| U.S. | IMPERIAL | METRIC |
|---|---|---|
| 2 TBS | 1 FL OZ | 30 ML |
| 3 TBS | 1½ FL OZ | 45 ML |
| ¼ CUP | 2 FL OZ | 60 ML |
| ⅓ CUP | 2½ FL OZ | 75 ML |
| ⅓ CUP + 1 TBS | 3 FL OZ | 90 ML |
| ⅓ CUP + 2 TBS | 3½ FL OZ | 100 ML |
| ½ CUP | 4 FL OZ | 125 ML |
| ⅔ CUP | 5 FL OZ | 150 ML |
| ¾ CUP | 6 FL OZ | 175 ML |
| ¾ CUP + 2 TBS | 7 FL OZ | 200 ML |
| 1 CUP | 8 FL OZ | 250 ML |
| 1 CUP + 2 TBS | 9 FL OZ | 275 ML |
| 1¼ CUPS | 10 FL OZ | 300 ML |
| 1⅓ CUPS | 11 FL OZ | 325 ML |
| 1½ CUPS | 12 FL OZ | 350 ML |
| 1⅔ CUPS | 13 FL OZ | 375 ML |
| 1¾ CUPS | 14 FL OZ | 400 ML |
| 1¾ CUPS + 2 TBS | 15 FL OZ | 450 ML |
| 2 CUPS (1 PINT) | 16 FL OZ | 500 ML |
| 2½ CUPS | 20 FL OZ (1 PINT) | 600 ML |
| 3¾ CUPS | 1½ PINTS | 900 ML |
| 4 CUPS | 1¾ PINTS | 1 LITER |

## oven temperatures

| °F | GAS MARK | °C | °F | GAS MARK | °C |
|---|---|---|---|---|---|
| 250 | ½ | 120 | 400 | 6 | 200 |
| 275 | 1 | 140 | 425 | 7 | 220 |
| 300 | 2 | 150 | 450 | 8 | 230 |
| 325 | 3 | 160 | 475 | 9 | 240 |
| 350 | 4 | 180 | 500 | 10 | 260 |
| 375 | 5 | 190 | | | |

Note: Reduce the temperature by 20°C (68°F) for fan-assisted ovens.

# index

# d